The Ojibwa Dance Drum

William Bineshi Baker, Sr., Ojibwa drummaker from Lac Court Oreilles Reservation, Wisconsin, with completed drum frame ready to receive its rawhide drumheads. (Photo by N. T. Wheelwright, 1970.)

The Ojibwa Dance Drum

Its History and Construction

Thomas Vennum

With a new afterword by Rick St. Germaine

MINNESOTA HISTORICAL SOCIETY PRESS

New material © 2009 by the Minnesota Historical Society. All rights reserved. No part of this book may be used or reproduced in any manner whatsoever without written permission except in the case of brief quotations embodied in critical articles and reviews. For information, write to the Minnesota Historical Society Press, 345 Kellogg Blvd. W., St. Paul, MN 55102-1906.

Originally Published in the United States by the Smithsonian Institution Press in 1982.

www.mhspress.org

The Minnesota Historical Society Press is a member of the Association of American University Presses.

Manufactured in the United States of America

10 9 8 7 6 5 4 3 2 1

♾ The paper used in this publication meets the minimum requirements of the American National Standard for Information Sciences—Permanence for Printed Library Materials, ANSI Z39.48-1984.

International Standard Book Number
ISBN-13: 978-0-87351-642-6 (paper)
ISBN-10: 0-87351-642-7 (paper)

Library of Congress
Cataloging-in-Publication Data

Vennum, Thomas.
The Ojibwa dance drum : its history and construction / Thomas Vennum ; with a new afterword by Rick St. Germaine.
    p. cm.
Originally published: Washington, D.C. : Smithsonian Institution Press, 1982.
Includes bibliographical references and index.
ISBN-13: 978-0-87351-642-6
    (pbk. : alk. paper)
ISBN-10: 0-87351-642-7
    (pbk. : alk. paper)
    1. Drum.
    2. Indians of North America—
        Music—History and criticism.
    3. Ojibwa Indians—Music—History
        and criticism.
    I. Title.
ML1035.V46 2009
786.9′21908997333—dc22
2008046158

Contents

Editor's Preface

In 1978 the Smithsonian Office of Folklife Programs established Smithsonian Folklife Studies to document, through monographs and films, folkways still practiced (or re-created through memory) in a variety of traditional cultures. Drawing on more than a decade of research accruing from fieldwork conducted for the Program's annual Festival of American Foklife, the studies are unique in that each consists of a monograph and a film, conceived to complement each other. The monographs present detailed histories and descriptions of folk technologies, customs, or events and include information about the background and character of the participants and processes through photographs (historical and contemporary), illustrations, and bibliographies. The films add a living dimension to the monographs by showing events in progress and traditions in practice, the narrative being provided mostly by the tradition bearers themselves. Thus, while each monograph is planned to permit its use independent of the film (and vice versa), their combined study should enhance the educational and documentary value of each.

Smithsonian Folklife Studies grew out of discussions begun as early as January 1967, when the Institution began plans to convene a group of cultural geographers, architectural historians, and European and American folklore scholars in July of that year. One recommendation of the conference stressed the need for new directions in documentation to keep pace with the ever-broadening scope of the discipline, as it extends from the once limited area of pure folk*lore* research to encompass all aspects of folk*life*. It was proposed at the time that the Smithsonian establish model folklife studies, although no specific forms were prescribed. (The Festival was one form developed to meet this challenge.) The new publication program, therefore, makes available studies that approach earlier research from new perspectives or investigate areas of folklife previously unexplored.

The topics selected for the publications range widely from such traditional folklore interests as ballad singing to newer areas of concern such as occupational folklore.[1] Included are studies of "old ways" in music, crafts, and food preparation still practiced in ethnic communities of the New World, centuries-old technologies still remembered by American Indians, and home-made utilitarian items still preferred to their store-bought counterparts.

Nearly all these traditions have been transmitted orally or absorbed through repeated observations. Several generations of Meaders family sons, for instance, began to learn pottery-making while at play around their fathers' shops.[2] As a youth, Cheever Meaders even built a miniature kiln, while his son Lanier remembers as a small boy being spun around on a potter's wheel for pleasure. Similarly, William Baker's exposure to Ojibwa Indian drum traditions began when he would sit on his father's lap and be allowed to tap on the drum with a small stick, but only softly and on its edge. Later, he and friends would "play" at having their own Indian dances behind the house in the evening, much to the amusement and encouragement of their parents. Learning traditions in this way, of course, extends beyond childhood. The degree to which oral tradition operates, even among today's blue-collar workers, has been described by Robert S. McCarl in a collection of essays on occupational folklore.[3] As McCarl points out, "technique [which] reflects the 'working knowledge' (what you need to know to do the work) of any work . . . is passed from one worker to another through imitation and instruction."[4] Because words cannot always communicate, apprentices must be shown the technique.

Many of the activities documented in the Smithsonian Folklife Studies, however, are practiced in a world apart from that of the factory; therefore, by modern standards of mass production, the technologies shown may seem inefficient and imprecise. In some of them, the proportions used, arrived at through years of trial and error, are often inexact (viz., Cheever's recipe for ash glaze, "roughly two churns of settlin's to three of ashes" or his recipe for lime glaze, which differs from his wife's recipe) or measured by using the human hand as does Paiute craftswoman Wuzzie George when she spaces the bindings on her duck decoys.[5] It is also a world in which the craftsman eschews technical terminology, preferring instead to attach names to his products that relate them to resemblances elsewhere, where a southern folk potter describes his kiln as a "railroad tunnel" or "ground hog," or an Ojibwa Indian refers to the cloth tabs decorating the sides of his traditional drum as "earflaps."

Many traditions presented in the Studies date to times when the pace of work and passage of time were relatively unimportant. It was an age when Cheever could spend hours grinding his clay with a mule-drawn pug mill ("I just like it that way") and William Baker could take pride in stitching by hand every inch of the several layers of cloth decorating his drum ("I could use a sewing machine, but I'd rather use my own handpower. You won't see anything on my drum made by machine.") Deliberateness is often commensurate with accomplishment, and, for the folk potter and Indian drummaker, quality in their products results from the care and time devoted to their manufacture.

The decline of many folklife traditions has paralleled the general social breakdown of communities, in many instances the result of advances in technology. Concurrent with this social dissolution has been the disappearance of many utilitarian items that the maker traditionally created for himself or his family. When commercially produced glassware appeared for home canning, it doomed to eventual extinction the churns and jugs that Cheever Meaders, the farmer/potter, had turned and fired for use by his wife and neighbors in making butter or pickling meat and vegetables. The closing of Nevada marshlands to Paiute Indians forced them to depend on food supplies from white trading stores. This precluded the need for Wuzzie George to weave from tule reeds small bags in which to collect duck eggs, a staple of generations before her. Or, as drummaker Bill Baker laments, today's Ojibwa singers find it expedient to purchase marching-band drums from music stores for their dances, thus marking the passing of the former practice of his people to construct a dance drum as a communal activity in which all took pride.

Many traditions are near extinction or live only in the memories of the oldest members of a community. Because a major role of the Smithsonian is that of a conservation institution, the Office of Folklife Programs accepts the obligation to document by word and film the traditional folkways it researches. During the 1967 Smithsonian conference, Ralph Rinzler's roughly edited film footage of Georgia folk potters was shown to demonstrate a new approach in describing the technology behind artifacts in the Smithsonian's collection of folk material culture. The edited version of the film *The Meaders Family: North Georgia Potters,* with supplementary film and soundtrack, has become number 1a in the series Smithsonian Folklife Studies. This screening of the pottery film took place at a time when film documentation of folklife was a novelty. In fact, in 1967 the American *Encylopaedia Cinematographica* listed a silent film on Amish breadmaking as its single motion picture entry to describe American folk culture.

This dearth of folklife films reflected the fact that, for the most part, folklorists were continuing to document the artifact rather than the craftsman. As Archie Green has noted, "the material favored, metaphorically or literally, by most American folklife specialists is still the boat or the basket, and . . . the object itself gets billing over its maker."[6]

Folklorists have not been alone, however, in being late to recognize film documentation as a necessary adjunct to verbal descriptions of culture. Anthropologist Margaret Mead, whose efforts helped to establish the Smithsonian's National Anthropological Film Center in 1975, took to task her own discipline's continuing refusal to appreciate the value of film documentation: "Department after department, research project after research project, fails to include filming and insists on continuing the hopelessly inadequate note-taking of an earlier age; while before the field-workers' eyes the behavior which film could have caught and preserved for centuries (preserved for the joy of the descendants of those who dance a ritual for the last time and for the illumination of future generations of human scientists) disappears."[7]

In expanding our study of folklife beyond mere artifacts and texts, we have come to recognize that much of what we witness is performance. And though performance can be described verbally or transcribed in print, only through sound motion picture can we hope to capture the complete flow of events and the character of the performers, their speech patterns, moods, and personalities. Hence, by incorporating artifact, text, and performance in our complementary monograph/film series, we bring to readers and viewers the immediacy and subtlety within folk culture. Essentially, it is our large aim to document folklife in all its dimensions.

Thomas Vennum, Jr.
General Editor
Smithsonian Folklife Studies

Acknowledgments

In preparing this study, I owe my foremost gratitude to William Bineshi Baker, Sr., who for nearly fifteen years has been my mentor in the ways of the Indian. This monograph and its accompanying film are as much his story as they are the story of the ceremonial Dance Drum. Baker's wisdom and expertise as a singer and traditional craftsman have guided me in discovering the great riches inherent in Ojibwa culture. Without him, this study would never have been undertaken.

I also must acknowledge my debt to the work of earlier students of Ojibwa and Menominee culture. In tracing the history of the Drum I have drawn repeatedly on information published, especially by Samuel Barrett, Frances Densmore, and James Slotkin. Their data were supplemented by three invaluable sources: Robert Ritzenthaler's extensive manuscript fieldnotes on the Ojibwa in the Milwaukee Public Museum; Gilbert L. Wilson's typewritten reports on the Mandan/Hidatsa, which I cite with permission of the Manuscript Division, Department of Anthropology, American Museum of Natural History, New York, and Division of Archives and Manuscripts, Minnesota Historical Society; and the many interviews with Minnesota Ojibwa collected by the University of South Dakota American Indian Oral History Project, which has allowed me to draw from them. Additionally, I wish to express my thanks to those who read the manuscript and offered suggestions for its improvement, particularly Margaret V. Daly, John C. Ewers, J. Richard Haefer, Charlotte Heth, Nancy O. Lurie, Earl Nyholm, Joe Rose, and Ernie St. Germaine.

Finally, that they may benefit from this study, I wish to dedicate it to the youngest generation of Ojibwa singers today—particularly my friends Keith, Siaki, Joe Dan, and the many Kingbird brothers. The future of Ojibwa music and the Drum is already in their hands.

T.V., Jr.

Foreword

Nearly all North American Indian cultures possess at least one type of drum as part of their song instrumentarium or collection of ceremonial objects. Only the rattle is more widespread and found in more varied guises thoughout the United States. Despite dozens of ethnographies and hundreds of recordings, little is known of the function and use of the drum in many Indian societies. For example, no broad-scale study of drum performance practices has been presented to date. The present volume helps to fill this gap in Indian musical instrument studies, as an investigation of the dance drum in Ojibwa culture and compendium of data pertaining to the dance drum as used by other Great Lakes and Plains Indian peoples.

The present study, developed through the collaboration of an Ojibwa drummaker/singer, William Bineshi Baker, Sr., and a non-Indian commentator, Thomas Vennum, Jr., provides an introduction to one type of drum—the dance drum—used by the Ojibwa. It is also a beginning step toward a comparative study of sound instruments used by North American Indian cultures.

Drawing on ethnographic data, Vennum first explains the role of the dance drum in Ojibwa society by defining its ceremonial use and discussing the relation of the dance drum to other sound instruments, especially other types of drums in Ojibwa culture. An examination of the uses of an instrument, determined by its decorative pattern, and the function of a drum, indicated by its size and shape, is presented as the authors reveal that the pulse of the drum is the very foundation of Ojibwa song. Throughout Vennum's objective descriptions of the function and use of the drum are found Baker's pragmatic statements explaining his traditionalist views of the world of Ojibwa sound instruments. Most emphatic is his belief that the dance drum must be made by those who are given the authority to do so and his parallel belief that the Anglo bass drum is definitely not Indian, which precludes his willingness to sing at such a drum. These statements lead one to believe that an inherent code of the dance drum is its function as an identity indicator; i.e., the drum is Ojibwa — is Indian.

The principle of tribal Indian identity embodied in the drum is further substantiated by the mythological origins of the instrument and legendary history of the migration of the dance drum from culture to culture. Relations between dance drums of the Ojibwa and other Great Lakes cultures with the earlier Sioux Grass Dance drum are explored, stressing especially attitudes about the use and care of the drum. The geographical distribution patterns of the large drum throughout the Upper Midwest are illustrated and, where possible, approximate dates are cited verifying the movement of the drum to particular cultures. A total reverence to the drum by the Ojibwa and their neighbors, the Menominee, is exemplified by their term of address for the drum—*gimishoomisinaan* (our grandfather). This embodiment of life within the drum further attests to the Indian identity belief surrounding the instrument.

The second major area of concern in this monograph is the technology of drum construction. Here Baker's influence is even more strongly asserted, as this section is not a mere description of technique but rather a strong statement of one Ojibwa's beliefs concerning each component of the drum. Baker reveals his ideology in a description of everything from the preparing of the hide for the drumheads to the minutiae of each decorative attachment. Nothing is allowed to be a part of the drum unless it was prescribed by the metaphysical powers and given its appropriate place within Ojibwa cosmology. To this base, Vennum adds details from other Ojibwa ethnologies to provide an extensive body of knowledge of drum technology within this culture. Although no linguistic analysis is presented, native lexemes or labels, which will benefit future comparative analysts of terminological data, are provided for many of the component parts of the drum. To the prescribed technological components both Baker and Vennum allow that numerous variants may be sanctioned for use as substitutes when needed for constructing, setting up, or playing the drum.

Throughout this description of a material object, emphasis is placed upon its spiritual as well as physical value for a given culture. It is stated that the drum may be seen as a "materialization of a vision as an artifact." May this vision continue to live and benefit the Ojibwa and their brothers. And, thanks to the willingness of William Bineshi Baker, Sr., to share his beliefs, may we, too, learn to respect and live by the tenets of "our grandfather."

J. Richard Haefer
School of Music, Arizona State University

History

The Ojibwa and Their Music

> They're losing their tradition. They don't care if they
> have a nice looking drum when they perform, when they
> have their dances. . . . And that's why I don't believe in
> that marching-band drum for the Indian to use. I believe
> in our custom. . . . They don't even take the time. They'd
> rather go and buy a drum for a hundred dollars instead
> of making one for the people. And then they don't even
> dress it up [decorate it]. They ain't anywheres *near* Indian
> [from the film *The Drummaker*].

These feelings were expressed in 1974 by William Bineshi
Baker, Sr., an Ojibwa Indian living on Lac Court Oreilles Reservation in northern Wisconsin, as a film was being made to document a tradition rapidly disappearing among his people—the
art of drummaking. While constructing a traditional dance
drum for the film, he noted with chagrin, and at times even with
anger, that acculturation had affected the musical practices of his
people to such an extent that he now considers many Ojibwa
musicians to have lost their Indian identity.

Baker's concerns are well founded. Although American Indian music generally is still very much alive, many facets of the
tradition have recently changed. Some of these changes are
attributable to social and political pressures, for as increasing
numbers of Native Americans left their reservations and moved
into urban areas, they had to abandon former tribal enmities and
suspicions in order to retain their Indian identity and unite for
survival in the cities. While politically expedient, such unification
has nevertheless resulted in the loss of many traditions—including musical ones—which once distinguished one tribe from another. Furthermore, as many Indians are now moving back to the
reservations, they bring with them recently acquired cultural
values that may be totally foreign to their own people. Where
once a rich variety of tribal styles could be found on this continent, today pan-Indian cultures are emerging.

One factor that has hastened the evolution of a pan-Indian
music has been Indian peoples' increased mobility. Although
tribes have always exchanged songs with each other, formerly
this sharing was gradual and usually restricted to neighboring

groups. Today, as Native American singers travel to distant pow-wows each summer with their cassette tape recorders, they return to their communities with entirely new repertoires of songs on tape. These songs have enormous appeal, especially to younger singers who are eager to learn them. Inevitably the new "foreign" songs supplant older ones, which the community may have preserved and identified as distinctly its own for generations.

It is precisely such older traditions that Indians like Baker are trying to conserve, often in the face of indifference and even ridicule. Conservation, as such, has always been an essential part of Indian life. Accustomed to harsh environments, Native Americans have always utilized whatever was at hand, wasting little and saving wherever possible. In marked contrast to the white man, who from his moving train shot buffalo for sport and left carcasses to rot on the Plains, the Woodlands hunter (or his wife) would carefully pack the deer he felled and carry it miles to his family with a tumpline on his shoulders. Upon arrival home, nearly every part of the animal was put to some use. What flesh was not immediately eaten was "jerked" (sun dried) to preserve it for future consumption. The brains were saved to make a slurry used in tanning, the skins were converted to clothing and moccasins or, if left untanned, were used for drumheads or rawhide thongs. Leg sinews were removed and separated to yield "Indian thread," and the bones were fashioned into knives and scrapers. Even the dewclaws of the deer were put aside to be strung together for a war rattle (fig. 1) or ankle decorations worn at dances.

Figure 1. *Ojibwa war rattle with bunched dewclaws of a deer. The indentations on the handle are for ease in holding the rattle when it is shaken.* (Photo courtesy Smithsonian Institution National Anthropological Archives [hereinafter NAA], neg. no. 493.)

The natural tendency to conserve has not precluded change in Indian life, however, for at no point in their history have Indian people been culturally stagnant. Indeed, long before the arrival of the European on this continent, through necessity Indians had become traders and sharers with their neighbors. From the moment an Indian had contact with New World settlers, he absorbed the goods of European manufacture into the mainstream of his life. Particularly when he perceived the utilitarian advantages of the white man's wares, the Indian quickly discarded many of his own. A galvanized pail, for example, was immediately recognized as far more durable than the traditional birchbark container (*makak*) of Woodland tribes and thus rapidly supplanted it for carrying water, cooking, and collecting maple sap.

In accepting articles of non-Indian origin, however, Indian people displayed ingenuity by adapting them to their own needs and tastes. Blankets, for instance, were cut apart and refashioned into hooded winter shirts (capotes) or unraveled for their yarn, which was redyed and rewoven using Indian techniques and designs. Even today the shiny tin tops of snuff boxes or beer cans are cut and bent into slender cones, which when sewn in rows onto garments make a pleasant jingling sound as part of a woman's dance costume.

Similarly, Indians have shown themselves capable of putting the white man's tools to their own quite different purposes. My own first awareness of this practice was during Baker's construction of a drum in 1970 while he was visiting me in New Hampshire. The time had come to remove the hair from the hides he would use for the drumheads. Traditionally, the Ojibwa accomplish this by draping the hide across a log called *zhizhaak-wa'igan* (beaming post) and scraping off the hair strip by strip with a tool called *naanzhii'iganaatig* (scraper). (On his reservation, Baker keeps his beaming post in his "workshop," as he jokingly refers to a clearing in the woods near his house.) Originally, such a tool was probably made of bone, but later it was replaced by a stick with a metal blade embedded along one side (fig. 2). The stick is grasped at each end and used somewhat like a spokeshave, although the Ojibwa in stripping the skin push the tool away from themselves (fig. 3).[1]

I had assumed that Baker—lacking a proper beaming post and scraper—had reached an impasse in completing the drum. Undismayed, he rummaged through my garage until he came across a sawhorse. Within a short time, he used his penknife to

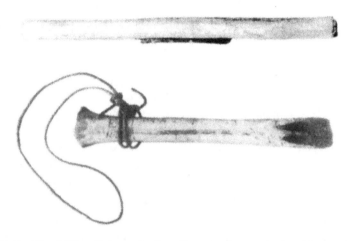

Figure 2. *Traditional Ojibwa flesher made of bone (bottom) and scraper (top) used for removing fat and hair from hides.* (Photo courtesy NAA, neg. no. 596-d-114.)

Figure 3. *Ojibwa woman dehairing deer (?) hide with beaming post and scraper, probably in preparation for tanning.* (Photo courtesy NAA, neg. no. 596-d-115a.)

whittle the top edges along part of the sawhorse crossbeam, rounding off its surface to simulate that of a log. After further search, he discovered an old file that he could use as a scraper and announced that he was ready to resume work. Sitting astride one end of the sawhorse, he draped the hide over the rounded section and began the arduous task of dehairing it just as generations of his Ojibwa ancestors had done before him.

Indian skill at adaptation and invention is also evident in the manufacture of musical instruments. Although pre-contact types of rattles are still made today from gourds, cocoons, hide, or bark as the receptacles for seeds or pebbles, a tin can filled with buckshot is just as apt to be found for the same purpose. Drum frames were traditionally made from hollowed tree-trunk sections or bent wooden splints. We now find, since the arrival of non-Indians to the New World, northern California square drums utilizing grocery box frames or a Montana Flathead drum with its skin stretched over an old radio speaker.[2] And while those tribes whose musical cultures included the flageolet (flute) generally made them of wood, the Winnebago on occasion used a discarded gun barrel.

The Ojibwa have been equally as assimilative as others in these practices, and Baker himself would be the last to eschew the advantages offered by goods manufactured outside his own culture. In fact, when Baker makes his drums, there is scarcely an article incorporated in the instrument or a tool used by him that does not originate with the dominant society: cloth from the fabric store; ribbon, needle, and thread from the five-and-dime; paint, nails, hammer, saw, penknife—all from the local hardware store. Even those articles provided by nature, such as feathers and fur, are attached to his drum with tacks or glue. But regardless of their origin, it is what an Indian does with such items and how he combines them that makes the final product so distinctively his own.

If, then, Indian people so readily adapt articles originating outside their own culture, why should Baker rail so against the marching-band drum used today so pervasively by American Indian singers of all tribes? Have they not put the commercial bass drum to their own purpose? Indeed, they do not perform with it as does the bass drummer in a marching band, who straps it upright over his shoulders and parades with it in consort with players of other musical instruments, swinging the drum beater from one head to the other in showmanship fashion. Instead, the Indian musician turns the marching-band drum on its side, lays it on the ground, and surrounds it with several men beating in unison on one head to accompany their singing (fig. 4). Also, many of these drums are "dressed up," or decorated, often the name of the singing group having been painted around the circumference of the exposed head, perhaps surrounding some Indian motif such as the image of a feather-bonneted warrior or a Thunderbird. Such drums are certainly considered by their

Figure 4. *Ojibwa singers from Bad River Reservation, Wisconsin, performing at a powwow on the Red Cliff Reservation. Commercial bass drums are commonly used to accompany singing at such secular events. Left to right: Siaki Leoso, Francis Stone, Joe Dan Rose (lead singer).* (Photo by the author, August 1980.)

owners to be "nice looking," Baker's opinion to the contrary.

It is at least partly to explain the nature of Baker's complaint that the present monograph has been written. To comprehend his consternation, we must first review Ojibwa history and the traditional role of musical instruments—particularly the drum—in Ojibwa life and describe the traditions that Baker feels are being lost.

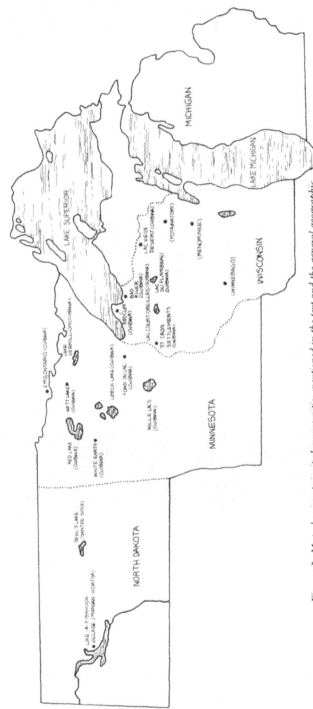

Figure 5. *Map showing principal communities mentioned in the text and the general geographic location of the southwestern Ojibwa today.* (Illustration by Daphne Shuttleworth.)

A History of the Ojibwa People until 1900

To understand fully the significance of the ceremonial Dance Drum to the Ojibwa (var. Chippewa, Ojibway, Ojibwe, etc.) we need to review the history of the tribe before the time they began to construct this particular instrument.[3] A knowledge of the Ojibwa past is also essential to comprehend this tribe's adoption of the dance in which the Drum was intended to be used. History shows that conditions in the nineteenth century created a climate conducive to new forms of ceremonialism, facilitating the rise of the Drum Dance and rapid spread of the Drum among the Ojibwa and their neighbors.

Originally an Algonquian-speaking people, the Ojibwa today are widely dispersed over a large area surrounding the western Great Lakes (fig. 5).[4] While many of them live in Canada, their principal reservations in the United States are located in the northern parts of Michigan, Wisconsin, and Minnesota. (Smaller enclaves exist in North Dakota and Montana.) Although legend places their origins far to the east of their present location, near "a great body of salt water," the Ojibwa were at the east end of Lake Superior at the time of their first contact with Europeans. There they lived in bands organized along totemic lines, occupying country to the north and south of the great fishery at Saint Mary's River (present-day Sault Sainte Marie).

Traditional Ojibwa life was based on obtaining subsistence, which fishing, hunting, and trapping provided them. Their religious beliefs appear at one time to have been limited to shamanism at a local level, although they participated in certain larger ceremonials when bands joined together in the summer months or met with other tribes. At some time in their history, a priesthood developed into an organization called the *midewiwin* (Grand Medicine Society), with limited membership achieved through "purchase" after lengthy instruction in occult knowledge.[5] Through time, *mide* priests became the tribal historians, bearers of herbal knowledge, and directors of elaborate ceremonials and curing rituals. Although certainly not chiefs in the political sense of other (particularly Plains) tribes, the *mide* in many ways functioned as community leaders. When the Ojibwa began their move westward, it was they who perceived the migration as a holy one dictated by the Great Spirit and celebrated it in legend and song.[6]

When the fur trade expanded west of Saint Mary's River, Lake Superior became the final link in a long chain of waterways leading to Montreal and thence to European markets; thus the Ojibwa found themselves in a crucial geographic position. As French explorers, missionaries, and traders poured into the area in search of fortunes to be made and souls to convert, the Ojibwa very quickly became middlemen in the fur trade. In fact, in a short time, the Ojibwa language became the lingua franca of the western Great Lakes area.

These contacts with Europeans resulted in acquisition of their trade goods including weapons, which put the Ojibwa in a position militarily superior to contiguous people west of them. Under pressures of the expanding fur trade, the Ojibwa began to move westward both to the north and south of Lake Superior. In doing so, they systematically drove out such peoples as the Huron, who occupied the territories at the time.

At first, the Ojibwa settled on the shores of Lake Superior, their centers established by the end of the seventeenth century. But the drive continued, and permanent villages were created inland on lakes and rivers. Once the great settlement of Chequamegon (present-day Madeline Island) was intact, the Ojibwa began to move southward into northern Wisconsin, driving the Fox and Dakota from the headwaters of the Saint Croix and Wisconsin rivers. Many villages founded at that time were later to be the sites of the Drum Dance, as it spread from one Ojibwa band to another. For example, Lac Court Oreilles, the home of William Baker, was established circa 1745 as one of the first inland villages, although for years before the Ottawa had used the lake as fishing grounds. Within two decades, it had grown to forty lodges and became the launching site for other communities, such as Lac du Flambeau. A century and a half later, Drums from Lac Court Oreilles would follow the same path and find their way to Lac du Flambeau.[7]

In the mid-eighteenth century, the Ojibwa were also moving into the territories west of Lake Superior (present-day Minnesota) where they continued to defeat the Sioux in their struggle to obtain new hunting lands close to trade centers. In the Battle of Kathio in 1750 they drove the Sioux from Mille Lacs; continuing the pressure, the Ojibwa then forced them from Sandy Lake, Cass Lake, and Red Lake, on the shores of which the new inhabitants founded communities that still exist today.

Throughout this period of intertribal warfare, the Ojibwa (and others) were becoming so reliant on the Europeans that their own culture began to disintegrate. In his *Indian Life in the Upper Great Lakes*, George Quimby summarizes the breakdown of tribal cultures in the period 1760-1820:

> By 1760 every Indian in the [Upper Great Lakes] region was in some way dependent upon the fur trade and thus in a sense was working for the white men. Animal skins, particularly those of beaver, had become money. And the Indians had to obtain this animal-skin money in order to buy the tools, weapons, utensils, clothing, ornaments, and even food that they formerly had produced themselves.[8]

Actually, the fur trade had perhaps a less disruptive effect on the Ojibwa than on other tribes. As many were dislodged from their homelands, the Ojibwa were, in fact, enlarging their own general land base and continued to subsist from hunting and fishing, without much interruption, merely by changing the location of these activities. It was not until they were forcibly settled on reservations that any real depression set in.

While warfare continued unabated between the Ojibwa and Sioux, white settlers were moving into the same areas to farm the land. For their protection and, to some extent, to regulate traders, the federal government began to locate military posts at intervals throughout the territory that ultimately became the states of Wisconsin and Minnesota; thus forts were established at Green Bay, at Prairie du Chien, and at the confluence of the Minnesota and Mississippi rivers at Fort Snelling. Moreover, the Indians were encouraged to meet at these sites in peace councils to settle their boundary disputes. Such a meeting between the Sioux and Ojibwa was in session at Fort Snelling in 1835 when the painter George Catlin arrived there. The large encampment enabled him to sketch a number of dances and artifacts of both tribes and describe other aspects of their cultures in his journal.[9]

Despite the presence of United States military, the fighting between the two tribes continued, albeit sporadically and in small skirmishes. Often, a war party was organized simply as part of a long chain of revenge matches, but the competition for game resources—particularly deer—played a role as well. The fighting lasted until the middle of the nineteenth century when, in the treaty of 1854, the Ojibwa gave up most of their lands and settled on reservations.[10]

Although initially the reservation did not drastically affect traditional Ojibwa life, ultimately the new restrictions would change every aspect of it and by the end of the century reduce the people to wards of the government. Probably the most immediate effect was to force a change in Ojibwa subsistence patterns, for the reservation period brought an end to their former semi-nomadic lifestyle. Most reservations were established on lakes where Ojibwa settlements already existed, yet the pursuit of game beyond reservation borders was now limited.

Formerly, each winter the Ojibwa would break up into small family units, fanning out over wide areas to hunt and trap. This created a seasonal pattern to their social and economic life which Alexander Henry, who lived among the Ojibwa in Michigan, noted in describing his family's departure in late August 1763 for their winter site:

> At our wintering-ground, we were to be alone; for the Indian families, in the countries of which I write, separate in the winter season, for the convenience as well of subsistence as of the chase, and re-associate in the spring and summer.[11]

At the end of the long winter, the Ojibwa moved into sugar camps to tap the maple trees and soon thereafter congregated in small villages on lakes or rivers for fishing and limited agriculture. In contrast to winter, this season became one of accelerated social life, as Ruth Landes has depicted it:

> The summering families moved in [to the villages] at slow stages until they were established by June. The summer-time activities sprang alive: tanning and cooking, berry-picking, games, visits, storytelling, puberty rites, marriages, dances, adulteries, divorces, war parties, religious performances. The crescendo hit a climax early in August. During visits, games and ceremonials, the villages mingled and approached some awareness of the broader horizons of a tribe. . . . Then a man was at his farthest remove from the winter's mode of isolation.[12]

At the end of summer, the wild rice was ready for harvesting, and soon thereafter families once again spread out into their winter hunting grounds as the cycle began anew.

Reservation life brought an end to this seasonal rhythm. The Ojibwa were now settled in permanent villages under government supervision. Beyond the borders of the reservation, fishing, hunting, and even ricing came to be controlled by the white political structure; as a consequence, traditional sources of food began to shrink even as the reservation populations began to increase. Because this new confinement precluded his traditional economic pursuits, the Ojibwa was forced to rely increasingly on trading stores for provisions. The resultant shift in diet has been frequently cited as a cause of the poor health endemic on reservations by the end of the nineteenth century. One Leech Lake Ojibwa, recalling his mother's remarks as she neared death, observed how changes in diet had been so depressing that she welcomed her impending release from life:

> "Everything is all different. Even what you eat is different," and she liked wild game food, boiled stuff. "That what you buy in the store," she says, "I don't think I feel very good to eat that. I like that wild game, but you can't have it. It just breaks my heart; you have to compete with the law; we ain't got chance to go out there and get it. I'm starving for it; I was brought up with that. I'll eat a woodchuck, anything, porcupine, just so it's wild game." That's how she felt.... "[Canned food and cured hams] I don't want that. . . . It isn't good for you. That's what's taking the life of people. Too much of that, it dries up your system. But I want boiled food, the old way. Cook it myself, and then after it sets while, then dish it out. That's good."[13]

Even when the reservation era began, dependency on the non-Indian economy meant facing a series of depleted food supplies for Indian people. About the same time that the Ojibwa began ceding their lands, the fur trade from which they had derived their principal income was reaching its end. In 1842 the American Fur Company went bankrupt. With the income for subsistence removed, Indians for a short time could survive the summers eating fish, but the reduced game supply meant less venison during the winter to feed their increasing numbers.

The history of the Ojibwa people for the last half of the nineteenth century is bleak, culturally and economically. The national policy regarding all Indians at the time was to bring them into the mainstream of American society, principally by inducing them to farming. That this plan would be futile in the Ojibwa case was clear by the end of the century: not only were there problems in converting north woods forests into farmlands, the growing season in that climate is short, and agriculture itself was foreign to a people whose traditional staples had been game animals, fish, maple sugar, berries, and wild rice. Further exacerbating the Ojibwa's economic conditions were the constantly changing and often whimsical policies of the government; far from smoothing the entry of Indian people into the dominant society, the policies left them frustrated and depressed. John Gillin has summarized the problem:

> Under "normal" conditions of acculturation the solution of the subordinate society's difficulties may be found in complete adoption of the patterns of the dominant culture. However, it is possible for the dominant society or its agents so to arrange conditions, either by accident or intent, that the subordinate group becomes chronically paralyzed culturally or chronically disorganized, or both. This is usually accomplished by the dominant society through capricious and unpredictable (from the subordinate society's point of view) alteration of social and cultural conditions. For example, through frequent and inconsistent changes of "policy" on the part of the Indian Office, conditions facing an Indian group may be so manipulated that *any*thing tried by the latter is punishing and the Indian group is unable to establish any system of cultural patterns capable of reducing anxieties.[14]

One example of government policy on reservations in northern Wisconsin should suffice to illustrate Gillin's point: the vicissitudes of the allotment policy and their effect on Indian timber rights.[15] To encourage farming among the Ojibwa, the Bureau of Indian Affairs began to allot the Lake Superior reservations into eighty-acre parcels given to heads of families. (After some earlier allotment experiments with various tribes, the Dawes Severalty Act of 1887 established this policy on a national level.) To "protect" these Indian tracts, the terms of the allotments stated that they could be sold only with the approval of the president of the United States. Almost immediately, however, the whole problem of mixed-bloods confused the rightful ownership of reservation land in such a way that allotments and their timber resources were often obtained illegally:

> In 1863, by ruling that mixed-blood scrip applicants need not have lived among the Chippewas of Lake Superior at the time of the [1854] treaty, the commissioner of Indian affairs threw open to white scalawags the lands ceded at La Pointe. Rationalizing that since all Chippewas were related (thereby all were Chippewas of Lake Superior), organizations at La Pointe and St. Paul ferreted out mixed bloods as far away as the Red River of the North and induced them to apply for government scrip. . . . Indian applicants subsequently executed powers of attorney to white speculators who were free to receive and locate the

tracts as well as strip them of valuable pine timber. A special commission in 1871 investigated these swindles and exposed a shockingly large number of fraudulent applications made by whites posing as Chippewas, by Indians applying more than once, by deceased half bloods, and by husbands and wives each claiming head-ship for the same family.[16]

To become tillable as farmland, the allotments needed clear-ing of their timber. To promote its removal, the Department of the Interior in 1882 gave timber cutting and selling rights to allotees. But despite the government's dispatch of professional farmers to the reservation to teach the new Ojibwa landowner, he was slow either to farm his land or even to move to live on it. Given the increasing demands for lumber nationally and history of fraudulent land claims, in 1889 the department reversed its policy and suspended Indian timber sales, authorizing instead commercial logging crews to cut on the reservations.

Ultimately, this cutover land, much of which had since turned into useless swamp, was all that remained of Indian property on reservations. Loopholes in the allotment policy had, over the years, allowed heirs to sell off their holdings to whites, resulting in the so-called checkerboard reservations. Such is Lac Court Oreilles today, where whites own nearly as many properties as do Indians, albeit irregularly scattered throughout the reservation (hence "checkerboard").[17] At Lac du Flambeau, by the time the Indian Reorganization Act of 1934 reversed the allotment policy to protect further erosion of the Indian land base, most of the valuable acreage—that adjacent to reservation lakes—had been bought by whites and developed into summer resorts. Of the original 73,600-acre reservation, in 1934 the Lac du Flambeau Ojibwa had only about 32,000 acres left in their possession.[18] (In Minnesota the situation is similar; in 1966 only nineteen percent of the Leech Lake Reservation was Indian owned.)

Land and timber issues were only some of the problems afflict-ing the Ojibwa during the first fifty years of reservation life. The annuities agreed upon in the 1854 treaty had expired by 1874, while the population had continued to grow. Where once an exchange of furs for goods sufficed, as settlers continued to move in around them, a new money economy was imposed on Indians. Many Ojibwa turned to white occupations for income—working in lumber camps or engaging in commercial fishing.[19] Already second-class citizens, however, they never really suc-cessfully competed with whites nor were they always fairly compensated for their labor; therefore, a gradual exodus, which has never really stopped, of Ojibwa males to urban areas began.

Gillin's study of the effects of the new economy has shown that Indian dependence on the manufactured goods of the dominant society and attendant fear of having no money with which to purchase them produced considerable group anxiety. With establishment on the Lac du Flambeau Reservation of an Indian agency, which constantly threatened the Ojibwa with punishment and opposed any aspect of their traditional culture, an era of prejudice and discrimination set in. The Flambeau Ojibwa had really only one of two choices: he could retire to the rather secluded Old Village, where he could continue to speak his native language, wear moccasins, keep his hair long, and retain other cultural symbols of his "deprived" status or he could join the "melting pot" of American civilization, convert to Christianity, and generally emulate white ways.[20]

During this period, Indian traditions were under pressure from other directions. The race itself was rapidly losing its purity as Indian women, in particular, married white men. By the time of the 1937 census at Bad River Reservation, there were only 74 full bloods in a population of 875.[21] Government schools were established in which children were forbidden to speak Ojibwa or otherwise retain Indian identity. Student absences during the times when, traditionally, families required all available hands to assist in making maple sugar or processing wild rice eventually led to the creation of boarding schools to solve the truancy problem.

By the end of the century, having lost most of their land, living in crowded one-room log cabins, subjected to an unhealthy diet, and plagued with tuberculosis and hereditary syphilis, with its attendant high infant-mortality rate, the Ojibwa were both culturally and materially impoverished. As Danziger summarizes their condition:

> Chippewa traditional culture was rapidly disintegrating; the first forty-five years of reservation life made them a people of two worlds. . . . They had become, in the process, the wards of Washington.[22]

It was in this climate that the Drum Dance was born.

The Role of the Drum in Ojibwa Life

Before turning to the history of the ceremonial Dance Drum, it is important to review the inventory of Ojibwa musical instruments and their traditional role in the lives of the people. It is equally necessary to understand what changes in Ojibwa musical practices were effected by reservation life around 1850, for these had a bearing on the receptiveness of the Ojibwa to the Drum Dance and the adoption by the Ojibwa of the large dance drum as their principal musical instrument.

Our knowledge of the history of American Indian musical instruments is very limited because of the paucity of early descriptions of Indian musical life. With few exceptions, the reports of explorers and missionaries in the American wilderness yield little if any detailed information about instruments used by the various tribes. These chroniclers generally held such a low opinion of Indian music that they devoted little space to it, except perhaps to mention it in passing as "barbaric." A typical example is offered by Henry Schoolcraft, an Indian agent in charge of Ojibwa territory. Despite his marriage to a member of the tribe, he held nothing but disdain for the music of her people. In his *Narrative Journal* (1821), Schoolcraft described his reactions to the singing and dancing he heard at Great Island in June 1820:

> It is perhaps all we could expect from untutored savages, but there is nothing about [their music] which has ever struck me as either interesting or amusing, and after seeing these performances once or twice, they become particularly tedious, and it is a severe tax upon one's patience to sit and be compelled, in order to keep their good opinions, to appear pleased with it.[23]

Even should a report such as Schoolcraft's describe a musical instrument, the data are minimal: the Indian is usually depicted as playing a "tom-tom," a word of Hindustani origin used by English speakers throughout the world to refer generically to drums of any "uncivilized" people. Early paintings and sketches of Indian dances also depict the instruments used to accompany them, yet, they nevertheless often provide conglomerate and misleading impressions. Sometimes, when the artist's memory may have failed him in completing his work once he left the field, the instrument shown is based on European models.

A case in point is Seth Eastman's depiction of instrumentalists accompanying a Sioux Scalp Dance, circa 1848 (fig. 6). From what we know of Siouan musical culture, certain details of the

Figure 6. *Detail from an engraving after the watercolor* Scalp Dance of the Dakotas *by Seth Eastman (circa 1848).* (Photo courtesy NAA, neg. no. 3711-c.)

"orchestra" in the painting—the type of drumstick used, for one—are credible, whereas others appear to be fanciful. It is unlikely, for instance, that one drummer would be seated and another standing, or that the latter would have his back to the dancers, or that a third drum would sit idle. Particularly hard to accept is the inclusion of the flageolet in consort with the percussion, for almost universally in North America it was a solo instrument used in courtship. Certainly it would never have been audible above the din of a Scalp Dance.

What little we know of the history and variety of North American musical instruments is, therefore, mostly restricted to specimens surviving in museum and private collections. Beginning about 1890, with the increased scholarly attention given to Indian music, the situation improved considerably. Publications, such as those of the Bureau of American Ethnology and American Museum of Natural History, have been indispensable in enlarging the timespan of our knowledge about Indian musical instruments. They also enable us to make some general statements concerning their contextual role.

It is essential to distinguish between the functions of musical instruments outside the American Indian culture and within it. In the Euro-American tradition, for instance, often the same instrument can serve a variety of purposes. Today, in America, the trumpet is used variously to coordinate the marching steps of paraders, awaken troops at reveille or bid a soldier farewell at his funeral, arouse crowds to excitement at sporting events, signal the arrival of important persons, or provide purely musical entertainment together with other instruments in jazz, dance, or symphonic ensembles.

Such a multiplicity of function for a given musical instrument is generally unknown to Indian people. The number of their instrument types is relatively small when compared to those of the Euro-American tradition, consisting mostly of membranophones (drums) and idiophones (rattles, rasps, clappers, etc.). Yet the variety to be found within these categories is enormous. Until recently, because of this variety, rarely did the same type of instrument serve more than a single purpose. While the Ojibwa possessed a number of tambourine-shaped hand-drums, their relative sizes indicated their functions: the drum used by the medicine man for doctoring was considerably smaller in diameter than that used to accompany gambling songs, which in turn was smaller than the drum a man took with him on the warpath. Even if the size and shape of drums were identical, different uses could still be specified for the instruments, often the distinctions indicated solely by the decoration of the drum, who owned it, who was permitted to perform with it, or what particular dance it was meant to accompany.

The almost exclusively secular use of musical instruments is another practice by which the Euro-American and Indian cultures diverge. Moreover, except perhaps for the pipe organ, which is associated with church, distinctions between sacred and secular instruments are not made by the Euro-American culture but are carefully observed by Indian peoples. For the most part, musical instruments have for the dominant society the function of entertainment. This is in opposition to most percussion traditionally used by American Indians, since for them drums and rattles have always provided the background for songs, and songs in turn for dance.

Because song and dance are traditionally considered to be sacred in origin, they are for Native Americans a form of prayer. Songs continue even today to be revealed to humans by supernaturals in dreams or visions often induced by ritual fasting. Thus they represent a symbol of one's spiritual bond with his tutelary spirit and are considered his property, sometimes kept secret, and always used with the greatest discretion. And because most song is accompanied by percussion of some sort—drums more often than not—the instruments themselves become sacred through their associations.

Those outside of American Indian culture have always been impressed with the pervasiveness of the drum among Indians, for rarely is there an Indian gathering without singing. From the time of their earliest accounts, travelers to the North American wilderness scarcely fail to mention the drums. The German Johann Kohl, on Madeline Island in 1855, was clearly impressed with the duration of drumming that accompanied the doctoring and mourning ceremonies of the Ojibwa living there:

> The drum had been beaten two evenings in succession in a lodge about half a mile from mine. . . . There was a sick and dying child there, which the [Indian] doctors attended daily . . . [after the child's death] such a consolation lasts a considerable time, for I heard the drums for several evenings while passing the house where my young mourners were residing.[24]

After centuries of such impressions the drum has so come to be identified with Indian life that when a child at play wishes to impersonate an Indian, his accouterments almost always include a rubber headed tom-tom, which can be bought at any five-and-dime store or tourist shop adjacent to a reservation.

The rhythm of the drum is the very foundation of Ojibwa song. Since the Ojibwa is continually exposed to song and dance from childhood, the sound of the drum becomes ingrained in him:

> As soon as [an Ojibwa] child "knew anything" it was held up and "danced" while some one made a drumming sound like that of an Indian drum. This was done before a child could stand alone, and perhaps it is for this reason that very young children react immediately to the drumming of the fingers on a table or any similar sound.[25]

A boy would have a small war drum to play on, a girl would make pine-needle dolls "dance" on a tin plate.[26] As Baker remembers, children at play would imitate the dances of their elders:

> When we were kids we used to have a powwow in the woods. Of course a bunch of girls and boys would get together; we used an old washtub for a drum. We used to have powwows among ourselves [at age ten to fourteen]. We tried to put on the dances ouselves, after we know it.

. . . Even at home in the evenings a lot of times we'd have dances and [the parents] would come out and say, "What the hell you guys doing?" Well, they'd sit down and help us—only way to learn.[27]

Because the drum served to remind the Ojibwa of his identity, it became a nuisance to those attempting to convert him to Christianity. Noted a missionary concerning "Heathen Dances and Their Influence" on White Earth Reservation:

When they become Christians, they themselves understand that they give up the heathen dance, for the two are the opposites of each other; but yet they are drawn into it again and again. There seems to be a chord that carries the throbbing of the drum into the Indian's heart.[28]

The drum played a role in traditional Ojibwa beliefs about the afterlife as well. Among the articles accompanying the deceased to his grave was his drum, needed for the four-day journey to the land of the dead. He would know that he was approaching the village of souls when he heard the drum, for the village had great singers who provided perpetual music. The Northern Lights (aurora borealis) are even conceived of as being the souls of the departed dancing to the beat of the drum.[29]

Most of the Ojibwa musical repertoire consists of dance songs that require a rhythmic accompaniment to coordinate the steps of the dancers; only story songs and women's love songs lack it.[30] Since the Ojibwa singer provides his own accompaniment, he so relies on the drum for "background," as Baker terms it, that he will insist on having a drum before he will sing. If one is unavailable, then he will look for a substitute to beat upon. Frederick Burton, researching Ojibwa music at the east end of Lake Superior in 1905, remarked on this need of the singer for percussion:

His dependence upon the drum for entire satisfaction is the feature of his art that separates him most widely from the musical manner of civilization. The Ojibway can sing without the drum, but he misses it. Even those who have grown up in semi-civilization prefer the thumping accompaniment, and when an Indian sings for me without his instrument he usually marks the rhythm by patting the table, or his knee with his hand.[31]

A variety of drum substitutes have been described in the literature. In 1832 Schoolcraft was entertained at Savannah Portage by two men and several boys dancing with guns in their

hands "while two men drummed, one on a [canoe] paddle handle, as they had but one drum."[32] Performing for a war dance at
La Pointe in 1855 was one singer who "had only a board, which
he hammered with a big knife, while holding his hollow hand
beneath it as a species of sounding board."[33] In Herman Viola's
study of Indian delegations to Washington, D.C., he described
an evening reception in 1875, given by an Ohio congressman in
his home, for an Ojibwa delegation who provided an impromptu
musical performance:

> The festivities got off to an awkward start. Everyone
> shook hands and stared at each other. Eventually, the
> Indians squatted on the floor and began to sing, keeping
> time by tapping their tomahawks on the floor. As one of
> the guests later remarked, "We made a show of them, and
> they made one of us. Which were the more civilized?"[34]

When Frances Densmore made her early recordings of Ojibwa
songs, at her request a singer once accepted a chalk box filled
with paper to pound on, for his drum was found to overpower
his voice and cause overmodulation on the wax cylinder. Singers
at Nett Lake, Minnesota, circa 1914 recorded war songs for the
Indian agent there using a pan or pail in place of a drum, and I
have often recorded Baker in his home accompanying himself by
tapping a pencil on an ashtray or empty beer bottle or using a
yardstick on a cardboard carton when a drum was not handy.
Because drums were not the only Ojibwa musical instruments,
however, the others deserve some mention in passing.

Stringed instruments were unknown to the Ojibwa, as well as
to most North American tribes. Their only melodic instrument
was the wooden courting flute (*bibigwan*), which at one time had
widespread distribution among Native Americans (fig. 7).[35] Like
a recorder, it was an end-blown duct flute, the tones of which
were regulated by a movable block tied to it. The flute ranged in
length from fifteen to twenty inches, although diminutive versions were made for children to play with. Most Ojibwa flutes had
five or six holes, and the melodies played on them were usually
love songs used by a young man courting a girl's affections.[36]
Flute playing seems to have died out earlier among the Ojibwa
than among their neighbors. Paul Parthun could find no flute
players in his study of Minnesota Ojibwa music,[37] and specimens
of Ojibwa flutes in collections are rare, whereas Menominee and
Winnebago examples are plentiful.

The idiophones most commonly used to accompany songs
were vessel rattles of various sorts. These were generically called

Figure 7. *Frank James playing courting flute at Lac Court Oreilles, circa 1941*. (Photo by Robert Ritzenthaler, courtesy Milwaukee Public Museum, Department of Anthropology, neg. no. 5762.)

zhiishiigwan (rattle; cf. *zhiishiigwe*, rattlesnake), a term that seems to have been borrowed from the Ojibwa by the French and universally applied to rattles of all Indians, including non-Algonquian-speaking tribes to their west. For example, Maximilian Neuwied refers to the Assiniboin rattle as "schischikue," and Catlin sketched two Siouan rawhide rattles that he calls "She-she-quois."[38]

Before Indian contact with Europeans, all rattles were made from natural materials. Although some Ojibwa used dried squash gourds, turtle shells, and even otter skulls, they seem generally to have preferred cylindrical shaped vessels. Thus examples survive with cylinders consisting of a section of animal horn, or thin wood, birchbark, and even hide—such as a moose scrotum—which are sewn together (fig. 8). Their open ends were stopped with wooden discs penetrated through their centers by the rattle's wooden handle, which was often indented for ease in holding when it is shaken (see fig.1). To produce their rattling sound, the vessels were partially filled with pebbles, dried kernels of corn, or small animal bones.[39]

Figure 8. *Frances Densmore's published photo of Ojibwa percussion instruments for her first monograph on Ojibwa music (1910). Left to right: birchbark song scrolls, small hand-drum for doctoring, medicine drum with curved drumstick, hoop rattle, and birchbark medicine rattles.* (Photo courtesy NAA, neg. no. 451.)

After white contact, the Ojibwa began to substitute ready-made cylindrical containers, such as spice boxes or baking powder cans, sometimes inserting lead shot or pebbles or both for sound production.[40] (This practice has led members of the Winnebago medicine lodge, where gourd rattles are used exclusively, to insist jokingly that the Ojibwa use beer cans for the same purpose.) The Menominee practice is similar to the Ojibwa, although their oldest form of rattle was described as manufactured from an inflated animal's bladder, its end tied until it hardened and could be used as a vessel.[41]

Traditionally, all Ojibwa rattles are considered to have supernatural power and are used exclusively by medicine men, either in *midewiwin* ceremonies or for curing, or by jugglers for prophesying in the shaking tent rite.[42] Since both men and women could attain priesthood, rattles and medicine drums were the only musical instruments played by women. In *mide* rites, such rattles were performed in consort with the medicine drum, the percussion pattern of the two being simultaneous. A typical performance took place at a *mide* feast on Lac Court Oreilles Reservation at Willie Webster's in July 1942, as follows:

> Around 6:00 Willie got out his water drum and gave it to John Mustache who put on the head and put water in it . . . then John Mustache filled the dishes that the people had brought and after all had received their dishes full of food, Willie again spoke, dedicating the food and then told the people to eat while he took the water drum and sang continuously all during the meal while Mrs. Webster shook the tin can rattle for him . . . during the meal the women got up and danced in place to Willie's drumming and singing.[43]

Later in the feast, the rattle was passed to John Stone, who sang while shaking it, while Willie Webster continued to drum.

While this type of rattle is the only one to have survived today, probably the earliest Ojibwa rattles were jingle rattles made of dried dewclaws of deer or moose. The dewclaws were either bunched together at the end of a stick (see fig. 1) or strung and tied around the ankle (and/or knee) as part of the dance costume. The strung type began to be replaced by hawk bells when they became available as trade items. Such bells, attached to leather straps, continue to be a standard part of today's male dance costume of many tribes.

Bunched dewclaw rattles were used by leaders of war parties to accompany songs of divination and by jugglers in the shaking tent.[44] Schoolcraft described the musical instruments of one of these "prophets" near Sault Sainte Marie in the 1820s:

> He had a little drum, the rim of which, was covered with hieroglyphics, and a curious stick, upon the end of which, was tied a string of deer's hoofs, which made a sharp noise at every stroke.[45]

One type of rattle, somewhat problematic in its classification, was the "doctor's rattle." Actually a small double-headed frame drum, it contained buckshot and was therefore called *zhiishiigwan* by the Ojibwa (fig. 8). The noted organologist Karl Izikowitz classified such an instrument as a rattle drum and proposed that it was in fact the progenitor of double-headed drums among

North American tribes. Since the topic of the present study—the dance drum—falls into that category, it is worth reiterating Izikowitz's speculation concerning its origin:

> [Rattle drums] in all probability originated by the Indians having put pebbles into a drum, precisely as they had done with a number of implements—often more or less sacred—with hollow bodies. In this way the pebbles have constituted an addition to or a substitute for the drum-stick. The rattle drums have, then, been capable of developing independently in such regions where the drum and the rattle have existed side by side. In consequence the drum must be completely closed and portable. This is in my opinion the source of the double-membrane drums in America.[46]

For such an instrument, the southern Ojibwa used a single circular frame in a number of sizes. Little Wolf's rattle drum at White Earth, Minnesota, in 1909, was about twelve inches in diameter, and the decoration of its head was not unlike that of the ceremonial Dance Drum.[47] Smaller drums, however, seem to have been more common. Fred Blessing described two Leech Lake drums, circa 1955; one was five inches in diameter with black cloth around its circumference and bits of ribbon attached, the other, worn by Chief Greenhill around his neck as part of his sucking doctor's paraphernalia was only 3 1/4 inches in diameter.[48] Among the northern Ojibwa, a special form of this drum was made by forming two adjacent circular frames with a handle between them (fig. 9) In Selwyn Dewdney's photograph of the

Figure 9. *Double-drum rattle of the northern Ojibwa (Saulteaux), Berens River, Canada.* (Photo courtesy Museum of the American Indian, Heye Foundation, neg. no 28765.)

Figure 10. *Canadian Ojibwa ceremonial Dance Drum belonging to John Keeper, after a photo by Selwyn Dewdney*. (Illustration by Daphne Shuttleworth.)

John Keeper Four Winds Drum, such a double-drum rattle is attached to one of its four support legs (fig. 10).[49]

A number of other idiophones have been used by the Ojibwa; their distribution in each case, however, seems to have been restricted to a small area. Among these were percussion sticks used by a medicine man at Grand Portage, Minnesota. They consisted of thin fourteen-inch boards, 3 1/4 inches wide, painted with red and black bands; in performance four narrow sticks were held between the fingers to strike against the board.[50] Also, seemingly unique to Lac Court Oreilles Reservation were hunting sticks (*mitigoons*) that consisted of four eighteen-inch pointed sticks, one-half inches in diameter, beaten together by two men singing hunting songs to attract deer. Noted one resident of the reservation, "John Mink said deer will come right into the wigwam sometimes when you sing with the sticks." Their power, however, was said to be ineffective if a close relative of one of the hunters was near death.[51]

By far the largest number of Ojibwa instruments, however, were the drums—*dewe'iganag*. Of the four principal types known to have been used, only the large homemade dance drum or its store-bought equivalent has any wide circulation today. Densmore's informants mentioned, as the oldest known drum, an entire animal hide stretched out over stakes in the ground, held in position by hoops, and pounded on by singers to accompany war songs.[52] That such a form of drum was known to other tribes is suggested by Edward Curtis's depiction of the percussion used in the Arikara Sage Dance:

> Sitting in a large circle near the altar, around an out-stretched, unworked rawhide, they beat upon it with long rods, and to the rhythm of this primitive drum sang songs of supplication for power to drive away illness.[53]

The second type of drum known to the Ojibwa was the water drum, still used exclusively by members of the medicine lodge. Called *mitigwakik*, meaning "wooden vessel," it averaged sixteen to twenty inches in height and was made from a section of basswood or cedar, hollowed by charring and scraping. A sepa-

Figure 11. *A priest of the Grand Medicine Society emerging from a wigwam with his water drum and drumstick. The lodge may have been used for ritual sweating prior to a medicine initiation ceremony.* (Photo by A. E. Jenks, Lac Court Oreilles Reservation, 1899, courtesy NAA, neg. no. 476-a-14.)

rate piece of wood—usually pine—was inserted and sealed with pitch to form the bottom of the drum. For a drumhead, a single rectangular piece of tanned deerskin was held in place with a removable hoop wound with cloth. The drum was partly filled with water through a bunghole in its side and played with a curved drumstick. Like all water drums, its high pitched tone could carry great distances and characteristic sound informed one instantly that a medicine ceremony was in session (see figs. 8, 11).

Another type of water drum was used by converts to peyotism. The Ojibwa used a cast-iron kettle or pot, the practice of groups elsewhere on the continent. As peyotism was practiced secretly in secluded settlements, such drums were rare among the Ojibwa. Blessing discovered one—which he describes as being three legged and cast in sand sometime before the Revolutionary War—in an abandoned house on the Leech Lake Reservation.[54] Some peyote drums at Lac du Flambeau had inner tubes for heads and were used in performance with gourd rattles—the customary practice of the Native American Church, the officially recognized peyote religious establishment.[55]

A large number of tambourine-shaped hand-drums comprise the third category of Ojibwa drums. These included both single- and double-headed drums, some of which were provided with internal snares—usually short sticks held against the drumhead by a thong. Such drums, similar to hand-drums of many North American tribes, were used principally on the warpath and later in the war dance but also in accompanying moccasin games and the Chief Dance, a curing ceremony. A typical example is the war drum of Gegoweosh, a chief in northern Wisconsin (fig. 12); the design on the drumhead can be assumed to have appeared to

Figure 12. *War drum of Gegoweosh in the collection of the Madeline Island Museum, Wisconsin.* (Photo by the author, 1970.)

him in a dream or vision. The [Thunder?] bird represented in its design was probably his protective spirit in battle.

The fourth and most recent category of drum types is the large dance drum that came into use beginning circa 1880. Originally, these drums were homemade and used for secular as well as sacred events. Increasingly in this century they have been replaced with the store-bought bass drums.

What happened to their musical instruments once the Ojibwa were settled on reservations? The social and economic changes brought about by reservation life directly affected the traditional contexts for music. As a consequence, the need for certain instruments began to disappear, while the climate was created for others—particularly the large dance drum.[56] To cite briefly but one example: following the former mode of courtship a young man would have played love melodies to his woman on a flute in semiseclusion; once reservation life began and younger members of the tribe were increasingly exposed to non-Indian pastimes, the musical context for courtship shifted to dancing, either in emulation of white patterns (the square dance) or participation in pan-Indian couples' dances, such as the Rabbit Dance or the 49 Dance (fig. 13). The traditional courting songs disappeared and with them the flutes on which they had once been played.

Generally speaking, after the mid-nineteenth century, we can perceive a gradual reduction in the number of contexts requiring music, frequency of performance, variety of song genres, and number of musical instruments. As the Ojibwa were restricted to reservations, the seasonal pattern of their social life changed, for the annual winter dispersal to isolated hunting areas was discontinued. The Ojibwa were now located in permanent villages, living year around as neighbors; and whereas summer had formerly been the only season for them to come together in social dances and large ceremonials, the opportunity was now ripe for year-round participation in such events. This helps to explain why the ceremonial Drum Dance came to be organized around four seasonal rites, whereas the older medicine lodge had held ceremonials only twice a year when the population was at its densest.

The change in lifestyle directly affected the contexts requiring specific musical instruments. With warfare forcibly ended, the drum an Ojibwa took on the warpath was no longer functional, although it did survive in some communities as the Chief Dance drum, where it was used solely in curing rituals. Pressure from missionaries drove into seclusion such "heathen" activities as the shaking-tent seances and medicine-lodge ceremonials and, with them, their traditional drums and rattles. The moccasin game drum in some places was eventually abandoned as the final stage in the decline of its song repertoire. Once a popular event, the game came under attack by Indian agents when gambling was judged excessive on reservations. As the performance of its songs became less frequent, the Ojibwa gradually relegated the moccasin game songs to memory, thereby removing the need for an instrument to accompany them. (Baker recalls moccasin game songs he once heard but usually only when he is chopping wood.)

In the meantime, deprived of former economic pursuits and reliant on the white economy, the Ojibwa found themselves with more free time for social pastimes. Secular dances provided entertainment that could be indulged in during all seasons. Under the general influence of musical practices of tribes to their north and west, singing became more and more a group activity. With the spread of the Grass Dance, singers began to perform around a single large drum. About this time a revelation to a Siouan prophetess took place that would induce the Ojibwa to adopt the large dance drum, their principal musical instrument today.

Figure 13. *Lac Court Oreilles singers provide indoor wintertime entertainment. The dancers perform the 49 Dance, a couples' dance popular with many tribes. The absence of eagle feathers hanging from the drum support legs indicates that the event is secular.* (Photo by Fred Morgan, courtesy W. A. Fisher Company, Virginia, Minnesota.)

The Origin and Early History of the Dance Drum

The Vision of Tailfeather Woman

Here is the story of the beginning of the ceremonial powwow Drum. It was the first time when the white soldiers massacred the Indians when this Sioux woman gave four sons of hers to fight for her people. But she lost her four sons in this massacre and ran away after she knew her people were losing the war. The soldiers were after her but she ran into a lake (the location of which is never mentioned in the "preaching" of the Drum's story). She went in the water and hid under the lily pads. While there, the Great Spirit came and spoke to her and told her, "There is only one thing for you to do."

It took four days to tell her. It was windy and the wind flipped the lily pads so she could breathe and look to see if anyone was around. No—the sound is all that she made out, but from it she remembered all the Great Spirit told her. On the fourth day at noon she came out and went to her people to see what was left from the war. (The date of this event is unknown.) The Great Spirit told her what to do: "Tell your people, if there are any left (and he told her there was), you tell your people to make a drum and tell them what I told you." The Great Spirit taught her also the songs she knew and she told the men folks how to sing the songs. "It will be the only way you are going to stop the soldiers from killing your people."

So her people did what she said, and when the soldiers who were massacring the Indians heard the sound of the drum, they put down their arms, stood still and stopped the killing, and to this day white people are always wanting to see a powwow.

This powwow drum is called in English "Sioux drum," in Ojibwa *bwaanidewe'igan*. It was put here on earth before peace terms were made with the whites. After the whites saw what the Indians were doing and having a good time—the Indians had no time to fight—the white man didn't fight. After all this took place the whites made peace terms with the Indians. So the Indians kept on the powwow. It's because the Sioux woman lost her four sons in the war that the Great Spirit came upon her and told her to make the Drum to show that the Indians had power too, which they have but keep in secret [William Bineshi Baker, Sr.].[1]

Probably in the 1870s and somewhere in west-central Minnesota, the above-described event is believed to have happened. For more than the next half century it would affect the social and religious life of many Indian people in the western Great Lakes area and on the Prairies. The exact details of the origin of the ceremonial Dance Drum will probably never be known, as the story is shrouded in legend and has been embroidered over the years through oral tradition. Even the earliest published accounts are conflicting and have led to scholarly debate. Because a definitive history of the Drum Dance awaits further investigation, I have, for the purposes of this study, restricted myself to reviewing the most pertinent data currently available.

The salient themes in Tailfeather Woman's story remain constant in the many versions collected. A Sioux woman, who fled United States soldiers who were killing her people, hid in a lake for four days. During this time, she was visited by the Great Spirit who instructed her to make a large dance drum and taught her the songs and (presumably) ritual details for their use. The Drum was then built as an instrument of peace and was meant to be copied and passed on to other tribes to bring an end to bloodshed.[2] The fact that all this was revealed to the woman in a dream or vision has resulted in references by some scholars to the adherents of the Drum ceremony as belonging to a "Dreamer's Society" and to the instrument itself as a "Dream Drum."[3] (Hereinafter the distinction will be made between *Drum*, indicating the ceremonial instrument, and *drum*, referring to its secular version or generically to other membranophones.)

The details of the story, which vary, are unessential to the basic theme. Some versions name a young girl as the visionary rather than a woman. She may be hidden behind bulrushes rather than under lily pads as in Baker's account. The length of time she hid is given as ten days in one story; some say she was taken bodily into heaven for the revelation. Although various dates—roughly between 1860 and 1890—are ascribed to Tailfeather Woman's vision, Ojibwa and Menominee readily admit to not knowing the exact time or place of the event.

Despite variations in detail from one community to the next, because the story is always "preached" at Drum Dance ceremonies, its basic structure remains constant. Thus the Ojibwa White Feather was able to relate exactly the same history of the

Drum at ceremonies in 1910 and again in 1928;[4] the story collected by Parthun at Mille Lacs in the 1970s from "an aged
medicine man [was] in the same detail and sequence" as versions
published by Densmore and Barrett.[5] The longest account in
print was given by the Menominee Johnny Matchokamow, who
insisted on parceling it out over two days' time and then further
elaborating on it with two additional narratives.[6] This conforms
to the practice of relating the *mide* origin tale—and most other
esoteric knowledge—a bit at a time.[7]

Some confusion regarding the date and place of the vision
originates with individuals from several tribes who over the years
have claimed to have the original Drum in their possession or
even to have created the Drum Dance itself.[8] This can be explained in part because Indian ceremonials—far from being
static institutions—are constantly subject to changes and accre-
tions through individual visions. Thus dances and drums, together with their "authorizing" legends, arose as variations
based on the original one. (This will be discussed more fully here
in the chapter "The Decline of the Drum Dance.")

One of the earliest controversies regarding the Drum's origin
was published in the *American Anthropologist* (1923-26) in a series
of brief exchanges between the linguist Truman Michelson and
anthropologist Alanson Skinner.[9] As their articles touch on the
early history of the Drum, the controversy merits summarizing
here.

Michelson began by noting in a report that previous researchers were not only unconcerned with the true history of the
Drum's origin but had overlooked one important source: Benjamin Armstrong's *Early Life among the Indians* (1892). In his
memoirs, Armstrong asserted that the prophetess herself, together with a large number of Ojibwa adherents, had brought
the dance to Wisconsin in the spring of 1878.[10] Further,
Armstrong claimed to have witnessed the ceremony, himself, at
that time in northwestern Wisconsin and to have interviewed the
woman, who described herself as a survivor of the Battle of Little
Bighorn of 1876. Michelson was quickly challenged by Skinner,
who contended that the Menominee had received the Drum
Dance from the Kansas Potawatomi as early as 1862.[11] The ceremony had so frightened the Indian agent that he wired Washington for troops to suppress it. Half a century later Skinner's
Menominee informants could still point out where the first ceremony was held and claimed that the owner of the original Drum
was a certain Ksweatosa.

Michelson retorted by discounting the reliability of Skinner's informants and cited correspondence in the files of the Bureau of American Ethnology to place the so-called Wisconsin Scare in 1878, a disturbance caused by "this new Sioux dance which is said to be a religious institution." In reply, Skinner continued to defend his information and challenged Armstrong's assertion that the Sioux woman could have been involved in the Custer massacre.

Ultimately, Michelson had the final rebuttal, for Skinner had died. In his "Final Notes on the Central Algonkian Dream Dance," he presented new evidence he unearthed in 1925 from a John Crow at Odanah, Wisconsin (Bad River Reservation), to support the Little Bighorn connection. Crow claimed to have seen the first dance, called *bwaaniniimi'idiwin* (Sioux dance) at Moose River in Minnesota and recollected it as taking place shortly after his daughter had been born, circa 1876. (There are two Moose rivers in Minnesota. One is in Marshall County in the northwestern part of the state; the more likely site for the dance, however, is the Dead Moose River in central Minnesota [Aitken County], which is near Mille Lacs Reservation and other communities, such as East Lake, where Drum societies have been numerous for years.)

Further obscuring the origin of the Drum was an initial confusion among non-Indians between the Drum Dance and the Ghost Dance, a well-known Indian messianic movement that culminated in the tragic massacre at Wounded Knee in 1890. Since both dances were fairly contemporaneous in origin and diffusion, general anxiety and unsettled conditions in "Indian Territory" in the late nineteenth century often led observers to mistake the Drum Dance for the Ghost Dance. Moreover, because of elements that the two held in common, certain essential differences in the underlying beliefs and ritual details of the two were usually overlooked.

Both dances were phenomena, which, from their points of origin "somewhere to the west" were spreading eastward from tribe to tribe. Consequently, reports of Indian "scares" led white settlers in Woodlands areas, where Drums were being given away, to misinterpret the intentions of Drum donors (cf. Michelson on the "Wisconsin Scare"). For instance, Clay MacCauley, connected with the federal census in 1880, learned from the Indian agent in Keshena that local Roman Catholics felt threatened by the new Menominee religious activities taking place in forest seclusion. There is little question that the Christians had the Ghost Dance in mind in depicting Drum Dance followers as "part of a league which is forming among all the Indians of the northwest [which] when the good opportunity comes, is to rise against and to destroy the white man."[12] Armstrong, describing the Sioux prophetess and her Drum Dance adherents as "moving in a easterly direction," circa 1878, even mistakenly calls it the "Ghost Dance."[13]

Missionaries in particular were sensitive to such threats of an Indian "return to the blanket." Whatever ceremony it was that the Reverend Gilfillan observed, he was alarmed over "the new 'Sioux dance'" brought the winter before Wounded Knee to White Earth Ojibwa in northern Minnesota where it "caught among them like wildfire." It was being taught to them by, in his opinion, "fifty of the worst Sioux," who, despite the attempts of missionaries to have them sent back, were nevertheless being given permission to visit every Ojibwa village as well as being fed with government provisions.[14]

Early reporters on the Drum Dance seem also to have been confused by certain aspects of the ritual. This is understandable given the fact that some of the very elements of the Grass Dance incorporated into the Drum Dance were at the same time being appended by some tribes to the Ghost Dance. The southern Arapaho and Cheyenne, for example, began to use the Grass Dance as an afternoon preliminary to their Ghost Dance, which took place in the evening. In his classic study of the Ghost Dance, James Mooney was quick to point out that the Crow Dance, a ritual within the Grass Dance complex, was clearly "auxiliary" and had nothing at all to do with the Ghost Dance. He interpreted it properly as "a modification of the picturesque Omaha dance [Grass Dance] of the prairie tribes, with the addition of religious features borrowed from the new [Ghost Dance] doctrine."[15]

The most prominent feature of the Crow Dance was the special feathered belt worn by the dancers. Next to the belt in importance, according to Mooney, was "an immense drum." That he and other such reliable reporters as Samuel Barrett were so perceptive to note the musical distinctions between the Ghost and Grass Dance types is to their credit. There was no instrumental accompaniment to the songs of the Ghost Dance, while great importance was attached to having a large drum accompany the singing in both the Grass and Drum dances. These scholars also noted the differences in the musical and dancing styles.[16]

Despite the confusion between the Ghost and Drum dances, as Barrett and others have contended, history simply does not support a connection between the two. In Mooney's Ghost Dance study, he carefully delimited its provenance as west of the lower Missouri River and stressed that most of the Santee or eastern Sioux—although they may have known about it—never accepted the Ghost Dance.[17] Moreover, almost all early reports of Drum Dance activity antedate by nearly a decade the last great flurry of Ghost Dance activity, which was ended at Wounded Knee and was effectively prevented from spreading further to the east.

While any direct connection between the two movements seems doubtful, Barrett nevertheless advances the notion that Tailfeather Woman may have been influenced by earlier prophets.[18] Conceivably, the Paiute creator of the Ghost Dance, Wovoka, himself, may have served as the model, for— like Tailfeather Woman—his visions initiated the movement and he personally disseminated the new doctrines to tribes east of his people. There is at least a suggestion that some of Wovoka's teachings found their way into the story of Tailfeather Woman or perhaps were added to it at a later time. Common to both was the concept of the invulnerability of the Indian in the face of attack from United States soldiers. Essential to Tailfeather Woman's story was the theme that, by building the Drum and dancing, the Indians would escape harm by inducing the white man to put down his arms. Some accounts elaborate on this point in such a way as to suggest parallel beliefs concerning the power of the Drum and that of the Ghost Dance shirts worn (mostly) by the Sioux.

The followers of Wovoka believed their specially designed Ghost Dance shirts with sacred emblems painted on them would serve as protective amulets in battle. As George Sword, an Oglala Sioux described them:

> "All the men and women made holy shirts and dresses they wear in dance. . . . On the shoulders and on the sleeves they tied eagle feathers. They said that the bullets will not go through these shirts and dresses, so they all have these dresses for war."[19]

This belief was reflected as well in the text of one of their Ghost Dance songs that included the phrase: *Ogale kin niniye-kta* ("The shirt will cause you to live").[20]

In Mooney's description of the early phases of the Battle of Wounded Knee, he implied the disastrous consequences to which the tenacity of this belief would lead the Sioux:

While the [United States] soldiers had been looking for the guns Yellow Bird, a medicine man, had been walking about among the warriors, blowing on an eagle-bone whistle, and urging them to resistance, telling them that the soldiers would become weak and powerless, and that the bullets would be unavailing against the sacred "ghost shirts," which nearly every one of the Indians wore.[21]

A nearly identical theme appears to have survived in (or been added to) origin tales of the Drum. In James Shaugobay's Mille Lacs (Minnesota) account of Tailfeather Woman's vision, the spirit promises her that once the Indians begin to dance, the soldiers will be unable to harm them:

"Soldiers wanted to kill the Indians off. . . . The Indians never made a move or stopped having a good time. Finally, the soldiers couldn't hurt nobody, *the bullets were disappearing* [emphasis mine]."[22]

Had historical events evolved differently, perhaps the Ojibwa would have accepted the Ghost Dance if it had reached them. Certainly their adoption of the revelations of Tailfeather Woman shows a readiness at that point to assimilate a new ceremonial and accept ethical precepts revealed in a vision to some individual. Indeed, other "prophets" continued to alter the Drum Dance as they added their personal revelations to those of Tailfeather Woman. This eventually led to cultism in some communities, weakening the general social position of the Drum Dance and perhaps hastening its ultimate decline.

Given their status at the end of the nineteenth century, the Ojibwa were ripe for the revelations of Tailfeather Woman. In accepting them, they reacted no differently than other peoples who, when subjected to outside pressures on their traditional mode of life, are prone to nativistic behavior. Even before the Drum Dance there is some history of Ojibwa attentiveness to prophets who, in effect, told them to change their ways. The Ojibwa historian William Warren described the influence of the Shawano cult on his people in the early nineteenth century. In the summer of 1808, messengers from the prophet arrived with blackened faces to tell the people to cease all their white-induced habits (particularly drinking), throw away all articles of European manufacture, give up their traditional religious practices, and adopt the new ceremonies the messengers were to show them. The effect was so profound, Warren tells us, that many Ojibwa at

Chequamegon (Madeline Island) discarded their medicine bags by throwing them into Lake Superior.[23]

Similar instructions were once imparted to the Pembina band of Ojibwa, according to John Tanner, who lived among them in captivity. The revelations from a prophet named Sky-Spirit were interpreted for them by Little Clam, who, after singing and praying, instructed the Pembina to cease fighting their enemies and give up drinking, lying, stealing, and the like. Tanner was clearly suspicious of the whole affair:

> In the spring of the year, after we had assembled at the trading house at Pembinah, the chiefs built a great lodge and called all the men together to receive some information concerning the newly revealed will of the Great Spirit. The messenger of this revelation was Manito-o-geezhig, a man of no great fame but well known to most of the Ojibbeways of that country. He had disappeared for about one year and in that time he pretended to have visited the abode of the Great Spirit and to have listened to his instructions, but some of the traders informed me he had only been to St. Louis.[24]

Despite his reservations about the authenticity of these "messages" from the Great Spirit, Tanner noted that they at least had a salutory effect on the band for a few years afterward.

The Precursory Role of the Grass Dance

There is general agreement among students of Indian history that the movement engendered by Tailfeather Woman's vision and disseminated to the Ojibwa and eventually nearly all other central Algonquian tribes had its origins in the so-called Grass Dance of the Plains. The unique contributions rendered to the Grass Dance by the Woodlands people were their acceptance of the role of Tailfeather Woman as a prophetess and—from the dictates of her vision—their particular attention and even devotion to the large ceremonial Dance Drum.[25]

The Grass Dance and its diffusion have been carefully covered in anthropological literature.[26] One of its most thorough researchers was Clark Wissler. In preparing an early and important paper, he had sifted through an enormous amount of data covering twenty-five tribal groups in an attempt to discover the origin of the dance and extent of its spread. In his "General Discussion of Shamanistic and Dancing Societies," published by the American Museum of Natural History in 1916, Wissler forwarded the premise that the dance could ultimately be traced to an older ceremony, the Iruska of the Pawnee Indians. This ceremony was characterized by the performance by its members of "fire tricks" to demonstrate bravery, such as reaching into a boiling pot for meat without being burned; thus it began to be called variously the Hot Dance or Fire Dance as it was adopted by other tribes (Omaha, Ponca, Osage, Kansa, et al.).

From the precursory Iruska ceremonial, Wissler perceived a geographic bifurcation of the dance from its origins "southeast,"[27] evolving into two modern ceremonies—the Grass Dance of the Plains, representing the "western type," and the "Dream Dance [Drum Dance]" of the Woodlands, representing the "northeastern type." Concerning the differences between the two, he wrote:

> The most striking aspect of this distribution is its general agreement with cultural and geographical distinctions. . . . The peculiarity of this correlation is that in each group we find a different form of dance and that each form tends to completely cover its culture area.[28]

The development of these ceremonials was during an extremely difficult time for American Indians generally, as white settlers continued to stream into western territories and the pace of frontier confrontations quickened. Especially on the Plains, a general depression had set in resulting from the disappearance of the buffalo and cessation of warfare between tribes. (Bravery in battle had been the accepted means of becoming prestigious.) Also a factor was the failure of Indians to convert, overnight, to farming, as was urged by the government. The general disorientation of Indian people during this period was reflected in increased alcoholism and suicide. Simultaneously, as Indian people attempted to readjust, a flurry of religious activity began, namely the Ghost Dance, peyotism, etc. As Wissler notes, the climate was therefore ripe for the rapid spread of the Grass Dance:

> The important point for us is that there was a strong stimulus to the diffusion and modernization of ceremonies at the time the grass dance was in full swing and it was this that carried it along to its present [circa 1915] development.[29]

It is generally accepted that the Grass Dance was based on an Omaha society, the Hethushka, whose membership was limited to warriors. Their meetings (dancing and feasting) took place within a lodge in which the seating location was specified by the offices held within the society. The music for the Hethushka dances was provided by two to four singers grouped around a single drum behind whom sat "a few women who possessed fine voices."[30] The leader of the ceremony needed to be someone of sufficient military rank to wear a special feather bustle called "The Crow," a decoration of the highest order, "said to symbolize a battlefield after the conflict is over."[31] When the Hethushka had evolved into the Grass Dance, the wearing of the Crow belt was retained. Wissler adds to his list of the dance's other important regalia: "a roached headdress of deer hair [like the Crow belt, another war badge], a food stick or spoon, *a large drum suspended horizontally* [emphasis mine (fig. 14)], a whip, a sword, and a whistle [and] a dancing house of definite form."[32]

Figure 14. *Assiniboin and Gros Ventre Grass Dance singers.* (Photo by Sumner W. Matteson, Fort Belknap Reservation, Montana, July 1906, courtesy NAA, neg. no. 34,055-k.)

As the Hethushka model was adapted by other tribes, they called it either the Omaha Dance or the Grass Dance. The latter designation was most certainly derived from part of the regalia worn by the Hethushka dancers: a long bunch of grass tied to the back of their belts to symbolize scalps taken in battle. But though the name Grass Dance was used, the original significance of the bunch of grass was soon forgotten by the new adherents; or they inferred the name's derivation from some local practice of long standing. Such an explanation was given by the Hidatsa Edward Goodbird (born circa 1868), for the origin of the term among his people:

> "In olden times when warriors of my own or other tribes went out on a war party, it was customary for each to carry a bunch of dry grass in the belt in damp or wet or cold weather. This was for two purposes: the dry grass could be used for starting a fire in damp weather when it was hard for the warriors to find anything dry enough for tinder; and in cold weather, the dry grass could be used to thrust into the moccasin in lieu of a stocking. The Grass Dance was to imitate a warrior's life, and I understand that the name Grass Dance comes from this old time custom of our warriors. In the dance, all warriors who had carried the dry grass in a war party did so likewise in the dance. . . . No one in the Grass Dance carried a *kip-tsi-ki* [something carried in the belt] of grass unless he had borne one on a war party."[33]

Fortunately for Native American history, information concerning the diffusion and practices of the Grass Dance was collected early enough—not only when elders were still alive who could document the dance in great detail but also when its spread was still underway. Former members of Grass Dance societies could even fairly accurately pinpoint its arrival date on a tribe by tribe basis. Thus we can follow, for example, one trail of the dance leading from the Omaha to the Teton Sioux, circa 1860;[34] from the Sioux to the Assiniboin in 1872; and from the Assiniboin to the Gros Ventre, circa 1875-80.[35]

As each group received the new ceremonial, they were evidently able to accommodate some aspects of it immediately to indigenous practices. In reviewing the variants of the Grass Dance, Wissler was able to perceive that the dance changed according to preexistent ceremonial customs of a given tribe:

> we find evidences of pattern phenomena in that some dominant ceremonial concepts of the respective localities have been incorporated in the grass dance and have inhibited the continuance of others.[36]

A clear example of this is the ritual consumption of dog flesh. Among the Dakota for whom the eating of dog flesh held great ceremonial value (see fig. 32), the Dog Feast became appended to the Grass Dance, so that by the time the Santee Sioux transferred the dance to the Mandan/Hidatsa, it was included as a ritual requirement. At the end of the first day's ceremony in transferring the ceremonial, the Santee Iron Cloud instructed them, as a matter of course, that "at every feast of this society must be brought a dog, well-boiled, with the head," which would then be divided and eaten.[37] Attempts by the Sioux, however, to transfer the Dog Feast to the Ojibwa were not always so successful, as the eating of dog flesh was considered abhorrent by most of them. In fact, sometimes Ojibwa referred to the Sioux derogatorily as *bwaanag* (roasters), alluding to the practice. Although the Dog Feast was retained by some Ojibwa in the Drum Dance, doubtless to comply completely with their instructions from the Sioux, often beef was substituted symbolically for dog (the man serving it was called bull cook [see fig. 33]) or the ritual was dropped altogether—confirming Wissler's point about the discontinuance of certain ceremonial concepts because of local inhibitions.

Some unfamiliar aspects of the Grass Dance represented such a novelty to its recipients that they had to be carefully learned from the donors. The Gros Ventre, who were camped on Milk River when they were given the Grass Dance by the Assiniboin, were obviously amused by what was for them its peculiar style of choreography:

> [They] had never had any dancing of that kind before and called it jokingly *inaetenin* (moving-buttocks) referring to the way [the Assiniboin] danced.[38]

Also to be learned were all the special songs and dances assigned to each ceremonial office of the Grass Dance Society; those appointed as ceremonial drumstick owners were responsible not only for learning all the new songs but for the exact order in which they were to be performed as well.

Grass Dance Drums and Their Transfer

One of the most important items to be transferred when the Grass Dance was given (or sold) to a tribe was the special large ceremonial drum. The drum itself was often something new, for most tribes to whom this dance spread were accustomed to using hand-drums, one to each singer. It is evident that the newly introduced musical instrument was accorded immediate respect by its recipients. For example, when the Gros Ventre moved camp, "the drum was packed on a special horse by itself and when they came to a stream, four men who owned the drumsticks carried the drum across, wading in without taking off their moccasins or other clothing."[39] Drum transfers and the subsequent attention and care given the drums by their new hosts were equally vital to the spread of the Drum Dance in the Woodlands.

Because the Ojibwa Dance Drum belongs to the same general category of American Indian membranophones as the Grass Dance drum, which predates it, one should look among examples of the latter for prototypes. There was considerable variety among Grass Dance drums, yet there were certain basic elements, which they shared.

To begin with, the large size of the Grass Dance drum is almost always mentioned in anthropological and historical literature as its paramount feature. Even though the drum may not be named, such adjectives as "big," "great," and even "immense" almost always signal that a Grass Dance drum is being described to distinguish it from a hand-drum. (The Ojibwa even today refer to their ceremonial drum as "The Big Drum.") This type of drum was clearly a new form of percussion for most recipients of the dance. Previous to that time, they had accompanied their dances as well as healing ceremonies, games, and even warfare with hand-drums. Turning to the use of any large dance drum, then, required a shift in performance practice and probably an attendant change in vocal style as well, particularly under the influence of the new repertoire of "foreign" songs transmitted with the drum. (See "The Music of the Drum Dance," pp. 92–103.)

Formerly each singer/drummer had his own hand-drum, which he used while he sang melodies in unison with other singers; each singer thus accompanied himself in a group arranged shoulder to shoulder in a row or semicircle facing the dancers or medical practitioners. (This practice still survives among some Native Americans—the Crow for instance—and is universal among circumpolar people, such as the Inuit.) The hand-drum was held almost vertically before the singer, either by a strap attached to it, if the drum were double-headed, or by crossed rawhide thongs on the back of the drum in the case of single-headed drums (fig. 15). With the introduction of a large drum suspended horizontally, singers now shared the same instrument; surrounding it meant facing each other rather than the dancers (see fig. 14).[40]

For the frame of a Grass Dance drum, the builder would either hollow out a section of a tree or cut off part of a barrel over which he then laced together the two drumheads of hide: horse, buffalo, or cow. The Arikara used part of a swamp willow; the

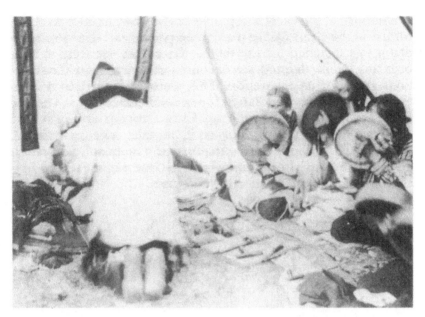

Figure 15. *Hand-drums used by Gros Ventre singers during the Bear Dance (or Medicine Pipe Dance).* (Photo by Sumner W. Matteson, Fort Belknap Reservation, Montana, July 1906, courtesy NAA, neg. no. 34,055-o.)

Figure 16. *Pause during a Grass Dance of the Oglala Sioux. Note the use of a commercial bass drum. The dancer second from the left is wearing the feather bustle called the Crow.* (Photo by James Mooney, Pine Ridge Agency, South Dakota, 1892, courtesy NAA, neg. no. 3318-a2.)

Hidatsa, a wooden washtub; the Blackfoot and Oglala Sioux even resorted to commercial bass drums, turning them on their sides for performance (fig. 16).[41]

Evidence of the early acceptance of the white man's bass drum for use in the Grass Dance makes one point clear: though a large drum was specified for the dance, there does not seem to have been any clearly defined way of constructing it nor ritual instructions given for its decoration. This is one of the crucial distinctions between the Woodlands ceremonial Dance Drum and the Grass Dance drum. Although one Grass Dance drum might have elaborate designs and symbols on it, another, once constructed, could be left simply as an unadorned functional percussion instrument or, as photographs indicate, one might even be purchased ready made from the white man.

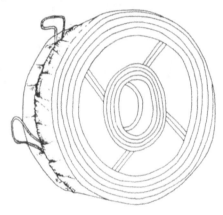

Figure 17. *Drumhead design on an Assiniboin Grass Dance drum, after an illustration by Robert H. Lowie.* (Illustration by Daphne Shuttleworth.)

The degree of attention to decoration varies considerably as does the style of ornamentation: the Assiniboin hollow-log drum described by Lowie was surrounded with red and blue flannel and had a variety of designs on it symbolizing, among other things, the sun, wounds, and slain enemies (fig. 17);[42] among Ponca drums was one "covered with red strouding from which a dozen eagle feathers were hung";[43] the Hidatsa's was simply painted black;[44] and one Winnebago drum photographed circa 1887-89 appears to be totally lacking in decoration (fig. 18). Such a plain drum would be completely unacceptable in the Ojibwa Drum Dance.

Although Grass Dance drums were sometimes beaten upon while resting on the ground, the use of support stakes to raise them for greater resonance was another common feature. Thus the Ponca Mowadani drum was "supported by four crooked sticks," the Blackfoot Hair-Parters drum was hung from curved

Figure 18. *Winnebago Grass Dance members and their drum.* (Photo by Alice C. Fletcher, Winnebago Reservation, Nebraska, circa 1887-89, courtesy NAA, neg. no. 4449.)

stakes, and the Arikara Young Dog Society's drum was "suspended by means of loops from four forked sticks driven into the ground for this purpose."[45] As we shall see, this purely functional item was greatly elaborated upon by the Ojibwa.

When the Grass Dance arrived on a reservation, it frequently replaced a dance complex belonging to some warrior society. As Flannery perceives its acceptance by the Gros Ventre, "so far as we can see, at the time of its adoption, the Grass dance was a case of pure substitution and one that fitted readily into the cultural situation."[46] Because the dance could be so easily accommodated by preexistent ceremonials, its large drum, in many places, seems simply to have been added to the arsenal of musical percussion already in use rather than supplanting it. Consequently, in the musical accompaniment for the Grass Dance we often find hand-drums continuing to be used by societies alongside the newly introduced large dance drum, although probably not for the same portions of the ceremony. That hand-drums were occasionally reserved for various rituals within the larger ceremonial complex is in fact occasionally suggested: while the Hidatsa used the large black drum they received from the Santee to learn the new Grass Dance repertoire of songs, they had used hand-drums during the ritual feeding: "the six or

Figure 19. *Hidatsa and Mandan singers using hand-drums.* (Photo by Gilbert L. Wilson, Fort Berthold Reservation, North Dakota, circa 1913, courtesy American Museum of Natural History, neg. no. 286365.)

seven drummers, beating their drums, began to sing" (fig. 19).[47] In some cases, the retention of hand-drums is explicit: in the Sarsi Hair-Parters dance, "a big drum is on the right side, supported by sticks stuck in the ground. . . . Four small drums lie in the middle"; these four hand-drums were censed with sweetgrass smoke before being given to the singers.[48]

The inventory of instruments to accompany the Grass Dance songs of some tribes extended beyond hand-drums to include rattles and other idiophones. Bear's-Teeth, the only surviving member of the Arikara Young Dog's Society, described the instruments available to the group's members, in Lowie's words:

> [Rattles which] consisted of a stick about one foot long, covered with hide, decorated with a feather at one end, and with buffalo dewclaws attached to it. . . . Pillows of tanned deer or elk hide, stuffed with buffalo hair, were beaten as if they were drums. Besides, there was one large drum hollowed out of a swamp-willow. . . . There were said to be five drummers, who were expected to be the best singers. Actually there were only four, one behind each forked [support] stick, while the fifth man stood up in the rear and acted as musical conductor; he was believed to represent the heavens.[49]

By contrast, the Ojibwa attached so much importance to the ceremonial Dance Drum, following closely what were assumed to be Tailfeather Woman's (and thus the Great Spirit's) instructions in building and decorating it, that no other musical instrument approached its status. As a result, the Ojibwa use of the single large drum exclusive of other instruments is an important distinguishing feature separating theirs from Grass Dance practices.[50]

The Ojibwa Attitude toward the Drum and Its Care

"Well, we treat [the Drum] as a person. That's the way we [Menominee] was preached [by the Ojibwa] . . . they even make special beds for that Drum. Keep it as a person. We Indians do that just for the sake of God; appreciate, take care of that Drum good, because that's his power. That's why we decorate that Drum, make it look pretty, clean, because it's from God."[51]

In every respect the Ojibwa regard the Drum as though it were a living being. Once engendered by the incorporation of some part of an earlier Drum, then dressed in ceremonial garb, the Drum is cared for as though it were an important personage commanding respect and requiring attention to its physical needs.

In describing the diffusion of the Grass Dance, Wissler noted that the distinctive aspect of the Ojibwa (and Menominee) version of it was their focus on the Drum as a sacred object.[52] Whereas a large drum was an important accessory to the dance as practiced by other tribes, it nevertheless remained a secular musical instrument. But in the Woodlands the Drum became so central to the dance that it was even invested with medicine attributes. This would explain why the Ojibwa are sometimes reluctant to have their Drums photographed[53] and why, whenever a broken drumhead is removed, the people surround the Drum to be imbued with the beneficial "power" released by the Drum.[54] For the same reason, one is not supposed to be stingy about keeping a Drum in his home but to share it with others.[55]

In revering the Drum, Ojibwa address it as *gimishoomisinaan* (our grandfather), the same term used by the *mide* to identify the guiding spirit in their westward migration.[56] Johnny Matchokamow explained the Menominee "grandfather" appellation by saying that in dreams the Drum turns into an old man. He related one dream in which the old man appeared to a woman in exactly the place where her Drum had been.[57] To attend a Drum meeting is even called by some "going to talk with grandfather."[58]

As much as the Drum has beneficial effects, its power enables it to inflict harm as well. This is consistent with the general Ojibwa belief concerning medicine: the more knowledgeable one becomes in its use, the greater his capacity for "bad medicine" as well—thus, the respect accorded medicine men, lest they turn to using it. This belief in the duplicity of power is implicit in one member's interpretation of the drumhead design. Noting that it was half red and half blue, he explained:

> "This religion is half good. The other way, [if] a person wants to make fun of it, he gets bad luck on that. We got to use that Drum in a good way. Like if I go to work and make fun of that Drum, I throw it away, someplace, like that, you know; if I don't treat it right, something will come up to me."[59]

Stories are told of those attempting to harm the Drum. Their efforts backfired as a result of the instrument's power: a man who once angrily pounded the Drum with his fist was crippled for life the next day in a car accident,[60] and when a Keshena woman tried to destroy her husband's Drum with an ax, her brother died immediately afterward.[61] The Drum is meant to be protected at all times. Because it must never touch the bare ground, mats, blankets, and rugs are placed beneath it. Where it "rests" in its owner's house, these coverings are called its "bed," and so that the Drum will not become lonely, a kerosene lamp is kept lit at night next to it.[62] Some owners even take their instruments with them if they are to be absent for a time; during the haying season one man kept his Drum with him where he stayed in the hayfield for four days.[63]

Drums are removed in the presence of objectionable people; should they disturb a dance, the Quitting Song is performed forthwith to dissolve the event, and the Drum carried out of the dance ring to protect it from trouble or abuse:

> "If you have song service at night, maybe somebody come kind of drunk and try to do something; try to join in there [and] disturb everything. Sing that song right away and then quit, before that person do a damage or something like that; and take care of the Drum and put him away."[64]

Out of respect for the Drum one is expected to maintain decorum in its presence. People should never vent anger over some matter or otherwise "act foolish" in front of it.[65] A young man from Round Lake, Wisconsin, who appeared at a dance without a shirt was publicly berated by one of the officials who complained of the "impropriety of the participation of a person in such scanty attire in the dances held in the presence of the drum and in its honor."[66]

A singer must be attentive to his performance on the Drum. If he hits it out of time, he must rise and "dance off" the error in place, "acknowledging his error, and signifying that no intentional slight to the drum has been committed."[67]

Like a close friend or relative, the Drum is meant to be visited. When presented with a Drum, in his acceptance speech, the Menominee Chief Wiskino promised his Lac du Flambeau Drum donors that when his friends came to visit the instrument about every four days, they would together ask the Drum to help them live a just life without harm to others.[68] When a former naval officer, who as a boy had belonged to a Potawatomi Drum, came home, "he felt personally compelled, as soon as he had returned to the reservation, to visit the Drum of which he was a member, to pay his respects, to make an offering and to caress the Drum lovingly."[69]

Drums are dressed, and their attire thereafter should be kept in good condition; they are ritually "fed" and presented with gifts; and before they are given away, Drums are bade farewell. When tobacco is donated at a ceremony, while the pipe tender receives some of it, the greater share goes to the Drum.[70] At the 1910 presentation Densmore witnessed, "certain delicacies had been 'presented to the drum'; these were placed beside the drum until the time of the feast, when they were divided among the singers."[71] In 1939 at Lac Court Oreilles, a special farewell song was performed for the Woman's Dance drum before it was taken down from its stakes for the last time to be given to the Winnebago.[72]

Clearly, then, the single large dance drum came to occupy the central position in the new Ojibwa ceremonialism by the end of the nineteenth century. Endowed with anthropomorphic characteristics, it was revered to a degree far exceeding its role in the Grass Dance. As we shall see in describing the technology of the drum, the Ojibwa, sparing no expense, devoted great time and care to its construction and decoration and also provided the instrument with elaborate accessories.

The process of transformation of the Grass Dance drum into the Ojibwa ceremonial Drum may have been gradual at first but accelerated once the vision of Tailfeather Woman was disseminated eastward. Conjectures concerning this process, however, must be based on a consideration of the most probable line of transmission as the Grass Dance spread to the western Woodlands.

The Santee Sioux as Transmitters of the Grass Dance

It is particularly important to examine the Santee form of the Grass Dance, for it must be from some band within this division of Sioux that elements of the Grass Dance reached the Ojibwa through the Siouan emissary, Tailfeather Woman.[73] Not only are the Santee geographically the most proximate group west of the Ojibwa, but the history of the enmity as well as peace and cultural contacts between the two tribes is noteworthy. In the Menominee stories describing the Drum's origin it is always the *wi-kwana-skiw* or "Minnesota [Santee] Sioux" who are being killed by United States soldiers.[74] Because the Drum was prescribed to bring an end to the warfare between the Sioux and Ojibwa, it is safe to assume that some member of this division was the intended recipient of the revelation.

For nearly two hundred years, until the middle of the nineteenth century, the Ojibwa had slowly and in small skirmishes forced the Santee from northern Wisconsin into southern and western Minnesota. After a Santee uprising in 1862 killing settlers in Minnesota, thirty Sioux were hanged—others escaping death through a pardon from President Lincoln. The Santee were then forcibly settled by Congress on three reservations in Dakota Territory. As late as 1935, when Ruth Landes conducted her study at Prairie Island, her informants:

> still told bitterly how their fore-bears had been driven from Lake Superior woodlands by the Ojibwa three centuries before. Their traditional life and memories were bound up with the Ojibwa, as centuries-long enemies, periodic truce-friends and source of marriage partners and continuous sharers in cultural exchanges.[75]

Landes heard tales of Ojibwa atrocities against the Santee (babies' heads impaled on poles) and found constant references to them in the war stories told at Prairie Island: "the Ojibwa were [the Santee's] preferred opponents; it was they who starred as enemies in the war tales. To the Santee, they seemed nearly the sole enemy among aboriginal neighbors."[76]

In the origin tale, the building of the Drum and dancing effectively caused the United States soldiers to stop their slaughter of the Sioux. Still, the emphasis is primarily upon using the Drum to end bloodshed between the Sioux and Ojibwa (cf. Baker's version). As the Menominee tell it:

> "Then, after awhile, the Great Spirit probably told [Tail-feather Woman] to make friends with those others [of different tribes], her fellow men, to give them that affair, to give them that Drum. These Sioux and the Chippewa . . . always fought with each other. Whenever they saw each other, they would immediately fight with each other, kill each other. That was the way they used to be."[77]

In the continuation of the story, the Ojibwa capture a Sioux boy who then acts as an intermediary between the two enemies. After the Ojibwa have prepared a large dancing area, they hear a drum in the distance. A fog descends and they hear the Sioux singing. When the songs stop, the fog lifts, revealing the Sioux who come forward to shake hands with them:

> "And so even to this day they are friends. There has never been any evil between them. Everything has been [good between them] since they gave them that Drum."[78]

While the band of Sioux to which Tailfeather Woman belonged may never be known, it is tempting to conjecture that she was a Mdewakantonwan or Mystic Lake Sioux, the most easterly of the Santee. Since it is not known where or what "Mystic Lake" actually is, Landes surmises that it "may not have been an actual body of water but possibly the site of a great revelation by vision."[79] (Could this have been the lake in which Tailfeather Woman hid?) Moreover, of all the Santee the Mystic Lake people had the simplest police system, in which case their version of the Grass Dance might have proven the most accommodating to the Ojibwa, for the Plains police systems were generally foreign to them.[80]

Much of the best information concerning the Santee Grass Dance can be found in the Gilbert L. Wilson manuscripts deposited with the Minnesota Historical Society. Wilson collected two accounts of the dance in 1914, one each from former members of the two Hidatsa Grass Dance societies, Edward Goodbird (born circa 1868) and Wolf Chief (born circa 1849).[81] Wolf Chief's description of the "purchase" of the dance from the Isanti Dakota and his recollections of the transfer and rituals are by far the longer and more detailed of the two accounts. Wilson had Goodbird review Wolf Chief's information; based on the review, Goodbird observed that the ceremonies of the two societies were identical and pronounced Wolf Chief's account as accurate.

When a Native American ceremonial belonging to one tribe is requested by another (i.e., they wish to "buy" it), the recipients always take great pains to learn exactly what it is they are supposed to do in perpetuating the ceremonial. This attention to orthodoxy involves everything from copying the ritual costuming of the donors in great detail, to spending lengthy song sessions together to learn the new repertoire of music meant to accompany ritual actions. The care with which these songs are learned has resulted in the widespread phenomenon of tribes singing songs containing texts in a language other than their own, the meaning of which is usually not understood by the performers. Wolf Chief, for instance, gave Wilson the text of a Grass Dance song he had learned more than thirty years earlier. The song was intended to be performed during the feeding ritual, but Wolf Chief seemed unsure of its translation. It contained one word, *wita*, which he did not know at all. "Perhaps it is a Santee word [said Wolf Chief]. I do not know what the song refers to."[82]

Rather than reiterating here all the ceremonial details given by Goodbird and Wolf Chief, I have integrated the relevant material from the two accounts into my later discussions, as the Santee-Hidatsa Grass Dance practices are compared with those of the Ojibwa-Menominee Drum Dance. For the moment, a brief outline of the events of the Grass Dance transfer will suffice.

Two Grass Dance societies were established at Like-a-Fish-hook-Village, the home of the Mandan and Hidatsa. Goodbird had joined the first of these, the Big Grass Dance Society, when he was fourteen years old. The Hidatsa had initially seen the dance at Devil's Lake and later formed a "purchasing party" circa 1879 to inform the Santee that they wished to obtain the dance from them.[83] The party consisted of about thirty people of all ages belonging to different societies. Goodbird's father, Son-of-a-Star, who had belonged to the Black Mouth Society before becoming a member of the Grass Dance, was a member of the group that went to Devil's Lake with their request. "On this invitation, the Santee came one summer to our village to arrange the purchase. My mother says that this was when I was about three years old."[84]

After the Big Grass Dance Society was founded, two years later a second one was purchased from the Santee. It was a smaller organization consisting mostly of young men who had been unable to join the first society; since they did not have the rights to the songs and rituals, they decided to purchase them from the Santee for their own organization. It was called the Night Grass Society because they frequently held their dances after dark. Wolf Chief joined when he was thirty-two years old.

The fifty Santee men and twenty-five women who had come some one hundred and eighty miles on foot were housed by the villagers, who gave them a feast the evening of their arrival. The Sioux were fed in Big Brave's earth lodge, which was cleared of furniture for the event (fig. 20). The speeches of the Santee Walking Soldier were interpreted into Hidatsa by the Mandan Big Thief. Walking Soldier began, as follows:

Figure 20. *Earth lodge on the Mandan/Hidatsa reservation (Fort Berthold), circa 1913. It was in a lodge such as this that the Santee transferred the Grass Dance circa 1882, once the furniture had been removed from it to allow room for feasting and dancing.* (Photo by Gilbert L. Wilson, courtesy American Museum of Natural History, neg. no. 288283.)

"Our friends, last summer we came to visit you at this place and at that time we promised you that we would sell to you our society. Also, those [Santee] visitors who came last summer—eight of them there were—sang the songs of the Grass Dance and your young men tried to learn them. You asked us to return and teach you the songs so that you would know them. . . . These men here, the Sioux, your friends, wish also to give to you besides the songs, the Grass dance outfits [beadwork, bells, head-dresses, etc.]. This dance society is a sacred society, and we observe it with reverence. When a war party is out they pray to these objects for success."[85]

Walking Soldier then mentioned that the Santee promise to transfer the dance was dependent upon a propitious moment.

They had learned that the Hidatsa had killed four Black Hills Sioux the winter before; the Santee interpreted the successful skirmish and subsequent rejoicing in Like-a-Fishhook-Village as the favorable sign needed to clear the way for the Grass Dance transfer. In Wolf Chief's account, the remainder of the evening was taken up by Walking Soldier, as he outlined the structure of the society for the Hidatsa, the various offices and their functions, and where those who held them were meant to be situated during the ceremonies. This was followed by a song rehearsal that lasted until midnight. Such rehearsing would have to continue for five nights, in Walking Soldier's estimation, after which the Hidatsa would be able to perform the songs properly.

The dance transfer was to have taken place the next day, once the Hidatsa had selected their officers. A grudge fight, however, broke out at the local trading store and ended in one man's death, causing the Sioux to postpone the ceremony for a day. When it resumed, all gathered once again in the lodge, the Sioux "very elegantly" dressed in their regalia, the Hidatsa and Mandan only in their finest clothes, for they had not yet been given their dance outfits. Walking Soldier announced the officers selected for the new organization, and the Sioux began the transfer during the singing of songs as each new officer was led to his proper place in the lodge.

Thereafter began the recompense to the Santee. In payment for the dance, Wolf Chief, who had been elected an officer, described his share:

> "my mother and sister and brothers had brought calico and goods, and they now laid these in a pile on the floor at my feet, together with a stick which represented the gift of a horse. Of course, a horse could not well be brought into the lodge, and so a stick was made to represent it. Some of the young men chosen to be officers gave as many as two or three horses. [The interpreter] Big Thief's relatives brought many rich gifts and laid them in a pile before him. . . . Before each of the newly chosen officers was a pile of gifts three feet or more in height. . . . Of horses given to the Sioux, I think the number must have aggregated about one hundred."[86]

The Sioux drum keeper then transferred the Grass Dance drum to the Hidatsa, picking up the pile of gifts in front of Big Brave, leaving the drum in their place, and giving him his new dancing "suit." Each Sioux officer of the society did likewise with his Hidatsa counterpart. Once they learned their proper ritual positions, all the new officers returned to their initial seats around the circumference of the lodge, and ten Sioux singers moved to surround the drum where it had been left untouched to the right of the door:

> "And now the visiting Sioux went through the ceremony of making friends of the Hidatsas and Mandans. A Sioux would arise and walk to the place . . . behind the fireplace and say, 'I want to make so- and-so my friend!' The Hidatsa or Mandan named would arise and go to him . . . when the Sioux would present him with the dance outfit that he carried on his left arm, and the Hidatsa, as he received it would say, 'I give you a horse!' and at once don his newly received outfit."[87]

The Sioux then rehearsed the ceremony with the recipients—how to open the dance, what the trail bearers should do with their feather belts, and so on. The proper songs to accompany each action were performed, interspersed with nonritual songs during which everyone (except the women) got up to dance, meandering wherever they wished while pantomiming war experiences. This continued until sunset, when the two Santee chiefs announced, "Your friends, the Sioux, are tired now, and so are you; we will quit now and dance again tonight." At this point, the elaborate Dog Feast was demonstrated to the Hidatsa, with four men who had been wounded in battle selected to be eaters of the dog's head. In the midst of that ceremony, the four belt wearers retired to a log house some thirty yards from the dance lodge where many kettles of various food items prepared for the feast had been kept. Upon returning, with soup, bacon, biscuits, fried bread, pies, and coffee, still wearing their feather bustles, they distributed the food to the assemblage. The Dog Feast rituals were resumed and completed with much dancing until the Santee began the Quitting Song:

> "Woman's Ghost [the Hidatsa wearer of the red feather belt] at once arose . . . from his place in the circle behind and between the two rear big central posts, [danced] past the fireplace on the left side, and toward and nearly up to the door of the lodge . . . [where he performed ritual feints of striking an enemy with a small red stick, dancing back and forth from the door to the fireplace and finally directly out of the lodge]. This was the signal for the company to arise, which we did; and with no particular order we went out of the door and to our homes."[88]

The Movement of the Drum

The Santee were prolific in their transfer of the Grass Dance, its drum, and its rituals. Although they traveled west to teach the Hidatsa, there is no question that their lines of communication were to the east as well. It is fairly safe to assume that the Sioux who brought to White Earth in 1891 their "new dance," which had so aroused the Reverend Gilfillan, were Santee and possibly even from Devil's Lake. The Ojibwa in accepting the dance were probably no different from the Hidatsa with one important exception: they had an obligation to copy the drum and keep it "moving."

Tailfeather Woman's revelation was explicit in its instructions for the future: the Drum was to be passed on to establish inter-tribal peace and brotherhood. In accordance with the wishes of the Great Spirit, then, the Drum Dance was actively disseminated from the Ojibwa to other tribes and within the next fifty years the proliferation of Drums would be great. As Drum members describe it:

"Them Drums, they keep travelling, keep travelling. They got to keep them so long; maybe four years. After four years come, you know, you got to pass them on."[89]

Beyond the Minnesota and Wisconsin tribes Drums found their way to the Fox in Iowa, the Potawatomi in Kansas, and as far as the Absentee Shawnee in Oklahoma and the Plains Ojibwa in Manitoba.[90] In its initial stages one can assume that the Drum Dance, once organized, spread fairly rapidly from its point of origin. Still, once a Drum was received, some time was needed for the ceremonial to take hold and the songs and rituals to have sufficient rehearsal to be comfortably taught to others. Also, there was the time needed in constructing a replacement for the "giveaway" Drum and assembling the material goods to accompany it before the Drum could "travel" again. It would seem that, in the early years of the Drum, at least a year or two would be required to accomplish all this. Although the Menominee said that the length of time was dependent solely on how long it took to accumulate the necessary gifts and that it could be as short a period as a few months, we must remember that this was told to Densmore some forty years after they had first received the dance; during that time they had received many Drums and were thoroughly acquainted with the rituals.[91]

Gradually it became accepted that the "ideal" length of time to retain a Drum was four years, the number clearly selected for its

ritual significance.[92] By this century, however, the intervals between Drum arrivals in some communities had lengthened to
about a decade: on the Menominee Reservation, the Whitefeather Drum arrived in 1911, the Pete Sam Drum circa 1918, the
Johnny Matchokamow Drum in 1928, and the Kemewan Drum
in 1942.[93]

Theoretically, the Drum is to travel in a clockwise direction.
This has its parallel in the general directional movements of
dancing among the people who adopted the Drum Dance. That
is, most of their dances—even secular ones—proceed clockwise
around a centrally located drum. This has ritual significance for
the Ojibwa, as it is meant to celebrate the order of birth of the
Four Winds.[94] Circling clockwise is so habitual for them, in fact,
that the occasional counterclockwise dancing of other tribes—
some Iroquoian dancing, for example—seems peculiar to them.
(Once, I was helping Baker cut a circular piece of plywood for his
drum frame. As he held a nail in the middle of the board
attached to a string with a pencil tied to its other end, I began to
draw the circle, proceeding in a counterclockwise direction. He
quickly interrupted me: "No, no, you're going the Mohawk
way!")

In outlining the Drum's history, John Bisonette, a Lac Court
Oreilles Ojibwa, provided Ritzenthaler with what he called "the
path of the Drum" by naming the sequence of donor communities from Minnesota through Wisconsin. (This is transformed
for the reader into the map in fig. 21. Cf. also fig. 5.)

Since the Sioux presented the first Drum to the Ojibwa, its
travel was set in motion from west to east. Once the Wisconsin
Ojibwa, Menominee, and Potawatomi had been reached circa
1875-80, the line of travel turned to the south, toward the Winnebago, and then west.[95] The Fox in Iowa, who had received it
from the Wisconsin Potawatomi, in turn transferred it to the
Potawatomi in Kansas, who then brought it to Oklahoma, and so
on.[96]

Bisonette's map is generally substantiated by the testimony of a
number of Ojibwa who received and/or donated Drums. We
know that Drums at Lac Court Oreilles came from the Saint
Croix Ojibwa: the Mitchell Quagon Drum was received circa
1917 from the Pine Lake band; the John Stone Drum came from
Lake Lena (a Saint Croix settlement) circa 1931-41 and was later
presented to Lac du Flambeau Ojibwa.[97] Also, while most Drums
at Flambeau were presented to them by the Lac Court Oreilles
people, some came from Bad River: circa 1920 Jim Crow of Lac

72

Figure 21. *"The path of the Drum" as given by John Bisonette of Lac Court Oreilles Reservation to Robert Ritzenthaler, circa 1941.* (Illustration by Daphne Shuttleworth.)

Court Oreilles gave Flambeau his Drum; they made a replacement Drum for him but he gave that at Lac du Flambeau as well;[98] in 1941 all three Drums at Flambeau were from Lac Court Oreilles (there had been a fourth belonging to George Brown, but he had given it to the Menominee); the Drum that Bijikens from Flambeau donated to the Menominee in the 1910 ceremony described by Densmore had come from Odanah (Bad River Reservation) four years earlier,[99] while the John Coon Lac Court Oreilles Drum went first to Flambeau and thence to the Keshena Menominee.[100] At the end of Bisonette's path, Drums were exchanged between contiguous Ojibwa bands: in 1918 the Lac Vieux Desert Ojibwa gave an eight-day dance at Antigo to present the Mole Lake Ojibwa with a Drum.

Bisonette's line of transmission is curious, however, in its omission of Mille Lacs, Minnesota, as a donor community. Not only have Drum societies been active there for years, but Mille Lacs is geographically intermediate between the Saint Croix bands and the two northwestern Minnesota reservations that Bisonette had indicated as at the beginning of the path. Moreover, in other data collected by Ritzenthaler from Lac Court Oreilles residents, Mille Lacs is specifically mentioned as having given Saint Croix their first and second Drums. Wasigisik even named the man who had brought the first Drum from Milles Lacs, "Zewabetago." It is quite possible that Ritzenthaler received incorrectly or misspelled in his notes the name Shewabigito (Resounding Metal) and that the person intended by Wasigisik was a well-known *mide* priest, Jiwabikito,[101] a Mille Lacs "removal" living at White Earth and one of Densmore's principal informants on the manufacture of bows and arrows.[102] White Earth was populated with Mille Lacs people relocated there by the federal government; because many of them had moved back to Mille Lacs, strong cultural and ceremonial ties existed between the two communities.[103]

White Earth is the westernmost of Ojibwa reservations in Minnesota and has a long history of contacts with the Sioux. It is

Figure 22. *Secular dance at White Earth Reservation, Minnesota, June 1906. Man at the right is Chief Wadena. The presence of small beaded pads in addition to the customary four large ones is unusual.* (Photo by Frank Churchill, courtesy Museum of the American Indian, Heye Foundation, neg. no. 27533.)

not completely clear as yet to what extent, if any, the Drum Dance was active on that reservation. At least one photograph taken there in 1906 shows a large drum, with decorations conforming to those of the ceremonial Dance Drum (fig. 22). Nevertheless, the context appears to be secular, and the drum lacks the ceremonial head decoration and rests on the bare ground. The Reverend Gilfillan, who complained of Siouan dances at White Earth in 1890, recalled an even earlier occasion involving a large drum. In a speech given in 1897, he recalled with his usual disdain for "native" activities the arrival in January 1873 of some sixty "old Grand Medicine men . . . bringing the big medicine drum with them from Red Lake. Their coming created a greater sensation than would that of Paderewski to your city. The big drum was brought out with all the old fellows from Red Lake singing around it." In response, the White Earth people were "whooping and dancing around the drum, telling stories about the Sioux they had scalped and having a veritable orgy which made night and day hideous for weeks."[104]

Gilfillan's account, which also mentions Dog Feasts, suggests some form of the Grass Dance, particularly in depicting the drum as "big" and noting the public recounting of war tales. Since some Wisconsin Ojibwa (including Baker) mention White Earth as the possible site of the original Sioux Drum transfer, it may be that the path of the Drum went from that reservation *through* Mille Lacs to Saint Croix. What seems more likely is that Mille Lacs was a dissemination center from which the Drum traveled both northwest to White Earth through its "removals," and east to Saint Croix.

While the path of the Drum given by Bisonette is generally accurate, as the number of Drums increased, the directions they took were not always directly along that path nor were they always clockwise. Histories of Drums are often obscure due to simple forgetfulness or a lack of communication between groups once a Drum was transferred. Thus, Lac Court Oreilles informants in 1940 thought there was at least one Drum at Mole Lake but were not certain, or Jim Crow, who gave two Drums away at Flambeau, admitted "a lot of other drums were given away but I don't remember who they belong to."[105] But what is clear is that the number of societies within a given community and the number of tribes practicing the Drum Dance increased and a pattern of giving away drums in *any* direction emerged. Intermediary groups along the path could be bypassed. For instance, John Pete's Uncle Carl at Lac Vieux Desert in Michigan on the far northeastern Wisconsin border got a Drum directly from Sose at Saint Croix on the Minnesota border circa 1921 and Steve Grover at Lac Court Oreilles eventually gave his Drum directly to the Kansas Potawatomi.[106] Or, as Drum activity increased, we also find Drums arriving in the same community from several sources, often at about the same time. Not only did the Kansas Potawatomi receive the Grover Wisconsin Ojibwa Drum, but in 1907 they had gotten two from the Kansas Kickapoo, then two more from the Iowa Fox, who gave them a third in 1923:

> The sixth Drum arrived improperly and uncer-emoniously in 1917 when its Chief and owner, a Kansas Kickapoo became enamored of a Potawatomi woman, married her and moved onto the Potawatomi reservation bringing with him his Drum and part of his cohort of Kickapoo officers. This Drum, appropriately enough, is nicknamed "The Visitor."[107]

There is even some suggestion that Drums traveled west to the Sioux, although this would certainly be discounted by Baker who has visited members of that tribe with the specific intent of finding the Drum but without success.[108] On two occasions during a 1911 Whitefish (Lac Court Oreilles) ceremony, visitors announced the presence of (presumably) ceremonial drums on Sioux reservations. A man from the Saint Croix area had visited some Sioux whom he found were lacking a drum. "They had formerly possessed one, but had given it away. He suggested the desirability of the people of Whitefish making a new drum and presenting it to these Sioux."[109] Another visitor, claiming to have participated in the Drum Dance among many tribes, found it to be the same everywhere. He had also taken part, he told the crowd, in a Sioux Drum Dance:

> [The dance took place] far toward the west, in the Sioux country, to the music of a drum which had been made by the Whitefish people and which had been presented to them by another community toward the west and which had eventually found its way to their comparatively remote region. He also told how the story of this particular drum's origin was still kept by its present owners, and how they always spoke with great respect concerning the people of Whitefish.[110]

How much truth there was to his assertions or whether they were merely fabricated to flatter the Whitefish community, as they did, is not known.

The Drum Dance and Its Functions

The Structure of a Drum Society

Walking Soldier arose and spoke: "Now I will call out the names of you who have been chosen for officers."... The Sioux now began to sing, and two of the feather belt wearers got up and began to dance ... [they] took Big Brave and led him back to a place in the rear of the lodge. ... They danced once around, singing, and chose me ... seating me ... facing the fireplace.... Before each of the newly chosen officers was a pile of [their] gifts ... and now the drum keeper, also a Sioux, arose and picked up all the gifts [piled before Big Brave] and in their place set down the big drum and gave to Big Brave his dance outfit.... Each one of the other officers of the Sioux ... gave to his corresponding office of our own party his dance outfit, and took up from the floor the gifts piled there by the relations of the young candidate [Santee/ Hidatsa, circa 1881].[1]

And when Kemewan start selecting each member in that Drum there, that member from Flambeau, when Kemewan selects one from here to take his place ... this [Ojibwa] gentleman, he's got a bunch of goods or something, you know, three, four blankets, or whatever he wants to give for his replacement. So when they came for me to go sit in that east stick [drum support leg] over there, well there was a guy there, sitting there already from the Flambeau reservation.... Well, he gets up, and then he puts that bundle [of gifts] down there, whatever it is, you know ... he kind of give you in return for taking his place [Ojibwa/Menominee, 1942].[2]

Perhaps the clearest evidence of the relationship between the Grass Dance and Drum Dance is the close parallel of the structure of the two societies. Not only is the membership of each divided into equivalent offices having much the same functions, but the officers themselves are called by equivalent names in the different languages, and in one instance—the *ogichidaa* (warrior)—the name itself (possibly of Dakota origin) became a loan word adopted by tribes practicing the Drum Dance. To show this relationship I have outlined in the appendix "Drum Society Structures," the structure of the Grass Dance Society as given to the Hidatsa circa 1881 and that of the Drum Dance some sixty years later at Lac Court Oreilles. A comparison of the two will show that the general outlines of the former served as the basis for the latter organization. Many offices appear to have been taken over by the Ojibwa intact, possibly as instructed by Tailfeather Woman herself.

The structure of nearly all Grass Dance and related societies of tribes other than the Santee conform more or less to the same type, with official drum owners, female and male singers, pipe lighters, heralds, waiters, and additional members. Variations between society organizations are usually insignificant: where the Ponca Iskaiyuha Society had but four female singers, the Iowa Helocka Society had eight—four chosen by the dance leaders, four by the male singers.[3] Since the function of each female singer was identical, the difference would be simply in the volume of their singing.

Variations in the structure of the societies can be attributed to several factors. For example, it was customary for Plains tribes to continue to add special offices to their dance once it had been transmitted to them. Some offices might have had a local history predating the Grass Dance; others might be adopted from Grass Dance contacts with tribes other than the original donor. New ways of performing the ceremonial seen elsewhere may have been appealing, particularly to younger members of the society. The Sarsi Grass Dance, "clearly a social organization largely in the control of the younger members of the tribe," had its origins circa 1883; certain additional elements, however, were obtained later from the Southern Piegan and were in use by 1905.[4] Some offices—usually the least important ones—were allowed to go vacant upon the death of those filling them; in time, such offices might be dropped altogether and forgotten.[5] Or, what had been the same office at one time in the societies of two tribes could change in name and function over several generations. This is particularly true when the duties of one office holder became absorbed by another. The Menominee formerly had two officials—the aide (*oshkaabewis*) and the belt man—with different songs assigned to each. By 1928 the office of aide and belt man had been combined.[6]

An example illustrating this discussion is the office of whip man, which, it will be noted, is absent from the Ojibwa Drum Dance Society as described in the appendix "Drum Society Structures." The office was not among those given to the Hidatsa by the Santee when the Grass Dance was sold to them but was added later. There were two Hidatsa whip men who sat at either end of the dancing circle. Their job was to whip the dancers—supposedly on the legs and lightly—"if they became indolent or sluggish."[7] In fact, they had the right to whip them harshly anywhere on the body—even drawing blood—if they compensated the dancer with a valuable gift, such as a horse.[8] How far back this custom existed in North America is not known. William Strachey in *The Historie of Travell to Virginia Britania* (1612) describes sacred processions led by men with rattles and followed by "certayne of the Chiefest young men with long Switches in their handes to keepe them in their places."[9] While this office is absent from the Ojibwa Drum society it seems to have survived in the Potawatomi Drum Dance. James Clifton has theorized the Grass Dance whip man as the prototype for the office the Potawatomi now call "Big Stick or Staffman" (*pakokwanni*). This particular position exists on only four of their seven drums, and, in his opinion, may have been used to symbolize Christ when the Drum was first given to them.[10]

One particular office in the Santee Grass Dance—the Red Feather belt man—was retained in the Lac Court Oreilles Drum Dance, although in the 1940s it was in the process of losing its identity and the requirements for filling the position. Its original intent was recalled by John Bisonette, and one of the ritual functions performed by the office was still being perpetuated in the 1940s. In the Santee Grass Dance four men were chosen to wear feather belts, one of whom wore a special belt with red feathers to signify that he had been wounded in combat. His most significant function was to close the dance, which he did by enacting a sham battle at the doorway to the lodge. As Wolf Chief described it, Woman's Ghost, the Santee Red Feather belt man, danced toward the door as the Quitting Songs began. Upon reaching the exit, "he paused and with a little stick painted red (as if the bearer had been wounded) he raised the stick as if he were about to strike an enemy," whereupon he danced backward to the fireplace. This ritual feigning was performed three times; "a fourth time he raised his stick, but this time brought it down as if striking an enemy, and at the same time dancing straight out of the door." The rest of the members followed him in no particular order and returned to their homes.[11]

In the Ojibwa retention of this ritual, to close the ceremony, the head warrior announces the four Quitting Songs. During the last two of them, an old man who has been appointed to the task leads the dancers around the ring four times:

Before he starts, however, he blocks the doorway with a coat set up to represent a Sioux and the Bullcooks start lowering the flags. After he has danced four times around the ring, he points his stick three times at the coat blocking the entrance and symbolically "shoots" it on the fourth. Then he goes out of the ring and the others follow. This used to be done by the man with the feather belt, preferably by someone who had been wounded by a Sioux. Nowadays, there isn't anyone around who has been wounded by a Sioux, so they just appoint some old man to play the role.[12]

A Drum Society was initiated much the same way as the Grass Dance was purchased: someone was selected or expressed his desire to be a Drum owner. Often the inspiration was motivated by a desire to conform to social and ceremonial patterns elsewhere in the community. This explains why eventually on most reservations there came to be a Drum in each of the principal settlements. On Lac Court Oreilles Reservation in 1935 there were five Drums, one each at Chief Lake, Reserve, Round Lake, Whitefish, and Barbertown.[13] On Menominee Reservation circa 1928, the people living at Zoar felt uneasy about not having a Drum while there was one at Keshena on the reservation ten miles away. The situation was rectified one day when Johnny Matchokamow's cousin from Lac du Flambeau brought him tobacco asking if he would accept a Drum. After it had been agreed upon, the cousin returned to Flambeau to inform his people and decide on a date for the Drum presentation. (This particular Drum giveaway was described by Densmore in *Menominee Music* [1932].)[14] Meanwhile, Johnny, who was to become the new Drum owner, selected the members he wished to fill the various offices, as is the owner's prerogative.

Once organized and possessing a Drum, a society is usually called by the Drum owner's name—the Kemewan Drum (Zoar), or the Henry Davis Drum (Mille Lacs), or the John Coon Drum (Lac Court Oreilles), although the entire membership of a given drum may be referred to informally by where they live—the Round Lake group or the Whitefish Drum.[15] (Community names are still used by a master of ceremonies at secular pow-wows where visiting drums perform in rotation at his direction over a public address system.) Additionally, Drums may be given nicknames that reflect local history or some aspect of the Drum's decoration: at Mille Lacs, the Rainbow Drum derives its name from the design painted on the drumhead; the Visitor Drum of the Potawatomi has been mentioned; the Potawatomi have another drum called the Joker that can be substituted for any of their other six drums.[16]

A relatively complete Drum society will have about thirty members, dependent, of course, upon how many positions are filled.[17] Drum societies tend to consist of bilineal relations of the Drum owner; usually the women of the Drum are the wives of its officers.[18] Membership is for life and reflects fairly accurately the social structure of the community. Vacancies are usually filled by relatives, or they may be voted into the society (see "Filling Vacancies," pp. 261–62).[19] When a Drum owner dies, inheritance passes to his son, assuming he is of a proper character and capable of assuming the responsibilities associated with the job.[20] One Menominee who inherited a Drum was deemed unsuitable to serve as its owner because he had married a Catholic; instead, another was selected to fill the office.[21] Despite variations in their organization, rituals, and songs, various Drums are associated with each other in larger ceremonials; the Drums taken together, as Clifton sees it, "form a religious congregation" (fig. 23).[22]

Figure 23. *A pause for food and refreshment during a Drum Dance at Lac Court Oreilles, July 1910. The membership of one Drum, including its warrior women, can be seen in the foreground surrounding the Drum. The women seated along the fence in the background probably belong to another Drum.* (Photo by S. A. Barrett, courtesy Milwaukee Public Museum, neg. no. 20206.)

The congregational aspects of Drum dances should be stressed: the belief is that if an individual belongs to one Drum he or she belongs to all of them. As the Menominee Rattlesnake put it, "There is really only one drum in this world."[23] For this reason, there was no problem appointing "49 Jim" Hart to be owner of one Lac Court Oreilles Drum, even though he was originally from the Pine Lake/Luck settlement, a community sixty miles to the southwest that had disintegrated. Moreover, because all Drums are considered equivalent, a member of one society has the right to the same office on other Drums:

> "No matter where you go, you go to the next reservation and drum there. Happen to get there, well, they're having a song service or something, well, you got rights to go over there and sit down there, too. That's the rules they got, anyway."[24]

This notion of communality is symbolized at the end of the Drum Dance, when singers from various Drums will join together to retire each Drum one by one.[25]

Because the Great Spirit imbued the Drum with his power, during ceremonies Drum members believe they are representing or "sitting in for" the various spirit helpers of the Great Spirit. The Drum is said to represent the world, and its members surround it just as the spirits surround the world. Even specific roles are played to symbolize the Drum's beginning: the Drum leader symbolizes the Great Spirit; during services "He sits there just like God, and watches what we do. If we do anything wrong [in the ritual] he is supposed to tell us. He is supposed to look out for us and not be stingy with anything."[26] The leading female member of the society represents Tailfeather Woman, while the janitors, whose duty it is to maintain the dance area, are believed to be standing in for their counterparts who serve the Great Spirit:

> "They claim that God made two janitors in heaven; it's these two spirits. And they clean up. They got brooms, and they take care of the sky and heaven [the fourth tier of the sky]."[27]

The dance itself is considered a reenactment of the vision story: it is begun in the morning because that is when the Great Spirit took Tailfeather Woman from her hiding place in the lake; women always take part in the afternoon ritual meal because it represents the meal brought to Tailfeather Woman when she was invisible.[28]

The Warrior Women (*ogichidaakwewag*)

From the time warrior societies developed the Grass Dance, dance organizations were principally male in membership. A special word, therefore, should be said about the women's role in the Drum Dance. In contrast to their position in the *midewiwin*, in which women could and often did advance as far as men in degrees, possession of power, and capacity to lead ceremonials, their position in the Drum Dance, while vital, was nonetheless subservient to the offices held by males. To rectify this imbalance somewhat, the Woman's Dance and its special drum were appended to the Drum Dance.

In any orthodox Drum society it would be inconceivable for a woman to be a Drum owner or pipe bearer or to hold any other office traditionally identified with men.[29] As a result, women's responsibilities were restricted to those duties that perhaps paralleled most closely their domestic chores: preparing the food, assisting the janitor in maintaining the dance grounds, making the beadwork clothing for the Drum, keeping the Drum and its paraphernalia clean and in good repair. ("Between times, [*ogichidaakwewag*] are supposed to—like the white sheet what the Drum wears, you know; they wash them, clean up everything.")[30] In all these instances and in joining the singers in performing the songs, the women are considered to be "helping."

Ideally there should be eight married women Drum members to represent the female spirits of the cardinal points and their assistants (sometimes called "substitutes"). They enter the dance ring in a specified order, beginning with their leader, then the west woman and her substitute, the north woman and hers, and so on.[31] Conversation among them during a service is restricted to decision-making concerning their duties; if they must quit the dance arena to prepare food, for instance, the west woman must request permission and offer tobacco, whereupon they depart single file once again in ritual order.[32] Their job is considered a serious one by Drum members, and where they do not seem to be participating fully, consternation has resulted. Matchokamow complained that Menominee women, out of bashfulness, sat on benches around the hall rather than near the Drum, as they were supposed to. (He cited Ojibwa women as models.) He was also upset because the importance of the role of Tailfeather Woman in Drum beliefs was not recognized. Even though it is perhaps incomprehensible to men that a woman was chosen by the Great Spirit as recipient of the first Drum, still it was she who engendered or gave birth to the Drum: "When this [Sioux] woman, when she got the Drum from the Great Spirit, Great Spirit told her, 'It's not only [for] you . . . that means for all women of different tribes [who] are your native sisters.'"[33]

The musical function of the women is particularly noteworthy and sets this style of music apart from others in the Ojibwa repertoire, such as those styles of singing reserved for medicine songs, gambling songs, or love songs. Densmore describes the performance of *ogichidaakwewag*, as follows:

> The women form a large outer circle, sitting with bowed heads, their mouths covered by their hands or shawls. The singing of the women, which is entirely through the nose, gives the melody with clear intonation, an octave above the voices of the men.[34]

Inside the dance ring the eight women are arranged behind the Drum outside the circle of male singers surrounding it and roughly paralleling the northwest sector of its circumference (fig. 24).[35] Such an arrangement was also followed in the relative positions of male and female singers in some Grass Dance societies.[36] In fact, the custom seems to go back for some time, possibly even predating the Grass Dance. In the Crow Hot Dance

Figure 24. *An informal moment during the Whitefish Drum Dance seasonal rites in 1910. One woman cares for an infant, while two elders in the background greet each other. The women of the Drum sit in a semicircle behind the male singers, who were absent at the moment.* (Photo by S. A. Barrett, courtesy Milwaukee Public Museum, neg. no. 2715.)

four women would sit near the drum and "help in the singing."[37]
The absence of female singers was probably unusual and perhaps attributable to shyness, as in the case of the Hidatsa. Wolf
Chief related the reaction of the women to their new appoint-
ments when the Santee transferred the Grass Dance offices:

> "The women singers chosen refused their offices. When
> they were named they declined and left the place. Some
> of the young men, half in sport, tried to drag them back
> but they would not return, so the office of the four
> women singers remained vacant."[38]

The inclusion of female singers to accompany Ojibwa dancing
predates the arrival of the Drum Dance by at least twenty years
and possibly more. Kohl in the summer of 1855 described the
dancers on Madeline Island circling around the group that
provided the music:

> The musicians, a few young fellows, cowered down on the
> ground, beat a drum, and shook a calabash and some
> other instruments, which were very primitive. One had
> only a board, which he hammered with a big knife, while
> holding his hollow hand beneath it as a species of sound-
> ing-board. The principal singers were a half-dozen
> women, wrapped up in dark cloaks, who muttered a
> monotonous and melancholy chant, while keeping their
> eyes steadily fixed on the ground.[39]

Kohl's description fits perfectly the mode of performance of the
women in the Drum Dance: they sit on the ground atop blankets
(MacCauley noted a circle of "straw and evergreen twigs"),[40] and
with their eyes cast downward hold their noses with one hand as
they sing (fig. 25). Formerly, they had shawls—Kohl's "dark
cloaks"—wrapped over their heads and covering their hands.
The quality of their vocal style, with noses pinched, undoubtedly
led Kohl to describe it as a "monotonous and melancholy chant."
    The Ojibwa call this style of singing zhaabowe (to pierce). The
word may describe the musical function of what they do, that is,
they do not sing the entire melody with the men but enter it
partway along during each of its repetitions, "piercing" the melodic line, or it may be simply a descriptive term to depict the
quality of nasal singing, as the tone flows through the nose.[41] It is
the practice of some Ojibwa singing groups for the men to drop
out completely once the women have begun their singing, to let
them finish the particular musical phrase; the men reenter after

Figure 25. *Women "helping" the men singing in a photo posed for Robert Ritzenthaler in 1941 at Lac Court Oreilles. Were an actual ceremony in progress the Drum would be raised on its legs and a fuller complement of Drum members would be present. Note the women's use of the hand to pinch the nose while they sing.* (Photo by Robert Ritzenthaler, courtesy Milwaukee Public Museum, neg. no. 5912.)

a cadence is reached and begin the melody anew.[42] In some Drum groups—Fox, for example—such women singers are called hummers.[43] Baker stresses the difference between women singing at a secular occasion, also called helping, and their performance at the ceremonial Drum Dance:

> That's what they call helping at a fun [secular] dance, they do that at home; but [during the Drum Dance] they don't stand up, those women sit behind the singers; there's eight of them; but *any* woman can sing during a fun dance, they can even sing while they are *dancing.* I call that foolishness, but still its fun.[44]

The Woman's Dance Drum

Since the woman's role in the Drum Dance is principally to "help" the men by preparing food and singing, they hold no office other than that described. Thus, they do not participate as dancers. For this reason a special Woman's Dance (*ikweniimi'idiwin*) was developed with its own drum and large repertoire of songs. The dance itself was learned from the Sioux and acknowledged as such (fig. 26).

Related to the ceremonial Drum but slightly smaller in size, the Woman's Dance drum is also believed to have originated in a dream.[45] Baker, who has made a number of these, explains their

Figure 26. *Oglala Sioux women perform a Woman's Dance (Squaw Dance) at Pine Ridge Agency, South Dakota.* (Photo by "C. F. M.," May 8, 1891, courtesy NAA, neg. no. 55636.)

origin: "The Indian's Woman's Dance drum is a pleasure [secular] drum for the woman, because she couldn't dance when the ceremonial was first put on the face of this earth."[46]

The Woman's Dance, sometimes called the Squaw Dance,[47] is distinguishable from the dancing in the Drum Dance by its rhythmic accompaniment and choreography. It is a circle dance, not unlike the round dances of many tribes: the dancers stand shoulder to shoulder around the drum and move sideways in a clockwise direction for awhile, then counterclockwise (fig. 27). Whereas the pattern of the percussion accompaniment for the regular ceremonial songs is in even strokes, singers accentuate alternate drumbeats for Woman's Dance songs.[48] Baker admits that this dance is similar to a round dance but characterizes it as "peppier."

The Woman's Dance was customarily held at the end of a Drum Dance. The one announced at the conclusion of the ninth day of the 1910 Whitefish summer rite was held outside the ceremonial grounds and lasted about two hours. Barrett described it as "an occasion of much mirth [that] contrasts very greatly with the solemnity and ceremoniousness of the dream dance itself."[49] It was a couples' dance in which one invited a partner by giving a present, which later had to be reciprocated with one of equal value. Such gifts were sometimes as costly as an entire dance costume, which could be exchanged for a pony.

The dance and its drum were considered to be owned by the women, who notified participants with the customary tobacco invitations.[50] At Mille Lacs, the Ladies Drum Society was similar in organization to the other Drum groups; if the drum owner

Figure 27. *Woman's Dance following a Drum Dance at Lac Court Oreilles, July 1910.* (Photo by S. A. Barrett, courtesy Milwaukee Public Museum, neg. no. 2732.)

died, her daughter or a close niece would assume the drum's ownership. Aside from sponsoring their dances, the women of the Mille Lacs society specialized in making quilts.[51]

At Lac Court Oreilles the Woman's Dance became so popular that it was held every weekend. It died out principally because the drums were given away, mostly to the Winnebago. The history of the instruments, however, is still recalled by local residents. Baker remembers that his family were living at Pigeon Lake near Drummond, Wisconsin, when they learned about the Woman's Dance. His uncle helped build a drum for it which Baker's mother and aunt decorated.[52] Another Woman's Dance drum from Lake Lena (Saint Croix) was given to Mrs. Gus Carl, who kept it for ten years and then gave it to the Winnebago. Mary Barber received her drum from Bad River Reservation in 1916 in a ceremony at Chief Lake.[53] It, too, went to the Winnebago when she died. In 1939 another Lac Court Oreilles Woman's Dance drum was removed from its support stakes after a special farewell song was performed for it before it was taken to the Winnebago.

Not everyone was pleased with the manner in which these drums were given away. Observed Bill Barber:

> "I used to belong to it. They just gave it away to the Winnebagos without talking it over with us. Didn't even notify John Mink [a noted medicine man]. It used to be a lot of fun, those dances. Some preaching, but not much . . . mostly singing and dancing."[54]

The Drum Presentation (*dewe'iganan omiigiwen*)

A Drum may be given away as a gesture of a donor's friendship, or it may be specifically requested by a group desirous of having one. In either case, deliberations are made before action is taken and certain preparations are undertaken before the actual transfer. Because a Drum presentation is such a serious affair, when a Saint Croix visitor at the 1910 Whitefish dance suggested they make a Drum for the Sioux, the leader of the ceremony cautioned that such a decision should not be made hastily for "in view of the importance of the making of such a drum, the matter should be thoroughly considered before any definite move [is] made."[55]

A Drum may be requested by another tribe or even another band from within the same community. At Mille Lacs, for instance, the transfer operates as follows:

> Occasionally, people in different areas of the reservation wish to have a Drum. Such people petition the people at the Mille Lacs Lake Indian Village for a piece of an original Drum. It takes a long time before the people will give such a piece to start a new Drum. The prospective Drum Owner must have appropriate dreams, and then a council of older men talk it over.[56]

The retention of some part of a Drum with which to generate another is at the basis of the concept of the relationship between all Drums and their common descent from a single source—the first Drum. In fact, a Drum donor has a right—some would say an obligation—to make a duplicate in this way to replace the one he has given away. Bijikens, when he gave his Bad River Drum to the Menominee, asserted his authority to make copies of it and to give them away at any time. Meckawigabau (Joe Kobe) had inherited a Drum formerly belonging to Lac du Flambeau Chief Medwayasun; when he gave it to a neighboring Ojibwa community, Kobe told of his intention to make a copy of it that winter and give it away the next summer.[57]

Presumably both men had retained some piece of the Drum or its accessory paraphernalia for, as Baker once stressed to me:

> When they give one drum away, take it apart, leave something [behind] . . . feather off a leg, pipe bag, head drumstick—that's the chief stick, like mine with fur and ribbon; if they give everything away you can't make that drum no more.[58]

To Baker's list of potential items with which to generate a new Drum, should be added drum legs (support stakes); Whiskey John mentioned the possibility of keeping one of the four legs and, in making a new Drum, replacing the three given away.[59]

While any member of a Drum Society can suggest giving away a Drum, after discussions it is usually the Drum owner who makes the final decision. Similar preliminary consultations took place prior to Grass Dance transfers. Among the Kansa, for example, "When it has been decided to get up a helucka [Grass Dance] society, before a drum is made all the prospective members get together and appoint the two chiefs. These two decide who shall be caretaker, or owner of the drum."[60] The purchasing party of Hidatsa who traveled to Devil's Lake with their request was described earlier. Precisely the same mechanism is involved in a Drum transfer, the usual procedure being to send a "runner" several months in advance to the other party.[61] This is probably what was meant by the Menominee when they told MacCauley that in the winter of 1879 their runners had been far to the west.[62]

Even in the initial stages of a Drum presentation an elaborate series of gift exchanges is set in motion. Because gift exchange of some sort characterizes most Native American ceremonials, it is important to understand its background. In the harsh environments often faced by Indians, the well being of each individual was linked with the well being of others. Consequently, communal sharing—a requisite for survival—was the expected mode of behavior: when someone killed a deer, everybody ate. Ultimately a system of ethics evolved in which generosity was expected; in sharp contrast to the values of the acquisitive white society, social status for the Indian was based on giving rather than acquiring material wealth.

The pattern of gift exchange to begin an Ojibwa Drum presentation is summarized by Densmore:

> As the gift of a drum involves the return of gifts supposed to equal in value the drum and the presents bestowed by the original drum party, it is customary for the man presenting the drum to ascertain from the one to whom he wishes to present it whether the latter desires to assume the obligations associated with its acceptance. This is done several months before the drum is to be given. It is the duty of the recipient to see that a suitable quantity of gifts is presented to the drum party at the ceremony, that one or more feasts are provided for the guests, and that their camp is supplied with food during their entire stay.

At some later date he must return a full equivalent of gifts to the donor of the drum. A year or two may elapse before he is prepared to do this. When he is ready he sends a messenger to the donor, and shortly afterward visits him with a large party carrying the gifts.[63]

Gift articles ranged from traditional items of Indian manufacture to material goods of the dominant society, which were expected to be new when presented.[64] They included among other things, blankets and quilts, rifles, traditional woven rush mats or yarn bags, clothing, beadwork, animal hides, and even money. The relative economic value of a Drum to the Ojibwa was high: around 1917 Mitchell Quagon gave forty dollars to the Pine Lake Band for his Drum; at that time such an instrument was equal in value to a horse, an otter hide, or two beaded bandoleer bags and a dancing outfit.[65]

Once the gifts are accumulated, the Drum is given away in a special presentation service called *dewe'iganan omiigiwen* (a drum is given away). The ceremony begins with four days of dancing either in the hosts' community prior to their departure or enroute to the site of the ceremony. A temporary camp is set up near the site to await the arrival of the runner from the recipient group's chief informing them they are ready to be received.[66] (Ideally, four "notification services" should be held on successive nights before a Drum presentation.)[67] When the Ojibwa brought their two Drums to the Menominee in 1910 they traveled most of the way by train; the last leg of their journey, however, was on foot, the mode of travel chosen by Santee some thirty years earlier in bringing their Grass Dance drum to the Hidatsa.

In the elaborate transfer ceremony, the Drum and accompanying gifts are presented to the leader of the recipient group by the leader of the visitors (fig. 28). In theory the ceremony should last four days and be followed by another four days of dancing together before the donors return home. (A more detailed description of the events is given in Bisonette's account of the John Apple Drum presented to the Lac du Flambeau band circa 1934. [See "The Presentation of a Drum," pp. 263–67]. This account may be compared to Densmore's in *Chippewa Music—II*, pp. 142-83, for changes transpired in the intervening twenty-five years since Densmore described it.)

Once a Drum has been given by one group to another, the latter almost always accept the former's version of the Drum Dance as orthodox and continue to rely on them as authorities should questions later arise. There is no clearer example of this

Figure 28. *Two of the four Drums used in the 1910 Ojibwa Drum presentation to the Menominee near Neopit on their reservation. Note the earth embankment, which serves as a bench, and the shadow of the flag raised for the ceremony.* (Photo by Frances Densmore, courtesy NAA, neg. no. 596-c-13a.)

than in the Menominee attitude toward the Ojibwa, the donors of nearly all their Drums. Often a Menominee Drum member began his observations on the dance for Slotkin, "The way the Chippewas told us . . ." or, if he did not have an answer to something, "You've got me. . . . Well, that's the way they preached us, them Chippewas and Sioux."[68]

Ojibwa Drum members are invited to Menominee dances and, should something go awry in the proceedings, are asked to intervene as authorities in setting things straight or settling arguments.[69] Rohrl notes that at Mille Lacs after a transfer, the donors visit the dances of the recipients "in order to make sure that the Drum is being cared for properly."[70] Johnson Awonohopay remembered one occurrence when the Menominee were rather shaky in conducting the belt ritual:

> "[The Ojibwa] did that altogether different from the way we do it. . . . Half the time we was stuck, over here; the song would start, you know, and [the Ojibwa would say] 'That ain't the one.' So finally— well—I sat still too, after a while, and I let them run it for us."[71]

The Ojibwa are relied upon to refresh the Menominee's memory in Drum matters. Johnny Matchokamow noted that "Every time the Chippewas come, we used to make them sit up pretty near all night and tell us about the Drum,"[72] and when he

complained about the general informality during Zoar services—disturbances created by children, for instance—he cited
what he had witnessed in ceremonies at Lac Court Oreilles as the
proper way to do things:

> "By rights, they ain't supposed to [talk informally during
> a service]. . . . And them kids should sit still. That's the
> way it's supposed to be. I know I seen that when I went to
> Reserve [the principal town at Lac Court Oreilles]; when
> one of them gets up and talk, the rest of them keep
> quiet."[73]

Finally, the incorporation of Ojibwa loan words into the Menominee Drum ceremony is also significant: the Great Spirit is not
called *mec-awetok* as in the Menominee Medicine Dance but
rather by the Ojibwa word *gichi-manidoo*; and as an Indian
"amen" to prayers in the service, the Menominee say *miigwech*,
Ojibwa for "thank you," because they consider it to be stronger
than the Menominee equivalent *wewenen*.[74]

The Music of the Drum Dance

> "My friends, we want to teach you all the Grass dance
> songs, and so we are going to stay and practice with you
> five nights. We shall closely observe how well you learn
> them; but I feel sure that in the five nights you will have
> learnt all the songs, and will be able properly to observe
> the dance" (Walking Soldier [Santee], circa 1881).[75]

> I dream a lot of times [of] singers; you see these old
> fellows singing for the powwow with the Drum. A lot of
> times I wake up; in my sleep I see them singing . . . and
> get in there [on the Drum] sometimes and sing with
> them, and I wake myself up singing [William Baker,
> 1971].[76]

The songs of the Drum Dance are considered prayers to the
Great Spirit and are believed to be the songs he gave to Tailfeather Woman when instructing her to build the Drum. "The
beating of the drum . . . together with the smoke from the
ceremonial pipes, is supposed to carry the invocations of the
participants up to the Great Spirit."[77] In the same way that the
Drum is meant to be "passed on," so are the songs. For this
reason they are carefully rehearsed to preserve them as they
were "given." As Baker stresses, simply knowing how to construct
a Drum does not give one the authority to do so; he must know

the songs that go "on the Drum" as well.

There is little question that the Drum songs are Siouan in origin; in fact they are acknowledged as such by the Ojibwa. As Baker puts it, "all that music comes from the west." In his travels among the Sioux seeking information on the origin of the Drum, Baker insists that they still perform the songs but have lost the ceremonial instrument meant to accompany them. As evidence of their identity, he has been able to perform for me without rehearsal certain Sioux songs upon hearing recordings that he recognizes as Drum Dance songs. Baker is upset that they have lost their ceremonial value with the Sioux, whom he berates for having converted one sacred soldier's song of the Drum Dance into a secular song performed for tourists.

Fortunately, a large number of Drum Dance songs were recorded early in this century and from several tribes. Truman Michelson recorded the Fox, and Densmore the Ojibwa and Menominee. Later, Slotkin recorded the Menominee again. Although this music awaits a full comparative study, it is evident from the recordings that the repertoire from tribe to tribe is closely identical and attests to an astonishing degree of accuracy in its oral transmission over time.[78]

The Ojibwa Drum Dance songs recorded by Joe Kobe (fig. 29) in 1910 at Lac du Flambeau for Frances Densmore provide fairly clear evidence of their Siouan origins. Stylistically they are sufficiently different from the traditional Ojibwa repertoire to constitute new music at the time they were received.[79] They also show the general Siouan influence on Ojibwa music, which continues even today,[80] doubtless from the long association of the two tribes through intermittent periods of warfare and peace. Ojibwa frequently identify certain songs as having been learned from the Sioux, and many songs contain Siouan words in their texts.[81]

Sioux songs, particularly those of the Grass Dance, have enjoyed widespread popularity for some time with many tribes. There is little doubt that the quality and style of the music was enormously appealing at the time the Grass Dance was in full sway. Wissler notes how the music was an attractive feature to Indian youth of other tribes at the time:

> There is, however, an important accidental factor, generally acknowledged by the Indians themselves, for to this modern revival of the grass dance the Dakota contributed some splendid songs and important social features. These songs make a strong appeal to Plains Indians and are said to have great individuality. They appeal par-

Figure 29. *Meckawigabau (Joe Kobe) of Lac du Flambeau, who recorded onto wax cylinders twenty songs of the Drum Dance for Frances Densmore in 1910.* (Photo.courtesy NAA, neg. no. 499.)

ticularly to young people and as we have noted, the great enthusiasm for new ceremonies came at the time when there were few outlets for the interests of young men.[82]

The Sioux at that time, in fact, had become recognized as *the* singers par excellence and were consulted for training. Wissler continues:

even where the [Grass Dance] ceremony was introduced by an intermediary the tendency was sooner or later to go to the nearest division of the Dakota for further song instruction. Often in response to an invitation a Dakota delegation would arrive to assist in conducting the singing and dancing.[83]

Because song instruction was vital to the accurate transmission of the sacred repertoire of the Drum Dance, it is conceivable that when the Drum was first given to the Ojibwa, they too, like Plains tribes, for a period had continual recourse to their donors for song instruction. Such "instruction sessions" were in fact still being ritually reenacted at Leech Lake in 1910. In the Dog Feast observed by Densmore there, two Ojibwa were playing the role of the Sioux who were said to be "teaching [the Ojibwa] the ceremony."[84]

Song instruction is a mandatory part of a Drum presentation. Although many singers may already know the songs from previous Drum transfers, there may be some in the group who need to refresh their memories and younger members who are totally unfamiliar with the repertoire. Despite their knowledge of the songs, singers, during these ritual teaching sessions, "are required to listen attentively and appear to learn the songs as carefully as if they were not already familiar with them."[85]

Baker recognizes slight variations from tribe to tribe in the performance of these songs; the Potawatomi, for instance, "have the same songs, but they've got a little different version to it." In fact, he can imitate the differences by singing in succession the same song in its Ojibwa and Potawatomi versions. Still, he insists, the repertoire is the same from tribe to tribe:

> Our original songs that was given to us, that's passed onto us, we always try to sing the way it was given to us. . . . You can't change our religion, the beginning is still the same today, and the songs are the same today as far back as I can remember, and you can't change them.[86]

In spite of the fact that song transmission followed the path of the Drum, that is, songs were mostly passed from west to east, members of the larger Drum community continue to consult each other to ensure the preservation of the repertoire. Thus an Ojibwa visitor to a Menominee Dance inquired about a song he had heard at a service the prior evening; he repeated enough of the song, albeit imperfectly, for the Menominee to recognize it and "correct" it for him by singing it through a few times until the Ojibwa had learned the proper way to perform it.[87]

Drum songs are performed by the headman, the four principal singers and their assistants (or substitutes), and the four drum heaters—the thirteen comprising a full Drum. They are seated on logs, benches, or, formerly, a slightly raised circle of pineboughs (see figs. 25, 28, 34). At times, if additional singers join them, they may kneel at the Drum to be accommodated.[88]

Any singer is free to start a song, although the better singers—certainly those most familiar with the songs and their proper order—are usually the ones to do so. The soloist signals the song's beginning with a sharp drum stroke, then immediately reduces the volume of his drumming as the other singers, having recognized the song, join him. Drum songs are expected to be sung for four repetitions, although in some instances additional verses may be added—particularly if some dancing "penalty" has been imposed on someone.[89] The common (less sacred) songs interspersed for general dancing may be extended indefinitely, just as they are at secular powwows: to continue to add verses, the lead singer will usually signal his wishes by raising a forefinger before the end of a verse.[90] If a singer begins a song and is not very strong with it, another will join him to "help out," but since sacred songs must be taken seriously and performed exactly, if a singer makes a mistake, e.g., hits the Drum out of rhythm with the group or departs from the accepted melodic line, he must dance in place to "atone" for his error.[91]

Drumming techniques are important, and if one is not secure with the songs or the drum, he is allowed only to beat on the drum's edge so as not to interfere. This is one way in which children absorb the tradition. As Baker recalls:

> I learned [the songs] from babyhood up. I used to sit on my father's lap and listen to him while the powwow was going on. I remember I had a stick, but I couldn't hit the drum, just played with the stick [see fig. 13].[92]

For the final songs of a service all singers beat on the edge of the Drum. This drumming technique is reserved solely for that part of the Drum Dance and probably signals that the Drum will retire. The performance of the accompaniment for concluding songs varies slightly with the group. The Menominee, when in a dance hall, even move their sticks to beat on the floor as follows: during the fourth special Quitting Song, the drum heater, at the end of the third repetition, raises four fingers to signal not only the fourth repetition but that following it will be four additional repetitions: during the first three of these, all singers beat on the edge of the Drum; the drum heater makes a "cutting gesture" (this is usually done with the forefinger across the throat), and the singers beat on the floor for the final repeat while the drum remains silent.[93] Slotkin, who was occasionally allowed to sit in at the Drum, described his impressions as a non-Indian performing a variety of drumming techniques:

> The drumbeat [was] with great variation and nuance. They would sometimes start pianissimo and work up to a fortissimo that involved the arm and shoulder muscles to such an extent that the men would become exhausted, and would make the whole room vibrate, and me as well. I never had such a sense of rhythm penetrating me. Their unison was extraordinary no matter how the tempo and magnitude of the beat was varied. . . . The drumbeat pervades the place. If I join the singers at the Drum, I soon became one with the music, drumming and singing almost automatically until exhausted.[94]

The songs of the Drum Dance can be divided into three basic categories: special songs for each of the officers, sometimes called "private" songs; songs to accompany ritual actions, and common songs. (These categories simply describe the use of the songs and are not meant to imply musical distinctions.) In the appendix "The Lac Court Oreilles Drum Dance, circa 1940," is given the order of the special songs for each position, which comprise the "private songs." During their performance the particular officer holding that position rises, dances, and is then joined in dancing by the others. After his song, he is obliged to "pay" for it by presenting someone at the dance with a gift. One by one in order the special songs are performed for the head chief (fig. 30), second chief, head speaker, sweeper, Drum owner, first, second, third and fourth warrior, and so on. As in the Grass

Figure 30. *Transcription of Joe Kobe's performance of the chief's song, recorded in October 1910.* (Transcription by the author; cf. Densmore's published version, *CM-II*, p. 150; original cylinder in the collection of the Archive of Folk Culture, Library of Congress, cat. no. AFS 10,555A2.)

Dance, these songs were assigned to them when they were appointed as officers.[95]

Aside from the officers' songs, there are special songs for other individuals, the performance of which depends upon their presence or whether the ritual involving them is included. For example, during the Old Man's Song, several old men could get up to dance, or during the Mourner's Song, a mourner, after he has been restored, rises and dances.

Songs accompanying ritual actions are also dependent upon the nature of the service. For instance, there is a special officer's song for the bull cook, and several songs are also performed at noon when the feast is ready. These concur with the ritual "hunting" of the food—a symbolic dance. The first of these songs is called the Looking around [for the enemy] Song. When the first pail of food is brought in and singers informed of its contents, they begin another song, the Runner's Song, while the symbolic "killing of the game" he has brought in takes place. All these actions are performed before the remainder of the food is brought in and distributed.

Other action songs not specifically assigned to officers are less often sung and depend upon decisions made during dances—if someone chooses to give away a horse or pony for instance.[96] If visitors are present, a special Traveling Song is performed at the end of the service just prior to the final four songs.[97] Unforeseen occurrences can prompt the performance of special action songs: a certain song is begun if the drumhead accidentally breaks during a dance, another if the rawhide drumhead becomes slack and must be taken to the fire outside the ring to be heated for tightening. Also, a special Quitting Song is used to terminate a dance suddenly if a disturbance erupts, caused, perhaps, by someone being intoxicated or otherwise rowdy.[98]

Individual officers' songs and ritual action songs account for less than a quarter of the music heard in a full ceremony.[99] Additionally, a large number of so-called common songs are performed between the special ones for general congregational dancing. Although they belong to the Drum Dance, they can be considered secular and considerable freedom governs in their selection. The repetition of their melodies usually is dependent upon the mood of the dancers.[100] Drum members may also add to the repertoire of common songs.

This distinction between the two repertoires—special and common songs—certainly dates from Grass Dance practices. There, too, the distinguishing characteristic seems to have been that the common songs had no gift requirements attached to them. As Wolf Chief marked their distinction:

> "we all danced while the Sioux drummers sang. . . . These songs were just dance songs, and did not pertain specially to the Grass dance society; also no gifts were given. However, they were Grass dance society songs in the sense that they were songs commonly sung by the members although they were not a part of the ritual."[101]

Evidently the general war songs of a tribe comprised most of these supplementary dance songs. Wolf Chief described how the Santee, after performing the Belt Dance, began another song, although not one belonging to the Grass Dance. During it, everyone (but the women) got up to dance—the old men pantomiming their war experiences.[102] Densmore found that the music performed by the Menominee and Ojibwa both before and after the actual presentation of Drums was germane to each other's regular secular repertoire, but that the Ojibwa used certain war songs at that time.[103] Slotkin found the same situation at Zoar and felt that their war songs were inconsistent with the peaceful intentions of the Dance. As his informant could not explain why war songs were being performed at that time, Slotkin assumed their performance to be a vestigial practice of the Plains Grass Dance.[104] Densmore heard Dream Songs performed at Menominee Drum Dances. The inclusion of special Bear and Buffalo songs at the end of the ceremony, however, during which only those may dance who have these *manidoog* as spiritual guardians seems a custom restricted to that tribe.[105]

Theoretically, the daytime dances are organized around the fixed sequence of the songs, often referred to as their "rotation."[106] Such fixed ordering of songs, of course, is common to most Native American ceremonials. Indeed, some sort of fixed sequence of songs for offices—although not necessarily the same for each tribe—was already widely practiced by Grass Dance societies. In the Crow Hot Dance, for example, the first song signaled that the dance regalia hanging from the lodge poles should be taken down, the second song was specified for the chiefs, the third for the crier, the fourth for the drummer, and the fifth for the drumstick owner, each of whom in turn had to rise and dance for his song.[107] In the Drum Dance it is considered equally vital that the songs be performed in their proper order, and the west, or lead singer (headman) is usually responsible to see that the order is followed, often by starting the songs himself.

When the Lac du Flambeau Ojibwa brought Kemewan his Drum, the Ojibwa Jim Corn took the trouble to write down the correct "rotation of the songs" so that the Menominee would not forget it.[108] Some societies will offer a prayer at the beginning of a service asking the Great Spirit's forgiveness if a mistake is made in the ordering of songs.[109] Baker, having heard Drum Dance songs performed in Montana and the Dakotas ad libitum in any order, is irked by their use of "private [officers'] songs" used as "pleasure songs" and feels that "those songs have just gone wild. The [western] people have forced the songs to be wild, they don't keep them in mind in the rotation."[110]

At the time Michelson collected from the Fox, circa 1916, at Tama, Iowa, where they live, several Drums appear to have been active and clearly adhering to a certain fixed order of performing songs. Although research is not yet complete on his data, the brief notes Michelson stuffed into the cavities of his cylinder recordings, now in the Archive of Folk Culture at the Library of Congress, contain such information as: "MacIntosh's and Mamasaw's songs, used first day only at beginning. After eating, MacIntosh's and then Mamasaw's songs." I assume that the two names represent owners of Drums and infer that the MacIntosh Drum is older, i.e., has seniority. On another note the collector has written, "Wanatie kecita [ogichidaa] songs (4) then 2 young chiefs then 2 housekeepers [janitors]." This suggests yet another Drum as well as a fairly elaborate Drum organization, since the positions of young chief and housekeeper are generally accorded one to a Drum.[111]

As the Drum Dance began to lose membership and attendance at dances declined, the fixed song sequence was among the first ritual requirements to be directly affected. By the time Slotkin studied the Menominee Dance (circa 1950), they had abandoned the song sequence for the first day of the ceremony for lack of officers to dance for their songs. What was performed depended upon who was there; although there are four drum heater's songs, since only two people held the office on the Kemewan Drum, only those two songs were performed. In order to have someone dance during the song for the waiter—a vacant position on the Kemewan Drum—a waiter had to be borrowed from another Drum.[112]

There is some variety in the songs from one Drum to the next because songs have been added to the standard repertoire through the years. Some were received through dreams, others simply composed by Drum members to commemorate an occurrence of special local significance. Many such songs become popular enough to travel to other Drums and other reservations. The inclusion of foreign texts is one indicator of their origins. For instance, except for a number of songs that "mention" Tailfeather Woman, most Drum Dance songs do not have texts and are sung to vocables.[113] Yet, some Menominee songs have words in Sioux, others in Ojibwa, and still others in Potawatomi.

The origins of new songs are usually quickly forgotten and evidently not particularly important. Slotkin once recorded a Potawatomi singing "the latest hit." When he played it for Pete Sam, it was identified as a song whose composer was anonymous and which had arrived in the Menominee reservation the previous summer, "passing from the north" somewhere. "It ain't been around very long. Something new. One of the latest songs, you know, in the—a regular Powwow song. I think it came from towards Odanah . . . or Flambeau . . . through that way?"[114]

Some songs may be peculiar to only one Drum. The special Virgin's Songs are performed only by singers on the Henry Davis Drum at Mille Lacs; they were received in a vision by a man living at Sawyer, Minnesota, and added to the standard repertoire.[115] There is a special Meeting Song at Zoar but only performed on the Johnny Matchokamow Drum and used when a Drum is given away or in inclement weather to petition the Great Spirit to clear the sky for the service.[116] Lac Court Oreilles Ojibwa have a song called *gaawe-nagamon* (lit., he is jealous song), which is performed somewhat in jest and said to refer to "the jealous ones" at the time peace was made with the Sioux. They are said to be those Ojibwa who refused to dance at the first Drum presentation.[117]

An early instance of special songs added to the Drum repertoire were two Danger Songs revealed in a dream to Bird-Sitting-Down, the father of Pete Sam, shortly after the Menominee received the Drum Dance (circa 1880). The songs were intended to safeguard Drum members when danger threatened. Ultimately, these protective songs were performed to keep their reservation from being taken from them and for the protection in battle and safe return of Menominee servicemen during both world wars.[118] Bird-Sitting-Down's dream was described as follows:

> "When he heard that [first] song . . . that's just like something heard up in heaven; kind of a light, when he heard that song. And this [second] song, when he heard that, he could see something straight west; looks like a railroad

track, a nice straight road; there's nothing in there . . .
just nice. That's what he said he seen."[119]

By 1950 the two songs had disappeared from general circulation; Johnny Matchokamow was the only Drum member who
knew both songs and Pete Sam, the son of their recipient, remembered only one.

One special set of four songs—the Shake Hands Songs—is
used to reenact a portion of the original Drum presentation.
When the Ojibwa and Santee Sioux met to establish peace, they
not only smoked the ceremonial pipe communally but also shook
hands to symbolize the end of warfare. As the story of this
meeting is told:

> Early in the morning, they really heard the Drum making
> a sound. Suddenly that Drum ceased. Then [the Ojibwa]
> stood up and left [their settlement], and those Sioux
> came nearer. It is said that a fog then descended; they
> could not see any distance, the fog was so thick. They
> could hear singing, though. When the Sioux stopped
> singing those songs, the fog rose. Lo and behold! the
> Indians then shook hands there.[120]

Because the Shake Hands Songs are believed to be the the first
that the Great Spirit gave to Tailfeather Woman to "put on the
Drum," they are also believed to be the first Drum songs heard by
the Ojibwa as the Sioux approached them to make peace. Consequently, these songs are performed at the very beginning of
any especially important service.[121]

Outside of song contexts a considerable amount of handshaking accompanies all Drum giveaways. This gesture of friendship
seems to derive from patterns of gift exchange in the Grass
Dance and is evident in the transfer of the ceremony from one
tribe to another:

> [After the offices had been transferred] the visiting Sioux
> went through the ceremony of making friends of the
> Hidatsas and Mandans. A Sioux would arise and walk to
> the place . . . behind the fireplace and say, "I want to
> make so-and-so my friend!" The [man] named would
> arise and go to him . . . when the Sioux would present
> him with the dance outfit that he carried on his left
> arm.[122]

References to handshaking are made in the speeches accompanying Ojibwa Drum presentations, such as "The Great Spirit

has seen us shake hands" or "We leave all differences behind us as we shake hands."[123] The "hands of God" are also part of the decoration of the Drum itself (see "Tabs," pp. 178–89), and ritual motions accompanying the songs symbolize shaking hands with God.

The performance of this gesture varies slightly from community to community. At Mille Lacs, on the Henry Davis Drum, all dancers stand in place facing the Drum; when the singing begins they slowly raise their right hands to shoulder height with open palms facing the Drum; at the end of the song, they lower them.[124] At Zoar, similar motions were at one time supposed to be performed for each of the four songs, but when the Kemewan Drum began to omit them from the first three songs, the other two Drums followed suit. The men began to dance only during the fourth song and at the beginning of each repetition of the melody, while everyone in attendance, including children, stretched out their right arms with palms down, then slowly raised their forearms until they were vertical. These motions are considered similar to what whites do with their hands when they pray:

> "That [gesture] means [you want the Great Spirit] to help you out and feel sorry for you. If you are in hard shape, something like that, to help you out."[125]

The Belt Dance/Dog Feast

> "'Now distribute the food,' said [the Santee] Matsiwashte to the three feather belt wearers. 'Cut the dog meat into small pieces and let everyone in the lodge have a piece as his share. And you, Bull-against-the-Wind, choose four men. If you wish they may be men who have made first coups on enemies; or they may be four men who have been wounded, or they may be four men who have been war party leaders. But for whatever war experience you choose them, that experience must be the same for all four. These four men are chosen that they may tell their various honours and rehearse their deeds.'"[126]

To provide some picture of the function of music in the Drum Dance, from among its many subrites I have chosen to examine that part of the ceremony that focuses on ritual food serving—namely, the Dog Feast. In describing the characters involved and the roles they play, I have noted the pervasiveness of song and dance used to accompany their activities (see appendix "The

Dog Feast"). Although the Dog Feast was discontinued, abbreviated, or blended with other ritual activities by some Drum societies, the Ojibwa who practiced it in its more elaborate forms, with song, dance, costume, and properties, had evolved a veritable theatrical showpiece from seminal practices of tribes to their west. However peaceful the intentions of the Drum Dance may have been, we are implicitly reminded of the dance's origins in the warrior societies of the Plains by the performances of the belt man, specifically in his blessing and distribution of food. The affairs of the Indian in his former role as a warrior are encoded in every detail of the ritual.

Because of its complexity the Belt Dance/Dog Feast is perhaps more subject to variation than other subrites from one Drum society to the next and even within the same community.[127] Still, one finds in all the same vestiges of practices on the Plains a century earlier. The picture is somewhat complicated by the fact that what originally in the Grass Dance were three separate offices—that of crier, ceremonial food server, and wearer of the feather belt—are combined in the Drum Dance, their duties allowed to overlap and be performed by only one officer of the Drum. Because this portion of the ceremony held such an important position and had so many special songs assigned to it, it is described here in detail.

The feather bustle or belt, called the Crow on the Plains where it originated, was a military decoration of the highest order; only those who had proven their valor in battle were eligible to wear it in the dances. Its design and symbolism varied with each tribe, although the belt's appearance and beliefs concerning it conformed roughly. The wearing of the Crow was a practice that was diffused with the Grass Dance, ultimately the avenue through which it reached the Ojibwa (see figs. 16, 31, 46).[128]

The distinguishing design of the belt consisted of feathers arranged in such a way as to form a bustle to which other bits of decoration might be added. In its later versions it is more common to find a number of detached feathers rearranged in some design and hanging downward from a cloth base. Originally, however, it seems that the entire skin of a bird served the same purpose. The Hidatsa Small Ankle described his tribe's form of the decoration as used in their Hot Dance of the early nineteenth century, a precursor of the Grass Dance: "The leader of the dancers had a raven skin, wings and all, which he tied to his belt on his back. This was the only officer's badge used in the dance."[129]

Figure 31. *Ojibwa eagle feather belt, as used in the Dog Feast/Belt Dance. Note the large silver discs and the two "horns" protruding from the top of the belt.* (Photo by the author, 1970, courtesy Madeline Island Museum, La Pointe, Wisconsin.)

The Omaha version of the Crow was considerably more elaborate, incorporating eagle and crow skins, a wolf's tail, and additional eagle feathers.[130] The Hidatsa Grass Dance belts, by contrast, had only four bands of four eagle feathers each; the Crow worn by a wounded warrior was distinctive by its dyed red feathers.[131]

Ojibwa and Menominee belts are almost always constructed of rows of bald or golden eagle feathers.[132] Although left natural, they may be tipped with ribbons or bits of white rabbit or weasel fur. Further additions to the belt might include beadwork, silver discs, and feathers from other birds (fig. 31). On some, two special feathers extend outward from near the belt's top—as Barrett aptly describes them, "like a pair of horns." This was a feature common to Crow belts and war bonnets of Plains tribes.

The belt, like the Drum, was revered by the Ojibwa as a sacred object. One indication of this was the care taken that the belt, just as the Drum, should never touch the bare ground. While it was usually worn around the waist, often attached to a store-bought belt, some feather bustles were of such length that they had to be held under the armpits to clear the floor. Also, if children danced with the belt, it would be tied around their necks to prevent the bottom feathers from reaching the ground.[133] Similar protection was provided by the belt man who, when seated, had a blanket beneath him (as did the Drum) so that the belt would not touch the earth.[134] He also carried a specially beaded baton with which to straighten out the feathers behind him, once he was seated.

The practice of suspending the belt off the ground goes back to Grass Dance days. We know that belts were carefully hung up when not in use and that ritual surrounded the putting on of the belt. The Santee instructed the Hidatsa "trailbearers [belt men]" that their belts were to be hung up on a post in the dance house. At the proper time, when the men were to don the belts, a special song was performed, during which the four men arose, danced four times around the fireplace, moved to the post where their belts were hanging, and stooped to touch the earth with the palms of their hands. After this, they put on the belts and, at the completion of the song, presented a gift to someone of their choice.[135] Suspending the belt before donning it survives in the Menominee Belt Dance, where at Zoar a five-foot forked stick mounted on a square wooden base is placed in the northwest part of the dance hall to hold the belt aloft.[136]

Some of the Crow's original symbolism is retained in Ojibwa and Menominee beliefs concerning the belt and its purpose. Among the Omaha, the Crow represented a field at the end of a battle. The feathers were meant to have fallen from birds fighting over the slain; the protruding "horns" were the shafts of arrows in their bodies. Some Omaha belt wearers extended the battlefield symbolism beyond the belt by painting white spots on their backs to represent bird droppings. Fletcher has decoded the Omaha belt's meaning as follows:

> This composite decoration illustrated certain ideas that were fundamental to native beliefs, namely: that man is in vital connection with all forms of life; that he is always in touch with the supernatural, and that the life and acts

of the warriors are under the supervision of Thunder as the god of war.[137]

The association of the belt with the Thunders or Thunderbirds came to be invested with even greater meaning in the Drum Dance at the very time that the belt was losing much of its symbolism on the Plains. There it gradually developed into part of standard Grass Dance costuming with no particular requirements for its wearing; contemporary versions of the Crow are commonly worn even today at secular powwows.

Birds—particularly eagles and Thunderbirds—are strong tutelary *manidoog* among the Ojibwa and have served traditionally as their protectors. This is one reason so many references to birds are found in English translations of Ojibwa surnames: Kingbird, Whitefeather, Whitebird. Baker's given Indian name, *bineshii*, is a generic term for small bird, and the text of his personal song describes his guardian agent who can be heard in the sky but cannot be seen.

The explanation of the belt's meaning given by Ojibwa and Menominee underscores this traditional belief in the power of these spirits. The incorporation of the Belt Dance in the Drum Dance can, therefore, only serve to strengthen the general beneficial effects of the Dance for its members. The belief was perhaps best summed up by the Menominee Johnny Matchokamow in the following discourse:

> "[The Great Spirit] made the birds, big birds and small birds. The big birds, God gave them lots of power; like these Thunderbirds and eagles and other kinds of birds. And he put one in the sky; that's the one that's looking after the Indians. And when God gave this Drum to this [Sioux] woman here . . . this Drum here wasn't so strong. And this big bird here, he puts more power in it and when he puts that power in this Drum here, this one was more powerful than it was before. Then he gave away his feathers to make that belt. . . . The American Eagle, when he knows that God give these Indians that Drum, then he thought that he'd give his power too. That's why this belt is included in these Drums."[138]

It should be clear, then, that the belt, like the Drum, is endowed with medicine attributes. Wearing it, dancing while holding it, being fanned with it, helping someone put it on—all these actions are believed to expose one to the belt's power and thus its protection.[139] Because of the power associated with it and the complexity of the ritual, the Menominee by 1950 had already omitted the Belt Dance for some time for fear of making a mistake and thus offending the *manidoog*.[140] Whenever they tried to revive it they consulted with the Ojibwa as authorities for assistance in performing it properly.

In the Santee/Hidatsa Grass Dance the belt wearers performed multiple functions. They assisted in the selection of the newly appointed officers: two Santee belt men danced four times around the lodge, making ritual feints as if to grab someone during a song, the text of which stated, "You are a man [but probably will be killed in battle, so] you will come to be a ghost." In this manner each new officer was led by the belt men to his position in the lodge and seated.[141] It was the wearer of the red feather belt who terminated the dance by feigning exits and ultimately leading the company out of the lodge.[142] But unquestionably his most significant and dramatic function was the ritual "feeding" of dog meat to the feathers of the belt.

Comparative accounts of the Dog Feast in the Grass Dance, as taught to the Hidatsa by the Santee circa 1880, and the feast as practiced by the Ojibwa in the Drum Dance some thirty years later are provided in the appendix "The Dog Feast." The correspondence of the two rituals even in minor details is striking, and the integration of the Belt Dance into the Dog Feast should be apparent in each version.

In the Ojibwa seasonal rites, the Belt Dance is supposed to take place during the final day. When consecrating the food, the belt man (*miigwanigijipizoowinini*) is considered to be representing the Great Spirit, but in feeding certain of the participants he is said also to represent an eagle (or Thunderbird) and those fed to be the bird's young.[143] Thus the ritual is at least partly intended to invoke the protection of these powerful agents.

The use of boiled dog meat for the feast and its ritual distribution by special ceremonial food servers was one of the more spectacular features of the Grass Dance and one reason it gained such popularity (fig. 32). Almost everywhere it was practiced on the Plains, the servers held special offices within the society, the badges of which were usually "a highly decorated pointed stick [and/or] a similarly conspicuous spoon."[144] Some tribes, such as the Omaha, had specific requirements for holding the office: each of the two Omaha ceremonial servers had to have broken an enemy's neck.[145]

Although a number of dogs might have been consumed in the feast, it was required that one carcass be cooked with its head left attached, for it held important symbolic significance. The head of the dog was considered to represent the enemy, and the manner in which it was used in the ceremony was considered to represent counting coup upon him. The Santee/Hidatsa had a special song during which the Grass Dance members would "dance against the dog's head [enemy]." Each member, dancing in place, would raise his right hand during the texted portion of the song, the words of which stated, "O Sun, be kind to us, the Grass Dance Society feasts."[146]

Figure 32. *Sioux Women in 1929 roasting dogs in preparation for Sun Dance ceremonial feast at Rosebud Agency, South Dakota.* (Photo by Bert Bell, courtesy NAA, neg. no. 3675-d-2.)

Essentially the Dog Feast can be divided into three phases: scouting the enemy, counting coup on him, and serving the meat to certain distinguished elders.[147] A comparison of the approximately contemporaneous versions of the Lac Court Oreilles Ojibwa ritual given by John Bisonette (see appendix "The Dog Feast") with the Zoar Menominee ritual as described by Slotkin show them to be nearly identical.[148]

At Lac Court Oreilles the feast begins around noon, as the singers start the Looking around [for the enemy] Song, while the three bull cooks dance once around the Drum and exit to fetch the prepared food (fig. 33). (At Zoar, first the Belt Song is performed, after which the belt man is asked by the west warrior to see if there is any food at the door. He circles the drum once

Figure 33. *Ojibwa bull cooks preparing ritual noontime feast at Whitefish in 1910. In their version of the Dog Feast, the Ojibwa often substituted beef or some game animal meat for dog.* (Photo by S. A. Barrett, courtesy Milwaukee Public Museum, neg. no. 2718.)

during the Looking around Song, then dances in place in front of the pail of meat.) The first Ojibwa bull cook arises and dances once around the pail then stops at each cardinal point, pretending to scoop up food and offering it. Then he dances three times around the pail, shaking his fist downward. On the fourth time, he bangs his fist down in a quick hard gesture to symbolize the killing of game (enemy); at that moment, the singers end the song abruptly. (At Zoar, the belt man brings the food to the center during an ordinary dance song. The lids are removed from the kettles and the speaker arises and blesses the food. Then, during the Dancing around the Food Song, he offers it to the cardinal points. The belt man takes his beaded baton, holding it like a spear and dances toward each of the cardinal points, acting as though he were stalking game [scouting the enemy]. Then he dances up to the pail of meat and makes a gesture with the wand as though striking his prey. All the men then dance in place.)

Such ritual gestures suggest origins that may predate the Grass Dance. Striking at the pail, banging down with the fist, skewering the meat—such enactments seem ultimately to derive from one of the "fire tricks" featured in the precursory Hot Dance of Plains warrior societies. As a demonstration of bravery, society members would reach into a boiling kettle to retrieve a piece of meat. To accomplish this without getting burned, the Hidatsa (and probably others) rubbed the juice of a certain root on their hand before undertaking its immersion in the boiling water.[149]

In the Drum dances of various tribes the ritual assumes somewhat different forms, all related to those described. For example, for the noon feast in the Iowa Drum Dance, the leader sings four songs while dancing around a food bucket. During the last song, he goes through the pretenses of taking food, dances toward each of the cardinal directions, pretending to throw food to them as well as to the zenith and nadir:

> Then he goes back, sings a song and dances up towards the food, but retreats as though in terror. This he does until the fourth song, when he whoops and snatches up the bucket. Then all present dance, and the feast follows.[150]

Similar ritual offerings are included in the Santee/Hidatsa rite where, after the kettle is censed with sweetgrass smoke, a speared piece of meat is presented to each direction while prayers are offered. This is considered to be "feeding" the cardinal directions.[151] (Joe Rose informs me that the feigning of food throwing to the directions was also the practice at Bad River Reservation. He remembers also that after this was done, the pail would be turned 180 degrees clockwise.)

The end of the ceremony is the distribution of the meat for human consumption. For this, special ceremonial serving implements are almost always employed. The Omaha Dog Feast servers used two sticks, the Ojibwa apparently used a small spoon attached to the end of a long stick.[152] Usually, the persons selected to receive the first portions of the meat must be warriors with distinguished military records. In Densmore's account, after the Drum owner is given the first bite, the head of the boiled dog is placed in a pan; four warriors are selected, seated next to the pan, and each given a portion of the dog to eat. The dog's skull is removed, placed on the ground, and each warrior in turn dances around it, makes a speech recounting his war deed, then sings his commemorative war song. Thereupon the remainder of the meat is distributed among the other Drum members (fig. 33). (The Menominee evidently elaborated upon the structure by including a special Old Warrior's Song for those selected to eat the meat. Each in turn dances holding the feather belt, fanning other members with it to drive out evil or illness. As with the Ojibwa, the Menominee after dancing relates his war exploit.)[153]

The Dog Feast among the Ojibwa and Menominee gradually disintegrated, perhaps for the very same reasons it did in the Grass Dance. The more removed in time these tribes became from the days of warfare, the less meaning the ritual had as former warriors died off. At the time of Densmore's fieldwork, circa 1910, the Dog Feast was still celebrated, could be held independently of the Drum Dance, and was, in fact, performed frequently at Lac du Flambeau.[154] Still it is doubtful that its intentions were "for the further cementing of the peace bond," as she notes. The feast was clearly a vestigial warriors' rite, looking backward in its celebration rather than to the future.

There is considerable evidence to challenge Wissler's assertion that the Ojibwa were among those who did not eat dog meat in the Drum Dance; all indications are that at one time they did.[155] Perhaps because the practice is considered generally distasteful to them, to eat dog meat must have been considered a demonstration of bravery indulged in only by warriors. Over time, however, other meats came to be substituted for dog—usually game meat, such as deer or raccoon, but later pork and beef, hence the designation *bull* cook. (The name is obviously derived from lumber camp days.) Johnny Matchokamow claimed the Menominee discontinued using dogs for the feast after 1905 when it was discovered that the animals were diseased, although Skinner found it continued on that reservation as late as 1911.[156] When the aide forgot to get an animal head for the 1950 rite at Zoar, Slotkin was requested to drive to Antigo to get a pig's head from the butcher shop. Since it was closed, he was asked to drive the Menominee to a place in the woods for them to catch a porcupine for the same purpose—porcupines being slow moving, thus easily (but cautiously) captured.[157]

Clearly some vestige of the Dog Feast is suggested by a Minnesota Ojibwa report of the Feast of Seasons celebrated at Red Lake before 1900. It included a dance with ten special songs, during which someone with a decorated stick poked at a pig's head in a pail. At a certain moment he speared the head and "the drum [went] to pieces, it [was] hit by all the drummers out of time." (Cf. the signal to stop the singing of the Looking around Song.) In the feast that followed, the first to be served were elders "with a record of bravery."[158]

Another stage in the gradual disintegration of the ritual was the substitution of a piece of bone for the animal's head. Describing the Menominee feast, Densmore observed that after people had finished eating with their fingers from the pail containing meat other than dog, "the pail was removed and a piece of rib was laid on a paper directly in front of the entrance. (This represented the skull of the dog.)" Later on, Rattlesnake walked around the bone making ritual feints as if to spear it; then it was taken by an Ojibwa visitor and thrown out of the dance ring. Doubtless recalling her Ojibwa data, Densmore added that "in older versions" the visitor would have then related one of his uncle's war exploits and performed a war song to commemorate it, as would have three other old men.[159]

Dance Sites

The Drum Dance takes place within a symbolically defined space reserved for it, either in the form of an open-air enclosure or dance hall. The boundaries of such sacred arenas, as Evon Vogt has suggested, serve to establish ritual purity within their confines and separate the events contained inside them from the disorders of the outside world.[160]

Whether or not the open enclosures predate the dance halls is not certain, for in most communities both were used. The earliest reporters on the dance—MacCauley, Hoffman, Densmore, and Barrett—all describe outdoors events, but it should be remembered that their observations were made in the summer or fall. Certainly in the northern climate, groups who strictly observed the four seasonal rites required protection from the elements for the winter and spring events, which only enclosed structures afford.

The adoption of open-air enclosures for the Drum Dance may have occurred during the transitional period when adherents of the Grand Medicine Society began to form the Drum societies. We know that for some time medicine ceremonies and Drum dances were contiguous events, with members belonging to both organizations. Moreover, in many communities the two enclosures were physically juxtaposed. The structure for a *midewigaan* (medicine lodge) can be seen in the field behind the dance ring at Lac Court Oreilles in 1899 (fig. 34) and the Mille Lacs dance hall in 1963 was situated across from a lot where *mide* ceremonies took place.[161]

The earliest dance enclosures may have been modeled on the medicine lodge, which, despite its name and wigwamlike sub-

Figure 34. *Probably the oldest photo (1899) of an Ojibwa ceremonial Dance Drum. The dance enclosure at Lac Court Oreilles appears to be very large. Three Drums are present, and a medicine lodge framework can be seen at the upper left outside of the wooden fence.* (Photo by A. E. Jenks, courtesy NAA, neg. no. 49,399.)

structure of saplings, was still left open at its top (fig. 35). The lodge was originally covered with pine boughs to a height of no more than three feet. Thus it permitted outsiders an unobstructed view of the procedings, at least for the "public" portions of the ceremony; as with dance rings, however, only authorized

Figure 35. *Medicine ceremony at Lac Court Oreilles, circa 1899. The photo appears to be taken from the western end of the medicine lodge. Some members seem to be circuiting the lodge in procession, indicating that medicine songs were being performed; others appear to dance in place at the left. The central figure is a* mide *priest, possibly playing a drum cradled in his arm, although it is obliterated from view by the woman to his right holding her otter-skin (?) medicine bag.* (Photo by A. E. Jenks, courtesy NAA, neg. no. 476-A20.)

persons were permitted within the sacred grounds.[162]

Aside from these basic similarities, the two structures differed apparently for symbolic reasons. A *long* rectangular or oblong structure, the medicine lodge was intended as an allegory to *gichi-gami* ("The Big Sea" [Lake Superior]), sometimes referred to in song texts as "the long, long room."[163] The circular Drum Dance enclosure symbolizes the universe, its shape paralleling the circular Drum in its center. In the earliest published account of the Drum's origin, the Great Spirit tells Tailfeather Woman:

"Do you see the sky, how it is round . . . go, then, and tell
your people to make a circle on the ground, just like the
round sky. Call that holy ground. Go there, and with a big
drum in the center, sing and dance and pray to me and
speak my works."[164]

According to most reports these enclosures varied in measure-
ment anywhere from thirty to eighty feet in diameter, the size
apparently dependent on the number of persons regularly using
it. The ring itself was formed in a number of ways, by an earth
embankment, logs, a low fence of some sort, or even a framework
of lumber with chicken wire. If an exact circle were impossible—
for example, when constructed from boards—it was made to
resemble one as closely as possible. Eventually, however, we find a
change from a circular to a square dance area (see fig. 25). This
seems to have been gradual and done for convenience: when an
octagonal enclosure at Whitefish was moved, it was found that
building a square hall at the new location was easier.[165]

Dance enclosures were also intended to provide seating space
for participants around their interiors. Members were free to sit
on the dirt embankment or on benches built around the inside of
the circle, where a fence might be built that served also as a
backrest (see figs. 23-24). Over time, apparently, the height of the
backrest increased as well; circa 1910 Barrett found six-foot-high
hexagonal enclosures at Lac du Flambeau and Round Lake.
Built of solid lumber, they would have blocked outsiders' view of
the happenings.[166]

As was also customary with the medicine lodge, participants
were expected to enter and exit through designated openings in
the structure. For the Drum Dance enclosures, these "doorways"
were always created at one or more of the cardinal points, although there is no apparent consistency in their location.[167]
Hoffman illustrates both east and west openings at two dance
rings near Keshena in the 1890s (fig. 36), whereas MacCauley
noted only a western one a decade earlier on the same reservation.[168] Densmore observed that the Menominee dirt embankment had openings at the south, east, and west, but that those at
the south and west had been blocked off by logs (fig. 37); thus
everyone entered through the eastern door while handing a
pinch of tobacco to an official stationed there. Her report is at
odds with Barrett's contemporaneous account, which states that
the western door was regularly used for entry.[169] (Barrett implies
a distinction between Menominee and Ojibwa dance rings: en-

Figure 36. *Menominee dance enclosure near Keshena in the 1890s, after an illustration by Walter J. Hoffman.* (Illustration by Daphne Shuttleworth.)

Figure 37. *Menominee dirt bank dance enclosure at Keshena, circa 1913. Since a ceremony is not in progress, the east and west openings have been "closed" with boards, probably to remind people not to enter.* (Photo by Alanson Skinner, courtesy American Museum of Natural History, neg. no. 105439.)

closures of the former all had western entrances, while those of the latter also had eastern entrances.)

Formerly, once a ceremony was in session, one was permitted to enter the enclosure or exit from it only through the specified doors. Even where the enclosure was low enough to step over—such as an earth embankment—one could do so at any other time but during the service was required to use the special gateways. To control traffic, guards were stationed at the openings. While their responsibilities included preventing dogs and objectionable people from entering and disturbing the ceremony, their principal function was "to permit no one to leave the area without the permission of the chief dancer, and then only upon a payment of a small fine, this fine being devoted to the benefit of the Drum."[170]

The posting of guards at meetings for practical reasons has a long history with American Indians—for example, at council meetings the League of the Iroquois had eastern and western doorkeepers. Still, the Woodlands practice has deep significance, namely, the containment of good and purity within the dancing ground and evil and danger outside of it. This is consistent with general Grand Medicine tenets concerning the thresholds of the medicine lodge, which are believed to be guarded by powerful spirits who must be placated before one gains admission.[171] In Ojibwa medicine ceremonies, for example, the leader makes four ritual feints toward penetrating the lodge before he can successfully gain entrance. At the end of the Menominee ceremony, the medicine drum is carried out the west end around to the east, where the leader attempts to bring it inside, but faces a sham battle from some of the participants to prevent his entrance.[172]

Beliefs concerning the beneficial power contained within the dance ring and maintenance of its purity are inherent in statements of Drum members as well as certain rituals in the Dance itself. Declaring that participants were not to leave once the dance had begun, Johnny Matchokamow noted, "They claim that outside the dancing ground some bad spirits are outside. That's why the people, they hang back. Maybe some of them, they don't come; maybe they go drinking someplace."[173] At the end of the Menominee Belt Dance ritual, to collect the evil that has been purged from the participants and remove it from the dance hall, a blanket is put on the floor by the entrance; the belt man makes four ritual feints to grab it and then gives it to the *oshkaabewis* who takes the blanket outside together with the "bad luck" believed to be contained within it.[174]

The Ojibwa use of a totally enclosed building for the Drum Dance was almost certainly borrowed from Plains tribes. Leaders of Plains warrior societies customarily kept drums in their homes, which then became the sites of their dances. Thus, Lump-Face, the headman of the Arikara Young Dogs Society, had the society's drum in his earth lodge where the dances were held.[175] When the Grass Dance was first accepted by these tribes, the custom continued; the dance would be held in the house of the new owner or leader of the dance, once all the household furniture was removed for the event. The Hidatsa Wolf Chief, for example, remembered when the Grass Dance was first brought circa 1881 to Like-a-Fishhook-Village:

"Big Brave's lodge had been cleared for the occasion. All the beds had been taken outside of the lodge. The bed posts had been pulled up out of the earth floor. The puncheon fire screen had also been taken down and carried outside, as had the big couch that stood against it facing the fireplace. All this was done to make more floor space for the feasting and dancing. We expected to replace everything after the [Santee] Sioux left our village."[176]

(With the Ojibwa, storing the Drum in the owner's home and holding evening dances and "song services" there seems to be a vestige of the original Grass Dance practice.)

In time, however, special dance houses came to be reserved exclusively for the ceremonies. The Kansa, who had formerly held their Drum Dance in the owner's house, had moved it to a round house with a cone-shaped roof by the time Skinner reported on them.[177] The Pawnee Skidi Iruska Society held their dances in a circular lodge with an eastern entrance; the large drum was located at the northeast, the ceremonial pipe at the west, and the members seated around the periphery.[178]

The importance of these dance halls led Wissler to observe that one prominent feature of the Grass Dance—whatever the name given to the ceremony—was "a dancing house of definite form."[179] The Blackfoot had three such houses for their Hair-Parters Dance (Grass Dance); the Oglala Sioux modeled their log dance hall after the Pawnee earth lodge (fig. 38, see also fig. 20).[180] Where a permanent enclosure was lacking, it seems, one could be improvised; the Sarsi Hair-Parters would place their

Figure 38. *Lakota octagonal log dance house, circa 1890-1900.* (Photo by James Mooney, courtesy NAA, neg. no. 3703.)

Figure 39. *Another Siouan dance hall of the same period built of board and made to approximate a circle. Nearly all such halls shared the peaked roof.* (Photographer unknown, courtesy NAA, neg. no. 53396.)

Figure 40. *Arikara dance house with turret and windows. The Hidatsa and Crow used a similar style of architecture for dance houses.* (Photo courtesy American Museum of Natural History, neg. no. 283721.)

Figure 41. *Old dance hall at Mille Lacs Lake, circa 1910. The architectural features are similar to those of the Arikara hall (see fig. 40).* (Photo probably by Frances Densmore, courtesy NAA, neg. no. 596-d-8.)

wagons in a circle leaving an opening to the south, the owner of the large drum seated opposite the entrance.[181]

Architectural evidence suggests that at least some of the older Ojibwa dance halls derived their shape and mode of construction from their western counterparts. The basic structural elements of the Sioux hall shown in figure 39 are nearly identical to the Ojibwa dance hall at Mille Lacs: a many-sided framework approximating a roofed and boarded circle. Another example is offered by the architecture of the Crow Hot Dance (Grass Dance) lodge. The Crow, who received the dance from the Hidatsa to their east in the early 1880s constructed a partially open hall for the Hot Dance. Later, more modern features were added to this structure—for example, a turret with windows (fig. 40).[182] These structural features are incorporated in the old dance hall at Mille Lacs (fig. 41). When a replacement dance hall was built for it, this tendency toward having a peaked roof was retained: the new hall, fifty feet square, reached a height of thirty-five feet in the center.[183]

There have been some recent attempts to revive the dance hall on reservations. In 1975 as a project of the Economic Development Administration an octagonal structure was built at Lac du Flambeau on the site of the old hall that had been stripped of its wood over time since it was last actively used in the late 1940s. The new hall is thirty feet across and reaches to a peak of fifteen feet (fig. 42). The building is oriented to provide an eastern entrance and western exit. Benches were constructed around six

Figure 42. *The Round House, a dance hall constructed at Lac du Flambeau in 1975. The octagonal structure has both east and west entrances.* (Photo courtesy Ernie St. Germaine, 1981.)

of the sides, and four central posts reach to the ceiling (cf. fig. 43). The posts are painted according to ceremonial color associations: red for the two south posts, blue for the north. The new dance hall is only about a third the size of the one it replaced, and some in the community feel that the resultant space restriction makes it too cramped for dancing. (The original hall is said to have accommodated eleven Drums at one dance.) Although the new hall occasionally serves for meetings of elders and was once used for a service prior to the reburial of ancestral remains, the building has never seen a Drum Dance.

Figure 43. *Arikara dance lodge under construction. The four central posts were a structural feature retained in some Ojibwa Drum Dance halls, such as that at Lac Vieux Desert and the hall (fig. 42) at Lac du Flambeau.* (Photo courtesy American Museum of Natural History, neg. no. 15981.)

The old Flambeau dance hall had been constructed of logs six inches in diameter that were later replaced with boards about 1930 when the hall was remodeled under the supervision of George Brown. At the time, a wooden floor was installed over the earth, worn smooth and hard over the years from dancing. Some people are still alive who can recall the seasonal alternation of using the Round House and the powwow grounds (fig. 44). After sugar making in the spring, Flambeau residents living near the dance hall would move to the powwow grounds, where they would set up wigwams, which they occupied through the rice harvest. Then they would move back to their homes and use the indoors facility for their dances because it was heated with barrel stoves. The hall was no longer used for "Big Drum" services by the late 1940s; the last affair to take place in it was a bachelor party for George Brown, Jr., before his marriage in 1952. By that time, the boards had already begun to disappear.[184]

In the Woodlands not only were dance sites frequently moved

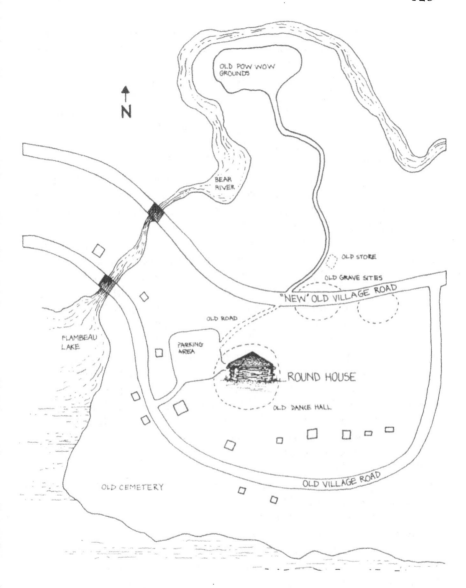

Figure 44. *Location of the new dance hall at Lac du Flambeau on the site of the old hall, after an illustration by Ernie St. Germaine.* (Illustration by Daphne Shuttleworth.)

to new grounds within the same community, but Drum societies also alternated their use of open-air enclosures and buildings, in accordance with changes in climate. A brief history of the dance locations on the Menominee reservation is fairly illustrative. The first site we know of was a "wide, enclosed circle" sufficiently large to encompass nearly one hundred people when MacCauley saw it used in the fall of 1880. It was located some miles from Keshena in "a large, oval clearing in the woods." By the 1890s there were three low circular wooden enclosures near Keshena such as the one published by Hoffman (see fig. 36). By 1911 Zoar had a circular earth ring, which was still in use as late as 1950 for summer ceremonies (cf. fig. 37). In the 1930s a circular dance hall was constructed, which eventually was abandoned after snow collapsed its roof. At Zoar in 1948 the reservation agency converted an old twenty-four-foot square lumber camp kitchen into a dance hall, which was in use in 1950 at the time of Slotkin's study. In the reconstruction of this building, the door was located by mistake on the north side.[185]

Over time and perhaps paralleling the decline of the Drum Dance most events were moved indoors, possibly as a means of protecting them. The people at Lac Vieux Desert had two buildings for their dances: the winter dances were held in the community hall—doubtless because it could be heated—while the summer dances were held in a special octagonal building.[186] Although daytime dances had been held indoors for some years in Zoar, a decision was made in 1950 to revert to holding ceremonies outdoors. Because it rained for the event, the weather was interpreted as a bad omen and no further dances were held outside.[187] At Mille Lacs, dances were moved indoors because the missionaries objected to such public displays of "heathenism." In addition to being removed from sight, for further protection the dates of the events were kept secret.[188]

Within the dance ring or hall, the Drum, of course, was the central object, but little consistency is evident in its location. Generally speaking, it would be placed somewhat centrally to permit dancing around it. The Mille Lacs Drum was exactly in the middle of the hall in 1953; at Lac Vieux Desert in the 1940s, however, it was in the southwest corner of the hall, and at Keshena in 1890 it was at the northeast corner.[189] If more than one Drum is present, they tend to be fairly evenly spaced around the ring, although, again, the arrangement varies with the community (see figs. 28, 34). This procedure is also followed today at secular powwows of most tribes, where each drum performs several songs before the next drum takes over. When kept in the dance hall, the Menominee Drums were arranged clockwise in order of seniority (i.e., when each had arrived on the reservation); for Kansas Potawatomi dances, the six Drums are spaced equidistantly around the ring, although the three within the southern half are not used during the daytime service.[190]

Flags

"'One thing should be added to this [Grass] dance; we [the Santee Sioux] want to give you [the Hidatsa] a flag. The man appointed to be keeper of the flag should bring a long pole with the flag upon it, and should rest it on the porch.' And here Walking Soldier pointed to the covered entrance way of the earth lodge. The Sioux had not brought a flag to give us, but after the feast was over they searched about the village and found an old Mandan who had a big flag with an eagle design on it. Afterwards we replaced this with a United States flag" (Wolf Chief, 1914).[191]

It is customary for Drum societies to raise one or more American flags at the dance site for the duration of the ceremony (see fig. 53). Like the Drum, the flag is meant to be put up at the beginning of the day and taken down at its end.[192] It may be flown over a dance hall or placed by the entrance to an open-air enclosure, although the number of flags and their location may vary. The Iowa had two American flags at the north side of the western opening, the Kansas Potawatomi had four at the same place, the Keshena Menominee had three flags directly over the western entrance, and the Zoar Menominee used but a single one near the eastern opening.

The inclusion of a flag for ceremonial events was evidently also adopted from the Grass Dance (cf. Wolf Chief's report above). Specific Woodlands interpretations have arisen concerning its significance. For some it is meant to represent the flag flying over the camp of soldiers seen by Tailfeather Woman in her vision.[193] More commonly, however, the flag is understood to symbolize peace between the Indians and the United States Government as well as among all tribes under American jurisdiction.[194] As a symbol of peace, the flag is also intended to offer protection to those practicing the Dance. As one Menominee noted, "When you got this flag up before the drum, that means no trouble whatever."[195] Similarly, the Potawatomi interpret the flag as "the guarantee of religious freedom in the U.S. Constitution. [They] say, that so long as those flags fly over their ritual center, they will be allowed to practice their ancient customs in peace."[196]

Although hoisted American flags should not be confused with the so-called medicine poles, they seem in fact to serve a similar protective function. Medicine poles were usually erected to ward off disease; they were also left standing as evidence that some ceremony had been held. Formerly, in front of houses in the old village at Lac du Flambeau, for example, there would be two poles six feet apart, one with a white flag bearing the totemic design of the resident, the other, a tall evergreen stripped of all but the top branches to show where a ceremony had taken place.[197] Medicine poles of various descriptions were also placed next to and even inside medicine lodges and dance enclosures. Their particular design was almost always dream dictated—hence the notion that a flag was included in Tailfeather Woman's vision. Near the dance hall at Lac Vieux Desert was a pole in the shape of a cross with clothing hanging from it; its design, instructed in a vision, was meant to prevent sickness.[198] Densmore visited a *waabanowiwin* lodge in July 1930 at Grand Portage, Minnesota, in which a healing ceremony had been held for a man with an ear abscess. Near the eastern entrance stood a six-foot post with a windmill on it as "an invitation to the east wind . . . [which] always came and made its presence known in this manner."[199]

When used ceremonially, the American flag may have been equated with the medicine pole and served a similar purpose. The Potawatomi interpretation of the flag, in Clifton's opinion, was "strongly flavored by magical implications."[200] Similar spiritual connotations are suggested for the two poles erected outside a Nett Lake medicine lodge in the early 1930s: at its southeast corner was a medicine pole with bits of calico tied to it "for the healing of the people"; at the other end of the lodge was an American flag.[201]

Preaching

Beyond promoting peace and brotherhood, the Drum Dance stressed the ethical behavior of its adherents. This was done both formally, through preaching during ceremonies (fig. 45), and informally when the occasion warranted it. Such discourses on morality were common to many tribes, as when an elder would address an assembly of his people either in some public forum or within the context of a ceremony. The Santee village chief, for example, "delivered his homilies by stepping into the open and addressing the close-packed tipis around him"; in his talk he would stress the importance of character and camp welfare, reminding his people how they should live together and avoid strife.[202] Similarly, between songs the Iowa Mawatoni drum chiefs "preached to the society on morality and right conduct."[203] Because of this widespread tradition in North America, Indians

Figure 45. *Steve Grover of Lac Court Oreilles Reservation during the Whitefish Dance in July 1910 preaching to the membership. Note the elaborate beadwork sewn onto the shirts of the singers. The crossed beadwork straps on the man in the immediate foreground are part of his bandoleer bags.* (Photo by S. A. Barrett, courtesy Milwaukee Public Museum, neg. no. 20203.)

generally became renowned for their great skills as orators.

Ethical behavior was a precondition for joining a Drum. Membership requirements at Mille Lacs stressed that:

> The members, and in particular the [Drum] owners must possess certain characteristics that ensure perpetuation of the Drum [and that] a person must be of good character and not too poor; in particular he must not be stingy.[204]

In Slotkin's discussion "Ethics and Eschatology" in the Drum Dance, he observed that the principle of the golden rule applied not only within one's own community but beyond to all other tribes who had the Drum:

> Essentially the ethical way to behave is to treat others as if they were members of one's own elementary family. . . . The people should cooperate with one another . . . and help one another.[205]

Further, he concluded, this attention to universal ethical behavior distinguished Drum Dance members from others in their community:

The distinctive contribution made by the [Drum Dance people] is believed by its members to be that it extended this behavior from fellow tribesmen to people of other Indian tribes as well. The ethic is "in the Drum," that is, it is an intrinsic part of the [Drum Dance]. Its validation arises from the fact that when the Great Spirit gave the Sioux woman the Drum, he also enunciated the ethic which belongs to it.[206]

This attitude would explain Rattlesnake's remarks to Densmore, "There is really only one drum in this world.... Whenever I run across a band of Indians with a drum, the people have been trying to do right."[207]

Since the decline of the dance, however, some of its ethical precepts have been weakened or abandoned. In the film *The Drummaker*, Baker notes with chagrin that the former spirit of cooperation among his people had vanished, as evidenced by the fact that he alone must build the entire drum with no help from others in the community: "Years ago they used to help one another. Now it's come to the time where nobody takes interest."

Cooperation with others was only one character requirement expected of members. In speeches at Drum dances the membership was constantly reminded in exhortations to avoid quarreling and to abstain from drinking, gambling, and stealing. Kindness and helpfulness were also attributes of Drum members, and impromptu solicitations could be provoked during the course of a ceremony, such as requests for aid for people in trouble and sickness or comfort for those in mourning. Once a young man had inadvertently seated himself at a Drum to which he did not belong. Rather than openly criticizing him, a member arose and spoke on his behalf, while others distributed tobacco offerings for him. He was then led to his proper Drum.[208]

Costuming

As the Grass Dance spread, special dance costumes were transferred to recipients as an important part of the regalia, but by the time of the Drum Dance, most of these items—once novel—were already in common currency among many tribes. Consequently, the lack of any great attention to dance costumes in Drum affairs merely increased the focus on the Drum as the paramount transfer item. Still, general costuming practices at the Drum Dance over the years deserve some discussion.

Wissler cites the Crow belt and roached headdress as the most distinctive costume items associated with the Grass Dance; yet the transfer of the dance often involved donations of complete dancing "outfits" consisting of many more items.[209] The new apparel was frequently a complete novelty to a group receiving it and provided one avenue of exchange of material culture that affected adaptations in tribal styles of ceremonial design and dress. Prior to receiving their new dance costumes from the Santee, the Mandan and Hidatsa were simply attired in their "Sunday best." As each new officer was named, he was given his new dancing outfit by the corresponding Sioux officer in exchange for the gifts that had been accumulated to pay for them:

> and now the drum keeper, also a Sioux, arose and picked up all the gifts piled before John Smith, or Big Brave, and in their place set down the big drum and gave to Big Brave his dance outfit: head dress, otter skin for the head, sleigh bells, and beaded work articles; the whole suit in fact.[210]

In addition to these articles the Hidatsa received yarn belts and beadwork armlets. These together constituted the new Grass Dance costume for them, although, as Wolf Chief pointed out, not everyone received all of the items.

Roaches and sleigh bells eventually became part of standard dance attire. The sleigh bells were used as garters around the knees and/or ankles where previously one might have worn strung dewclaws of some animal for the same percussive purpose. The roach headdress, today commonly worn by dancers of many tribes, was made of a deertail reinforced around its perimeter with porcupine guard hairs, moose bristles, or horsehair. It was held in place by a hole in its center through which a lock of the wearer's hair was pulled and fastened with a thong.[211] (When the roach is worn, the image may remind most non-Indians of the "Mohawk"-style haircut affected by American youth in the early 1950s.) Roaches of all tribes conformed to the same general type; differences for the most part arose from the materials available for their manufacture. For example, where porcupines were scarce, the entire roach might be made of horsehair. The Woodlands style is exemplified by the roach made by Baker. For its base he unravels gunnysacks and reweaves their threads into a tight thick mat in the desired elongated shape. The perimeter is then surrounded with a row of the thinnest porcupine hairs and the fine white hair from the tail of the Virginia deer. Each tuft of

Figure 46. *Drum Dance at Lac Court Oreilles in 1899. At least three Drums appear to be present. Belt man of one Drum can be seen center left. Note crossed shoulder straps of bandoleer bags on man to his left.* (Photo by A. E. Jenks, courtesy NAA, neg. no. 476-a-57.)

hair and quill must be sewn individually to the base. The roach fairly bristles when worn by a dancer, producing the desired effect.[212]

Generally speaking, by the time of the Drum Dance, members simply wore what had been their ceremonial garb for previous occasions. Since many had belonged to the Grand Medicine Society, there was really not much distinction in the styles of costuming for the two events—that is, by circa 1880 white and Indian clothing were combined. (War clubs, tomahawks, roaches, and feather bustles, however, were absent from medicine ceremonies.) The women would dress conservatively in conventional full-length dresses with shawls (sometimes fancy hats) over their heads; by contrast, the men were more elaborately dressed, the degree and style of their costuming dependent upon their position within both the community and the Drum Society. Former warriors would wear roaches, might carry war clubs or wooden guns (see fig. 22), and paint their faces; elders, particularly medicine men, would wear elaborately beaded bandoleer bags over their shoulders. If the dancers did not wear roaches, they wore black felt hats of non-Indian manufacture (fig. 46).

The style of costuming reflected local customs of ceremonial dress at the time. Clay MacCauley depicts a fairly elaborate assortment of articles that made up the costume of the speaker at the Menominee function he witnessed in 1880:

> He wore a black cloth frock coat and trousers like leggins, down whose outer seams were broad, black, embroidered

flaps. Bright red and yellow handkerchiefs hung from his right shoulder. Bound around his legs just below the knees were more gaudily coloured articles of the same kind [probably loom-beaded garters tied at the back by means of yarn tassles attached to them]. A string of shells was hung, as though it were an amulet, about his neck; long silver rings dragged down his ears; a long tufted rod stood up straight from the back of his neck; fancifully beaded mocassins clothed his feet, and in his hand was a gaily decorated wand with which every now and then he emphasized his speech.[213]

By the turn of the century, it is evident from photographs that a less elaborate style of costuming had become acceptable. It is fairly safe to say that formal wear of some sort was expected, but usually following white dress fashions of the time (or slightly earlier), with the addition of some token of Indian identity—moccasins in place of shoes, for instance, or bandoleer bags slung over a suit coat, or a beaded apron worn over trousers, or minor facial painting. By and large, however, the singers were less apt to have Indian articles incorporated into their dress as were other office holders, such as the Drum owner or the bull cook (see fig. 33). The generally conservative nature of the dress, however, should be stressed: a young man at Whitefish in 1910 was severely reprimanded for appearing at a dance stripped to the waist and wearing war paint on his upper body, even though it may have been a sincere gesture on his part to honor the Indian mode of dress of former times.[214]

At all ceremonies, heads were covered, and although the broad-brimmed turn-of-the-century black felt hats and derbies gradually gave way to caps, which continue to be worn even today at secular powwows (see figs. 4, 25). In the Drum Dance, caps (or hats) are only removed when one makes a speech, possibly following white custom or perhaps as a conservative Indian gesture.[215] Earl Nyholm suggests that because white men were always depicted by Indians as wearing hats of some kind, when an Indian removes his hat to deliver a serious address, it may be a stressing of his Indian nature.

The failure in recent times to incorporate even some small item of Indian costuming is surely evidence of the decline of the importance formerly accorded the Drum Dance. As Slotkin observed in the summer rite at Zoar in 1951, the absence of any Indian dress at all was consistent with the tardiness of the people and scarcity of singers at the Drum.[216]

The Decline of the Drum Dance

"Us [Drum Dance] people, we ain't much of us left. All them old people [are] all gone now; most of them [are] young people living now. And we are short handed today. We ain't got enough people to fill out the Drum [Society] the way it's supposed to be. That's why we have to invite the other people [from other reservations] to come and help us in our ceremonies every season. Every season we invite other people to come in order to [help] run this ceremony of ours. . . . You know, this Powwow [Drum Dance] is going dim all over. It's just us [and the Chippewa] that have that belief. The Potawatomi don't have no dances no more. Especially in Wabeno [Wisconsin]; they got Drums, but they don't use it" (Johnny Matchokamow, 1950).[1]

The day that I first learned, I was told the Great Spirit has the power to put tobacco on that Drum . . . and every Drum should have a tobacco box. Today they make a fool of that Drum. I *know* that ain't supposed to be that way. They just make the Drum and pound the hell out of it, no tobacco, no nothing. What happens? A lot of things [it always rains for their dances, for example], but they don't stop to realize as long as they're just having fun, that's all that's necessary. But I don't feel that way myself. I walked *away* from those dances last time for that reason, that's how much I think of it, and I'll think of it until my last day on this earth, and that's why I carry that tobacco with me [William Bineshi Baker, Sr., 1971].[2]

When the Menominee requested James Slotkin in 1950 to write his study on their Drum Dance, their intention was not only to have him preserve the details of their ritual in writing as a sort of handbook but also to break a deadlock that had arisen between the generations: the young were complaining that their elders did not want to teach them the dance, the elders that the young were not interested in learning it.[3]

Although the Drum Dance continues to be viable in some places, especially among later recipients of the Drum, there is no question that beginning around 1930 it experienced a sharp decline in Minnesota and Wisconsin. Except in isolated settlements today or for an occasional ceremony, such as a funeral wake, for all practical purposes, Drums are now inactive and have been for some time. The most significant evidence of this decline is found in dwindling membership, disintegration of orthodox ritual, and disappearance of the Drums themselves.

Loss of membership was experienced everywhere. Densmore noted that, although many more could have been accommodated in the dance ring, fewer were in attendance at the 1928 Drum presentation she attended than were present at the similar event in 1910. In 1941, despite three Drum societies at Lac du Flambeau, there were not enough people to hold a spring dance.[4] When Slotkin tried to compile a list of Drum members for the Menominee, no one could remember exactly who belonged. To find out, he called a meeting to bring the members together, but only about a third attended.[5] Some disinterested officers who were not fulfilling their obligations asked relatives to join, but they rarely accomplished their new assignments.

To fill empty places on Drums, the Zoar people borrowed officers from other societies and even resorted to using young boys. (Slotkin himself was sometimes tapped for service.)[6] Or, they invited people from other reservations. For a June Dance in 1950, a letter sent to the Ojibwa telling them of the planned two-day event concluded: "If we have more company, maybe we'll have four days dance [as is ritually prescribed]."[7] When they tried to put a dance together, even the traditional tobacco invitations were ignored. Said Matchokamow ruefully:

"But, you know, it's pretty hard, nowadays, to gather all them members. We tried that a good many times, and passed tobacco around [to] the ones that belong to the Drum, and they don't come. I don't see why that people done that; they don't come. If they'd come, everything would go right. But this way, there's very few of us [who] go over there and decide what we are going to do in that day [dance]."[8]

Baker has met with the same indifference from his people. Several years ago he wished to honor the memory of his mother through a dance with his drum. When he sent the traditional tobacco invitations around, they were declined. For him, the experience was a bitter one.

Because of declining interest, societies were forced to practice multiple membership. (This was already in effect by 1910.)[9] That is, an officer from one Drum would serve on another to fill a vacancy and not necessarily the same office he held on his own Drum. While there were supposed to be four directors for each instrument, at Whitefish the same four people had to serve for both Drums in 1910.[10] In 1941 Jim Billyboy belonged to two Lac Court Oreilles Drums and one at Hertl, Wisconsin; Willy Bisonette declared he belonged to all three Drums on his reservation because "there aren't enough singers to go around anymore"; Wasigisik joined the Mitchell Quagon Drum "because there was a shortage."[11]

Ritzenthaler's listing of the personnel for three active Drum societies at Lac Court Oreilles circa 1940 shows their membership to range in size from the largest group with two Drum owners, twenty-five male members, and twelve female helpers, to the smallest number with nineteen males and only six females (see appendix "The Lac Court Oreilles Drum Dance, circa 1940"). On closer examination of the lists it is clear that by 1940 the societies had resorted to dual and even triple membership to fill as many as possible of the requisite positions. Nearly half of the forty-six male members belonging to these three Drums served on more than one instrument, five held positions on all three. Since the same man served different functions on different Drums, it is clear that "filling in" had become the accepted practice. Thus Willie Webster served as speaker for two Drums and as a warrior on a third; Joe Benton was bull cook for two Drums and pipe tender for the third; John Jack, lead singer on the John Martin/Pete Quagon Drum, was assigned to the west stake on the John Pete Cloud Drum and served as warrior on the John Stone Drum.

Such multiple membership, however, seems not to have been practiced by the women of the community. Most were wives of Drum members and served only in the societies for which their husbands held a post. Of the twenty-seven women listed, only one—Annie Dandy—belonged to two Drums.

While certain assignments were absolutely mandatory—the four warriors, at least one singer per stake, and the speaker, for instance—lesser offices appear to have become optional, such as the sweeper, boss, and tobacco pouch tender. Also, only one of the three Drums had young warriors, and only two at that when four were required.[12] That the same situation existed among the Menominee is confirmed by Slotkin's table 1 "Membership in the Three Drum Organizations, 1951."[13]

Drum adherents were clearly concerned about this practice of multiple membership; some could discern in it a weakening of the Dance. As George Kapishkowit was told by his father:

> "'One Drum is just as strong as the others' he says, 'so you don't have to be in every one of them Drums; that's too

much work for you. . . . If you happen to be a good singer, or something like that, it's going to play you out to go into every Drum.'"[14]

Concurrent with the decline in membership was a loosening of orthodox procedure in ritual. As elders died, the meanings of certain parts of the ceremony and the correct way of performing them were lost. Consequently mistakes began to occur, and a general sloppiness developed in conducting services. This affected the singing as well, as Baker noted: "Even yet they're trying to sing, but they've lost their way—they know the songs and all that, but they've lost their way." Where there was once a prescribed order of songs and different tempos specified for their performance, in Baker's opinion, "now there's only a mixup affair nowadays; you don't even know what it is, a powwow [Drum Dance] or a hoedown."[15]

As examples of the disorganized state of the services and general lackadaisical attitude prevailing circa 1950, Slotkin lists, among other things, people being late or absent, leaving early, entering in the wrong order, and sitting in the wrong places, female members not singing with the men; and few officers at the Drum.[16] Additionally, the oshkaabewis at one dance forgot to purchase the animal head required for the Belt Dance, the man owning the big stick had lost it, and members forgot that they should give food to the Drum owner.[17] Ritual taboos were not only ignored, but some did not even know of their existence—sexual abstinence before the seasonal rites, for instance.[18] What he found led Slotkin to entitle his publication *The Menominee Powwow: A Study in Cultural Decay.*

The Drums themselves at this time had uncertain futures. The whole mechanism for their presentation, upon which the Drum Dance depended for its viability, was in jeopardy. With people increasingly reluctant to accept Drums, the whole reason for building them was obviated. Jim Crow, around 1920, gave his Drum away at Lac du Flambeau: when the replacement Drum was made, he also gave it to Flambeau people. That was the last Drum he would own; no replacement was made, and he refused several times the chance to become owner again.[19]

Inactive Drums faced uncertain fates. Whereas they were once kept in their owners' houses with a light burning before them, in the spring of 1951 the Zoar Drums were moved to the Dance Hall and left there.[20] While there was some activity in 1941 with the three Flambeau Drums, the Woman's Dance drum on the reservation sat idle at Fence Lake.[21] A Drum given by that reservation to Lac Vieux Desert had been without a custodian since its previous owner died in a fire;[22] another in the same community was said to have been buried—a traditional Ojibwa method for disposing of medicine paraphernalia when no successor was in line to assume responsibility for their care;[23] and Norman Feder asserts that inactive Drums were converted into coffee tables.[24]

Some Drums were sold, like other Indian artifacts and almost always to whites through some furtive transaction to obtain drinking money.[25] The fourth Drum of the Menominee was sold to the Oshkosh Museum in 1931 because its society had dissolved.[26] Because collectors and museums today desire such objects, their value escalates each time they change hands. (I do not know what a Minneapolis collector paid for a very old Nett Lake Drum; I do know, however, that he recently sold it to a third party for $1,000, who in turn sold it to a museum for $1,500.)

The history of a Drum once belonging to Baker's grandfather is typical. It passed from Joe Baker and Frank Dodd to Frank Geezhkok at Bad River, who had it until he gave it to Henry Martin. In 1968 Jesse Martin for some reason either gave or sold it to a white man in Iron River, Wisconsin, some forty miles west of the reservation. A fanciful feature story was published in a Saint Paul newspaper in 1969 claiming the Drum to have been Sitting Bull's and that Martin had given it to his white friend for safekeeping.[27] (A photograph of the new owner's wife posed holding two drumsticks as though the instrument were a snare drum was published with the article [fig. 47].) The Drum has since been sold to someone in Florida.[28]

Other factors contributing to the decline of the Drum Dance were economic and religious pressures, an accelerated disintegration of traditional Ojibwa culture with an attendant generation gap, and the rise of cultism among Drum adherents.

Keeping the Drum movement alive involved expenditures of time and money, which were less and less available to Indian people in this century. Just to construct and decorate a Drum properly required the combined efforts and cooperation of several people, to say nothing of the time and expense involved in obtaining the required materials—hides, velvet, and beads. The fact that Baker must accomplish all of these tasks himself, as the section on construction in the present study illustrates, is a sign of his great dedication to perpetuating the tradition. His uniqueness is underscored by the fact that much of the work he must do was formerly performed by the women of the tribe. Whereas hunting and skinning animals was the man's duty, preparing

Figure 47. *Drum built by William Baker's grandfather. This Drum met the fate of many such instruments as the Drum Dance began to decline; it found its way into non-Indian hands.* (Photo courtesy the Earl Chapin Collection, Area Research Center, University of Wisconsin-River Falls. Reprinted, by permission, from *Saint Paul Pioneer Press.*)

their hides and tanning them was expected of his wife. At one time nearly every Ojibwa woman (as well as women from most tribes) knew how to do this and had her own tools for the job (see fig. 3). By the late 1940s there were only a few specialists in the art to whom hides were taken to be tanned for two to four dollars apiece.[29] But hide preparation is only one such task formerly assigned to women that Baker must now do himself, for he does all the sewing and beadwork for his drums as well (fig. 48).

At about the same time the Drum Dance began its decline, the traditional Ojibwa artwork that had characterized drum decoration of the past was also disappearing. The reasons for this are complex but certain contributing factors are obvious. Whereas young girls in the past learned beadwork from their mothers, they were now attending school and had less time available to absorb the tradition. The gradual lack of interest in traditional

Figure 48. *William Baker working alone at his table, sewing part of the belt for one of his drums. Formerly, the women of the Drum made the belts for the instruments.* (Photo by Mike Herter, June 1974.)

art is attributable in part to the fact that it simply took too much time.

In her study of Ojibwa decorative arts in the 1940s Coleman was able to discern that, even when traditional crafts were being kept alive, the market drastically reduced the quality of the goods:

> Many tourists demand low-priced articles; consequently, the worker puts out low-grade, hastily made objects. Of

the articles that were analyzed, quite a number of pieces of beadwork were carelessly made; some of the baskets were haphazardly constructed; and many pairs of moccasins showed slovenly workmanship.[30]

Similar shortcuts were conducive to the adoption of bass drums, as Ojibwa singers found it more expedient (and perhaps even less expensive) to buy a marching-band drum than to go to the trouble of making one according to traditional methods.

The spread of the Drum Dance was also interrupted by problems in its transfer. Not only were Ojibwa becoming unwilling to assume ownership of a Drum, but the transfer to other tribes was not always successful either. This was particularly the case with the Winnebago, who—as evident from the path of the Drum— were intended recipients along the line. The Winnebago did accept some Drums, particularly during the 1920s when the Ojibwa were proselytizing, but they did not always take seriously the obligations accompanying them nor accept the tenets of the Drum Dance. This is understandable for a people already saturated with religions, who had viable alternatives through their active involvement with the medicine lodge, war bundle feasts, peyotism, and Christianity.

While the Ojibwa traveled the considerable distance to southwestern Wisconsin to deposit their Drums with the Winnebago, what subsequently happened to the instruments was scarcely the donors' intent. In most cases, once the Ojibwa had departed, the Winnebago simply used them in their secular dances (fig. 49) or even dismantled them and used the beadwork decorations elsewhere. John Bisonette's observation—"With them the Drums just go to pieces"—was literally quite true, for in one case a sacred beaded tab was attached to the end of a Winnebago dance wand as though it were a war trophy. Similar problems in keeping the Drum "traveling" were encountered by the Potowatomi whose attempts to transfer the Drum to Oklahoma Indians were disastrous: "One Drum was immediately sold to a museum for spending money, while the recipient of another became drunk and set his house on fire, destroying the Drum."[31]

One reason people were reluctant to accept Drums was the expense involved: in this regard, the Drum Dance was under the same economic pressures as the Grass Dance. Because the considerable changes the Grass Dance underwent parallel to some degree similar changes in the Drum Dance, it is useful to review them, as they help to explain the ultimate decline of the Drum Dance.

Although the Grass Dance has experienced periods of dormancy since the end of the last century, it never really disappeared. At times it was given a different name by non-Indian observers. Tourists witnessing the Grass Dance on the Plains frequently called it "The War Dance" because of the frenzied style of dancing of its younger members (fig. 50). In its modern form, in the powwow, the dance has survived tenaciously and is today one of the most vital links Indians, including the Ojibwa, have with their past.

In her study "The Changing Form and Functions of the Gros Ventre Grass Dance,"[32] Regina Flannery has traced the history of the dance among these people from the time they received it from the Assinniboin, around 1875, to its disintegration, 1916-20. As was the case with nearly every tribe who accepted the dance, it filled a void created by conditions in the late nineteenth century. Before then, the entire Gros Ventre ceremonial life had been dependent upon a nomadic existence in pursuit of buffalo and acquisition of prestige through demonstrations of bravery in warfare, such as counting coup. In each tribe there had been one or more warrior or soldier societies whose functions, besides organizing war parties and fighting, had included maintaining order in camp, policing the buffalo hunts, and holding ceremonial dances.[33]

The last buffalo hunt for the Gros Ventre was in 1884; intertribal warfare as well as freedom of movement was brought to an end when they were settled on Fort Belknap Reservation in present-day Montana. The new conditions imposed on them precluded any need for warrior societies, but when the Grass Dance was transferred to them, it was easily substituted for the dance formerly belonging to one of the two Gros Ventre warrior societies. Local ceremonial customs of long standing, such as ritual "begging" and patterns of gift bestowal, were simply incorporated into the Grass Dance.

After 1890 the dance became more elaborate, with the accretion of certain rituals and more regalia (such as four special feathered warbonnets); furthermore, since the dance was no longer the function of a true warrior society, participation was now open to everyone, including children. (Formerly, Flannery points out, children would have been forcibly removed from a dance lodge.) The addition of round dances in particular allowed former spectators to take an active part in the dancing and marked an increasing secularization of the event. Gradually, the other Gros Ventre dance society, the Star Dance, became less

Figure 49. *An Ojibwa ceremonial Drum being used for a tourist show in Black River Falls, Wisconsin, in 1908 to celebrate the fiftieth anniversary of the town's newspaper,* The Badger State Banner. *The drum next to it is a typical Winnebago nail keg drum. It is played by a man wearing a Chinese coolie hat, an item popular with local farmers and available in a Black River Falls dry goods store. The tabs on the Ojibwa drum and the beadwork are in a general state of disrepair.* (Photo courtesy American Museum of Natural History, neg. no. 2A7253.)

Figure 50. *Siouan dancers performing a Grass Dance, circa 1907. Note the many feather bustles, elaborate costuming, and frenzied style of dancing.* (Photo courtesy NAA, neg. no. 55903.)

popular, losing membership to the more spectacular Grass Dance; with such attractions as its Dog Feast, feather bustles, and society officers, "it had more to it."

The Gros Ventre Grass Dance began to disintegrate around 1916. Flannery ascribes its decline principally to two factors: increased poverty on the reservation, which put an end to the lavish gift exchanges of former times, and the dying off of former warriors. Because participation in the ritual Dog Feast had been restricted to them, that part of the ceremony disappeared by 1920. Ultimately, all that remained of the Grass Dance were the round dances.

Similarly for the Ojibwa, particularly during the depression, the price required to keep the Drum Dance viable became prohibitive. (The *midewiwin* was also experiencing a decline for much the same reasons.) An enormous amount of goods was expected to change hands in Drum transfers: such giveaways were not only a matter of course during the dances, they were also ritually required. Whenever the song of a particular officer was performed, he would stand and dance in place but was then obligated to present someone with a gift. So, if an individual belonged to more than one Drum, the financial obligations could be great indeed. Traditionally, these gifts were not just small tokens, but truly expensive ones. In fact, on Baker's reservation a song was created to commemorate an incident when someone had tried to get by with presenting only a trifling gift. The text of the song states, "What I am given here is too small; I reject it."

Because generosity, associated with all Drum members, was a particular requirement of the Drum owner's character, he was expected to be a man of some means. This put demands on him and his family when the instrument was kept in his house, for he was expected to receive any member who wished to visit the Drum and provide him with hospitality. Thus the removal of Drums from owners' houses and their relocation in dance halls may be taken as a sign that such economic obligations were straining the owner's resources to the point that it was no longer feasible for him to keep the Drum at home.[34]

The Drum Dance was also affected by economic, religious, and social pressures from the dominant white society. People had so adjusted to the white economy that they would not take time off to attend ceremonies for fear of losing their jobs. Consequently, to accommodate their work schedules, the Drum Dance was shifted to weekends and abbreviated. The last Menominee four-day service—one day on each Drum—was circa 1935; thereafter it was compressed into a two-day weekend affair.

With only three Drum societies still active, one Drum was used all day Saturday and the other two divided the time on Sunday.[35] Even the Saturday services were poorly attended; following white patterns of social life, Friday night had become a time for Indians to relax in the taverns.[36] Matchokamow blamed his people's absences on evil spirits and warned of the consequences:

"What they told me, if I don't go to [the rites of] my religion, [if I do] not show up a good many times, that means that I'm not going to live very long. . . . That evil [spirit] is holding [back] the people, not to go to this place [i.e., the dance hall] here. He tell[s] them, 'You ought to go to a show, you ought to go to tavern and have a good time. Let this [other] one go [to the rite].'"[37]

The Drum Dance had met with opposition from Christian quarters since the time Catholics became alarmed by the "Wisconsin Scare" in 1878, an event that lives on in the oral history of the Drum. As Matchokamow recalled it:

"You know how this Catholic people are; they kind of always be against something in the Indian way. And some of them men, they went and told that agency, 'Them people are doing something over there [i.e., having a Drum Dance]. I think they're going to start up a war or something.' . . . Them soldiers come on the reservation and they were going to march over. . . . And they pretty near had trouble over that Powwow."[38]

Missionaries like Gilfillan at White Earth were relentless in their opposition to any form of Indian religion. At Mille Lacs, as mentioned, the church was successful in driving the dances indoors and out of sight, causing the members thereafter to keep fairly secret the dates of their meetings.[39] Conceivably, it was church members who supported the forcible dispersal of one Lac du Flambeau Dance by the reservation police, who "told the people to go home and [that] the government didn't permit Indian religion any place in this country."[40] Many Ojibwa were converting to Christianity at this time, often through dream dictates. When Paul Buffalo at Leech Lake had pneumonia as a baby, his mother dreamt of a man in a black gown who told her the baby would live, which induced her to become baptized immediately.[41] Converts such as these became vocal opponents of their former religions. Rohrl's interpreter at Mille Lacs, who turned Christian in 1958, admitted being afraid of Drum Dances because "evil spirits were represented [there] related to the Devil.["42] In so unsympathetic a climate, it is little wonder that Matchokamow was not only reluctant to give away his Drum for fear others would abuse it but felt also that for security he must keep his beliefs quietly to himself:

> "Sometimes I'm singing in my heart. You know, some people make fun of somebody [about] their religion way; when I see some people that don't belong in [the Drum Dance] then I don't like to start out anything in my way [aloud]; I just sing in my heart. When I get through singing, then I pray for myself."[43]

Competition from another religion—peyotism—was also detrimental to the Drum Dance. Instead of attending the 1951 Zoar service, Kemewan and members of his Drum were at a peyote meeting, and a minor one at that.[44] The *midewiwin* suffered a similar decline during this period, as evidenced by the drastic reduction of the number and frequency of its services. Menominee who belonged to the medicine lodge had, at the most, one ceremony a year in July. In 1950 there were none; members wishing to participate had to travel to Wisconsin Rapids to take part in Winnebago rites.[45]

Concurrent with the decline of Indian religions, the increasing exposure to white culture widened the gap between older Ojibwa attempting to maintain the Drum Dance and their more acculturated children. The loss of the language due to schooling made ceremonials conducted in the native tongue difficult to follow for those under forty. White forms of entertainment and government sponsored alternatives for social organizations were attracting the young. At Odanah (Bad River Reservation), a community hall, completed in 1937 with funds from the Bureau of Indian Affairs and constructed by WPA workers, became a social center for secular dances; twenty-four boys and thirty girls joined 4-H clubs, as the government continued to encourage Indians to farm; athletic teams and a fair board were also organized.[46] Even a community band was begun at L'Anse, Michigan, with instruction provided by a WPA musical director, Herbert Welsh, ironically, like Tailfeather Woman, a Sioux (fig. 51). Baker remembers that such pastimes have always competed with the Drum for attention. In the 1910s and 1920s it was the square dances:

> They didn't put on the powwow [Drum Dance] at the same time when they had these other [secular] dances, only at the four times of the year at a certain part, like

145

Saturday and Sunday. Most likely some places would have an [old-time square] dance on Saturday night; well, there was some would go to it, even the older [people] would go, but not anyone who had a position on the Drum, they never went, it's the ones that didn't belong on the Drum . . . the young generation, the 1900s half of that generation that turned [from the Drum] and after they found out that they did wrong by turning, well now they want to come back.[47]

The gradual secularization of Indian life in the twentieth century was partly a result of the desire—mostly of younger people—to bring it up to date, to modernize it. To provide musical pastimes, Indians learned to perform on the instruments of the dominant society (see figs. 51-52). It was also be-

Figure 51. *Ojibwa at L'Anse, Michigan, receive musical instuction on band instruments from WPA music teacher Herbert Welsh.* (Photo courtesy National Archives, neg. no. 69-N-23525.)

Figure 52. *Fiddle and guitar entertainment in an Ojibwa berry-picking camp in northern Minnesota, September 1937.* (Photo by Russell Lee, Littlefork, Minnesota, courtesy Library of Congress, neg. no. 11248.)

cause of this trend that the Ojibwa (and others) came to accept the white man's drum to accompany Indian songs. This substitution was possible only after the Drum Dance lost its original function and, like the Grass Dance, had become so secularized that it was principally a social gathering. Ultimately the Drum Dance no longer encompassed ritual events such as divorce or the removal of mourning; eventually, too, it lost its medicine attributes and ceased to be used for curing. Thereafter, the kind of drum used became unimportant.

Modernization seems to have been the principal reason behind the acceptance of the bass drum in the Grass Dance as well. As we have seen in the case of the Gros Ventre, by about 1910 most Grass Dance societies had lost most of their ceremonial significance. Such groups as the Kansa still retained some of the regalia for their Helucka Watci, but since it was purely a social organization by 1914, the meaning of the regalia had been forgotten.[48] Similarly, the Oglala Sioux still had their Omaha Society, but it was now purely social in nature.[49] When in 1911 the Pawnee Eagle-Chief announced he wanted to organize a new Iruska (Grass Dance), it was simply pro forma for him to take up a collection to purchase a new bass drum and sleigh bells for the dancers to wear, or for the Arikara Young Dog Society's officer in charge of renewing the drumhead if it needed repair to recommend replacing the homemade instrument formerly used with a white man's drum.[50] To further modernize his society the same man suggested using a bell to announce the dances rather than the traditional crier, who had always climbed to the top of an earth lodge to inform the members of the event.[51]

In the Grass Dance, however, the drum itself was never so sacred an item as the Ojibwa ceremonial Dance Drum; consequently, the turn to using a commercial instrument would have created little turbulence among its members. But in the mind of Baker and others who believe in the Great Spirit's revelation to Tailfeather Woman, it is incumbent upon the Indian to continue to copy the first Drum, for "that was given to us for [a] purpose; that other [bass] drum wasn't given to us." Baker is therefore adamant in his refusal to perform on any but a homemade drum; in fact, he cites one occasion where the introduction of a white man's drum effectively dispersed an otherwise enjoyable dance:

> [George Brown], oh sure, he's got a drum like like that [homemade]. . . . He don't believe in that bass drum; he's the one that told me to tell them people there, they had

no business bringing that [bass] drum over there, spoiling our dance. They did spoil our dance. There were two nice drums, one from Odanah, and they were having a good time, until they came in and them people kept going away, by God; we didn't have no dancers after awhile, on account of that bass drum, the *chimookomaan's* [white man's] drum.[52]

Drum Dance Variants and Cultism

No culture, no matter how ancient or isolated, is static. . . . Some combinations of tensions within the system . . . and the propensity of men to "play" creatively with their cultural patterns probably best explains the "drift" characteristic of all cultures [Evon Vogt, *Tortillas for the Gods*].[53]

A review of the Drum Dance during the period of its decline would be incomplete without some mention of directions taken in several communities where the dance departed from the orthodox model sufficiently to be considered a variant. In two of the three cases to be discussed, the dances were so focused upon a central figure that they approached cultism. It is debatable whether such departures from orthodoxy were the result of the general decline of the Drum Dance or were in themselves a contributing factor in that they posed a threat to its larger congregational basis. In any case, the departures from orthodoxy exemplify Vogt's "drift" of one important aspect of Ojibwa culture in the twentieth century.

All three variants were based on revelations to individuals in which ritual details and songs were dictated. Wissler outlined this general process in reviewing the origins, which he found to be roughly the same, of various Pawnee ceremonies:

An individual begins to make revelations of visions respecting some one of these ceremonies and by accumulation forms a ritual with songs. The songs usually possess some individuality but the ceremonial procedures generally take forms already developed.[54]

The cultivation of dreams or visions has a long history with the Ojibwa; it was their principal means of obtaining the spiritual power necessary to survive sickness, battle, starvation, or any other adversity. The vision quest, undertaken when an individual was a youth, had been the traditional mechanism for receiving such power. Landes indicates that the Ojibwa's neighbors to the west also cultivated visions similar to theirs but "externalized" them in material artifacts, such as war bundles:

> One such "dream" could serve generations, possibly centuries through its materialization; the original experience of dreaming then became a sacred tale explaining the origin and powers of the bundle.[55]

If we can interpret the Drum as the materialization of a vision in an artifact, then it is clear that the Drum functioned for the Ojibwa much the same as a medicine bundle.[56] Its authorizing story explaining the Drum's origin and power put in it by the Great Spirit did indeed "serve generations." As will be seen, the three vision-dictated rituals in question were built to a greater or lesser degree upon the existing framework of the Drum Dance by adding to or varying its contents. I will summarize them briefly in historical order.

The Steve Grover Dance at Whitefish (Lac Court Oreilles Reservation)[57]

At some time before 1900 Steve Grover had a series of visions, which were met with skepticism when revealed to others. Around 1900, an eight-to-ten-year-old girl named Maggie Quarters received the same visions; because Grover was convinced that she, too, had been chosen by the Great Spirit as a messenger, he recorded Maggie's visions in a book. In her first vision the Great Spirit appeared in a cloud over the Drum Dance enclosure and warned its members against gambling and drinking. Her second revelation occurred one day while she was walking to school. Maggie was suddenly transported into heaven: "She was taken directly to the abode of the Great Spirit himself, which she found to be a large palace of many rooms."[58] The Great Spirit told her among other things that his people should respect the cross and offer it tobacco. Other visions followed; in one, Maggie was led by angels who asked her if she knew the meanings of red and black marks on a scroll: "The leader then said, 'I am going to show you how the earth will be washed by and by.' She then threw a bucket of water on the ground and the whole earth was flooded."

Following the visions, Steve Grover had a large red cross erected in the dance ring, apparently of the kind that was used in the medicine dance (fig. 53). Additionally:

> Upon the top of this cross was placed during each day a

tablet covered with blue cloth and provided with loops of the same material which extended from corner to corner along its four edges. It was said to symbolize the heavens . . . this object was removed every evening, wrapped in a large silk handkerchief and carefully kept overnight, being returned to its place on top of the cross on the following morning.[59]

Other details were added to the Drum Dance to conform to Grover's (and Quarters's) vision dictates: for instance, Grover wore a special cross around his neck and, at one point in the service everyone venerated the cross, with ritual obeisances similar to those performed in the Dog Feast.

Grover's version of the dance and Maggie's visions became widely known. A Menominee who had learned of it as a boy was able to relate Maggie's story in some detail and was even fairly accurate about the date of the revelations.[60] This new form of the dance evidently had enhanced the reputation of Grover's community as a sort of mecca, for one visitor to their dances "took occasion to mention especially the importance of Whitefish as a center of this creed."[61]

Figure 53. *Ceremonial removal of mourning during the Steve Grover Drum Dance, 1910. The mourners are being "fixed up," that is, having their hair combed and face paint applied to them. They are seated in front of the special cross that was dream dictated to be in the dance enclosure. Note the tablet atop the cross.* (Photo by S. A. Barrett, courtesy Milwaukee Public Museum, neg. no. 20216.)

The Maggie Wilson Dance at Emo, Ontario[62]

Beginning in 1914, the Canadian Ojibwa Maggie Wilson began to dream a great war dance, which, through its performance, was intended to protect the relatives of people in her community who were fighting overseas in the armed forces. In her dreams she was visited by the Thunders (Thunderbirds) who taught her eighty songs for the ceremony; they also dictated the special costumes and choreography to be used in the dance and outlined the structure of its offices. (Ceremonial waiters, for example, were to be included.) The fifth time the Thunders appeared to her with a drum and indicated to her how to construct it and how it was to be used in the dance. The drumhead was to be decorated in the manner of the ceremonial drum, with red and blue fields divided by a yellow stripe (cf. "Drumhead Decorations," pp. 201–8); a white Thunderbird was to be superimposed on the basic design. For the next seven or eight years other people dreamed more songs for the ceremony. The service was supposed to be held five times a year but was usually only conducted in the fall or spring.

The Henry Davis Dance at Mille Lacs, Minnesota[63]

Sometime before 1924 an Ojibwa named Drifter (Siyabas) from Sawyer, Minnesota, dreamed that he was visited by the Virgin Mary who told him how to make and decorate a drum and conduct a special service with it. In addition, certain new songs were to be added to those of the Drum Dance as well as a particular ritual involving the participation of a young girl. At some point the drum and ceremony were given to Henry Davis's father, who later passed them onto him. The ceremony is commensurate with Easter weekend, and at a certain time during the afternoon of the Sunday service a small girl dressed in white is brought in, seating herself on a special quilt laid out for her. The singers perform a special Virgin's Song during which the young girl raises the palms of her hands toward a pile of blankets to bless them. A pipe is then passed to her, and, after she smokes, she passes it to the various officers of the society, whereupon blankets and other gifts are distributed.

These three examples by no means exhaust the ceremonial variants known to have evolved from the Drum Dance. People of other tribes were also dreaming their versions of the dance with varying degrees of success in gaining adherents to their new rites. For example, Wissler learned of a Potawatomi formerly living at Saint Mary's Mission who claimed to be the founder of the Drum Dance; around 1895 he tried unsuccessfully to transfer it to Oklahoma tribes. Later, Billy Fawfaw, an Oto, dreamed a new version of the dance but met with similar failure in its dissemination.[64]

Each of the described variants, however, was able to take root and flourish for some time, no doubt due to its incorporation of at least some of the mechanisms and rituals already familiar to its adherents from the Drum Dance. Two variants, for the most part, are simply elaborations on its basic structure.[65] Because of the crucial position of Tailfeather Woman in Drum Dance beliefs, it is significant that common to the origins of all three variants was a female recipient or dictator of the revelation and that in two of them the recipients were told how to make and decorate a special drum. It is important to observe the initial reception of these new rites in their communities and their ultimate fate, for there is some indication that they were viewed by the Ojibwa as evidence of the general decline of the Drum Dance.

Maggie Wilson's dance dissolved after eight years. She blamed its demise partly on the cost of the ceremony, a growing suspicion in her community that she was an evil shaman, and the conversion of the dance's members to Christianity: "The people became mean and jealous, and the whole thing too expensive. If anyone sickened or died, it was blamed on me."[66] When the ceremony was abandoned, she took its ritual paraphernalia into the woods, leaving it there exposed to the elements and eventually to rot—the *mide* practice in disposing of sacred artifacts.

Steve Grover, whose inital visions had been scorned, continued to be regarded as a heretic in his community. His claims of going to heaven and speaking with Jesus were discounted. Whiskey John at Lac Court Oreilles berated Grover as "messing in the dream business"; John Mink added his criticisms as did Baker.[67] Ultimately, Grover gave his Drum away to the Potawatomi in Kansas.

The situation at Mille Lacs was quite different. The Davis rite, when Howard witnessed it in 1963, was still a viable and well-attended event some forty years after its inception. Furthermore, at the time, the Drum societies were generally in full sway despite the opposition of the missionaries. The collective Drum congregation at Mille Lacs, however, appears to have been somewhat exceptional and perhaps, therefore, more receptive to variations in ritual with a local history.

Mille Lacs had long been a center of orthodoxy for the medicine lodge.[68] Because of its relative isolation until this century, it was able to safeguard traditions that other bands in Minnesota territory—particularly the Mississippi bands—had lost because of early exposure to settlers. Furthermore, in many ways there appears to have been a certain self-imposed isolation of Mille Lacs in relation to the larger Ojibwa Drum community, which might explain its omission from Bisonette's path of the Drum.

Mille Lacs has often laid claim to possessing the original Drum. Parthun in his study of Ojibwa music in Minnesota once participated there in a ceremony in which the original Drum was said to be used and was told that the first Woman's Dance drum was also still intact in the community.[69] In the same vein, Thomas Shingobe, a medicine man at Mille Lacs, claimed the Davis Drum as the "only real one."[70] Furthermore, it was Rohrl's impression that those belonging to Mille Lacs Drums considered themselves more orthodox than others; one member had once met Canadian Ojibwa on the border while ricing and was astonished to see they had brought their Drums with them, for Mille Lacs Drums are never allowed to leave the reservation—an example of the greater "piety" of its societies' members.[71] This community has also been very conservative about giving away Drums, demanding that prospective owners have appropriate dreams before they would transfer instruments to them. Although it seems unlikely that Mille Lacs people were unaware of the long and active Drum tradition at Lac Court Oreilles, they at least acted oblivious to the fact in telling Rohrl that Indians at "Heyward [sic], Wisconsin" had been requesting in vain a Drum from Mille Lacs for years; "it is said that if the Wisconsin people do get the Drum, it will be an occasion for festivity."[72]

The nature of the unorthodox aspects of the Davis rite may also have been less disruptive to the Drum Dance than the rituals indulged in by Grover. To begin with, there is no evidence that Drifter, the vision recipient, ever emerged as a cult leader in the sense that Grover appears to have. Furthermore, the once-a-year introduction of the small girl dressed in white to four songs unique to her brief performance seems hardly obtrusive in a ceremony that lasted two days—and totally lacking in the flamboyant obeisances insisted upon in venerating the cross at Whitefish. While a surfeit of accommodation to Christian beliefs seems represented by both these variants, what the Mille Lacs girl actually enacts has in fact deeper roots in the medicine lodge than in Christianity: sitting on the blanket blessing gifts about to be distributed has its parallel in the medicine ritual called "Seating the Candidate." During *midewiwin* initiations, the candidate is brought to the west end of the medicine lodge where he or she sits on the pile of blankets to be given the membership.[73] For this reason, the brief ritual with the girl may have been interpreted by Drum members—many of whom belonged to the *midewiwin*— more as a conservative gesture than a radical departure from orthodox procedures. Over time, this localized ritual was simply accepted as part of the customary Henry Davis Drum rite and tolerated as a minor embellishment of the general procedures of the other Drums.

The Future of the Drum

For the past decade there has been a general resurgence of Indian pride in their heritage. Native American studies programs have been developed at the university level to assist young Indians who would understand their traditional culture and perhaps revitalize it. Language and culture classes are offered at all levels, taught by native-speaking elders and financed by the very same government that once forbade their instruction. Pan-Indian political movements have confronted the dominant society repeatedly to decry the abrogations of treaty rights. As Indians have achieved a new political awareness, we have witnessed a takeover of the Bureau of Indian Affairs in the nation's capital, a standoff at Wounded Knee, and young Indian runners reenacting the Pueblo Revolt against the Spanish in a tricentennial celebration.[74]

Throughout this period music and dance have continued to be vital links with the Indian past. Although much has changed in Indian music since the nineteenth century, good singers of all ages continue to enjoy status among their people and provide an invaluable service in the retention of Indian identity. Tribal styles have blended, pan-Indian repertoires have arisen and spread, song texts in the traditional languages have disappeared leaving only vocables to carry the melodies; yet the vitality and spirit of the singing and dancing attest to a lively tradition.

What does the future hold for the traditional Ojibwa Dance Drum in this milieu? The answer, I believe, lies with today's Indian youth, who must decide if the Drum Dance can serve to solidify their communities as it once did. This will require them to seek actively a rapprochement with their elders in the traditional manner. There are still enough members of the oldest generation whose memories of the songs and ritual details remain an untapped source; it is to them that the young Ojibwa, tobacco in hand, must go to request this knowledge, and they must do so repeatedly and with patience, as did their forefathers. And they must go to men like Baker, who have kept the traditions alive, despite his isolation and the general indifference of his people; to him they must go to learn to build the drums they were once instructed to make by the Great Spirit.

The Drum, as the central icon of the dance, can continue to serve the Ojibwa as it did for more than half a century. It can be a source of comfort to those who lose a relative, just as it was to Joe Martin's wife, who joined the Drum when her child died and was led to her place behind the singers at the Drum through the ceremonial removal of mourning.[75] The dance enclosure can become once again a place where people can feast communally on Indian foods. And it can become a forum wherein former warriors who have defended their country can recall their deeds. Though the days of fighting the Sioux were long since over by the 1940s, when Drums were presented at that time, the position of *ogichidaag* was easily filled by veterans of the two world wars, who recited their battle experiences before the drum stakes were put in the ground.[76]

Clifton has argued effectively that the Drum Dance of the Potawatomi is essential to their cultural survival. During their four-day dance, they come together "to reinforce their collective identity." Also, "within the Drum ring the structural values of a former style of village life are symbolically operative and expressively acted out."[77] The same scholar noted that "by 1962, the message of the Dream Dance religion had become one of peace and brotherhood, and its promise was cultural continuity; if the rituals are practiced and the songs sung, the Potawatomi will persist as a culturally distinct people."[78]

Much of the strength of the Drum Dance lies in its accommodative nature. Although its ritual outlines can be found in the Grass Dance, the association of the latter with warfare separates it from the Drum Dance, for Tailfeather Woman's message was one of peace.[79] Requirements for the drum transfer to the Hidatsa were fulfilled by their killing of Black Hills enemies; the requirements of an Ojibwa Drum recipient are only that he be generous and of good character.

The Drum Dance has not been totally lost to the Ojibwa and their neighbors, for it continues quietly and unobtrusively in isolated pockets of traditionalism. For instance, Wisconsin Rapids Potawatomi maintain an active Drum tradition. In other communities the "Big Drum" has even experienced a revival; when the Menominee reservation was restored to them in 1973, many returned to the Drum, including former Catholics. Nor has drum building "the old way" died out completely, even though Ojibwa singers continue to purchase bass drums. When Joe Rose built his drum (see fig. 95) at Bad River in 1978, he had the enthusiastic help of his son, Joe Dan, and other younger singers (see fig. 4) who were involved in the project.

The time may not yet be ripe, however, for an active revival of the Drum Dance on many reservations, particularly where factionalism continues to undermine community morale or political leadership is shaky. I was once on the trail of a ceremonial Drum, which had disappeared more than a decade earlier from a reservation and had probably been sold secretly for spending money. In my attempt to recover the instrument, I was cautioned that, even should I find it, the political turmoil on the reservation at the time would be exacerbated by the Drum's reappearance. As a result, I was disuaded from my efforts to find the Drum.

In the meantime, the present study and its accompanying film are intended to show an aspect of traditional Ojibwa life threatened with extinction. Should the Ojibwa wish to reverse this trend, it is hoped that these documents will serve them in reviving some of the beauty of their past. By following the section on construction and viewing the film, one can learn to make a proper drum—although as Baker has stressed, just knowing how or seeing it done does not necessarily give one the authority to make a ceremonial Drum.

Details of the rituals and descriptions of the belief are preserved in writings and photographs. Many Drum Dance songs were graciously recorded by singers such as Joe Kobe at Flambeau half a century ago. Whether or not the Ojibwa choose to revitalize these traditions is their decision alone; at least the historical evidence of their past will be available to them. It is for this reason that Baker permitted the film to be made and why, near its completion, he stated: "I don't give a damn if I get anything out of this or not. I don't care, but I want my people to see this, and I want that film here, and I'm going to show it to my people."

Construction

The Drum Proper

The making of one of these drums and of the accessories which accompany it is the occasion of very elaborate and solemn ceremonies, and requires a considerable length of time for preparation and several days for the actual execution of the work itself. Such a drum is not made except for some very special reason, such as the loss through breakage of an old drum, or such as the desire to present one of these drums to a friendly neighboring community. When it is agreed by the various members of a given community . . . that such a drum should be made, the actual work is placed in the hands of certain people especially appointed for the task. The materials are assembled and minor ceremonies are held over the production of each of the important parts, such as the making of the beaded band about the upper head of the drum, and such as the painting of the drum heads. A considerable amount of money and goods is required to enable the members . . . to produce one of these drums, since each person who has in hand the production of some particular feature of the drum must be paid an amount commensurate with the importance of the part which he is producing, and also commensurate with the amount of work entailed. Also the materials must be the best obtainable, and the large pipe and other accessories must be provided.[1]

The following section on technology describes each step in the building and decoration of the traditional Ojibwa dance drum and such accessory articles as its support legs and drumsticks.[2] The descriptions derive from the author's close observation of Baker's construction of several drums over a five-year period (1970 through 1974).

Though among the last practitioners of the craft, William Bineshi Baker, Sr., is still only one of hundreds of Ojibwa who have built a large repertoire of dance drums over the years. While his style and way of doing things in many respects are uniquely his own, the final object is unmistakably Ojibwa. Therefore, the description of each stage of Baker's work is preceded by a discussion of the general practice of the Ojibwa. Here the reader will find, among other things, a discussion of historical evolutions of style and regional variations as well as my speculations concerning the origins of certain items or practices. Data are taken from specimens in museums and private collections, augmented by descriptions and photographs of drums in the general literature on the Ojibwa. Within this context, then, Baker's work can best be measured and his place and contribution in the history and development of the Ojibwa dance drum ascertained.

The Frame

For the frame of the drum the Ojibwa have traditionally used a wooden washtub over which they stretch and lace together rawhide heads. If a washtub were unavailable, they would use a barrel, cutting it off about a foot or more from its bottom. While the metal hoops or wire surrounding the staves were left intact for support, the bottom of the vessel was at least partially removed to provide greater resonance to the double-headed drum.[3]

Tubs and barrels became known to Woodland Indians in the early days of contact, for nearly every military and fur-trading post had its cooper's shop. Barrels arrived continually with provisions—food, whiskey, nails—while local produce, such as Lake Superior fish, was packed in them and shipped east. By the late nineteenth century when the Drum originated, such vessels were commonplace in rural life (fig. 54).

Indians eventually adapted wooden vessels of European origin into ready-made frames for their drums, for they obviated the need to cut, char, and scrape sections of trees to hollow them for drum frames—the practice before the arrival of settlers in the New World. Thus the Hidatsa replaced their cottonwood drum frames with wooden tubs for the Grass Dance drum; the Winnebago stretched a single rawhide head over a nail keg for both a medicine and dance drum, securing it with sticks that were then used to carry the drum in processions (see fig. 49), and the Sioux used a similar keg to accompany the Scalp Dance by 1848, if Seth Eastman is reliable in depicting their drum (see fig. 6).

The decline in making the large dance drum according to traditional methods among the Ojibwa (and others) can be attributed in part to the disappearance of wooden vessels from general circulation in this century as they were replaced by galvanized tubs and, thus, made obsolete. As one Ojibwa re-

Figure 54. *Smoking fish outside a farmhouse in central Minnesota, circa 1895. Wooden barrels such as in the left foreground and washtubs (between the woman and boy)—commonplace frontier items—were converted by Indians into drum frames over which they stretched rawhide heads.* (Photo by Joseph Brechet, Glencoe, Minnesota, courtesy Minnesota Historical Society, neg. no. 16570.)

cently remarked, "Those wooden washtubs are hard to get nowadays!" Because of their scarcity, Baker had salvaged the staves and metal hoops from an old drum that had fallen apart. In the film, the frame reconstruction required the assistance of several friends to hold the staves in position while Baker drove down two metal bands to force the staves together.

Because washtubs and barrels came in standard sizes, a certain uniformity in the dimensions of drum frames is evident. Drums average about twenty-four inches in diameter across the top head, sloping to about twenty-two inches at the bottom, with usually about thirteen inches between the heads. Some typical specimens measured had the following dimensions:[4]

Builder, Owner, or Collector	Locality and Approximate Date of Construction	Dimensions in Inches		
		Top	Bottom	Height
Walter Drift (owner until ca. 1950)	Nett Lake, Minn., ca. 1880?	21⅝		14
Albert B. Reagan (collector)	Nett Lake, Minn., ca. 1890?	25½	21½	12
Bijikens (owner 1906–10)	Bad River, Wis., 1906?	27		12
Earl Nyholm (owner since 1963)	Bad River, Wis., ca. 1916	23	21	10½
Henry Davis (owner; Drifter, builder)	Sawyer, Minn., pre-1924	25	22	
Johnny Matchokamow (Menominee owner since 1928)	Lac du Flambeau, Wis., 1928?	25	22	12
William Baker (builder)	Concord, N.H., 1970	24	20	13½
Joe Rose (builder)	Bad River, Wis., 1980	22	21	10½

Drums that vary greatly beyond these dimensions are exceptional and unacceptable for ceremonial use (see "Variants"). Some general distinctions, however, in the overall sizes of drums reflect the purposes for which they have been constructed. The Woman's Dance drum, for instance, is slightly smaller than the Drum used for the seasonal rites. Also, if two or more drums are presented in the same ceremony, they may vary somewhat, both in size and elaborateness of decor, depending upon the status of the donor and recipient. When the Lac du Flambeau Ojibwa presented two drums to the Menominee in October 1910, Bijikens gave to Wiskino, leader of the West Branch settlement, a Chief's Drum (*ogimaa dewe'igan*), while another member of the

Ojibwa delegation presented a Menominee from a different settlement with a slightly smaller Warrior's Drum (*ogichidaa dewe'igan*).[5]

At some point before the drum is completed, four looped straps are attached about a third of the way down the outside of the frame and equidistant from each other. This is most easily accomplished before the heads or decorations have been put on the drum. The straps serve to suspend the drum from the four support stakes, thus allowing it to resonate freely, which it would not were it resting on the ground. Occasionally, when the drum is not in its carrying cover, a strap may be used by a drum tender to transport the instrument slung over his shoulder (fig. 55).

Figure 55. *Ojibwa ceremonial Drum slung over a drum tender's shoulder and carried by one of its straps inside the dance ring at Lac du Flambeau, October 1910. He also carries the support stakes, or legs, upon which the Drum is suspended for performance. His assistant appears to hold such accessories as the Drum's cover, tobacco box, and drumsticks. The ceremonial design on the bottom head of the Drum is repeated on the top head.* (Photo by Frances Densmore, courtesy NAA, neg. no. 596-c-12.)

The straps are of leather or rawhide and occasionally of otter fur, sometimes twisted for strength.[6] They are nailed into or bolted to the frame. Often a metal washer is used with the nail or bolt to prevent the metal head from tearing through the leather under tension. The straps are about an inch wide but vary in length depending upon their position on the drum and location of the support hooks on the stakes. They must, however, be sufficiently long to raise the drum a few inches off the ground when it is set up.[7]

Invariably there are four straps—one for each of the four support legs symbolically assigned to the cardinal points. For this reason, Hoffman's circa 1889 illustration of a White Earth (?) drum showing only three legs and straps equidistantly spaced appears to be fanciful (see fig. 82).[8]

Before their heads are put on, some ceremonial drums have one or more hawk bells suspended inside them on a leather thong or twine partways down across the diameter of the frame.[9] The bell—usually a sleigh bell or pony bell—produces a pleasant jingling sound whenever the drum is struck or carried. When present in a ceremonial Drum, it is referred to as the "the heart of the Drum," the heart being the essential symbol of life. As such, it also represents the heart of the Great Spirit who, in the origin tale, told Tailfeather Woman that to bring an end to intertribal killing, he had placed in the Drum "only that which is good."[10]

Traditionally, the invisible sound such as that produced by the hidden bells has spiritual connotations for Indian people. For example, the Ojibwa shaking tent (jiisakaan) often had bells inside it that would ring loudly as each spirit entered the top of the tent. Therefore, the sound of the Drum's bell, which itself is not seen, indicates a direct communication between the members of the Drum and the Great Spirit. As the Drum is beaten during the performance of ceremonial music, the sound of the bell signals that the Great Spirit is hearing the songs.

The condition of the wood in the frame is important because of the tension on the frame when the rawhide drumheads dry. In selecting his barrel or tub, Baker will, therefore, reject it if the staves are found to be at all rotten. If the wood is suitable, he measures and marks the vessel about thirteen inches from its bottom and cuts it off with a handsaw to the desired height. Then, to ensure sturdiness, he inverts the frame on the floor and drives the metal hoops toward the larger end with a hammer and screwdriver to force the staves tightly together (fig. 56). (In the film he hammered the edge of a flat file against the hoops for the same purpose.) Once the staves are tight, Baker cuts a round hole from the center of the bottom. The size of this hole varies somewhat, but he usually leaves two to three inches of the original planking intact. Thus, from his 1970 drum frame, the bottom diameter of which was twenty inches, he removed a twelve-inch circle.

Because the removal of portions of the original planking weakens the overall frame, Baker reinforces it with a "doughnut" cut

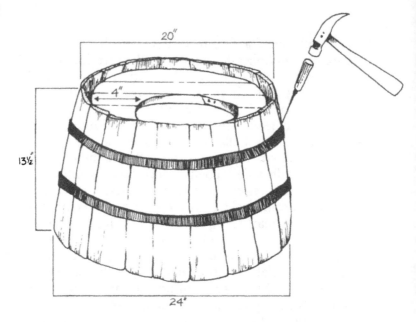

Figure 56. *Wash tub used as drum frame. Hoops are hammered down to ensure tightness of the staves. Circular hole has been cut to improve resonance.* (Illustration by Daphne Shuttleworth.)

from plywood to match the leftover bottom planking. This is measured from the inside of the frame so that, when it is screwed down to the bottom of the frame, it butts tightly against the staves, offering a uniform bracing to the opening and preventing any shifting of the loose planking (fig. 57).

For his drum straps, Baker uses scraps of finished leather. These must be thick and wide enough so that the weight of the drum, which can be more than fifty pounds, will not break them. For his 1974 drum, he made his straps from an old leather belt. First, he removed the stitching along either edge of the belt with a penknife, then he cut along the lines formed by the needle holes and trimmed the new edges smooth. Each strap was made from a fifteen-inch length, looped and bolted to the drum. Two bolts with washers—one an inch above the other—were driven through each strap, anchoring it about five inches from the top of the frame. The bolts were long enough to penetrate the staves and be tightened with nuts from inside the drum frame.

Baker's final preparation of the frame is to "trim the top" of the drum, as he calls it. With a penknife, he whittles the outside edge of the top where he has cut it off. This is to provide a smooth uniform roundness that will not cut into the hide when the heads tighten as they dry. At this point the frame is ready to receive its drumheads (see frontispiece).

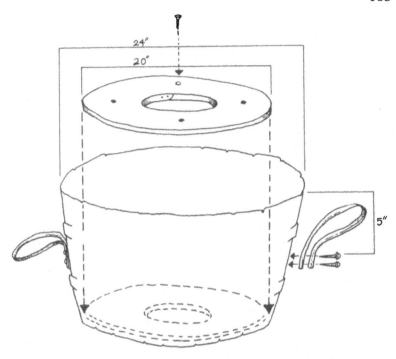

Figure 57. *View of drum frame showing circular plywood "doughnut" screwed to the bottom to prevent shifting of loose bottom planking and attachment of the leather support straps.* (Illustration by Daphne Shuttleworth.)

The Drumhead

For his dance drumheads the Ojibwa has always selected the hide of a large animal—most frequently cow or moose but also horse. Such hides are dehaired, left untanned, and stretched hair side out over the frame. Although deer hide was commonly used for smaller drums, such as the hand-drums and medicine drum, it was unsuitable for the large dance drum. Deer hide is simply too thin to withstand the tension of a drumhead that must span two feet and endure constant pounding from eight or more singers. Moreover, skins from larger animals are not only thicker and, therefore, stronger, but a single hide suffices to provide both drumheads and the requisite lacing, which a single deer hide would not.[11]

Such hides may once have been by-products of home butchering, but for some time now Indian drum builders have found it more expeditious to obtain them from slaughterhouses, where the work of skinning the animal has already been accomplished. Menominee drummakers, for example, got hides from a slaughterhouse fifteen miles away in Antigo, Wisconsin, Lac Court Oreilles Ojibwa from one in Minong, thirty miles to the west and a rendering plant in Barron, forty miles southwest of the reservation.

Cowhides, if purchased, must be in a "green" state—that is, they must be obtained before the slaughterer has salted them down to preserve them enroute to a tannery. If salt has been applied only recently with little time to penetrate the skin, the hide may be washed and soaked to remove it. Hides must also be carefully examined for imperfections, such as holes or lesions in the skin that would tear under tension. Particularly to be watched for in selecting a cowhide are holes caused by botflies (a common cattle affliction), which have burrowed through the skin to the animal's flesh. Such holes render a hide useless for a drumhead.

Drumhead hides are prepared essentially the same way deer hides are made ready for tanning: the outside must be dehaired and the skin side cleaned of bits of flesh, fat, and membrane (fig. 58). Dehairing requires soaking the hide in water for several days until it begins to putrefy sufficiently for the hair follicles to loosen their hold on the hair roots. (In the case of cowhides, the hair is short enough to be scraped off as is; the thick and longer fur of some game animal, particularly if it is a winter hide, may require some preliminary cutting of the hair to shorten it.) The hide is then draped hair side up over a beaming post and scraped clean of hair with a beaming tool (*zhizhaakwa'igan*).

The earliest fleshers were made from shin bones of deer or moose that were chiseled to provide a serrated cutting edge (see fig. 2).[12] Scrapers were similarly fashioned from antlers or cannon bones. Such bone implements were still being made in the late nineteenth century.[13] By circa 1940 the typical beaming tool used by the Wisconsin Ojibwa was a round cedar pole 1 1/2 feet long and 2 1/2 inches wide, which had a table knife embedded along one side.[14] The edge of the knife was filed flat to prevent its scraping the hide too sharply. (Baker's beaming tool conforms to this type.)

The beaming post—a four-to-five-foot log with bark removed—is propped up to waist height at one end with the other end resting on the ground. The worker stands behind (or sits beside) the raised end of the post as he or she grasps the beaming tool at either end with the blade tilted slightly backward so as not to cut into the hide. The worker pushes the tool away from him and against the grain of the hair (see fig. 3). Because the post has

Figure 58. *Baker cutting membrane from the inside of cowhide skin to prepare it for a drumhead.* (Photo by Mike Herter, 1974.)

a rounded surface, each stroke removes a swath of hair only about one-half inches wide, making dehairing an arduous and time-consuming chore. The hair removed from the hide is discarded, formerly it may have been cleaned and used to stuff mattresses and horse collars.[15]

Once cleaned and dehaired the hides are ready to be cut to size for drumheads. Because the wet rawhide shrinks considerably when it dries and because part of the hide must protrude over the edge of the frame to be attached to it, the circumference of each head must be larger than the frame opening it covers. While some drumheads have been found to be simply nailed or tacked on about an inch from the frame openings, most drums have their two heads laced together with rawhide or rope, although some examples have been both tacked and laced.[16] Leftover rawhide may be cut into strips for lacing. Otherwise, clothesline or some heavy twine may be threaded back and forth around the drum from one head to the other to bind them together securely on the frame.

After the heads are attached, the drum is hung up for nearly a week to dry. This is usually done indoors—the drum hanging from the rafters, perhaps, with string tied to its straps. When the heads have thoroughly dried, the drum is ready to be decorated.

Figure 59. *Ernie St. Germaine helps Baker plot out the location of the drumheads on a fresh cowhide before Baker begins to cut off the extremeties and divide the hide into two pieces for soaking.* (Photo by Tom Iglehart, 1974.)

For drumheads Baker's preference is a hide from a two-year-old Holstein cow or bull. (He considers Angus hides too heavy for a drum.) When ready to build his instrument, he will drive to the Link Brothers meat plant in Minong, having first determined what day they will be slaughtering so that he can get a hide fresh from the carcass before it has been salted down. Such a hide may weigh from thirty to fifty pounds, and while the prices charged by a meat plant fluctuate according to the market, in 1974, when the film was made, the cost of the hide came to about fifty cents a pound for a total of twenty dollars. (By contrast, Indians at Lac Court Oreilles in 1945 sold complete deer hides to each other for as little as seventy-five cents apiece.)[17]

Stretching the hide on the ground skin side up, Baker uses a sharp pocketknife to cut off the four corner pieces that had been peeled from the animal's legs (fig. 59). He discards those pieces. Then, with a tape measure, he plots out the location of the two heads, making each diameter about twelve to fourteen inches wider than the opening it will cover (figs. 59-60). The circular heads are not cut out at this point, but the hide itself is cut into two unequal parts to facilitate soaking, cleaning, and dehairing. Baker puts the two pieces in a galvanized tub filled with water, places rocks on them to keep them submerged, and covers the tub with a piece of plywood to prevent neighbors' dogs from disturbing the hide while it soaks.

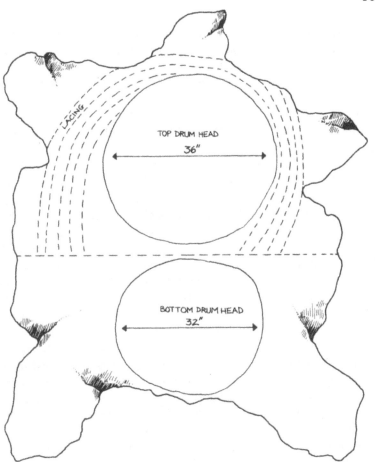

TOP DRUM HEAD
36"

BOTTOM DRUM HEAD
32"

Figure 60. *The heads and lacing as plotted out on a single cowhide.* (Illustration by Daphne Shuttleworth.)

Whereas a deer hide may be ready for dehairing after only three days of soaking, a cowhide being thicker usually requires as much as a week in water. The length of time depends somewhat on the weather, for if the nights are cold, as is usual in northern Wisconsin until about mid-July, the putrefaction of the hair follicles is slowed. Although the process can be hastened somewhat by adding warm water to the soaking solution, Baker is adamant in his refusal to add any chemical that might speed up the putrefaction.

To expedite the completion of the instrument, Baker customarily uses the soaking period to prepare the frame and begin the decorations. Almost daily, however, he checks the hides, stirring them up "so that the water will ferment and sour," scrapes them in several places to see to what extent the hair will come off and adds more water to replace what has evaporated. Also, during this time he removes the fat and membrane from the skin side of the hide—a laborious task that he spreads out over several days. Taking each piece in turn from the bath, he carries it to the edge of the woods behind his house, where he has lashed a cross pole between two trees about five feet from the ground. Baker drapes the hide over the pole and with a sharp knife cuts away all the flesh, fat, and membrane still adhering to the hide (fig. 58).[18] Then the hide is returned to the tub for further soaking.

When the hair can be scraped off easily, Baker attaches a rope to the soaking tub and drags it to a clearing in the woods about one hundred yards behind his house where his beaming post is set up—his "workshop," as he calls the spot. There, the dirty water is dumped out and each piece of hide dehaired in the traditional fashion. This work may take as much as two days and is carried out away from his house because of the foul odor of the dirty water and removed hair. (For sanitation, Baker wears an apron while dehairing hides.)

After the hair has been completely removed from both pieces of hide, Baker covers the beaming post with an old raincoat to prevent its rotting, hangs up his apron in a tree, and drags the hides back to his house, where they are rinsed several times to remove dirt and loose hair. By then, the hides are ready to be cut to size.

Once the circular drumhead has been cut from the middle of each piece, the leftover rawhide is cut in spiral fashion to provide lacing. About ten yards of lacing strips one inch wide are needed for the drum, and since the spiral cutting cannot be continuous, given the shape of the leftover rawhide, strips of lacing must be spliced together as needed.

To apply the heads, Baker first improvises a table in his yard by setting a plywood tub cover on top of an oil drum. The smaller head is laid flat in the middle of the board, skin side up, the drum frame centered on top of it, right side up, and the top head draped, skin side down over the exposed larger opening on the frame. Incisions about 1 1/2 inches wide are then made to receive the lacing. They are cut about 1 1/2 inches in from the edge of each head and parallel to it at approximately three-inch intervals. (If, as sometimes happens, the hide has a hole or two in it, Baker will plot out and cut the head so that these holes can be utilized in place of incisions.)

The threading is begun after an incision like the eye of a

needle has been made at either end of the first piece of lacing. One end is then threaded through an incision on the top head, and its other end doubled back through the eye on its opposite end and pulled taut to tie the lacing to the head (fig. 61). The lacing is threaded alternately from one head to the other, with additional pieces spliced as needed—the eye of the last strip serving the same way the first incision was used, that is, a new piece is threaded through it and back on itself through an incision in its opposite end and pulled taut to effect the splice.[19]

At first, the lacing is left relatively loose. After he has completed the threading, Baker goes around the drum several times to determine that the heads are properly centered and the tautness of the lacing uniform, all the while gradually tightening the lacing by taking up slack in it until the edges of the two heads are nearly touching (fig. 62).

It is crucial that whatever slackness is left is uniform, for it may affect the tone of the drum when it dries. (Baker recalls one drum builder who at this stage had left the bottom too tight and the top too loose; the drum has a good tone when beaten on its bottom but produces only a dull "flap" when hit on the customary top head.) Finally, the excess lacing is cut off and the end of the last piece threaded through the last incision and knotted to itself. Baker then takes the drum indoors, where he hangs it up to dry from ropes attached to the ceiling and tied to the four straps.

The rawhide takes from four days to a week to dry sufficiently for the drum to be taken down and decorated. Even in that state, the hide has not completely "set," and it may be a week or so before the heads are dry enough for the drum to be played upon. When first hung up to dry, the drumheads appear much too

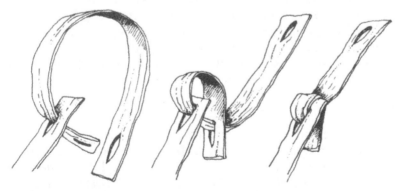

Figure 61. *Steps in splicing the lacing.* (Illustration by Daphne Shuttleworth.)

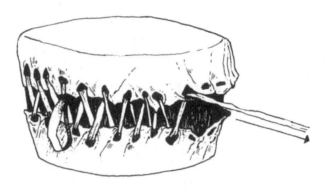

Figure 62. *The lacing of the two drumheads nearly completed.* (Illustration by Daphne Shuttleworth.)

limp and the lacing too loose to tighten, but in drying the heads shrink as much as four inches in diameter. As the rawhide dries, the moisture collects in the middle of the bottom head, causing it to bulge somewhat like a balloon, and seeps through it. The top head is, therefore, the first to dry and may be completely dry while the center of the bottom head is still moist. Because the rawhide retains an unpleasant odor, Baker frequently sprays his drums with disinfectant for several days after they are taken down and before he applies the decorations.

Decorations

Decorating the bare drum is considered "dressing it up." Almost all materials used by the Ojibwa and items attached to the drum have a long history predating the Drum's arrival. Some items—metal pendants, for example—date back to pre-contact times. When the French arrived in the western Great Lakes area, their unlicensed traders, the *couriers du bois,* introduced the Ojibwa to needles, thread, beads, yarn, broadcloth, velvet, and earbobs—in short, all items that would ultimately be incorporated in the decoration of the dance drum after 1880.

The Skirt

After the heads have dried, the skirt is the first article of decoration affixed to the drum. Although it is possible to attach the skirt together with the other circumferential decorations to the drum frame simultaneously by driving nails first through the fur strip, tabs, belt, skirt, and finally into the frame, the general

Figure 63. *Drum with decorations pulled away to expose lacing, frame, and straps.* (Illustration by Daphne Shuttleworth.)

practice is to add each item separately (fig. 63).

The skirt is just that—a simple rectangular cloth flounce surrounding the drum.[1] When the drum is suspended for use, its skirt hangs freely from around its top to a few inches below its bottom, thereby effectively covering the lacing, frame, and bottom head. Some examples survive for which the skirt has been made to adhere tightly to the shape of the frame—the Wiltschut Drum, for instance, the skirt of which is nailed at the top and bottom—but these are less common. More often the skirt hangs freely without touching the ground, its two ends sometimes merely overlapping for a few inches where they meet rather than being sewn together. Frequently, a muslin backing is sewn to the back of the skirt for durability.

Of the variety of materials chosen by Ojibwa for these flounces, velvet (or velveteen), flannel, and broadcloth have prevailed. An unpatterned cloth of a single solid color typifies skirts on the earlier drums, although patterned materials have been recently adopted. The colors most often found are black, red, and blue—exactly those colors in which broadcloth was first available to the Ojibwa and which they later fashioned into leggings and bandoleer bags during the period when floral applique beadwork was the style. Some drums, however, have skirts divided equally into two colors—usually blue and red to conform to the symbolic color design (see "Drumhead Decorations," pp. 201–8).[2] (The Walter Drift Drum skirt, one of the oldest examples, is exceptional, being divided into black and brown velvet [see fig. 68].) Accordingly, this blue/red color divi-

Figure 64. *Detail of Ojibwa dance drum in the Madeline Island Museum, La Pointe, Wisconsin. The skirt has been left plain in contrast to the fully beaded belt and tabs. The absence of symbolic representations on the tabs and the plain unpainted rawhide drumheads indicate that the drum was meant for secular rather than ceremonial use.* (Photo by the author, 1970.)

sion is normally assigned to the north and south sides of the drum, although the Henry Davis Drum skirt is divided horizontally, with its top half blue, its bottom red.[3]

In a Menominee legend of the Drum's origin, the division of the skirt into red and blue fields was, in fact, one of the instructions given by the Great Spirit to Tailfeather Woman for the first Drum.[4] Even when the material selected is of only one ceremonial color, some reference to the other may be included in simple ribbon edging or applique. The Bijikens Drum skirt made at Bad River sometime before 1907, for example, was of red flannel with blue edging, and when Baker chose red velveteen for the skirt of his 1970 drum, he sewed strips of three-quarter-inch satin ribbon around it halfway down the skirt. He selected blue ribbon for half the circumference and orange for the other, the orange ribbon possibly a substitute for red ribbon, which would not have shown against the red velveteen.

In general, the Ojibwa devote far less attention to the skirt than to the belt and tabs of a drum, which in almost all cases are elaborately decorated. Typical of this proportionate attention is an old dance drum in the Madeline Island Museum (fig. 64), the tabs and belt of which are fully beaded but the skirt is merely of unadorned cotton cloth. In fact, there are drums having a belt, tabs, and fur strip but no skirt at all. Thus the elaborately beaded skirt on the Potawatomi Drum in figure 65 would be atypical of the Ojibwa.

There is evidence, nevertheless, suggesting that the earliest drum skirts were more elaborate than they are today. One origin legend states that the first Drum had hammered silver discs on its skirt; Bijikens may thus have added the "pierced silver discs" to his Drum skirt to conform to the Great Spirit's dictates.[5] A Menominee Woman's Dance drum skirt of patterned red cotton has Indian-made German silver brooches sewn at various places on it. Since such brooches were common on Indian women's blouses, the association with the Woman's Dance in this case seems clear.[6]

Some older drum skirts—particularly those of black velvet—have beaded designs sewn on them. Most common are floral and leaf designs—the influence of "flowered chintz and calico" in Densmore's opinion.[7] The floral motifs are either filled in or merely outlined in beads (usually white), although animal and star designs are on the skirts of some of the oldest drums.[8]

Baker's drum skirts hang freely to about four inches below the bottom head and are hemmed under by hand, as is customary with all his sewing. The two ends of the flounce are either stitched together, the seam facing inward, or left unsewn but overlapped for a few inches. As mentioned above, there is a three-quarter-inch ribbon halfway down and around the skirt, a design feature common to all his drums. This ribbon is the only decoration applied to the material and is stitched perhaps every one-sixteenth of an inch along the top edge of the ribbon.

Figure 65. *MacKinley Wowyotten, Potawatomi owner (?) of this ceremonial Drum. The skirt as well as the belt and tabs of the Drum are fully beaded.* (Photographer and date unknown; courtesy NAA, neg. no. 47,747-G.)

While Baker has used solid color velveteen for some of his earlier drums, increasingly he has turned to patterned materials for the background of his skirts, belts, and tabs. Whenever they are available, he salvages old curtains or draperies having fairly elaborate patterns and color combinations depicting various subjects. Baker admits his preference for such materials "because of the color." He will select a large curtain from a cardboard box kept under his bed and begin by dismantling it, cutting the thread of all seams, and removing any backing material. Having taken apart the white man's curtain to adapt it to his own purposes, Baker is then able to lay out his patterns for the pieces with which he will dress the drum.

It is important to stress that, in cutting out these pieces, Baker ignores completely the original design printed on them and its intended orientation; he seems clearly more interested in the overall texture provided by the pattern than in its representational form. The material used for the drum skirt in 1974 is a case in point. In its original state, as seamed together to be hung before a window in some home, the drapery depicted a rural plantation scene with a stately mansion surrounded by lofty trees. The pattern was repeated at frequent intervals. Yet as Baker superimposed his own patterns and cut out the requisite forms, the plantation scene disappeared into a jigsaw puzzle of dismembered pieces—trees and houses were cut indiscriminately into sections and later juxtaposed without regard for their original arrangement. When completely decorated, the drum had on it such anomalies as portions of tree trunks diagonally abutting inverted sections of houses or leafy tree tops.[9]

There is some suggestion that skirt decorations may have been altered when Drums exchanged hands. Rohrl notes that at Mille Lacs:

> [The Drum Owner's] wife keeps the beadwork . . . in good repair, and he builds and repairs his wife's wooden loom. When there is a change in the leadership of the Drum, the Drum Owner's wife rips out the appropriate beadwork symbol from the covering of the Drum and sews in a new set of beads.[10]

The Belt

After the skirt is attached, yet another piece of material, the belt, is added over the skirt surrounding the drum at its top head. Although not all dance drums have them (see figs. 22, 68),[11] the belt is nevertheless a design feature of some of the oldest drums and, according to legend, was dictated by the Great Spirit to Tailfeather Woman to be included in dressing the Drum: above the half blue and half red skirt was to be a broad band of black velvet fringed with ribbon.[12] Belts may be four to six inches wide, although a Menominee Woman's Dance drum has a two-inch wide belt, possibly to match the smaller proportions of the drum.[13]

Whether or not the belt is beaded, its top and bottom edges are usually finished with silk, grosgrain, or satin ribbon selvage. (Only the bottom edge is completed this way if a fur strip covers the top of the belt.) Ribbons in various widths were introduced as trade or gift items in the Great Lakes area and were sewn by Indians as edge trimming onto their garments, moccasin cuffs, and cradleboard binding bands. Such ribbons on all drums examined by Densmore "were of a texture in use about 1860 to 1870, indicating the age of the drum."[14] When beadwork is present, as it is on a great many ceremonial drum belts, the designs may be only in outline form.

More common, however is the fully beaded belt. Patterns included in its design range from the simple to the complex: an uninterrupted zigzag "otter trail" around the ceremonial Drum at Whitefish photographed by Barrett in 1910 (fig. 24), so called because when otters are pursued they keep changing course to elude their captors;[15] typical Woodlands fanciful curvilinear floral meanderings on a Madeline Island secular drum (see fig. 64), the design continued on its tabs; or the fairly complicated geometric design complex with pyramids repeated twelve times on the belt of the Drum given the Menominee by the Lac du Flambeau Ojibwa (see fig. 81). Although most of these belt designs are nonrepresentational, the last cited was claimed by its Menominee owner to be a Siouan design with meaning: the sides of the pyramids show the four steps to heaven and the cross indicates that it is a religious drum.[16] Possibly this interpretation was imparted to him by the Ojibwa donors at the time of its transfer in 1928. The great variation permitted in belt beadwork even within the same community is nowhere more evident than in Ritzenthaler's photograph of three Whitefish ceremonial Drums side by side (see fig. 77). Apparently the belt was one of the few elements of drum decor that allowed Drum members free rein of artistic expression.

According to Baker, the work of making the belt was traditionally divided among four women, each of whom prepared an

Figure 66. *Multifaceted brass tacks are used to impale ribbon bits against the fur strip on Baker's 1970 drum. The tab design for this secular drum is purely decorative.* (Photo by Daphne Shuttleworth, 1981.)

eighteen-inch segment. Presumably, the segments were sewn together when completed to form a continuous strip in the way that some skirts were put together. The belt was then tacked onto the drum at intervals around its rim. If a fur strip were not to cover its top, rounded or faceted brass tacks (as well as nails or carpet tacks) might be used to attach it to the frame (see fig. 64).

Baker's belts range from about 4 1/2 to 6 inches wide and may or may not be from the same material as the drum skirt. If the belt extends below the level where the drum straps protrude from the frame, he must cut slits in the belt (as well as the skirt) to pull the straps through them (see fig. 71). Because all his drums have the fur strip, he needs only to hem under the bottom edge of the belt. To join the two ends of the belt he may sew them together, hiding the seam with one of the drum tabs. Or, as is the case with some skirts, he may simply overlap the two ends for several inches (see fig. 71).

A single length of ribbon is the only decoration (other than tassles) added to Baker's belts. This is applied with seed beads between stitches along the ribbon's upper edge in the same way that ribbon is applied around the drum skirts. On the narrower belts, the ribbon forms the bottom edge of the belt; on the wider belts, it is sewn partway down, but above the level of the drum straps (fig. 66).

Tabs (*mazinigwaajïganan*)

Four mitten-shaped pieces of material are attached to hang freely over the belt or from its bottom, spaced equidistantly between each of the straps that suspend the drum. (The sixteen tabs on a White Earth drum [see fig. 22] are exceptional; the smaller ones appear to take the place of a belt.) These tabs thus face the northeast, northwest, southwest, and southeast when a drum is positioned for ceremonial use. Their appellation by some as "earflaps" may simply serve to describe their shape and size, for in appearance they are not unlike the flap extensions on winter caps or earmuffs commonly worn for a good part of the year in the northern Woodlands climate. Still, some an-thropomorphism seems inherent in the earflap designation, for it is through the Drum and its songs that the Great Spirit "hears" the petitions of its members.

The Ojibwa consider the tabs vital elements of a Drum and require that they be kept in a good state of repair. Since one responsibility of the drum heater is to see that the decorations are in order, when checking their condition he is particularly atten-tive to the tabs and will pull on them to ensure that they are securely fastened.[17] The lack of regard for tabs by those to whom they have no particular significance is evident in figure 49, where the tabs on a ceremonial Drum being used for a secular event of another tribe have been allowed to become so loosely attached that they are in danger of falling off.

Information concerning the shape, design, and purpose of drum tabs is scant. Before circa 1880 no such decorations were attached to Ojibwa musical instruments, although prototypes for them abound elsewhere in their material culture. Tobacco pouches typically were of that general shape and, like some drum tabs, had fringed bottoms and beaded floral motifs on their fronts,[18] while Lyford, in her study of Ojibwa design, noted the frequent occurrence of four "ear-like" flaps at their tops.[19] Also similar in design to drum tabs are objects belonging to people with whom the Ojibwa were in contact. For example, the Canadian National Museum of Man possesses a pair of circa 1830 tab-shaped mittens, probably Huron, with exquisite moose-hair embroidery in floral designs against black buckskin,[20] and Sioux women and girls carried small beaded tablike pouches with fringes of cone jingles.[21] By the late nineteenth century, Ojibwa

Figure 67. *Fully beaded coin purse with Ojibwa floral design and looped strung bead pendants. Vermilion Lake, Minnesota, ca. 1920 (?)* (Photo by David K. Bateman, 1981, courtesy Mesabi Community College, Virginia, Minnesota.)

women were decorating commercial coin purses by covering them with beadwork much in the same way that they would decorate a drum tab (fig. 67).

Conceivably, the significance of drum tabs is derived from medicine bags. It had long been customary for Indians of many tribes to utilize entire skins of small animals as ready-made pouches and to add bits of decoration to them, particularly if they were to be religious artifacts. On almost all skin medicine bags of those tribes belonging to the Grand Medicine Society is found beadwork (sometimes quillwork), metal cones, bells, yarn fringes—in short, all those decorative items that made their way onto the skirts, belts, and tabs of the Ojibwa dance drum. Invariably, those parts of the hide decorated with such attention were the feet and the tail. In describing Ojibwa "Bags of Skin" Lyford points out that "though the [decorative] pieces were small, especially on the paws, and simple in design, the work was always carefully done, undoubtedly because the bags had ceremonial significance."[22]

There is evidence to suggest a possible connection between drum tabs and animal feet converted for utilitarian use. We know that actual hoofs were incorporated into pouches. A late-nineteenth-century Blackfoot example survives made of elk skin with its hoofs attached at the bottom as pendants.[23] Or, if the actual animal part were absent, some vestigial reminder of it may have been expressed in another material. Thayer, in discussing an old Delaware (possibly Montaignais) fire bag made from wool trade cloth, asserts that, since the bag was a substitute for an animal skin, the four pendant tabs at its bottom were meant to represent the four legs of the animal.[24] And on a recently built variant of the dance drum, Fred Connors of Bad River Reservation has attached split deer hoofs, splaying them to resemble tabs.

Whatever their precursors may have been, the tabs are certainly the most significant ornaments on the drum, for many of them are fully beaded and their designs contain symbols central to the beliefs of the Drum members. While the drumhead may convey some general symbolism through geometric fields of color, the tabs are the only items on the Drum for which representational forms are chosen to convey specific catechismic tenets. For this reason, they are called "pictures" (*mazinigwaajiganan*; var. *mazinibii'iganan*).

The tabs on almost all traditional Drums are encoded with symbolic forms.[25] The tabs of secular versions of the dance drum are generally less elaborate and lack symbolic meaning. Even fully beaded tabs may be made from the same material as the belt and simply continue the texture and conventional motifs of the belt's design. Fairly common are secular tabs with floral beadwork against a solid color background—usually sewn onto black velvet or worked into a solidly beaded white background (see fig. 64).

Of the representational forms found on Ojibwa drum tabs, the two occurring with the greatest frequency are an open human hand and a humanlike figure, complete, bustlike, or with only a head shown. Furthermore, where one of these two general forms is depicted, almost certainly the other will accompany it on an adjacent tab (see figs. 34, 99). The use of the same representational form for all four tabs is exceptional, however. Because each tab on the Henry Davis Drum at Mille Lacs bears the figure of a hawk and the design is further repeated on the cover for the drum, this symbol was probably especially significant for the owner and was probably dictated through a dream.[26]

The human hand has been used as a design element and variously interpreted in many world cultures—for example, in the decorative arts of African as well as Afro-American traditions. On a twentieth-century applique gown from Ghana, one entire panel is devoted to a hand,[27] as is a panel on an 1898 quilt created by a Black American in Georgia to depict biblical as well as local events. As the Ojibwa interpret the hand design as the "hand of God," it is intriguing that Harriet Powers, the creater of the quilt, explained her symbol as also representing God's hand, which prevented a calamity in her community by stopping the stars from falling in 1833.

Hand designs were used by American Indian tribes outside of the Woodlands as well. The Osage sewed hands onto blankets as cloth appliques and wove them into beadwork for knee garters;[28] a large hand appears on a Zuñi face mask used to represent the god Anahoho, the hand encompassing the eye and mouth holes of the wearer.[29] Two red and blue hands against a white background on a Sioux pipe and tobacco bag were intended to depict a war exploit of its owner: the red hands symbolized his having wounded an enemy with his bare hands, while the blue showed him to have carried away by force the enemy's women and children.[30]

The use of the hand symbol by the Ojibwa certainly predates its incorporation into Drum decor. We have an example of a hand carved of deer antler to form the handle of an awl.[31] A hand could also be made of buckskin, stuffed, and dyed black to be sent as a summons to enlist support in organizing a war party. Pictographically, it served a political use when drawn on legal documents or etched in peace pipes to signify the honor of the tribe.[32] It could also be "read" into esoteric sacred drawings. An interpretation for a hand that was part of a design complex was given to Coleman by an Ojibwa who had been instructed in its meaning by his grandfather, a noted storyteller from Bear Island (Leech Lake):

> He referred to this pattern as the meeting place of the sky and the water which is considered to be the home of the manidos. Either the hand of Kije Manito [the Great Spirit] or the paw of the bear, the guiding spirit of the Midewiwin is seen in the sky.[33]

This equation of the Great Spirit's hand with a bear paw can be attributed to *mide* teaching, for according to some legends, Bear served as God's messenger spirit leading the tribe on its westward migration.[34] (Traditionally, bears are thought of as having human attributes, and their paws were often used as medicine bags for the higher degrees in the medicine lodge.)[35]

The hand of God interpretations given by Drum members for the symbol vary somewhat, but all derive from the story of the Drum's origin and conform to the basic religious themes preached at Drum gatherings. Some say the hands depict those of the Great Spirit in the act of giving the Drum to Tailfeather Woman, in which case the humanlike figures on the other two tabs may be interpreted as representing these two principal characters in the origin story.[36] Rattlesnake, the Menominee recipient of the 1928 Drum presented by the Flambeau band, told Densmore that the symbols signified that "we are all in the hands of God."[37]

The symbol is imbued with further meaning by the special Shaking Hands [with God] Songs performed at the beginning of ceremonies, at which time there is a ritual presentation of the singers' palms to the Drum. John Bisonette noted that, while performing them, the singers would "hold up one hand in certain parts of the song" and that Alice White had explained this as "an offering of thanks to the Drum."[38] Johnny Matchokamow acknowledged the deep personal meaning of this gesture:

> "when we raise our [right] hand; well, I think about God, you see. Alright. God is up there; that's just like, you know, I got a hold of his hand. I got that habit, when I bring my hand down, well I just hold it like that . . . it's just like I'm holding his hand there, see?"[39]

Since the singer customarily beats using his right hand, to perform the ritual gesture while still continuing the percussion accompaniment to the song, he must shift his drumstick momentarily to his left hand—because "the right hand is God's side."[40]

The depiction of the hand is nearly identical from Drum to Drum, variations in its design being restricted to how much space it occupies on the tab or whether the fingers point upward or downward or such details as fingernails are included. By contrast, the other symbol—the humanlike figure—may appear in any of a number of forms: a whole human figure with arms, legs, and head, outlined only or solidly beaded in one color, or more complete with the addition of facial features (eyes, mouth, and sometimes teeth) and given a few strands of hair, or the figure may consist only of a head, of a head and torso with or without facial features and with the possible addition of horns.[41] (The faceless head and torso resembles the human cutout used in the Ojibwa bowl and dice game. The cutout is one of several objects painted light on one side and dark on the other. The highest points are won if, after being agitated, all the human cutouts show one color and all the other pieces another.)[42] Occasionally, the figure may be holding some object. On the John Martin Drum the tab assigned to accompany the west leg shows a man holding what appears to be a medicine drum,[43] whereas the tab design on the Pete Sam Drum is meant to show the figure holding an American flag. Also holding what appears to be a small flag is a figure wearing a hat and a frock on the tab of another Drum. The flags are said to refer to those raised for ceremonies as a symbol of peace to indicate that the members are as one person and are supposed to help each other.[44] On yet another tab the object held is clearly a pipe and is probably meant to represent the pipe with the elaborate ceremonial stem that is part of the Drum's accessories.

Although the figure on all of these tabs shows human characteristics, it is intended to represent a spirit, usually the Great Spirit. This is evident not only from explanations given by Drum members but also from the design elements themselves, most of which predate the origin of the Drum. A human figure, for instance, was used to represent the Great Spirit on the "healing turban" given to John Tanner during his Indian captivity in the early nineteenth century.[45]

Horns added to the heads of human and animal figures had been symbols used traditionally to denote spiritual power long before they ever appeared on drum tabs. Eagle claws were attached as horns to the heads of some animal-skin medicine bags, for example.[46] Horned figures were frequently etched on birchbark instructional scrolls of the midewiwin[47] and carved into the sides of medicine drums. Two of the four figures on the mide drum collected by Densmore at Ponemah in 1907 have horns, eyes, and mouths incised in the wood.[48] Manidoog (spirits) almost identical to these were beaded by Lac du Flambeau Ojibwa for two tabs of the Drum given to the Menominee in 1928; clearly the spirit design was simply transferred from medicine drums to Dance Drums (see fig. 8). Bilateral strands of hair projecting from the top of the head on one drum tab suggest that they are vestiges of animal horns.

The hand and spirit figure symbols are used in pairs, invariably on opposite sides of the Drum, and with some consistency in ascribing ritual directions to the two designs: Lac Court Oreilles Ojibwa in 1910 assigned the hands to the northeast and southwest tabs as did Zoar Menominee by 1950.[49] Even nonsymbolic designs on secular drums are paired in this way. On the Madeline Island drum, for example, a bilateral floral design (see fig. 64) is repeated on its opposite side as is the less fanciful flower and leaf design on the other two tabs. The two extant tabs on opposite sides of the Walter Drift Drum (fig. 68) show human figures, even though one is maroon in color, the other black. Upon close examination the Drum shows evidence indicating the prior existence of two other tabs; presumably they showed hands.

The only adequate explanation for the invention of drum tabs is that they serve as some sort of dream icons bearing symbols central to the beliefs of Drum Society members. (The dream iconography is implicit in the many references to the instrument as the "Dream Drum.") The tabs thus function in a sense as talismans to provide spiritual protection, health, and power to the Drum and through it to its members. For much the same purpose, in fact, both the hand and spirit symbols had been displayed on the heads of Ojibwa hand-drums. If a moccasin game drum had a hand painted on it, doubtless the symbol had appeared to the drum's owner in a dream or vision and its display ensured him success in the game.[50] *Waabano* drums almost always had a human figure on them to indicate that the (eastern?) spirit had visited the owner in a vision and offered him protection.[51] Such a drum in the Ayer collection at Mille Lacs Indian Museum has a large faceless figure on one head and a smaller version of the same figure enclosed in a circle on the reverse side. The drum closely resembles a hand-drum being played by the eastern Ojibwa singer Tetebahbundung in a photograph published by Frederick Burton in 1909 as a frontispiece for his study of music at the east end of Lake Superior. The faceless spirit on this drum suggests it also to be a *waabano* drum and apparently quite old, for the design has been partly worn away by repeated pounding on it.

In applying dream-inspired symbols to material objects, the Ojibwa conformed to practices and beliefs common throughout North America. Plains warriors of many tribes had dream symbols painted on their rawhide shields to provide spiritual protection in battle. In one of the best-known instances, the Sioux adherents to the Ghost Dance religion applied dream symbols to their special shirts and dresses that, when worn, they believed would render them impervious to the white man's bullets. Mooney described the use of such vision symbols on their faces as well as their garments:

Figure 68. *Walter Drift Drum, Nett Lake (Bois Fort) Reservation, Minnesota, ca. 1880 (?). The two remaining tabs show spirit figures, indicated by the claws and the lifeline from the mouth downward to the heart.* (Photo courtesy Glenbow Museum, Calgary, Alberta, Canada, neg. no. R2209a.)

After the sweating ceremony the dancer was painted by the medicine-men who acted as leaders, of whom Sitting Bull was accounted the greatest among the Sioux. The design and color varied with the individual, being frequently determined by a previous trance vision of the subject, but circles, crescents, and crosses, representing respectively the sun, the moon, and the morning star, were always favorite figures upon forehead, face, and cheeks. . . . After the painting the dancer was robed in the sacred ghost shirt. . . . This also was painted with symbolic figures, among which were usually represented sun, moon, or stars, the eagle, magpie, crow, or sage-hen, all sacred to the Ghost dance among the Sioux.[52]

The Ojibwa had several means of obtaining dream symbols. One could receive his own personal symbol from a spirit— particularly during the vision quest undertaken by young people in isolation. Ajawac's six-inch black cloth figure of a "flying man" was made to look as he appeared to her in her youth whenever she fasted.[53] Or, a symbol could be sought in a dream specifically for someone else by an elder in the community, usually a medicine man. Often the names for children were dreamed in this way and bestowed on them together with the symbol in a special Naming Ceremony. During a Drum Dance at Lac Court Oreilles in 1960, a small child's great-uncle informed the assembly that in each of four dreams he had seen a bolt of lightning illuminate the boy's face; therefore, he gave him the name One Lightning.[54]

The symbol could serve a particular purpose, as the one "prescribed" to John Bisonette for healing his paralyzed son. For the treatment, the local juggler (*jaasakiid*) instructed Bisonette to draw with blue chalk a Thunderbird on white cloth, tie two strands each of red and blue yarn at its bottom, and then hang this flag from a sapling that had all but its top branches removed.[55]

Once received, it was customary to display a dream symbol in one of several ways, such as on the cloth covering hung over the entrance to the wigwam. Its esoteric significance was considered to be private and could only be interpreted by its owner. In fact, having received a symbol, one showed it as evidence to the community that he had been successful in his quest for a spiritual guardian. Such dream designs could be painted, woven, or applied as cutouts to cloth.[56]

Because many of the oldest symbols are of birds and animals, they may once have derived from totemic practices now long forgotten. This is certainly suggested in Radin's accounts of a hunting practice of the eastern Ojibwa:

> Once a man made a bag and he drew the image of his totem upon it. Then whenever he went out hunting, those who had the same totem would give him some tobacco . . . and once a year they gave a feast and they would eat this animal. An image of it would be made and this would be painted in three colors. The image would then be placed in the center of the lodge where they were eating.[57]

A vestige of this practice was continued by the Menominee into this century, for at dances whenever a bear or buffalo were mentioned, all those who had dreamed of the animal were expected to rise and dance in place.[58] (As examples of dream symbols, Densmore published, in addition to the flying man, beaded bear and turtle dream figures, a carved knife and a Thunderbird/sun dream complex drawn on a blanket.)[59]

The custom of wearing a dream symbol as a means of displaying it may provide a further clue to the reason for drum tabs.[60] Because all other decorations are part of the Drum's apparel, the tabs must also be considered to be worn by the Drum. In this way, tabs are bestowed upon Drums just as dream tokens were sometimes given to children when they received their names[61] or, on some reservations, were worn around the neck as scapularlike badges in religious ceremonies. These badges were usually made

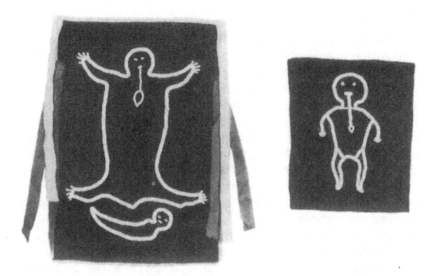

Figure 69. *Sign badges of the Bungi (Manitoba Ojibwa) medicine lodge, showing spirit designs with claws and lifelines beaded on black cloth. These were worn around the neck in initiation ceremonies and had sacred white shells sewn beneath the hands and feet of the figures.* (Photo courtesy Museum of the American Indian, Heye Foundation, neg. no. 41138.)

of black cloth or velvet and had sacred cowrie shells (*miigisag*) sewn between the cloth layers behind the head, hands, and feet of the spirit figure (fig. 69). The Indian agent at Nett Lake, Minnesota, described the ritual surrounding the initiation of young women into the medicine lodge prior to their instruction:

> Soon after dark these *mide* [priests] all met at the ceremonial tepee and commenced to give the young lady instructions in the order. A sign-badge was embroidered on cloth and suspended from her neck with elaborate ceremonies.[62]

Reagan's published photograph of the "sign-badge" worn by one initiate at Nett Lake shows it to be almost identical to one of the tabs on the Walter Drift Drum from the same reservation (see fig. 68). (Canadian Ojibwa wore around the neck *baagak* dolls with ribbon fringes and even human hair attached.)[63]

The appearance after 1880, then, of the same symbols repeated on the tabs of all Drums and the freedom with which Drum members could explain their significance marks a shift in traditional Ojibwa attitudes toward the dream symbol: it could now be communally owned and its meaning was no longer covert.

Whereas tabs on most older drums are fairly oblong, Baker's tend to be more rectangular. Still, he rounds the free hanging end either just at the bottom corners or beginning about two thirds of the way down the tab, effecting a gradual curve. Averaging four inches wide and hanging from just under the fur strip to about six inches below its bottom edge, Baker's tabs are invariably made from the same material as the belt, although not necessarily from the same material as the skirt (see fig. 66).[64] Since the beadwork on his tabs is minimal, the pattern of the material is nearly completely exposed to view.

Baker's design for tabs varies greatly from one drum to the next. But common to all is a continuous ribbon selvage sewn around the exposed edges of the material. For this he uses the same technique for attaching the ribbon to the skirt and belt, that is, a basting stitch with two seed beads at each stitch.

The patterned material chosen for the tabs serves as a background for some sort of geometric nonrepresentational design—either beadwork, ribbon, or some combination of the two. Although the same design is repeated on each of the four tabs, he is careful to change the color scheme, so that no two tabs on the drum are alike. Although his tabs lack the symbolic pictures of the sacred Drums, by changing colors he at least stresses the individuality of each tab and its assignment to a specific direction.

Some idea of the variety of his color combinations is indicated in the following schema for tab designs on his 1970 drum (fig. 70). (In assigning directions to the tabs I am basing my assump-

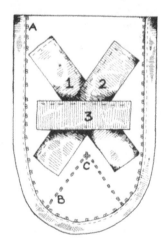

Figure 70. *Design by William Baker for the drum tabs on his 1970 drum.* (Illustration by Daphne Shuttleworth.)

tion of their intended location on the ribbon around the skirt, which is blue for one half the circumference, and orange [red] for the other.) The background material selected for the belt and tabs of this drum was a drab madras with stripes in muted shades of black, dark red, dark green, and dark yellow. The cloth was cut so that the stripes ran vertically around the belt and horizontally across each tab. Three pieces of ribbon were cross-stitched and sewn in the tab's center, and lazy-stitch beadwork paralleled the inner edges of the selvage and crossed up into the center to meet four somewhat larger beads arranged to form a cross:

Color Schema: red velvet skirt, madras belt with yellow ribbon fringe basted with light blue beads.

Ribbonwork:			Beadwork:	
Northeast tab	1	orange	1	blue
	2	pink	2	red
	3	blue	3	clear
	4	white		
Southeast tab	1	red	1	clear
	2	blue	2	white
	3	pink	3	blue
	4	orange		
Southwest tab	1	orange	1	red
	2	pink	2	clear
	3	white	3	white
	4	blue		
Northwest tab	1	orange	1	white
	2	pink	2	green
	3	white	3	clear
	4	red		

The Fur Strip

Almost all dance drums—certainly every ceremonial Drum— have a thin fillet or strip of fur about 1 1/2 inches wide surrounding the frame at its top (fig. 71).[65] Even on the oldest drums, though most of the hair may have fallen off, usually some evidence of the strip remains (see, for instance, fig. 49). The fur strip generally is dark and dense, with longish hairs. Otter fur is commonly selected, although the pelts of beaver and other small animals have also been used. As the last item of decoration to

Figure 71. *Dark beaver fur "turban" or strip surrounds the top of Baker's completed 1974 drum.* (Photo by Tom Iglehart.)

encircle the drum, the fur strip covers the tops of the skirt, belt, and usually the tabs and is glued or tacked into position. On drums where tacks with large heads are found, such as ornamental brass tacks, bits of ribbon may be impaled beneath the tack heads and against the fur (see figs. 34, 66).

The origin or meaning of the fur strip is obscure, but the juxtaposition of hair to skin—in this case, the drumhead—is noteworthy, for fur fillets have always been characteristic of Ojibwa decorative art, not only for material objects but also for bodily adornment. Traditionally, young men wore narrow fur bands as wristlets and anklets.[66] This might help to explain their transfer to the "legs" of the drum as well as to ceremonial drumsticks, said in legends to be extensions of the human arm.

Fur turbans were widely popular as headdresses (fig. 72). In fact, many Ojibwa singers who recorded for Densmore were photographed wearing fur turbans in their portraits published in *Chippewa Music*. She also photographed Little Wolf wearing such a headband while he was doctoring at White Earth in 1910.[67] The turban could be a simple fur strip; often, however, it was quite elaborate. Some Ojibwa wrapped yarn sashes and loom-beaded strips around these bands. Otter-fur turbans were sometimes decorated with quillwork or, if a whole skin were used, it might have beaded tabs attached to its tail. In addition to otter fur, skunk skin was favored. Burton found skunk turbans the typical headdress of the eastern Ojibwa, describing them as

Figure 72. *Fur turban worn by Swift Flying Feather, a Leech Lake Ojibwa, in Washington, D.C., in 1899. While there on tribal business he made the first known recordings of Ojibwa songs on wax cylinders for Alice C. Fletcher.* (Photo courtesy NAA, neg. no. 509A.)

having "two feathers attached over the forehead, pointing in opposite directions," their makeup similar to the headpieces worn by Densmore's informants at the opposite end of Lake Superior.[68]

The band of fur may also be a vestige of the hoop on the medicine drum. This wrapped wooden hoop was a functional device to fasten the deer skin head on the drum frame, since the head was not permanently attached. Because the hoop was wrapped with strips of cloth in a kind of spiral, the visual effect is not dissimilar to the twisted bead, cloth, or fur turban worn by Ojibwa on the head (see fig. 8). (Although some old drum hoops lack the cloth wrapping, they were almost certainly once wrapped, as the bare hoop itself fits too loosely to hold the skin in place, whereas the cloth would flesh it out to provide a cushioned but snug fit.) Similar hoops at one time had sacred associations and were worn on the head during curing ceremonies. John Tanner in the early nineteenth century was given a curing hoop that had the figure of a snake on one half and a representation of the Great Spirit on the other half.[69] Paul Buffalo at Leech Lake noted its practical and spiritual connotations:

> [The Spirit in heaven] got a band on his head. What does that mean? It's altogether . . . keeps his brain steady, smooth, warm, all there . . . hold down pressure inside. We wear them here. We got a headache, pull it tight, goes away. Mine works good. . . . Years ago they use to have them all the time when they get old.[70]

(Some Drum members have interpreted the "binding" notion of the otter fur strip as a reference to Otter's role in the Ojibwa flood legend. In some versions of the story it is Otter who is sent beneath the water to bring up the piece of dirt from which the new world is created. Since the Drum metaphorically represents the world, otter fur is used to bind the world together.)

The fur strip applied to Baker's 1970 drum conforms to his general design for the fillet and appears to be a common feature of Lac Court Oreilles Drums since at least the turn of the century (see figs. 34, 77). From an old mink coat Baker cut a two-inch band of fur, attaching it in its middle with carpet tacks about every six inches around the top of the drum frame. The hair was sufficiently long and dense to cover the heads of the tacks. He then impaled two-inch lengths of three-quarter-inch ribbon in a variety of colors with multifaceted furniture tacks, two ribbons of different colors to each tack, with no discernible overall color scheme. Under each tack, a horizontal ribbon strip was placed over a vertical one. The tacked ribbons were located first over the center of each tab in the middle of the fur strip, with others about six inches to each side, resulting in twelve such decorations in all (see fig. 66).

Pendants

> Below this beaded [belt of the drum] and attached to the
> "skirt" . . . are fastened pendants of various kinds, some
> made of beadwork, others of coins, and still others of
> various other metal objects. In fact, almost anything may
> be used which will produce a pleasing jingle and add to
> the good appearance of the drum. Frequently, also, the
> bottom of this skirt ends in a fringe made of buckskin
> strings provided with small conical metal objects: such as
> coins, thimbles, and in fact almost any object which will
> jingle as the drum is being beaten.[71]

Customarily, Native Americans have accentuated the outlines
of garments, tools, and ceremonial objects. Be they simple leather fringes or elaborately constructed pendants, such decorations
not only enhance the visual beauty of the object for its maker or
owner but also identify the use to which it is put. Whereas a plain
unadorned otter skin kept somewhere in the wigwam might
receive little attention until its fur were to be cut for some piece of
apparel, an otter skin with beaded tail and paws and metal cones
hanging from its edges would be immediately recognized as a
medicine bag and carefully stored away—venerated or avoided
as belonging to powerful ritual paraphernalia (fig. 73).

Drums are no exception, and the inclusion of fringe decoration in their overall design indicates the great value placed upon
them. The wide variety of pendant types affixed to the skirts,
belts, and tabs of Wisconsin ceremonial Drums early in the
century was noted by Samuel Barrett. Basically, these appen-
dages fall into two categories: metal pendants that make a jingling sound when struck against each other when the drum is
beaten and those of nonmetallic materials such as purely decorative beads or yarn.

Among metal pendants, homemade cones cut and fashioned
from sheet tin, silver, and—less commonly—copper, appear to
be the oldest and most frequently used. A form of border decoration popular long before the arrival of the Drum, they are
found on, among other things, shoulder pouches, moccasin
flaps, medicine bags, and cradleboards.[72] A typical use is indicated in figure 74 showing an Ojibwa ceremonial war club,
probably from Lac Court Oreilles circa 1900.[73] The ball of the
war club is carved to resemble its being held by eagle (?) tallons,
while the handle is covered with fur to which a number of metal
jingles have been attached. The ornamentation suggests that the

Figure 73. *Otterskin medicine bag with black and white beadwork, tin jingles, and red-dyed deer hair. From the Michilimackinac Fort Miami region. Possibly Ojibwa, Ottawa, or eastern Sioux. From the Major Andrew Foster Collection, 1790-95.* (Photo courtesy Museum of the American Indian, Heye Foundation, neg. no. 38402.)

item was part of the dance accouterments of a former warrior.

Similar cone fringes are attached to objects from many tribes in the Great Lakes and adjacent regions, some items dating to the eighteenth century. For example, a circa 1775 Iroquois bag has several metal cones still intact along its bottom edge where once a complete row must have existed.[74] Some cones have moose (?) hair protruding about two inches from their open ends, a feature unquestionably common to all the cones in their original state. Similarly, a circa 1820 buckskin bag of the Sauk and Fox, which makes use of quillwork and duck skin in its design, has its bottom finished off with eighteen tin cones.[75] They, too, contain hair and are joined to the bag by thongs threaded through large red and white beads. To the middle of the same bag, six more cone

Figure 74. *Ceremonial warclub, possibly from the Lac Court Oreilles Reservation, circa 1900 (?), with homemade metal cone jingles attached to the handle. It was probably carried in dances by a former warrior.* (Photo by the author, 1980, courtesy Charles Trudelle.)

pendants are attached beneath the quillwork and hang freely over the area covered with the neck skin from a male mallard duck.

Adding cone decoration to Woodlands ceremonial Drums when they are dressed suggests a transfer of the use of cones in adorning articles of clothing or the human body itself as earrings. Archaeological evidence suggest this to be an old custom in North America, predating contact with Europeans. Burial sites have yielded ample evidence that in the western Great Lakes area people rolled thin sheets of copper into tubes as hair ornaments. The Dumaw Creek Indians of central Michigan buried their dead wearing many such "hair pipes." Strands of hair were threaded through the pipe and knotted at its bottom to hold the copper tube in position; the protruding hair was then colored with red ocher.[76] This seems clearly the origin of metal pendants with colored hair (later yarn) protruding from them. In fact, in a transitional stage, human hair was used for the ornament. Quimby describes the seventy-two brass pendants on a costume found in a Gros Cap burial near Saint Ignace, Michigan, which he dates 1710-60 and identifies as from the Ottawa tribe:

> Many of these tinkling cones . . . were filled with tufts of human hair at the open end and had twisted cord or leather fragments at their apexes indicating that they had once been attached to something.[77]

The tinkling cone survives today as part of the traditional woman's costume at Woodlands' powwows,[78] the popularity of which extended to tribes as distant from the Ojibwa as the Mescalero Apache.[79] In making this dance costume, cones fashioned from tin or in recent times cut from the tops of Copenhagen snuff containers are sewn horizontally in rows at several levels onto the buckskin or cotton dress. As the dancer moves, a pleasant soft jingling sound is produced. The concept for such a dress is old and certainly not exclusive to the Ojibwa. During the Missouri River Expedition (1833-34) Karl Bodmer painted a Yankton Sioux woman whose dress has rows of metal cones near and along its bottom. Maximilian, who led the expedition, described their construction: "[the dress is] trimmed as usual at the bottom with fringes, round the ends of which lead is twisted, so that they tinkle at every motion."[80]

Metal cone jingles, like bells, appear also to be substitutions for the dried dewclaws of a deer, though occasionally dewclaws are found on drums in conjunction with cones.[81] Dewclaws had long been attached to objects carried in war dances or tied together as bunch rattles (see fig. 1) or strung on costumes or around parts of the leg for dancing.

The cone-shaped jingle may also relate to earrings once worn by Ojibwa men. Originally such earrings, like silver brooches, were probably trade items or gifts, but by the middle of the last century Indians were fashioning them from sheets of nickel silver. Densmore in her *Chippewa Customs* (1929) described the former popularity of these earbobs, particularly among old men:

> The most common sort of earring consisted of a bunch of small, elongated metal cones, suspended at the tip. It was not uncommon for so many of these to be worn that the ear was weighted down with them.[82]

Several eighteenth-century German-silver earrings of this description were recently unearthed on Madeline Island and are displayed in its museum. Each slender cone depends from a thin ring, the total length of the ornament being 1 1/2 inches.

Of the metal pendants attached to drums, thimbles follow cones in frequency of use. Brass thimbles, early trade items, were converted almost immediately into tinklers by Great Lakes Indians as revealed by archaeological evidence from the Bell site in Wisconsin (Fox) and Escanaba site in Michigan (Ojibwa).[83] As nearly all these thimbles have colored hair or yarn protruding from them, evidently they were simply adopted by Indians as ready-made objects to serve the same purpose as the homemade cones. (Thimbles are also reported to have been used in the Woodlands as receptacles for magical potions; the Menominee once carried love powders in them, wearing the thimble around the neck or hung from clothing.)[84] More frequently, thimble pendants are used to finish off the ends of beaded bands, such as on the Bijikens Drum photographed in 1910.[85]

Where yarn or hair extends from the mouths of thimbles or cones the choice of color is frequently symbolic. On a drum purchased from the Winnebago in 1913 (but almost certainly not of their manufacture) the color selection of red and blue yarn for the thimbles conforms to the red and blue flannel skirt, each color extending halfway around the drum. Continuing the color symbolism associated with ceremonial Drums, two thimbles each with yellow yarn are located at the east and west sides of the instrument, the points where the skirt color changes.[86]

On occasion, the Ojibwa have used coins as pendants in place of homemade cones or in conjuction with them. The Henry Davis Drum at Mille Lacs had along the bottom of the skirt not only jingles but also Canadian dimes, which were perforated to hang from the belt.[87] In all instances where coins are part of drum decoration, they have been silver dimes or quarters. This is doubtless for appearance's sake but perhaps also as a gesture of bestowing wealth upon the drum. (The words for "silver" and "money" are the same in Ojibwa, zhooniyaa.) Moreover, the ritual use by minority cultures of the coinage of the majority culture has occurred elsewhere in North America. Evon Vogt depicts the "riot of color" effected by ceremonial necklaces of the Tzotzil Indians of Mexico. The necklaces have silver coins attached to a gold colored band by red and pink ribbons threaded through holes drilled in them. While Vogt interprets the coins as a possible symbolic reference to "the little sun," he proposes a more significant meaning as well:

> in a contemporary world where the Indians believe the ladinos [whites] have most of the money and they (the Indians) are impoverished and need to increase their supply of money . . . the necklaces are composed of money which is counted each Sunday in a kind of "increase" rite.[88]

Hawk bells may also have once served as pendants on drums, although I have never seen them attached externally except on drum legs.[89] (See fig. 84. As described earlier, bells are usually not visible but contained within the drum frame as the "heart" of the drum.) Bells have been used elsewhere in the manner of the other pendant ornaments discussed—to decorate the tails and paws of otter-skin medicine bags, for instance—and bell anklets worn by dancers are sometimes used for percussion by Ojibwa singers if a drum is not available; thus their sound is clearly associated with drum beats. This would explain why, in one of Steve Grover's visions, circa 1905, at Lac Court Oreilles, a man appeared before him to instruct Grover in the use of the Drum, then disappeared into the sky:

"As he arose I thought I heard the sound of jingling bells and upon again looking in the direction in which he had gone I saw, not a man, but a drum such as we have before us."[90]

For the "silent" category of pendants applied to drums the Ojibwa have used yarn, loom beadwork, pony beads, and animal hair in all sorts of design combinations. Again, the idea supporting their use seems to have been the same as that behind their common application to other material objects. Yarn tassles were commonly sewn onto knife sheaths as well as onto elaborate Ojibwa ceremonial shoulder or bandoleer bags.[91] A particularly handsome bandoleer bag in the Fort Wayne Military Museum bears in beads the date of its completion (?) and name of its probable maker or owner, doubtless a descendant of a French voyageur (fur trader): "Joseph Lant/re Mars 21, 1851."[92] The bag is richly adorned with two tiers of more than fifty yarn tassles each.

Often yarn tassles were used to complete a narrow loom-beaded band (fig. 75), itself a sort of pendant found on many of the oldest drums. The Drum of Baker's grandfather, for one, has this feature (see fig. 47), although such fully beaded ornaments are as rarely made for drums today as the bandoleer bag prototypes from which they were probably copied. One museum collection has a circa 1890 Ojibwa navy wool shirt with beadwork panels in otter-tail designs as well as beadwork bands ending in yarn tassles on the shoulders and front of the shirt.[93] Lyford published a photograph of a velvet bag with applique beadwork floral motifs: the bottom half of the bag had been cut and edged in such a way as to suggest the maker desired to imitate loom-beaded band pendants, finishing their ends with pony beads and yarn tassles.[94] In place of a yarn tassle, the Ojibwa would sometimes sew strings of beads around a ball of soft material and attach it to the narrow beaded band.[95] Whether or not this was done to resemble a hawk bell is not known.

Almost all of Baker's drums have tassles along the bottoms of their belts and tabs. His 1970 drum without tassles constructed in New Hampshire is exceptional, but Baker, somewhat pressed for time to complete the drum, may have intended to add them later. (The legs for this drum were also left incomplete, Baker promis-

Figure 75. *Beaded apron, Vermilion Lake, Minnesota, showing both loom-beaded geometric and applique floral Ojibwa beading styles. Yarn tassles are attached to each of the bottom tabs.* (Photo by David K. Bateman, courtesy Mesabi Community College, Virginia, Minnesota.)

ing to complete them at home that summer.)

Baker's tassles invariably incorporate yarn and large pony beads. To my knowledge, he has never used metal or beaded pendants on his drums. A typical arrangement is shown in figure 76, each tassle having been assembled and then added to the drum individually. As ten tassles span the distance along the belt between each tab and three are applied to each tab, fifty-two yarn tassles in all adorn this drum.

To expedite their manufacture, Baker has developed a sort of production-line approach to assembling the tassles. With skeins of five different colored yarns anchored on the table before him, he pulls toward him the five loose strands and doubles them

200

Figure 76. *Baker's yarn and pony bead tassles attached to his 1974 drum. The background cloth chosen for the belt, skirt, and tabs is from the same drapery.* (Photo by Mike Herter.)

twice over the fore- and middle fingers of his left hand. Using yarn threaded on a large needle, he knots together all the strands where they are looped at one end and cuts off the yarn to match the width of his two fingers. The end opposite the knot then has ten free ends and five looped ends, so that by inserting a pair of scissors simultaneously through the five loops and cutting them, Baker produces twenty free strands altogether for each tassle.

The free ends of the tassle are secured together by wrapping yarn several times around them and tying it about three-eighths of an inch from the first knot, thus forming a small loop between the two knots. Next, Baker ties the end of threaded yarn to this loop and from a dish of large pony beads on the table selects four of different colors to thread on the yarn. Then the tassle is attached to the belt or tab by inserting the needle through the material near its edge, pulling the tassle tightly into place, wrapping it once or twice with yarn between the top bead and edge of the material, and pushing the needle once again through the cloth to tie the yarn behind it. This entire procedure is repeated for each tassle attached to the drum.

One variation in Baker's mode of tassle design appears to derive from the earlier practice of using thimbles as pendants with strands of horsehair or yarn protruding from their bottom openings. For this type of pendant, Baker collects the yellow plastic mouthpieces or tips of Tiparillo cigars and adapts them in much the same way as his predecessors had used thimbles. That is, he threads strands of yarn in several colors through the thin slot in the mouthpiece end of the plastic tip, allowing them to hang freely down from its larger end for about one half inches. These tassles are then attached to the tabs and the belt in the manner described.

Another tasslelike appendage, seemingly unique to Baker's drums, is fashioned from a yellow string, the synthetic threads of which are woven to form a very thin rope. After the belt and tabs have been attached, he cuts four lengths of the yellow string and with a comb feathers out the strands at one end so that it resembles a yarn tassle. The string is sewn at the top middle and the very center of each tab, the feathered end hanging freely to about two inches below its anchor.

Drumhead Decorations

[For] the moccasin game, they use the same [hand] drum, but it's not painted, it's not the sacred form of the drum. They just make them [secular drums] for the purpose to use. But you take a sacred Chief Dance drum, that's decorated; it's painted with the idea of nature up above—Thunderbird and eagle [from the film *The Drummaker*].

The heads of secular dance drums are rarely painted except perhaps for insignificant trim around their border. The plain rawhide is left just as it dries, in spite of the fact that it may have a mottled appearance if the removal of fat and membrane from its under side had been uneven. If an Ojibwa drumhead bears any kind of symbol, it is an almost certain indication that the drum itself is put to some sacred use.

As Baker points out, the only real distinction between a moccasin game drum used for amusement and a ceremonial Chief Dance drum is the fact that the head of the former is left plain, while the head(s) of the latter will have some representational or abstract painted design.[96] Indicating a spiritual bond between its owner/user and his *manidoo* protector, the design was always dictated by the spirit in a dream or vision, at which time certain songs were taught the recipient to go with the drum. It was in this manner that Tailfeather Woman was told how to build and decorate the first Drum and was given the songs meant to be performed on it.

The decor on the sides and support legs of ceremonial Drums varies considerably; the design for their heads, however, is standard: a narrow yellow band across its diameter, dividing the remainder of the circle into solid fields of red and blue. Thus the rawhide is completely covered with design. Following a practice of the *midewiwin*, this three-color pattern (or some variation of it) is repeated on the bottom head of the Drum (see fig. 55), even though it is rarely seen.[97] Vegetable dyes appear to have been used for the colors on some of the earliest Drums, one reason why on some old instruments the design has faded nearly beyond recognition. On the Walter Drift Drum (see fig. 68) only the central stripe is still faintly discernible, and the red has faded to a pink. The designs are created today using commercial paints and as part of general maintenance are meant to be repainted each spring and fall.[98]

The three principal ceremonial colors of the drumhead and their assignment to the cardinal points are reinforced by their application elsewhere, not only on other parts of the Drum but in ritual objects used in the dance. The repetition of these colors may be noted in yarn tassles, ribbon and beadwork on skirts and tabs, decor on drum legs and tobacco boxes, and applique designs on drum covers. Additionally, the officers of the Henry Davis Drum wear badges of red, blue, and yellow ribbons.[99] The four center posts of the old octagonal dance hall at Lac Vieux Desert as well as the new one made in 1975 at Lac du Flambeau are painted—those on the north side blue, on the south red.[100] The Pete Sam rawhide drum tobacco box also had the drumhead design duplicated on it.[101] Whether or not it was intentional, most tobacco offered to Drums at Mille Lacs in the early 1960s was "in the form of Velvet pipe tobacco, Copenhagen snuff, or Pall Mall cigarettes, all of which have red wrappings."[102]

While this generalization describes the orthodox design for the ceremonial drumhead, some latitude is permitted in varying it slightly. For instance, to highlight the yellow stripe, frequently additional thinner stripes in red and blue may be painted along both sides of the yellow. Barrett gives the proportional dimensions for such an arrangement at Lac Court Oreilles circa 1910: the yellow band is 1 to 1 1/2 inches wide, the blue and red stripes 1/2 inches wide.[103]

Because of the symbolic association of the colors, the Drum is always kept properly oriented to the cardinal points, even when it is "closed" in its owner's home.[104] In fact, the placement of Drums pictured in historical photographs can serve as a sort of compass: the alignment of the yellow stripe will usually confirm an east-west axis, and the blue and red fields on the head, which appear dark and light respectively in black-and-white photographs, should indicate north and south. In perhaps the oldest photograph of a Drum we have, made by Jenks at Lac Court Oreilles in 1899 (see fig. 34), the yellow stripe can be seen to run parallel to the frame work of a medicine lodge in the background. These structures were always erected along an east-west axis, with an entrance at the east end, an exit at the west. Figure 77 shows three Drums forty years later on the same reservation,

Figure 77. *Drums belonging to three societies at Lac Court Oreilles, circa 1941. The central yellow stripe on their heads is aligned to the east-west axis of the dance enclosure. All three tobacco boxes are present as well as Drum covers and legs (still wrapped) of at least one Drum. The number of quilts and mats beneath the instruments show the great care taken that Drums never touch the bare ground.* (Photo by Robert Ritzenthaler, courtesy Milwaukee Public Museum, neg. no. 5902.)

aligned with each other inside a rectangular dance enclosure. Like the medicine lodges, such enclosures were always oriented to the cardinal points with sides running north to south and east to west. Since the drum owners in this instance took care to align the three stripes parallel to one of the sides, it is safe to assume an east-west axis for the stripes and the bench running parallel behind them. As the lighter, red half of the drumheads faces away from the viewer, the southeast corner of the dance enclosure is the suggested location.[105]

The origin of the drumhead design is obscure, and the decoding of its meaning by the Ojibwa is anything but consistent. It has been suggested that its correct interpretation was limited to only a few people, particularly elders, who would pass on their knowledge to a new Drum owner together with "the laws and rules of the Drum."[106] This would conform to the protection given esoteric knowledge in the *midewiwin*, were it not for the apparent willingness of Drum members to interpret the design for outsiders as well as the general and widespread understanding of the representational figures on drum tabs.

There seems to be more agreement about the yellow stripe than the other two colors. Most Ojibwa recognize it as symbolizing the path of the sun across the sky but occasionally attribute to it a second meaning derived directly from *mide* teachings concerning "the good road." Grand Medicine preached that, to attain the goals of longevity and health one should follow an upright and moral path through life. *Mide* priests represented this pictographically on birchbark (and later paper) instructional scrolls as a straight line with occasional short "branches" leading away from it; the branches were meant to signify temptations along the way.[107] The straight line, then, was the preferred "good road." This explanation supports the interpretation of the yellow stripe as what whites call the golden rule: "If you believe . . . in God, and obey him . . . your road is good all the way through; nothing's going to happen to you."[108]

The interpretation given the red and blue fields is less consistent and, like the yellow stripe, frequently open to multiple explanations in decoding. The two fields are usually expressed as representing opposite pairs: a Mille Lacs Drum member asserted that the red denoted war, day, and evil, while the blue denoted peace, night, and good.[109] Similar notions were expressed concerning the "ritually defined colors of ceremonial dancers" at Fond du Lac circa 1900: red meant strife, strength, and manhood; blue, peace, modesty, and the Great Spirit.[110]

Directional symbols had appeared on Plains drums (fig. 78) but without such rigid color associations. Because of the directional orientation of the Ojibwa Drum by color, however, the most frequent explanations relate the colors to concepts concerning the north and south. Thus the red can represent "the brightness of the sun and light toward the south. . . . The blue symbolizes the darker sky toward the north."[111] John Mike, circa 1940, elaborated on this, pointing out that north was where the harsh spirits who brought winter lived. He also drew attention to the association of blue with mourning and red with its removal ("the brighter side").[112]

Some precedence for the association of colors with directions and phenomena existed in the *midewiwin*, although a different assignment of colors is evident. Hoffman, in describing the *mide* wooden posts for the fourth-degree initiation, noted they were painted the following colors: east/white (for the source of light, the rising sun), south/green (green and blue are equivalents in the Ojibwa language), west/red, and north/black (representing cold, disease, and desolation).[113]

This discrepancy in color assignment between the two ceremonials and stylistic features of drumhead design itself combine to suggest that it is not Ojibwa in origin but probably Siouan and may have been taken from the first Drum. Recalling that, in the origin legend, the Drum was established to halt bloodshed between tribes, it is striking that interpretations of the ceremonial colors collected in Minnesota include references to warfare nota-

Figure 78. *Mandan buffalo hide drum. Directional symbolism is painted on the drumhead.* (Photo courtesy Museum of the American Indian, Heye Foundation, neg. no. 29133.)

bly absent from Wisconsin interpretations. In fact, one Mille Lacs Drum member decoded the entire drumhead as symbolizing the end of fighting between the Sioux and Ojibwa: red denoted the blood shed by the two tribes, yellow represented the boundary line made when peace was established, and blue symbolized the treaty and justice.[114] This interpretation could have derived from color symbolism of the Sioux military, for which red represented blood or wounds and blue (formerly black), victory or enemies killed.[115]

As the first Drum was believed to have been made in central Minnesota by the Sioux and possibly given to the Mille Lacs people, conceivably the "end-of-warfare" interpretation or something similar to it predates the purely directional connotations of the three colors and may have been lost in the transfer of drums eastward. If that were the case, the directional symbolism may have been "read into" the design by later recipients of the Drum in lieu of other explanations.

While military associations for the drumhead design may have been obscure to the Wisconsin Drum societies, there is at least vestigial evidence on two of their drums that may link the design to Siouan origins. On the John Stone Drum at Lac Court Oreilles and the Kemewan Drum at Zoar, six horseshoes have been incorporated into the design.[116] Because the Kemewan Drum has the red horseshoes painted single file over the yellow stripe, it is noteworthy that the Sioux military color symbol for horses was yellow, and that, when asked the meaning of the horseshoes, the Menominee explained that when the Sioux made the first Drum they gave away forty ponies.[117]

The design itself—primary colors in a geometric arrangement—is more typical of Plains than Woodlands art. Those who have studied the development of Ojibwa artistic styles, however, note a change about the time of the Drum's origin and through the period of its initial flourishing. While Coleman has written that "Ojibwa design of this period [1870-1920] shows a decided bent for color. In fact, realism is often sacrificed for color,"[118] Lyford proposes that the typical Ojibwa use of color was to select a variety of shades and combine them.[119] Thus a Siouan influence may be reflected when primary colors are used alone.

The topic of Ojibwa drumhead decoration would be incomplete without forwarding another possibility, that painting the head of the drum is conceived of as analogous to painting the face. The application of ritually prescribed designs to the skin "face" of the Drum would seem a natural final step in its dressing, and in fact there is evidence to support this contention, specifically in Drum rituals involving mourners.

Face (and body) painting, as is generally known, are centuries-old customs with almost all Native American peoples. The paintings were done for purely cosmetic as well as ritual reasons. In the latter case, the design was often dream dictated, in which case face paint was considered the equivalent of good medicine. During his captivity among the Ojibwa, John Tanner in the early nineteenth century came to practice this art and had a song that accompanied his face painting, the text of which stated: "My [face] painting; that makes me a [spirit]."[120] For their colors, the Indians used natural substances, such as clay or earth and berry juices. Blackfeet warriors decorated their faces with blue earth obtained from the foothills of the Rocky Mountains and mercury vermilion, an early trade item from China.[121] In the summer, Red Lake Ojibwa around 1870 would plaster white clay on their backs as a background color for figured designs.[122]

Among patterns used by the Ojibwa, it was not uncommon to divide the face or body into two halves of contrasting colors. McKenney in 1826 described Fond du Lac Indians near present-day Duluth, Minnesota:

> Some were painted black; others one half red and the other black, and the colours were separated by a nicely dividing line down the spine of the back and in front.[123]

Kohl on Madeline Island in 1855 learned that La Pointe Ojibwa attributed the invention of face painting to Wenebozho, who to frighten his enemies took red earth, burned it, and smeared it on his face before battle.[124] Remarking that the Indians changed the pattern of their facial painting almost daily, Kohl noted:

> They like contrasts, and frequently divide the face [vertically down the nose or horizontally] into two halves, which undergo different treatment. One will be dark— say black or blue—but the other quite light, yellow, bright red, or white.[125]

Among facial designs employed by White Earth *mide* priests in 1889, the design published by Hoffman for the third degree is similarly divided, the upper half green (an equivalent of blue), the lower half red.[126]

There is, then, a precedent in Ojibwa face and body painting for the sort of color arrangement found on the face of the Drum. Although the topic of ritual design exchange between American

Indian musical instruments and the human body has not been fully investigated, we do know of instances on the Plains where this exchange was customary. Copying ritual patterns from rattles onto faces has been reported for the Omaha in the Wawan ceremony. As Fletcher describes them, the primary colors and stripes transferred from gourd rattles had directional associations not unlike those of the Ojibwa drumhead design:

> During the singing of the first stanza the man held the paint in its receptacle over the head of the child and showed it to all present. He first made a feint as if to touch the child with it. As the second stanza was sung he put red paint over the face of the child, then he drew a band of black across the forehead, a stripe down each cheek, one down the nose and one at the back of the head. This design had the same meaning as that on the gourds. The band across the forehead represented the line of the sky; the stripes were the paths at the four directions whence the winds start; the red paint symbolized the light of the sun and the gift of life.[127]

In the Ojibwa ritual removal of mourning during a Drum Dance, a similar transfer takes place while a special song is performed. Although the designs of the face painting vary somewhat, one or more of the three ritual colors is used. For example, during a dance in 1910 at Lac Court Oreilles, a singer who had lost a son five days earlier expressed a desire to have his mourning removed the next day. (Ordinarily, the waiting period is either six months or a year.) During the following day's ceremony, he was seated on a blanket, his face and hands bathed, and a new shirt put on him. His face was then painted with a diagonal blue and red streak, and after a speech, he was led to his drum. In another removal of mourning that occurred a day later, red, yellow, and blue were painted on the mourners' faces in the same arrangement as these colors were applied to the drumhead.[128] And in perhaps the most explicit gesture to connect the two, in the Lac Court Oreilles Drum Dance of the 1940s, the leaders of the ceremony in preparation for the removal of mourning actually rubbed the blue face paint on the blue field of the Drum before applying it to the mourner's face.[129]

Accessories

Pipes and Tobacco Boxes

Next to the Drum in importance is the ceremonial pipe, which is smoked four times during each day of a Drum Dance during the special Song of the Pipe. It is rotated to each of the cardinal directions by the pipe tender, who faces east.[1] The first smoke is offered by him to the spirits of each direction before members seated around the periphery of the dance site and singers at the Drum smoke, passing the pipe to the left.[2]

As the topic of pipes, tobacco, and smoking customs of the Ojibwa and Menominee has been thoroughly discussed by Barrett, the reader is referred to that source for more information.[3]

As is generally known, tobacco continues to be held sacred by the Indian. Not only did the Ojibwa send it with runners to use as invitations to ceremonials or for organizing war parties, but because of the belief in its inherent power, it was used to ward off storms or other catastrophes. As an offering, the Ojibwa would sprinkle it on the water before harvesting their wild rice or, if they took something from the ground, they would always deposit a pinch of tobacco in the hole as a replacement to show their gratitude.[4] Similarly, in the Drum Dance, members present tobacco offerings as they enter the dance enclosure. Each spring they are supposed to put a pinch in a special buckskin pouch (*gashkibidaagan*), which is tied to the west support stake, to invoke the Drum's protection for its members.[5] Tobacco can be taken to the Drum to petition its assistance—in hunting deer, for instance. When this is done, one addresses the Drum, saying "Well, we are going to hunt deer, something to eat. I want you to help me out, get me what I want."[6]

Ideally the tobacco used should be "Indian tobacco" (*kinnickinick*), a mixture of leaf tobacco with scrapings from the inside bark of the red willow. Actually, however, any kind of tobacco is acceptable—snuff, plug tobacco, even packs of cigarettes torn apart to obtain their tobacco. Just as the Great Spirit is believed to hear the Drum Dance songs, the smoke and aroma of the burning tobacco are thought to rise to him, like incense, carrying to him the petitions of the members. Whenever the Drum's pipe is used, its smoke is considered particularly powerful:

> Especially efficacious is the smoke from the drum's own pipe, since this is a pipe of special importance, and since

the tobacco which is smoked in it comes from the special pouch which is fastened to the loop which supports the drum on its western stake, and which is therefore especially potent.[7]

The Ojibwa use pipes with wooden stems and removable catlinite bowls of the elbow-pipe variety. There are usually two pipe stems per Drum: a short plain stem used in ordinary Drum rites, such as evening song services, and a much longer, elaborately carved and decorated stem, used in the seasonal rites (fig. 79). Baker is expert at stem carving and particularly adept at creating the illusion of a twisted stem, a hallmark of the Ojibwa ornamented stem (fig. 80). He carves his stems from sumac, a wood chosen for several reasons: its bark is easily peeled when still green; the wood is soft enough to facilitate carving; the layers of wood, when carved, exhibit a handsome marbled appearance; and its pithy core is easily hollowed out for a smoke passageway by pushing a heated coathanger through its length, thereby burning a smoke hole through the center. Such stems, once carved, are then surrounded with fur in places and have ribbons attached to them. More elaborate pipes may even contain metal inlays.[8] Special songs are sung during which the pipe tender will dance carrying the stem without its bowl.

Figure 79. *The long ceremonial pipestem is smoked from during a 1910 Whitefish Dance. The pipebowl rests on the ground.* (Photo by S. A. Barrett, courtesy Milwaukee Public Museum, neg. no. 20200.)

Figure 80. *Pipestem and bowl carved by Baker showing the characteristic twisted effect on Ojibwa ceremonial stems. As he lacked catlinite for the bowl, Baker used wood and painted it red to resemble the customary pipestone.* (Photo by Dane Penland.)

Because of the great importance of pipe rituals within the Drum Dance, a special wooden tobacco box or tray is part of the Drum's accessories. In it are kept the tobacco, matches, and pipe bowl. Resembling somewhat a rectangular box for shoe polishing gear, its handle is formed over the open top and its interior is usually divided into compartments (see figs. 34, 77). When not in use, the tobacco box is covered. During dances, in some places it is put at the entrance to the dance enclosure, and people entering deposit their tobacco offerings in it.[9]

Drum Legs (*waaganaakobijiganan*)

Of the drum's components, perhaps none are more imposing in appearance than the elaborately decorated support stakes, called the "legs" of the drum. When positioned, the stakes with their graceful bend reach up and outward from the top head of the drum by as much as three feet, spanning perhaps more than six feet. As the eagle feathers, ribbon streamers, and tufted ends of cow tails attached to the stakes move freely in the breeze, the total effect of a drum supported on such legs is that of something almost organic and alive (fig. 81).

Figure 81. *Lac du Flambeau Drum raised on its legs at the time of its presentation to the Menominee in 1928 at Zoar.* (Photo by Frances Densmore, courtesy NAA, neg. no. 616L.)

Figure 82. *A White Earth (Minnesota) dance drum, circa 1889, after an illustration by Walter J. Hoffman. The use of only three legs and the manner of supporting the drum from them appear unlikely.* (Illustration by Daphne Shuttleworth.)

The four stakes are used to align ceremonial Drums according to the cardinal directions, so that the yellow stripe runs from east to west and the red half faces south. Each leg is designated as belonging to a direction and has a song assigned to it. The four songs are performed in a prescribed order. To my knowledge, the Ojibwa have never used a greater or lesser number than four legs, even for secular instruments. Thus Hoffman's depiction of a White Earth circa 1889 dance drum (fig. 82) with three drum legs appears to be fanciful.[10]

Ceremony surrounds the putting up of a ceremonial Drum on its legs and its removal. Distinctions between daytime and evening services are reflected in the ritual requirement that the legs support the Drum during the day from sunrise to sunset, but are removed at night, when the Drum must rest on the ground or floor. The legs are so vital that each leg has a special song—an honor bestowed on no other piece of Drum equipment. When a drum is given away, very often a leg is kept behind to go with the replacement drum that must be built.[11] Incorporated into the paraphernalia of the new drum, the leg thus becomes a symbol of the kinship between drums. One could see the importance the Ojibwa attach to drum support stakes at a 1973 summer dedication of one of Baker's replacement drums. Already constructed for him to retain, it was set on its cover to one side of the singers who surrounded the giveaway drum. One of the old legs selected to go with the new drum was stuck in the ground beside it (fig. 83).

The Ojibwa and subsequent recipients of the drum have always devoted considerable attention to the construction of these support stakes and lavished them with decoration. The design of any Ojibwa drum leg may incorporate a wide variety of mate-

Figure 83. *A drum dedication at William Baker's house in 1973. A replacement drum built by him to keep is in the foreground. One drum leg from the giveaway drum (to the far left) has been retained to remain with the newly constructed drum to symbolize their kinship.* (Photo by the author.)

rials: buckskin, paint, beadwork, fur, feathers, ribbon, yarn, cloth, horsehair—usually these will be found in combination along the slender length of wood. Furthermore, there may even be variation in the combination and color scheme from leg to leg on the same drum.

While support stakes for some Plains Grass Dance drums possessed similar features, they rarely approach the elaborateness of western Woodlands drum legs. For example, W. T. Thompson's 1893 photograph of a Grass Dance drum on the Standing Buffalo Reserve in Saskatchewan (fig. 84) shows it to have a skirt and bells—items also found on the Ojibwa dance drum. Although long like the Ojibwa drum legs, the stakes are thinner and only slightly bent (see also fig. 14), and the tuft of hair or cotton on their tips and the feathers hanging from them are less prominent than those on their Woodlands counterparts. Still, the several design elements shared by Ojibwa and Plains Grass Dance drum legs provide further evidence of the relationship between the Grass and Drum Dance complexes. A portion of the leg, for instance, may be wrapped with a continuous spiral of threaded beads in one color for several inches, changing to another color for several more. Or, the end might be wrapped

Figure 84. *Grass Dance drum on its support legs on the Standing Buffalo Reserve, Saskatchewan, Canada. Note the bells attached to the legs, plain drum skirt, and thin almost vertical shape of the legs.* (Photo by W. T. Thompson, 1893, courtesy NAA, neg. no. 55,638.)

with a band of fur and tufted with a feather and horsehair. These particular features, evident in Sumner Matteson's 1906 photograph of an Assiniboin (or Gros Ventre) drum used for the Grass Dance on the Fort Belknap Reservation in Montana (see fig. 14) can be found as well on the Ojibwa examples given in figures 34 and 81.

Why should the Ojibwa have devised a drum support apparatus the elaborateness of which far exceeds its function, which is merely to hold the instrument off the ground? Historically, none of their other drums had any but the simplest means of support. The hand-drum was equipped with only a thin rawhide thong; the medicine drum, if not resting on the ground or cradled in the

Figure 85. *Baker with one of his drums in the Lac du Flambeau "Indian Bowl" prior to a performance before tourists. The drum legs here are purely functional and lack the elaboration of ceremonial legs. Baker is reaching into the bag he has made to hold his drumsticks.* (Photo by Mike Herter, 1974.)

arm, was held by the edges of its deer skin head, which protruded beneath the hoop. In fact, even for nonceremonial occasions, such as dances held for tourists, the Ojibwa have recourse to a completely functional and unadorned set of legs. These legs, of ordinary unpainted wood, are cut off just above the support hook, so that they project only slightly, if at all, above the head of the drum (fig. 85).

Several customs in which the Ojibwa use drum legs for purposes other than suspending the instrument point to origins in the war practices of the Plains, although the original connection has probably long since been forgotten. These practices suggest that drum legs may in fact be vestiges of the special lances that were part of the ritual paraphernalia of Plains warrior societies. That connection may help to explain their shape and elaborate decoration.

To begin with, Densmore was told that the reason for having "four leading dancers [*ogichidaag*, warriors]" was that there was to be one for each leg of the Drum.[12] Further evidence of a connection with warfare is the occasional reference to one of the four legs (usually the south leg) as the Wounded Drum Leg.

Densmore and Hoffman each found this name given by the Menominee, though neither scholar offered an explanation for it. Densmore notes without comment that of the songs for each of the four stakes, the song for the south leg is called Song of the Wounded Drum Stake, and Hoffman states that the name Wounded Drum Leg was given to the female singer who sat next to that particular stake. Apparently he received no elucidation on the meaning of the name, for he surmised only that "as the drum is supposed to rest on four legs the name is only an illusion."[13]

The Wounded Leg designation appears to be borrowed from tribes to the west of the Ojibwa. We know of the existence of the Wounded Leg Society (Omaha Kaiyotag) of the Oglala Sioux, for Wissler listed it in enumerating the tribe's various warrior societies. Although similar to the other *ogichidaa* societies, it was not recognized as one by the Oglala. In the origin story given Wissler by Calico, he learned that the Wounded Leg Society Dance had been revealed to a shaman in a dream in which members of the society were asked what they most desired:

> "One asked to be wounded. The shaman said, that if he so wished, it would be; but that the chief function of the regalia and formula was to prevent wounds. The member still persisted. 'Well,' said the shaman, 'then you shall be wounded and afterward may wear a small bell upon you to mark the place of injury.' True enough, this man was shot in the leg and at the next dance appeared with a bell on his legging. This was popular and many wished to be wounded so that after a few expeditions many of the dancers wore bells."[14]

Such a story may offer an explanation for the occasional bells attached to drum legs of Plains Grass Dance drums (see fig. 84).[15]

Rituals in which the Ojibwa use the legs for purposes other than a drum support also suggest that their original function may have had more to do with warfare than with musical instruments. During Drum giveaways, for instance, the Drum is taken down from its legs and transferred to the recipients, but only when the accumulation of donated gifts is considered sufficient to accompany its transfer.[16] At this time, there is considerable ceremonial handing back and forth of the drum legs. During the 1928 Drum presentation Densmore observed at Zoar, after the first day of singing, the Ojibwa left the Drum behind but took the stakes with them. Returning later, they presented a leg to each of the principal Menominee singers, though the legs were not inserted in the ground at this time:

> These stakes were formally accepted by the four Menominee "old men," each of whom took a stake from a singer, made a speech, and returned it, after which the singer planted the stake in its proper position for supporting the drum.[17]

The nature of the speeches given on this occasion lends further support to a connection between drum legs and warfare. While holding a drum leg, each elder described some feat of battle accomplished by an ancestor, as though the leg were some war trophy. In fact, only those whose ancestors had been valorous in battle were entitled to put up drum stakes at a dance. Densmore noted that Rattlesnake, the Menominee Drum recipient, could put up a stake because his father, while a scout for General Sherman, had escaped hanging by shooting his captors with a gun he had hidden. Similarly, Kimiwun, the Ojibwa donor, was entitled to put up two stakes, because his uncle had killed an enemy during the Civil War.[18]

The shape and decoration of the Ojibwa legs and the fact that they are on occasion carried in the dances seems to relate them to ceremonial lances and coup sticks of Plains warrior societies (fig. 86). Early travelers to the wilderness were often impressed by the elaborateness of such lances. Maximilian, for instance, describes four Mandan ceremonial lances seven to eight feet long, which were decorated with otter-fur bands, feathers, and strips of skin.[19] Similarly adorned were the special "crooked spears" carried by four of the six leaders of the Ponca Iskaiyuna Society. These, too, were wrapped with otter fur and had eagle feathers hanging from them; they obligated the warriors carrying them to remain steadfast in battle.[20] Some were pointed at their ends and, like drum legs, could be stuck into the ground or used to stab an enemy. The Mandan/Hidatsa Fox Society lance carrier sometimes presented his to a woman who performed Scalp Dance songs in the victory celebrations, thereafter making a new one for himself.[21]

The lances of the Pawnee bundle societies bear perhaps the most striking resemblance to Ojibwa drum legs. Particularly close in appearance are the Red Lance Society lances, as illustrated by Murie (fig. 87)—especially that of the Skidi branch of the Pawnee. Like a drum leg, its shaft wrapped with otter fur was bent over at the end, eagle feathers both erect and pendant were attached, and symbolic colors were applied—"dark for the north side lance, reddish for the south." A red stone was imbedded on

Figure 86. *Sioux dance wand (left) with eagle feathers (82 inches long) and Teton Sioux coup stick (right) wound with otter fur (69½ inches long). Such war emblems would appear to be the prototypes of the Ojibwa dance drum leg.* (Photo courtesy Museum of the American Indian, Heye Foundation, neg. no. 22537.)

the string tied to its crook. Such lances were carried into battle for protection and later in victory dances.[22] (The Teton Sioux usually buried them with their owners.)

Similar lances played a role in a Gros Ventre origin story of their Drum Dance, said to have been in existence in the early nineteenth century but extinct at the time Cooper collected his information. In the story, one of a party of Gros Ventre venturing into the Black Hills became lost, was near starvation, and found a dry lake bed in which to die. After four days there he heard a voice criticizing Drum Dance members for not coming to his aid. When he heard drumming and singing coming toward him, he sat up:

> It was broad daylight and as he looked toward the direction whence the voice and drumming and singing had

Figure 87. *A Pawnee Skidi Red Lance Society lance, wrapped with otter fur and decorated with pendant eagle feathers, after an illustration by James R. Murie.* (Illustration by Daphne Shuttleworth.)

come, he saw two lances (or sticks) curved (crooked) around on the upper end (like a shepherd's crook) come up from the ground of the dry lake bed. Three times they came up and after each time disappeared in the ground. The fourth time they came up, there were two men carrying them.[23]

Pairs of dancers followed the lance bearers, and two men at the rear of the procession carried two more lances. Of the four lances described to Cooper by his informant, The Boy, two were wrapped with otter-fur bands at four places, two with rabbit fur, and each had two eagle feathers hanging from the fur bands.

Lances, batons, and ultimately drum stakes seem to have played parallel if not identical roles in Indian ceremonial dances. During the period of intertribal warfare and before the arrival of the drum, it had long been common in victory dances for people to dance while holding some object aloft, whether some special badge, such as the lances described, or a war trophy. Frequently a scalp stretched on a hoop and attached to a stick served as the trophy (see fig. 6)—a practice the Ojibwa shared with tribes to the west. After peace had been forcibly imposed on the tribes by the United States Government, former warriors continued to dance with special batons or wands to represent such war trophies and to boast of past military exploits, thereafter presenting gifts. As recently as the 1940s such a stick was kept in a hole in the central table of the dance hall at Lac Vieux Desert, Wisconsin. Evidently anyone was free to take it out and dance with it, but if an elder did so he would always relate a dream or war story that told of killing. (Women, of course, had no such story but were obligated to give away a dress or shirt to someone the next day if they danced with the stick.)[24]

In at least one Drum Dance, a drum stake served a similar ritual function. The Henry Davis Drum at Mille Lacs had five legs, the fifth being twice the size of the others and reserved for people to dance with who wished "to donate on behalf of the drum" but were ineligible to do so through the regular legs.[25] This practice may have in fact been ritualized in the Menominee Drum Dance, for they designated two leaders, called Chicken Men, to carry special crooked staffs three feet in length and wound with otter fur, as a special song was sung for each of them in turn.[26]

In constructing their drum legs the Ojibwa customarily select saplings lacking branches for four to five feet from their base, the diameter of which is about 1 1/2 inches. White ash is a frequent choice, as it is easily peeled just after being picked (before it dries) and the curve at its end is made without breaking the sapling. (For the same reason, white ash is used for lacrosse sticks.) The short, stubby canelike legs in Hoffman's illustration (see fig. 82) are most unusual and probably are not very representative of what he saw. The carved spiraling is generally reserved for pipestems, and the thickness of the crook is atypical and probably impossible to effect without breaking.

Before the legs are decorated, they must be made to accommodate the straps attached to the drum frame. For this, either the leg itself is carved in such a way as to provide a hook or some sort of hook is attached to the leg. A wooden hook is usually lashed to the inside of the leg with rawhide (fig. 88), while a metal hook is screwed or nailed into it.[27] (Hoffman's illustration [see fig. 82] shows the hooks on the outside of the legs, which is improbable

Figure 88. *Hook attached to drum leg built by Fred Connors of Bad River Reservation. The hook is lashed to the leg with rawhide, the deerskin strap has been twisted for strength.* (Photo by the author, 1980.)

and would in any case prove awkward in setting up the drum.) If carved into the leg itself, the hook may consist simply of a diagonal notch cut perhaps no more than one-half inches deep into the round wood. In a more elaborate arrangement, the notch may be deeper and mark the point at which the leg changes its shape and begins to curve. The hardwood legs of the Whitefish Drums in 1910 were rectangular (two by three-quarters inches) for the lower two-thirds of their length and changed to a rounded section beginning where a notch two to six inches deep had been cut vertically into the wood down the center of the stake.[28]

When adding decoration to the wooden leg, the Ojibwa appear always to have accepted considerable latitude in design. Barrett, discerning the variations among sets of Ojibwa and Menominee drum legs that he had examined circa 1910, wrote, as follows:

> The ornamentations of the stakes . . . do not appear to differ in any systematic way in any given set of four

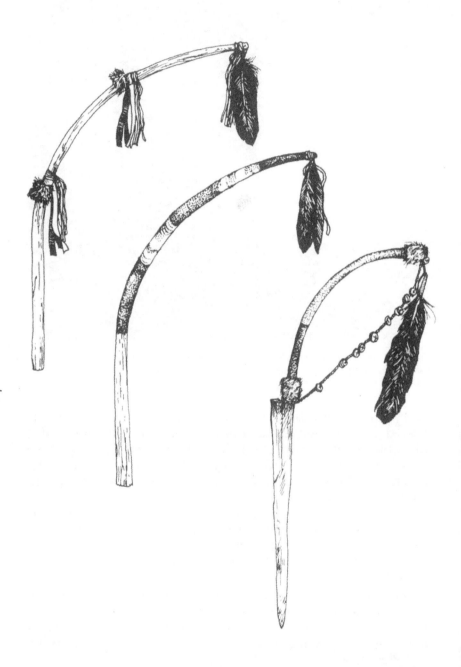

Figure 89. *Drum legs designed by three different builders. Left to right: William Baker Drum, 1979; Lac Court Oreilles Drum, 1899; David Goss Drum, circa 1876.* (Illustration by Daphne Shuttleworth.)

stakes, though as a matter of fact in almost all cases no two stakes are exactly alike. So far as could be learned, however, these differences have no special significance. A very considerable variety is found in the different sets of stakes, each set being evidently made and ornamented according to the personal preference of the particular makers of the drum to which the stakes belong.[29]

For comparison, figure 89 shows drum leg designs by three different builders.[30]

While the four legs of a given set were basically alike, there were usually certain distinguishing marks put on them to identify their various assignments to the cardinal points. These might be brass tacks on the inner surface of the hook—one, two, three, and four tacks indicating their respective directions—or notches carved into the stakes for similar identification. Also, the west stake customarily had a tobacco pouch (*gashkibidaagan*) tied to it. Where the color red was prominent in the ribbons or paint, it signified an east or south stake, the color blue a west or north stake. There is no evidence, however, that a different type of wood was selected for each stake for symbolic reasons, as has been reported for the Menominee juggler's tent.[31]

Whatever its other design features, nearly every set of drum legs was provided with eagle feathers—usually one per stake, hanging from its tip or placed erect in a socket partway along the bend in the stake, such as those on the Bijikens Drum (see fig. 90). These sockets might be of fur or even a bone swivel, like those found on the traditional porcupine- and deer-hair roach headpiece.[32] (In the Hidatsa Grass Dance a warrior could have erect feathers in a bone socket on his roach "if [he] had one strike on an enemy to his credit.")[33] For the Menominee, at least, having the feathers pendant or erect was a distinguishing feature used to signify the genre of the drum: hanging downward from the tips of the stakes the feathers indicated a Warrior Drum, but if erect in a socket, a Chief Drum.[34] (Earl Nyholm informs me that the distinction indicates the length of the dance, whether a four- or eight-day ceremony.) The feathers are believed to have power of their own and offer protection when attached to a stick in the ground. As Paul Buffalo of Leech Lake, who kept a green feather hanging from a light string in his house, explained:

> When it storms, big typhoon coming, hang that outside of it. Tie it on a stick, stick it on the ground, you watch that storm go around the other way. . . . Put a feather out, any feather . . . that's nature, you could do it with any bird up

Figure 90. *Bijikens's drum legs before the Drum is suspended. Note the pipebox, with ceremonial stem partly carved to give a twisted effect, and the mats to protect the Drum from the ground.* (Photo by Frances Densmore, courtesy NAA, neg. no. 596-c-11.)

> there that flies, that flies pretty fast . . . hang that outside
> on the doorknob, the storm will go around it.[35]

(Indians of many tribes keep a feather over their house door to protect them against lightning. The Thunderbirds see the feather and know that it signifies an Indian house, so they throw their bolts elsewhere.)

As with the drum and drumsticks, its legs and feathers were customarily kept covered and apart when not in use, the legs in a special cloth bag and the feathers in a box similar to the Drum's tobacco box. (The feathers are considered by some to be more important than the legs; for secular events they are often left off the legs [see fig. 13].) When the legs are put up, each of the four principal singers attaches the feather assigned to his stake. The legs are generally not used at night or, if they are, certainly not with the feathers attached. Explained John Mike:

> "They never put a Drum on its stakes at night. I suppose
> it's because the feathers hanging on the four stakes repre-

sent the Indian 'flag' and shouldn't be flown at night, just like the American flag."[36]

To support the drum, the legs themselves must have their bottom ends firmly imbedded in holes, either in the ground or in some sort of fixed stand. Barrett describes Drum members prior to the 1910 ceremony at Whitefish carefully orienting the location of the holes and then making them by driving a crowbar into the ground at the cardinal points.[37] The ends of the legs, which were tapered to a point, were then inserted in the ground. Where ceremonies were held in dance halls, holes were often made in the floor to serve permanently. The southwest corner of the Lac Vieux Desert dance hall had a cement base that contained the four holes;[38] similarly, the Mille Lacs dance hall, where the Henry Davis rites took place, had holes cut into the floor and lined with metal.[39] At sundown, the Mille Lacs drum heaters would take the Drum off its stakes and leave it for the evening service resting on the floor.[40] Wooden stands are also used, however. They are generally made from two-by-four-inch boards with holes drilled in them at the four points, either in a crosspiece (x) or a square frame arrangement (fig. 91).[41]

For drum legs Baker uses white ash saplings about an inch in diameter. He cuts these to uniform lengths, approximately four to five feet and peels the bark from them almost immediately, while it is still moist and easily removed. To effect the bend near the thinner end of the leg, Baker takes advantage of exposed wooden studding, such as those found inside a garage or tool

Figure 91. *Typical wooden stands into which drum legs are inserted.* (Illustration by Daphne Shuttleworth.)

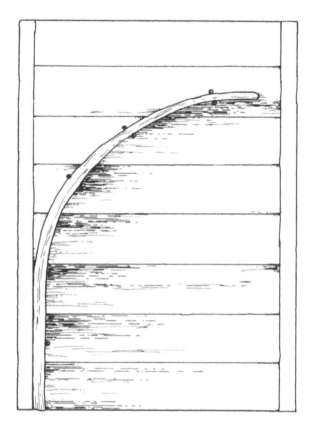

CROSS SECTION
DETAIL OF
WHITE ASH LEG

Figure 92. *Baker's manner of effecting a bend in the drumlegs by nailing the white ash between studding in a shed or garage and allowing it to dry in that position.* (Illustration by Daphne Shuttleworth.)

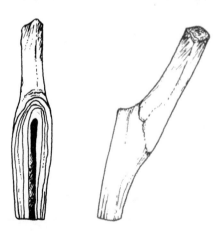

Figure 93. *Branch and part of sumac stem carved for drum support hook.* (Illustration by Daphne Shuttleworth.)

shed, by nailing each leg against the wall between the studs. The thicker end of the ash sapling butts against a stud for about two thirds of its length, and the thinner end is forced into the desired shape and nailed against the planking in that position (fig. 92). When the sapling has dried thoroughly, it will retain the bend when the nails are removed.

Hooks are carved from sumac usually collected at the same time Baker goes in search of this wood from which he carves his spiral pipestems. He selects a part of the bush where a branch projects from the main stem. The branch and trunk form a natural V-shaped hook from which to suspend the drum with its leather strap. Six-inch lengths of sumac are sawed off, peeled free of bark before they dry (see frontispiece, lower right), and the branch suspending-hook further whittled down to about one-half inches in diameter. With an ax Baker splits the piece of sumac vertically. Then with a pocketknife he hollows out the back side of it to match the roundness of the leg to which it will be lashed (fig. 93) Wet rawhide is used to strap the hook to the leg, being wrapped continuously around the hook and leg, thus binding the two tightly together as the rawhide dries (see fig. 88). Baker affixes the sumac hooks to the legs at a point where they will raise the drum three to four inches off the ground.

In decorating his drum legs, Baker shows the same flexibility that characterizes his approach to all design. While probably no two sets of legs he has made look exactly the same, some consistency is evident in his choice of materials and colors and their placement on the leg. Almost all of his legs are decorated with paint, fur, ribbons, yarn, and eagle feathers, with the three principal ceremonial colors predominant.

A typical set of legs is decorated as follows: each leg was divided and marked off into three equal sections, the two extremities painted red, the middle section, beginning just above the hook, blue.[42] (Dividing legs this way into sections of different colors appears to be fairly common practice at Lac Court Oreilles. Blessing describes a set of legs at a 1960 dance wrapped with yarn in blue, red, green and orange, the color changing every six to eight inches.)[43] These color fields were further delimited where they joined each other by having a two-inch wide fur strip glued around the leg at that point. One-half-inch-wide ribbons were tied just above the fur strips, and red, yellow, and blue yarn immediately above the ribbons. The varied color combinations for the ribbons above the fur was chosen, as follows: blue and red for the south leg, yellow and red for the east, white and blue for the north, and yellow and blue for the west. Ribbons and yarn in the principal colors and an eagle feather hang from the very tip of each leg. The base of each feather is wrapped with yarn—blue for the west and north stakes, red for the other two—and has a buckskin thong attached with which to tie it to the leg. Because the feathers are removed from the legs when the drum is not in use, Baker may carve a narrow groove around the leg near its end to tie the feather thong securely and prevent its slipping.

Drumsticks

From what we know, Ojibwa singers (and most other Native Americans) have always performed with a single stick to accompany their songs when using a drum.[44] Even the oldest form of drum mentioned by Ojibwa who remember hearing about it—a large piece of rawhide stretched and pegged to the ground—was beaten with sticks.

Although data is insufficient to establish any chronology of drumstick types known to the Ojibwa, the curved drumstick used in the Grand Medicine Society to beat the *mitigwakik* may be the oldest. According to legend, when Wenebozho (the culture hero) and the other spirits decided to give the Ojibwa the medicine dance, in addition to the drum they presented them with the curved *baaga'akokwaan* (lit., an object with which to strike something to make a noise).[45] The legendary origin suggests that the medicine drumstick predates the other two types—the stick whose beater end forms a hoop and the straight stick, the kind most commonly used today. In any case, the *mide* stick and the water drum used with it so closely resemble their present-day Iroquoian counterparts that they must date at least from the time when the proto-Ojibwa lived at the east end of Lake Superior and possibly earlier.

The medicine drumstick is characterized by having a gradual bend beginning near its beater end. The bend usually terminates in a small knob (see figs. 8 and 11);[46] thus the very tip of the curved stick strikes only a small area of the drumhead to produce the characteristic high pitched punctuations of the water drum, audible at great distances. (The knob at the end of the tip may or may not have a small buckskin or cloth covering tied around it with a leather thong.)

Usually a foot long, the medicine drumstick was used ritually to perform a rapid tremolo over which the priest sang "preaching songs" or a measured cadence to accompany general dancing as well as his circuits of the medicine lodge (*midewigaan*).[47] A Grand Medicine master instructional scroll from White Earth, Minnesota, which Dewdney reproduced for the cover of his study of Ojibwa sacred scrolls, shows no less than six medicine drums being played—the performers standing, sitting on the ground, or dancing in procession.[48] While most sticks depicted on the scroll are typically curved, one is represented in an angular L shape; the drawing may be intended to represent a variant of the curved stick in which a crosspiece is lashed vertically near the end of the handle to form its beater.[49] This crossbar type of stick may have had secular uses as well, for Densmore photographed a Grand Portage (Minnesota) Ojibwa using it with a hand-drum.[50]

Although most *mide* sticks in collections are of plain unadorned wood, some have survived with cloth wrapped handles, undoubtedly to prevent slippage in the performer's hand.[51] For the same reason others have toothlike finger indentations carved on their undersides, a feature shared with Woodlands war clubs, for which a firm grip was also important.

The medicine drumstick was considered a sacred and powerful item, often more valuable than the drum itself. As with most *mide* ritual paraphernalia, it could be used for evil as well as beneficial purposes. Kohl collected a story of an Ojibwa beating on water with a special staff resembling the drumstick in order to invoke an evil spirit,[52] while the medicine man John Mink, noting the tremendous spiritual power possessed by the stick, was reluctant to discuss it:

> "The drumstick can be used in place of a medicine bag to throw the migis [sacred shell used in Grand Medicine 'shooting' ceremonies], but it is very powerful and should only be thrust lightly. Don't like to even mention those manidos names because they are so powerful. There's a lot to that drumstick but it shouldn't be mentioned."[53]

Some drumsticks of this type were occasionally carved or decorated to represent animals, a practice apparently retained by some Drum societies. The Reverend Peter Jones collected an antler drumstick before 1844, probably Missisauga (an eastern band of Ojibwa) in origin. Looking not unlike a seahorse, it is a foot long and curves toward a small bulbous beater end, presumably meant to be the creature's mouth or beak; a hole drilled through it represents an eye, and jagged indentations along its topside suggest a mane or feathers.[54] Densmore observed that a special Drum owner's stick more than three feet long appeared at a certain point in the presentation of the Bijikens Drum. Unlike the other sticks used with the drum but similar to the *mide* stick, it had a curved end "over [which] was slipped the skin from the neck of a loon, its glossy black feathers dotted with white."[55] She described the ritual use of this stick after the Drum was transferred by the Ojibwa to the Menominee, as follows: the singers began by tapping on the ground with their drumsticks (the straight variety); as the special dedicatory stick was brought forward, everyone but the singers arose; the new Drum owner directed the Drum to be suspended on its legs, after which the singers began tapping lightly on the transferred Drum's edge as they sang:

> After this song Wiskino stood beside the drum, holding in his hand the long drumstick with the loon neck at the end. With this he pretended to strike the drum three times and as many times drew back. The fourth time he touched the drum lightly, and at the same time each of the four leading drummers struck it a sharp blow with his decorated drumstick. . . . The striking of the drum by Wiskino was done with great dramatic effect; his feints at striking held the people in suspense, and the final tap was welcomed as relief from the tension.[56]

The second type of drumstick used by the Ojibwa resembles identically their lacrosse stick minus its webbing. The end hoop is formed by carving the stick into a thin flat strip at one end and looping this strip back around and into the cavity on the handle. (John Keeper created similar loops at the tops of his drumlegs. See fig. 10.) There it is fastened into place with a thong drawn through holes drilled in the end of the flat strip and the handle. To pad the beater end, the entire hoop section is wrapped with cloth, leather, or rawhide, this despite the fact that only the very bottom of the hoop actually comes in contact with the drumhead.[57]

The Ojibwa have used the hoop drumstick with a variety of drums. Baker says that it is meant for the moccasin game drum, but I have seen Canadian Ojibwa using it with the modern bass drum as well. Moreover, there is evidence that the hoop drumstick has enjoyed widespread use with other tribes for nearly two centuries. Maximilian's expedition encountered it in the Minnetaree Scalp Dance and in the Mato tope ceremonial dance,[58] and Eastman depicts it used for the Dakota Scalp Dance (see fig.6).

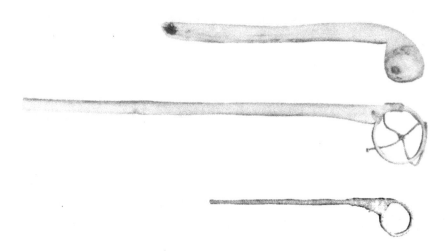

Figure 94. *Top to bottom: Ojibwa warclub (Desbarets, Ontario), lacrosse stick (Red Cliff Reservation, Wisconsin), and hoop drumstick (Bad River Reservation) in the author's collection.* (Photo by the author, 1982.)

Data for the Ojibwa hoop drumstick is minimal; information from their close neighbors, the Menominee, however, indicates the close association between music, games, and warfare among those tribes using the hoop drumstick. The connection between warfare and lacrosse with the Menominee is explicit in their belief that the first war bundle contained a war club, which the Indian then copied for his lacrosse stick. "Both war and lacrosse came from the thunderers, and they directed that the lacrosse racket be shaped like a war club. The game was supposed to resemble a battle."[59] Some dreams dictated to their Menominee recipients that they should make a small war club and keep it in a bundle with a lacrosse ball.[60] (The lacrosse games of the Choctaw, as sketched by George Catlin in the 1830s, were surrounded with ritual and were preceded by the "ball-play dance," with players massed around goal posts, banging their sticks together while singing.")[61] The similarity between a war club, lacrosse stick, and drumstick of the Ojibwa in my collection (fig. 94) suggests a similar close association, if not an actual evolution of form.

The most common type of drumstick among the Ojibwa, however, was a straight stick from twelve to eighteen inches long, its beater end fleshed out with some sort of padding (fig. 95). According to Baker, there is no prescribed mode of construction, singers being free to make and decorate them "the way they want to fix them." His statement is borne out by the great variety of

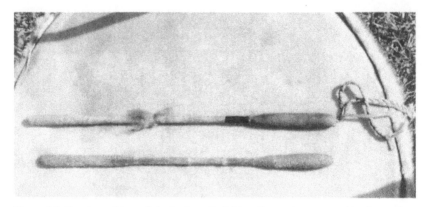

Figure 95. *Two drumsticks made by Joe Rose (Bad River Reservation) on top of his drum. These thinner, fully covered sticks are of an older variety than those commonly used today. Note the braided tassle at the end of one stick, also its fur strip.* (Photo by the author, 1980.)

sticks of this type used with every form of hand drum as well as the ceremonial and secular versions of the dance drum.

Drumsticks of this type figure prominently in stories of the Drum's origin. In a Menominee version, when Tailfeather Woman opened her eyes and saw the Drum for the first time, she heard singing and saw sticks hitting the Drum but moving of their own power without singers behind them.[62] An Ojibwa origin legend tells of the first two singers to play on the Drum, who dropped dead with the first stroke of their drumsticks.[63]

The sticks used with the ceremonial dance Drum are of ash, white oak, or hickory. They tend to be longer than those used with the hand-drum and are certainly more elaborate in design.[64] Barrett gives the Wisconsin Ojibwa dimensions as twenty-four inches long and three-eighths inches wide, while Slotkin describes the Menominee as slightly shorter at twenty-one inches.[65] The beater ends of straight sticks are fleshed out with buckskin or strips of cloth tied with twine. Furthermore, distinctions in their decoration affect their use assignment. Densmore, basing her description on circa 1910 practices, found the drumsticks used by the four principal singers in Wisconsin Drum societies to be covered completely with buckskin, with an otter-fur band and long ribbon streamers.[66] (Cf. Baker's mode of decoration, fig. 97.) That practice, however, appears to have died out by the 1940s, for the Lac Court Oreilles singer John Mike asserted at that time that formerly each of the four head singers had decorated sticks (he mentioned fur and beads), but that now all sticks were plain except for those of the "boss singer."[67] Baker recalls this distinction:

> I remember them sticks when I was a kid. My dad was the first one I ever seen to make a private stick for himself, decorated it. All the rest of them was just wrapped up with rags or something . . . and then later on they put buckskin on it.

The less ornate sticks were kept in a bundle or cloth bag before the west singer at the beginning of ceremonies, each singer simply selecting a stick from the bunch.[68]

The head singer's stick, however, should not be confused with the special dedicatory stick such as the one with the loon's neck described above in the Flambeau-Menominee transfer. Barrett speaks of such a stick as being beaded and used only during the ceremony of dedication when the Drum is hit once with it.[69] Nor is the "boss singer's" stick the same as the special beaded baton that was danced with in ceremonies or the nearly three-foot beaded stick kept by the *oshkaabewis* or belt man who used it to arrange the feathers on his bustle when he was seated.[70]

Such distinctive ceremonial sticks appear to be leftovers from ritual items associated with the Grass Dance drum. The specially decorated Grass Dance stick, however, served more as an office badge than as a musical accessory, although in some instances it was used in the same manner as the Ojibwa dedicatory stick. In the Crow Hot Dance:

> The drum used was held sacred and at first only two special officers were allowed to touch it. One of these held as an emblem a drumstick decorated with feathers and ribbons. . . . After the two drummers had hit the drum four times, the singers sat in a circle round the drum and were then permitted to hit it.[71]

A similar practice was taught the Hidatsa by the Santee when they transferred the Grass Dance to them. Four special officers were designated as "drumstick carriers"; to open the dance, each in turn would strike the drum with his specially decorated stick, while some female relative of his would come forward bearing gifts, which he would then present to an elder member of the society. Wolf Chief, who had served as a drumstick carrier, was careful to make a distinction between the four special sticks and the more common ones used by the singers for the dance itself. Unlike the latter, these were 2 1/2 to 3 feet long, their shafts covered with blue and white strung beads. The beater end apparently was also covered with beadwork, whereas a normal drumstick would be merely fleshed out at the end with rags and

Figure 96. *Young singer at 1980 summer powwow at Red Cliff, Wisconsin, with drumstick typical of the type with the soft beater end, preferred by singers today who use the commercial bass drum.* (Photo by the author.)

possibly covered with buckskin. Additionally, according to Wolf Chief, the special drumstick might have feathers or weasel skins tied to it.[72] This seems to be the origin of the custom surviving in the Drum dedication ceremonies of the Ojibwa.

Most Ojibwa singers today, particularly younger ones, use drumsticks that, be they homemade or purchased, are distinguishable from the older types of stick by their large fluffy beater ends. The beater may be of white cotton in a cat-tail shape (fig. 96) or some synthetic material in a "day-glo" color, such as fuschia or chartreuse. The choice of such a soft substance is clearly attributable to the plastic heads of the commercial bass drum. The older, thinner—and consequently harder—beater end of the older type of stick, while perfectly suited for hide heads, produces less resonance on the modern drums and too sharp a tone for the singers' tastes. Baker eschews the modern drumsticks, referring to them disdainfully as "big fat hairy things."

By contrast, the drumsticks Baker makes conform to a style already in use at Lac Court Oreilles by 1899 (see fig. 34) and still preferred by most older and some middle generation singers. For example, Joe Rose of Bad River Reservation, seventy miles northeast of Baker's home, makes sticks nearly identical to those of Baker. Averaging about eighteen inches long, these sticks are characterized by their uniform thinness, elasticity, and buckskin covering that envelopes the entire drumstick (see fig. 95).

For the substructure of his drumstick, Baker uses discarded fiberglass fishing poles from which he removes all the metal fixtures.[73] One pole will usually suffice for at least two drumsticks; from the thicker end (the part nearest the reel) a single eighteen-inch section is cut, while thinner sections cut to the same length can be taped together to achieve about the same thickness. He then wraps strips of cloth for padding at both the beater and handle ends of the stick (figs. 97-98). The cloth fleshes out the stick to about a one-half-inch thickness and extends inward from the beater end for approximately six inches, and from the handle end for about four inches. Before the stick is covered with buckskin, the cloth padding is held in place with thread, which is wrapped crisscross and tied around it. From photographs, it is evident that many sticks were formerly left as completed at this stage (cf. fig. 34).

Baker finishes off his drumstick by covering its entire length in buckskin. He stitches the covering together with thread using an overlapping whipstitch to pull the edges together until they abut. A single buckskin strip may be cut in a shape to allow for the

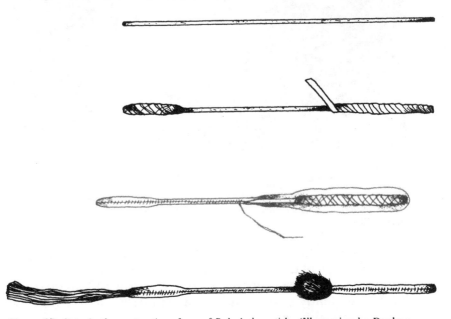

Figure 97. *Steps in the construction of one of Baker's drumsticks.* (Illustration by Daphne Shuttleworth.)

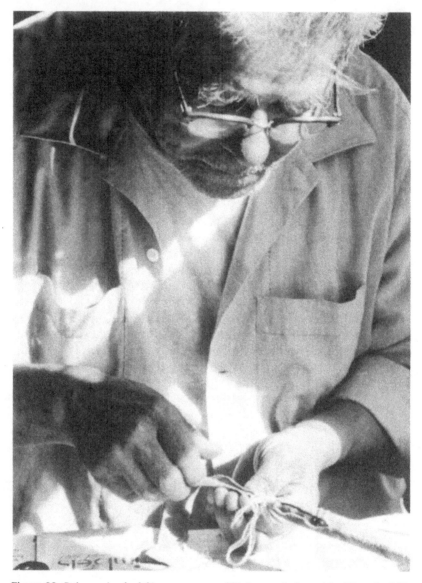

Figure 98. *Baker sewing buckskin cover on one of his homemade drumsticks.* (Photo by Mike Herter, 1974.)

fleshed out portions of the stick or three separate pieces may be used, one each of the same width to cover the handle and beater, a thinner one to cover the bare section of plastic rod. In this case, Baker frequently covers the two splices between sections with black electrical tape.

In contrast to the simpler unadorned stick used today by most

Ojibwa singers, Baker's stick, he feels, is prepared just as is his drum, to offer some visual beauty beyond its mere musical function. Pointing to a stick not yet covered with buckskin, he noted, "Years ago this would have been alright for you to hit that drum with, that's OK, but I finish them up so they look good, that's the regular custom. I make that decoration so that she'll look good."

As final decorative elements, Baker sews a long buckskin fringe at the end of the handle and a strip of beaver or otter fur at the base of the beater. (Joe Rose follows the same practice but uses straps of braided leather as a fringe; see fig. 95.) Historical accounts describe similar elaborately decorated sticks for which long ribbon streams were used in place of buckskin fringe.[74]

Drum Covers

Ceremonial Drums are accorded as much respect when not in use as they are during ceremonies. The Drum is protected at all times; just as it is never meant to rest on the bare ground, it also must be covered when idle. Such a covered instrument is referred to as a "closed Drum," the duration of this condition ritually prescribed.[75] (Similarly, to uncover the instrument is to "open up" the Drum [see fig. 99].) A Drum is kept closed in its owner's house, where it is treated much like a religious object in a shrine, with a dish set before it to receive tobacco offerings. In some homes small kerosene lamps are kept burning before Drums, much like votive candles before a saint's statue. Densmore provides a typical picture:

> [The Drum] was placed on a low box in one corner of [Bijikens's] room [in his house]; the box and the floor around it were covered with a clean white quilt. Beside the drum were the various articles belonging to it, the pipe filled and ready for use, and the drumsticks in neat cloth cases.[76]

The common Ojibwa (and Menominee) method of covering a drum is with a deep cloth bag slightly larger in circumference than the drum (fig. 99). The bag, frequently of mattress ticking with a drawstring, serves not only to cover the instrument but also enables it to be carried. Although it is possible to transport the drum by one of its straps (see fig. 55) or by bunching up a blanket or sheet around the instrument and carrying it by the gathered edges of material (fig. 100), the bag manufactured for the same purpose has a neater appearance and avoids the risk of the blanket covers coming untied.[77] The deep carrying cover

Figure 99. *Drum owner folding the carrying bag for his instrument. Note the fully beaded head and hand symbols on the tabs.* (Photo by Robert Ritzenthaler, 1941, courtesy Milwaukee Public Museum, neg. no. 5903.)

Figure 100. *Joe Rose, singer and drummaker, carrying his drum by means of a blanket, which also serves as its cover.* (Photo by the author, 1980.)

facilitates draping the drum over one shoulder, while the bunched knot offers a firm handle. Furthermore, the bag enables some drum keepers to suspend the Drum in the home. Hoffman provides a sketch of a Menominee Drum hung this way in a corner of a room from a rod fixed into the two walls.[78] Beneath the suspended instrument is a mat on which rest the drum pipe and dishes containing the customary tobacco (?) offerings together with the tobacco box and another folded cloth. (Bushnell visited a large wigwam north of Ely, Minnesota, in the winter of 1899, where "a carefully wrapped drum" was kept in one corner with its owner sitting on the ground near it. This could just as well have been a medicine drum as a Dance Drum.)[79]

In the literature on dance drums it is not always clear whether by "cover" an author refers to an actual covering bag, such as described, or whether is meant the skirt and/or belt of the drum, which, of course, "cover" the frame and lacing between the two heads. Usually, these side covers seem intended if elaborate decoration is mentioned, viz. Rohrl noting that the women of the Mille Lacs Drum societies fix up "the beaded coverings for the drums" in preparation for the fall and winter dances.[80] Still, there have been instances where a specially designed cover has been created in addition to a carrying bag. Such was the square cloth placed on top of the Johnny Matchokamow Drum when it rested in a corner of his house. (Although the Drum had been received from the Flambeau Ojibwa in 1928, this particular cover was not made until 1950.)[81] Visually striking, the handsome applique cover duplicates the ceremonial designs and colors of the drumhead but additionally includes the same symmetrical leaf motif in each corner and three five-pointed stars on each side of the yellow stripe down the middle, the designs reflecting the background color (red or blue) of the opposite half. The corners of the square cover are slightly rounded and the edges of the material trimmed with ribbon.[82] Variations in design for such covers, according to Johnny Matchokamow "depend on how you [are] going to treat that Drum."

Such attention to a "closed Drum" is further indication of the anthropomorphism inherent in attitudes toward the Drum. In the case of the Matchokamow Drum, it was provided with considerable comfort as it "rested" on a table in the northwest corner of the room.[83] On the table was a folded blanket beneath a two-foot circular rag mat, which cushioned the Drum; the Drum itself was in a carrying bag of ticking closed with a drawstring, the bag in turn covered by a clean white bedsheet—a luxury item rarely afforded by its Zoar custodians.[84] Finally, the specially designed cover was draped over the top of the Drum, much as an idle chalice resting on a credence table is adorned with a paten and cover of linen.

To make the cover/carrying bag for his 1970 drum, Baker selected a heavy cotton material patterned in red and blue stripes over white, his choice perhaps influenced by the ceremonial connotations of the colors. Although patterned in more than one color, the texture of the material and weight of the cloth together with the overall design effect are not unlike ticking. He cut the cloth in two pieces: a circular bottom piece twenty-one inches wide, slightly larger than the bottom of the twenty-inch drum, and a rectangle that when sewn together forms a tube eighty-eight inches round and forty-three inches deep. (The lines in the pattern run around the tube, parallel to the top opening.) The bottom of the tube was gathered every few inches and sewn to the circular bottom piece; a four-inch vent was left at the top where the material met to permit insertion of the drawstring into the 1 1/2-inch hem around the open end.

Carrying bags of this type were common at Lac Court Oreilles. When drums were displayed or played upon without being supported on legs, it was customary simply to peel the bag down and leave it in place around the bottom of the drum. Each of the three ceremonial Drums shown in figure 77 show this despite the many other coverings and mats beneath them. Baker leaves his secular drums "open" in this way in one corner of his house. When the drum is supported on its legs, however, usually the bag is folded and placed between the drum and the stand that holds the legs.

Variants

Because all dance drums conform to a standard type, presumably based on the original Drum, technically speaking they are all variations of one design. In fact, the Ojibwa, in considering all drums to be related, recognize this conformity. The situation is somewhat analagous to the phenomenon of "tune families" in folksong: that is, versions of a given melody can be assumed to be related having descended from a common source. By rewording Samuel Bayard's classical definition of tune families, we can fairly well explain the evolution of the multiple forms of the dance drum "family," not only among the Ojibwa but among the other peoples who subsequently received the drum:

> These drums taken together show basic interrelations by means of constant correspondence in their mode of construction and decoration and presumably owe their mutual likenesses to descent from the first Drum that has assumed multiple forms through processes of variation, imitation, and assimilation.[1]

Throughout this study we have observed how the Ojibwa have been free to vary the tradition in building new drums. No two dance drums are exactly alike; variation in the design of a drum is freely indulged in even by the same builder, as we have seen in Baker's case. Nor except for the drumhead decoration is there any ritual insistence on slavish imitation when a new drum is constructed. Still, despite the variety of such elements as beadwork styles or the decorations of legs, one can recognize a given drum as belonging to the "family" through the common features shared by all its members: the relative size of the instrument and its rawhide heads, curved support stakes, skirts, belts, and tabs. All are combined to distinguish the traditional dance drum from the commercial bass drum widely used by singers today.

There are, however, examples of Ojibwa handmade dance drums that, while owing their inspiration to certain design features of the prototype, are nevertheless sufficiently distant from it in other ways to comprise a category outside the tradition. These are the drums I have chosen to call "variants." Some are selective in their imitation of the dance drum by incorporating only one or two features of the model; others are fanciful reexpressions of the ceremonial Drum; still others bear only vestigial reminders of the orthodox dance drum in some subtle way, suggesting that the builder may not have been consciously aware of the source upon which he drew. Because it is impossible to classify these variants according to types, it is more fruitful to discuss each instrument individually, drawing attention to those features that relate it to the traditional drum and those in which it departs from it.

We have noted, for example, that drumhead decoration was subject to variation—the Kemewan Drum for one, with its six horseshoes along the yellow stripe, or the Albert Reagan Nett Lake Drum, where the stripe itself is black instead of yellow. The Woman's Dance drum, itself a variant if only because of its smaller size, shows no discernible conformity in its drumhead decoration. While Baker's drumheads of this genre are left in their rawhide state without decoration, examples of painted heads on Woman's Dance drums are plentiful. The head on the "Ladies' Drum" at Mille Lacs was entirely red;[2] a Menominee example in the Heye Foundation collection is divided into the red and blue fields of the ceremonial Drum, not by the yellow stripe but by juxtaposed blue and red stripes adjacent to their opposite colors. When I asked Baker why the yellow stripe was absent from the Woman's Dance drum, with his forefinger he silently described a circle in front of him, meant to indicate that the movement of the dance was circular and facing the drum.

The absence of the yellow stripe from the Woman's Dance drum, then, would seem explainable as follows: on the ceremonial Drum, the stripe symbolizes the path of the sun from east to west. The ritual requirements of orienting the path as well as putting the Drum up at sunrise and taking it down at sunset would seem to bind the participants in a Drum Dance to be encompassed by the passage of "sacred time," as it were, while normal everyday secular events are halted.[3] Because the Woman's Dance is basically a secular event, then, which can be held anytime and takes place outside the dance enclosure (see fig. 27), the decoration of its drumhead omits the symbolic reference to the passage of sacred time.

Another Drum with unusual head decoration is the Henry Davis Drum. Other features of the instrument and the Davis rite itself that depart from tradition have been enumerated: the hawks on all four tabs, Canadian dimes as pendants, and the special Virgin's Songs. Although the three ceremonial colors have been painted on the heads, their design is peculiar to this instrument: the top head has a red ring around its circumference and a red, yellow, and blue curved stripe intersecting it about a third of the way in. (This must be what Rohrl calls the

"Rainbow Drum.")[4] Rather than the bottom head decorated with a repeating design, as is the case with ceremonial Drums, the head is completely red with a small blue ring in its center.[5]

One variation in drumhead decoration of which there are several known examples is the imposition of a Thunderbird figure over the traditional three-color background. On the Maggie Wilson Ontario Drum, this particular design was dictated to her in a dream. As Ruth Landes points out, painting drums according to such "mystic directions" was one way of providing a "memento of the manito bond."[6] One interesting depiction of the Thunderbird is on a drum in the Madeline Island Museum (fig. 101). The instrument's diminutive size, seventeen by fifteen by

Figure 101. *Thunderbird Drum in the Madeline Island Museum. The zigzag lines above each arm and extending from the figure's right arm signify spirit power; the feathers hanging from the arms and tail show that a Thunderbird is meant to be represented.* (Photo by the author, 1979.)

nine inches, and dream symbolism suggest that the drum must have been built for some special purpose, probably for private devotionals, since its smallness would preclude more than one performer. Although no documentation accompanies the instrument, from the beads on it the drum appears to be relatively old (it lacks any of the later faceted or metallic beads). The

Thunderbird figure is greatly anthropomorphized, with its nearly human appearance. It is clear, however, that a Thunderbird is intended by the beadlike cap, feathers extending from the arms, and zigzag lightning bolts emanating from the head. The background colors also depart somewhat from the standard design—light blue instead of red, for instance.

The origin of these Thunderbird designs is fairly obscure. Occasionally they were put on *mide* drums. Coleman describes one such design, the spirit divided into half red and half blue.[7] The prototypes for the design may have been the decorations often found on circular Plains shields, where a large Thunderbird will be represented sometimes with its wings spread across the diameter of the shield, much like the yellow stripe of the Drum. The Denver Art Museum collection includes such a Sioux shield dated circa 1890.[8] A similar design is found on a pre-1902 double-headed Pawnee drum. Its top head is divided by the wingspan of a large Thunderbird dividing the background colors into approximately equal size blue and yellow fields. Additionally, twelve small swallowlike Thunderbirds are arranged against the yellow background.[9]

The David Goss (possibly Guss) Moon Drum in the Heye Foundation collection is a curious Plains Ojibwa variant. The early date ascribed to it suggests it to be a transitional type somewhere between a Grass Dance and a Drum Dance drum. The instrument shares many elements with the ceremonial Drum: its four legs, 2 1/2 feet long, are each wrapped with red and blue cloth just above the support crotch carved into the leg. The eagle feathers hanging from their ends have their tips wrapped in blue or red flannel, with some blue and red bead windings. The head, however, is most unusual, having been left in a plain rawhide state except for some inscriptions, as follows: painted in yellow is "CHIEF = 2 / MOON DRUM June 18.76"; written in pencil to one side of this but now nearly illegible is "War Dance [?]" and "David Goss 18.78." The signing of names and places on drumheads is a custom still practiced at powwows on the Plains, although the meaning of these inscriptions is not documented.[10]

In making drums today, some craftsmen take a very liberal approach in incorporating one or more aspects of the design of the traditional ceremonial Drum. As already mentioned, the John Keeper Four Winds Drum (see fig. 10) in most respects resembles the traditional drum except for its legs. Rather than bending outward, they loop inward at their tops so that they resemble the hoop drumstick. Certainly one of the most prolific drum builders among the Ojibwa today is Fred Connors of Bad River Reservation, Wisconsin. He has built over the years hundreds of drums; at one time, he tells me, he had thirty-five under construction in his house. Although his instruments are made in a variety of styles and sizes, all can be shown to be dance drum variants in one or more of their details.

The Peterson drum (fig. 102) purchased from Connors as a souvenir item circa 1970 is a diminutive version of the dance

Figure 102. *Secular drum by Fred Connors of Bad River Reservation. Note the fur strip at the bottom as well as top circumference and the wooden stick carved to resemble a stick fleshed out with rags.* (Photo by the author, 1979.)

Figure 103. *Another secular drum by Connors with unusual legs that incorporate deer antlers to effect the curve. Note the deer hoof support hooks and Thunderbird beaded tabs.* (Photo by the author, 1980.)

drum measuring only eighteen inches across and eight inches high.[11] Over the frame the builder has laced together white buckskin in place of rawhide heads of a larger animal. As may be noted in the photograph, the top head has been torn, undoubtedly because such thin skin will not stand up under severe pounding. The curved legs with their eagle feathers and fur bands conform to tradition; the use of two fur strips—one each around the top and bottom—however, depart from it. Two of the three drumsticks pictured show an interesting variation of the lozenge-shaped stick such as is made by Baker and Rose (who lives near Connors). Rather than fleshing out a beater end and covering it with buckskin, Connors has imitated its shape and appearance by carving the entire stick; the beater end is left intact with bark, the length of the handle reduced in circumference through whittling.

One of Connors's most fanciful variants, the Miller drum (fig. 103), was for several years used in a small "Indian Pageant" for tourists in front of a tavern in Mercer, Wisconsin.[12] Probably its most unique design element are the legs that utilize deer antlers at their ends to continue the bend and inverted deer hoofs as supporting hooks. Consistent with the builder's incorporation of "products of nature" is the stand used to hold the legs in place. Whereas the stand built for the Peterson drum is made from commercially available planks, here Connors has used simple

Figure 104. *Fred Connors with his otter drum. Note the two fur strips, pendants which come from the middle of the top strip, also the use of small eagle feathers on the legs in addition to the larger ones.* (Photo by the author, 1980.)

unhewn branches from a tree much as they might be found in the forest. Other unusual features of this drum are the diamond shaped tabs with Thunderbirds on them, of which there are three (instead of the customary one) between one leg and the next, and the decor of the drumhead with a representational symbol (the Thunderbird) and an abstract design that seems to incorporate an arrow. (If this is indeed an arrow, it may represent a "signature." Connors's Indian name is Chief Strange Arrow.) The two designs are paired opposite each other and between the drum legs exactly as are tabs on ceremonial Drums.

Connors's largest dance drum, shown in figure 104, measures thirty-seven inches wide and was built in the summer of 1979.

Figure 105. *Commercial bass drum decorated with design features of the ceremonial Drum: the red, yellow, blue stripe across the middle of the top head is made from plastic tape; the "fur" completely covering the side of the drum is of an orange synthetic material.* (Photo by the author, August 1980, Red Cliff Reservation.)

The buffalo hide used was obtained at considerable trouble and expense. The side decorations are unusual: in place of a skirt, the wooden frame is simply painted in a diamond pattern and, as with the Peterson drum, two fur bands, evidently from different animals, surround it. The round metal discs are used in the way Baker impales crossed ribbons with brass tacks over his fur strip. Most uncommon, however, is the arrangement of the bead and buckskin thong pendants brought out through the center of the fur strip.

Another unique feature of the drum's design is the arrangement of eagle feathers on each leg. The long feather hanging from the end is typical, but the addition of three small feathers spaced a few inches apart is not. On traditional drums, if more than one feather was used per stake, they were of the same length and usually hung together at the same point (see fig. 81). Whether or not the spacing of the feathers here was inspired by the prongs along the deer antlers on the legs in figure 103 is not known, but visually the effect is similar. The use of an otter design in the center of the drumhead seems to derive from the earlier practice of depicting animal *manidoog* on hand-drums. Otter is very sacred to the *midewiwin* and figures prominently as a spiritual leader in the legend of the tribe's migration west.[13]

There have been instances recently in which the commercial bass drum has somehow been altered or adapted to conform to certain design features of the traditional dance drum. For example, a drum currently being completed by a group of Ojibwa school children in Detroit Lakes, Minnesota, uses the frame of a bass drum that has been stripped of its heads and hardware to accommodate rawhide drumheads in the traditional manner. Instead of curved stakes, for support this drum is suspended from the simpler functional ones (cf. fig. 85). In place of attached hook projections, crosspieces are doweled through the support leg and drum straps are looped over these to raise the instrument.

Another bass drum left intact but decorated in a manner reminiscent of ceremonial drums was photographed by the author in 1980 at a summer powwow on Red Cliff Reservation, Wisconsin (fig. 105). How consciously aware of the traditions behind their efforts the young Ojibwa were who designed the decoration is not known. Consistent with the plastic heads of this store-bought drum are the modern materials added to it: the red, yellow, and blue stripes across its diameter were effected with plastic tape and in place of a strip of animal fur around its top, the entire side is covered with orange synthetic fur, such as is sometimes used on beater ends of modern drumsticks.

Appendixes

The Dog Feast

The first of the following two accounts of the Dog Feast is as it was taught by the Santee to the Hidatsa around 1880 at the time they transferred the Grass Dance to them. The information was given to Gilbert L. Wilson in 1914 at Fort Berthold, North Dakota, by the Hidatsa Wolf Chief. The second account, by Frances Densmore, is her composite creation, published in *Chippewa Music-II* (1913), pp. 173-80. She based her information on her own witnessing of a ceremony at Leech Lake, Minnesota, during Fourth of July ceremonies in 1910, and corroboration from the Ojibwa Meckawigabau at Lac du Flambeau, Wisconsin. From Densmore's text I have edited out principally her musical transcriptions of the songs and analyses based upon them. To provide the reader with some impression of where music is performed in these ceremonies, the text is presented in UPPER CASE during those portions of the ritual in which singing occurs.

Santee/Hidatsa, circa 1880

When the society was ready to eat, the officer with his skewer . . . took up one of the kettles of [cooked dog] and set it between the two big rear central posts of the earth lodge. Then he went back to one of the three other officers who wore the feather [belts] and asked for his own [belt] and brought it and laid it before the kettle. So did he also with the other three trails. THE FOUR OFFICERS NOW KNELT DOWN EACH BEHIND HIS OWN TRAIL AND THE SIX OR SEVEN . . . DRUMMERS . . . BEGAN TO SING [during which] THE FOUR OFFICERS DANCED, KNEELING WITH THEIR HANDS RESTING PALM DOWN ON THEIR THIGHS, IN FRONT. THE OFFICERS DID NOT SING, ONLY DANCED: BUT NOW AND THEN THEY RAISED THEIR HANDS, PALM DOWN, WITH ARMS EXTENDED OVER THE FEATHER [belts] . . . AS IF PRAYING OR ELSE ASKING A BLESSING UPON THE [belts]. THE SONG WAS SUNG FOUR TIMES, WHEN IT CHANGED AND THE FOUR OFFICERS AROSE AND DANCED BACK THEN FORWARD TOWARD THE [belts]. THE FOURTH TIME THE SKEWER CARRIER CAUGHT UP HIS [belt] AND PUT IT ON.

[This is followed by censing with sweet grass smoke, ritual feeding of the feathers on the belt, and offering food to the cardinal directions. Later in the ceremony, a performer dances around a dog's head, each time pointing his skewer at the dog's head as if he were going to spit it on the skewer, at the same time he cries, "Hu'i, hu'i, hu'i."]

Iron Cloud [the Santee teaching the Hidatsa] arose and spoke, "You feather belt owners take up your belts; they are yours and I have taught you our rites. . . . Bull-against-the-Wind, do you take the dog's head out of the kettle and put it in a small pan and place it on the west of the fire between the two big west posts of the lodge. [The group gathers, a SONG IS PERFORMED, taboos against sexual intercourse and the dropping of food are mentioned.]

"Now distribute the food," said Matsiwashte to the three feather belt wearers. "Cut the dog meat into small pieces and let everyone in the lodge have a piece as his share. And you, Bull-against-the-Wind,choose four men. If you wish they may be men who have made first coups on enemies; or they may be four men who have been war party leaders, but for whatever war experience you choose them, that experience must be the same for all four. These four men are chosen that they may tell their various honours and rehearse their deeds." [The selection takes place one at a time, each is led and seated beside the dog's head.] These four wounded men now sat around the dog's head which rested on a pan placed between the two rear posts of the lodge. SOME OF THE OLD MEN OF MY TRIBE NOW BEGAN TO SING A GLAD SONG. [Each then rehearses his story of surviving a wound in turn.]

Ojibwa, circa 1910

The four chief actors in the ceremony were two Chippewa representing, respectively, the oc'kabe'wis (aide or messenger) of the entire Drum-presentation ceremony and the [aide] of the Dog Feast and two Chippewa representing the Sioux [enacting the ritual teaching of the ceremony to the Ojibwa]. These men wore elaborate native costumes and feather garments [belts]. . . . THE FIRST SONG WAS SUNG AS THE MESSENGER OF THE DOG FEAST BROUGHT IN THE KETTLE CONTAINING THE COOKED DOG. HE PLACED THIS KETTLE NEAR THE ENTRANCE OF THE CIRCLE AND DANCED DURING THE SONG; when the song was finished he removed the kettle to the western side of the enclosure. . . . DURING THE [next] SONG THE FOUR MEN KNELT ON THE GROUND, THE TWO [aides] ON ONE SIDE AND THE TWO MEN REPRESENTING THE SIOUX ON THE OTHER SIDE OF THE KETTLE AT A DISTANCE OF ABOUT SIX FEET. AS THE SONG WAS SUNG, THEY RAISED THEIR ARMS HIGH ABOVE THEIR UPTURNED FACES, THEN LOWERED THEM UNTIL THE PALMS OF THEIR HANDS ALMOST TOUCHED THE GROUND. THIS WAS REPEAT-ED FIVE OR SIX TIMES, THE SWEEPING DOWNWARD MOTION OF THE ARMS BEING SIMULTANEOUS. THEN [without interruption] THE SECOND OF THE GROUP OF SONGS WAS SUNG, THE MEN RISING AND DANCING AROUND THE DRUM, LED BY THE [aide] OF THE DRUM WITH THEIR HANDS EXTENDED IN TURN TOWARD THE NORTH, EAST, SOUTH, AND WEST.

AFTER DANCING AROUND THE DRUM THE FOUR MEN SIDE BY SIDE, WITH ARMS UPLIFTED, ADVANCED TOWARD THE KETTLE CONTAINING THE DOG. AS THEY APPROACHED THE KETTLE, THEY LOWERED THEIR HANDS, EXTENDING THEM OVER IT. THIS WAS DONE SEVERAL TIMES, THE MEN FORCIBLY EJACULATING "HO HO HO HO" [ritual cadences from the *mide* ceremonies]. THE LAST TIME THEY LOWERED THEIR HANDS RAPIDLY, AS THOUGH ABOUT TO STRIKE THE KETTLE. This motion was the signal for the drumming and singing to cease.

THIS SONG WAS FOLLOWED BY A GENERAL DANC-ING SONG, THE OC'KABE'WIS SIGNALING ALL TO RISE AND DANCE. After [the general dancing song] the [aide] of the Dog Feast took a small piece of meat from the kettle. It was said that he selected the piece nearest the head of the dog and that he took it on a small spoon fastened at the end of a long stick. AFTER DANCING AROUND THE DRUM HE PRESENTED THE PIECE OF MEAT TO THE OWNER OF THE DRUM WHO ACCEPTED AND ATE IT.

[Then] the head of the dog was taken from the kettle and placed in a pan at the eastern side of the dancing circle. THE [aide] OF THE ENTIRE DRUM-PRESENTATION CERE-MONY THEN DANCED SEVERAL TIMES AROUND THE DRUM after which he selected four men from the assembly, leading them forward one at a time and seating them beside the pan. These were warriors of the tribe who had distinguished themselves by deeds of valor. THEY ATE THE MEAT FROM THE DOG'S HEAD . . . [then] returned to their places. . . . [WHEN THE WARRIORS SONG WAS SUNG] THE WARRIOR WHO WAS FIRST SELECTED DANCED AROUND THE DOG'S SKULL, WHICH HAD BEEN TAKEN FROM THE PAN AND LAID ON THE GROUND. After dancing he made a speech regarding one of his most distinguished victories and SANG A SONG COMMEMORATING THE EVENT. A SIMILAR COURSE WAS FOLLOWED BY EACH OF THE THREE OTHER WARRIORS WHO HAD EATEN OF THE DOG'S HEAD. . . . At the conclusion [of these war songs] the kettle containing the remainder of the dog was passed to women of the company, some of whom ate small pieces. The kettle was then passed to the men and in a short time the feast was concluded.

The Lac Court Oreilles Drum Dance, circa 1940

The following account is an edited version of Robert Ritzenthaler's fieldnotes on the ceremonial Drum Dance as practiced on Lac Court Oreilles Reservation in the early 1940s. This information was given to him by John Bisonette and can be found in notebook 9, pp. 11-41, in the archives of the Anthropology Department, Milwaukee Public Museum. An additional copy of Ritzenthaler's fieldnotes is deposited at Columbia University.

The Origin of the Drum Dance

A Sioux girl, to escape the United States soldiers who were pursuing her people, hid among some lily pads in a pond near an army encampment. A spirit came and told her to follow him. They went into the camp and she sat down and ate right with the soldiers, but because she was invisible, no one saw her. Then the spirit told her to make the big Drum and described just how to do it. When the army caught up with the Sioux, the people were dancing with the new Drum and the soldiers became so absorbed in watching the dance that they forgot to fight. As a result, peace was made.

The Drum Equipment

The John Stone Drum is slightly different from the other two Lac Court Oreilles Drums. When they gave it to John, they told him this was the "boss Drum" (*ogimaa dewe'igan*) and that it was the first one like that ever made. It only has two beaded pads hanging on the sides instead of the usual four because there are only two drum heaters on the John Stone Drum. Also the drumhead has six horseshoes painted on it along the yellow stripe. No other Drum has this.

If a Drum is given away, the members can get together and make a new one for the owner, like they did with John Stone. A big Drum is made from a wooden washtub, but they are hard to get nowadays. A hole a foot in diameter is cut in the bottom, and the top and bottom of the tub are then covered with a raw hide from a yearling calf. If the calf is any older, the skin will be too thick and won't sound good. Before the heads are put on, however, a strip of leather with two bells on it is stretched across the inside so as not to touch either head. These bells ring whenever the Drum is moved or struck.

The decorations on a Drum are done by the Drum women. They make the four beaded pads for the sides of the drum where the four drum heaters sit as well as the beaded belt (about four inches wide) which goes around the top of the Drum.[1] They also put on the band of otter fur (about two inches wide) around the top rim, sew on the ribbons, bangles, and metal decorations, and also sew on the beadwork and the ribbons on the four stakes.

Drum members talk of the Drum as the Earth, and the yellow stripe down the middle of the Drum head represents the path of the sun. I never heard why they paint the north half blue and the south half red, but I think it is because it is darker in the north and lighter in the south. They used to pass tobacco and try to eat exactly at noon, because at that time the sun would be nearest to them. At that time they would offer the food and tobacco to the sun spirit (*giizis*).

There are usually four beaded pads for the four drum heaters, and each one sits facing his pad. The design for each pad is different: one is a hand (in beads), another a figure of a man holding a flag, another a figure of a man with a red heart, and the fourth a head of a man.[2] I don't know what these mean except that each drum heater must sit by his pad.

Each of the four drum stakes is usually made from a single piece of second-growth hickory. The stake is about five feet long and is rectangular, tapering up to the prong which suspends the drumstrap. From there up the stake is circular. The circular part is beaded and the rectangular part is bound with fringed ribbons—blue for the north and east stakes, and red for the south and west. Stakes are usually set into the ground to a depth of about 1 1/2 feet, and each stake has a feather suspended from its prong. All the feathers are identical, so they can hang from any stake.[3]

Drumsticks are made of hickory or second-growth swamp oak about twenty to twenty-four inches long, about three-eighths inches at the center but a little thicker at each end. The ends are bound with cloth or buckskin to protect the drumheads when beaten.

The Drum Dance

When a Drum Dance is to be held, the four warriors (*ogichidaag*) from each Drum hold a meeting to decide on a date and place. If just one Drum initiates the dance, its warriors send any member of the Drum as a runner with tobacco that has been taken from the tobacco pouch on the Drum to invite the other Drum owners. Sometimes they also mail a dime down to the Saint Croix band, inviting them by letter and telling them that the dime is for tobacco to be put beside their Drum. The members then hold a meeting and smoke the big pipe after singing a few songs, whereupon the Drum owner gets up and tells them when the dance will be held here and that anyone can attend that wants to.

The members of the three Lac Court Oreilles Drums get together at the house of one of the Drum owners the night before the dance is to start and have an evening dance. (The supporting stakes are never set up for the evening dances.) The drum heaters decide how long they are going to dance that evening. One of the warriors gets up and gives a talk in which he hopes that the weather will be nice for the dance the next day and that a good crowd will be there. He reminds them that they already know what is going to take place and tells the drum heaters that it's up to them to decide how long they want to sing.

Around nine o'clock the next morning, the first day of the Dance, one of the drum heaters from each Drum gets his Drum and takes it to the dance ring. The first thing that the drum heaters do is put up the three flags. Then they dig holes for the stakes and set up the Drums, always orienting the yellow band painted on the drumheads to point east and west.

Sometimes those members already there gather around one Drum and sing a few songs while the people are arriving. The Drum women bring food and set it on a table just outside the dance ring. As the members arrive, they deposit their gifts usually on a blanket laid out for the purpose and then go to their assigned places at their Drums. (Later, this bundle of gifts will be distributed to visitors.) After the women have deposited their food outside and laid their gifts on the blanket, they come into the ring and go to the owner of their Drum, give him tobacco, and sit down in their places behind the men gathered around the Drum. One Drum owner then takes some of the tobacco out of the tobacco box next to this Drum and hands it around to the people, putting a pinch in the boxes of the other two Drums as he passes them. The other two Drum owners do the same. These maneuvers are always performed in a clockwise direction.[4]

One of the visiting Indians who is a good speaker then gets up and makes a speech accepting the tobacco and thanking them for it. He wishes them all good luck and hopes for a good day. Then, if three visiting bands were present, the Drum owners would split the pile of gifts into three parts and one Drum owner would take a third of the pile over to one of the old men representing a band, give him a blanket and tobacco for himself, and tell him to give the rest of the gifts to anyone he chose. The other two Drum owners do the same. Then each one of the three visiting elders gets up and thanks them for the gift of the bundle. Sometimes the bundle is then split up among the other visitors right there. This ends the visitors' part in the preliminaries.

After the distribution of gifts, the Drum singers start a song and the people dance, usually until noon. When the singers decide it is time to eat, they sing the bull cook's special song (*nandawaabanjige-nagamon*), the Looking around Song, also called the Hunter's Song, and the three bull cooks get up and dance around the ring once clockwise and then exit. The first one then brings into the ring a pail of food containing, perhaps, wild rice, and sets it down in the middle of the ring. As soon as he sets down the food and tells the singers what kind of food he has brought, they stop and begin another song, the Runner's Song (*oshkaabewis-nagamon*), while the head bull cook gets up and dances once around the pail of food.[5] He stops at the south side of the pail, reaches his hand into it as if scooping up some of the food, and offers the food to the north. Then he stands at the east and makes the same motions toward the west, similarly at the west and north directions.[6] Next he scoops down and holds food up, offering it to the spirit (*manidoo*) in the sky and scoops again, pointing his hand down to the spirit below. Then he dances three times around the pail of food, shaking his fist downward. On the fourth time around he bangs his fist downward hard, and the singers stop. This motion represents the symbolic "killing of the game" he has just brought in. Finally, he calls in certain new members to help him bring in the food and set it on the mats or blankets in the center of the ring, and he fills the plates of each of the visitors. People who haven't brought dishes gather around the food in the center and eat there. The singers and other Drum members remain seated around their Drums where they are fed. (Usually one person brings out food for the members of each Drum.)

After the food has been dished out, one visitor will give thanks to the women who prepared the feast by saying "thank you, Drum women" (*miigwech ogichidaakwewag*) and everybody eats. When the feast is over, the bull cooks and their helpers take the empty dishes and pails back out to the table outside the ring. The singers start a song and the people dance for about half an hour to an hour. Then the speaker (*gaagiigidoowinini*)—there is one to each Drum—gets up, announces that they are going to start the special songs, and designates which Drum they will use. Usually it is the John Stone Drum because it has the most members.[7] Formerly, they used all three Drums and would play special songs for each member of each Drum, but now they "club together" and use just one Drum for awhile. All members of a Drum gather around the Drum and play just one song for all three Drums—for example, they just sing one song for all three speakers.

The Order of the Special Songs for Each Position

1) As the song of the head chief (*ogimaa*) is performed, he gets up and dances and then all can join in. After his song, he "pays for his song" by giving a blanket or something to someone at the dance.

2) Second chief does the same for his song, then

3) head speaker (*gaagiigidoowinini*), then

4) sweeper (*niimi'idiiwigamig genawendang*), then

5) the Drum owner (*dewe'iganan debenimaad*). When he finishes dancing, he takes a quilt he has brought and spreads it on the ground near the Drum.

6) First warrior (*ogichidaa*) puts his gift on the quilt just laid out.

7) Second warrior does the same, as do the

8) third warrior, and the

9) fourth warrior. Then

10) boss, or head singer (*niigaaniiniimi'iwewinini*), who has the special large drumstick, puts his gift on the blanket.

11) The pipe tender (*opwaaganan genawenimaad*) puts his gift

on the blanket. He must fill the pipe four times during the day. After he fills it, he holds it above his head and turns it slowly four times. Then he passes it to the head singer and lights it for him. The head singer takes a few puffs and hands it to the singer at the next stake, then it goes to the third and fourth singers. (This can be done any time during the day.) Then it goes to the four partners of the four singers, then to the head drum heater, then the other three drum heaters, and finally to the Drum owner, who finishes what tobacco is left and gives the pipe back to the pipe tender.

12) The tobacco bag tender (*gashkibidaaganan genawenimaad*) takes care of the pipe if the pipe tender isn't there, but has no other duties at the dance. His job is to keep fresh tobacco in the bag hanging on the Drum while the Drum is in the home. Usually one keeps plug tobacco in there, just putting fresh tobacco in before a dance. He puts a gift down on the blanket after his song like the others.

13) The job of the head drum heater (*niigaanabiigizigewinini*) is to heat the drumhead before it is used to make it tighter. Also, he puts a blanket on the pile of gifts.

14) The second drum heater does the same, as do the

15) third drum heater and the

16) fourth drum heater. If they dance four days, the head drum heater heats the Drum the first day, the second drum heater the second day, and so on.

17) The bull cook (*oshkaabewis*) puts his gift on the pile.[8]

18) The head Drum woman (*ogichidaakwe*) gets up first and then all the women get up and walk around the Drum, each with her partner behind her. Then they each put a gift on the blanket.

They used to have a feather belt and a man to take care of it. He was called *miigwanigijipizoowinini*. When the Drum women were through putting their gifts on the blanket, the singers would perform the belt man's song and he would take the belt off the stick which kept it off the ground and put it on and dance wearing it. Then he would put it back on the stick, and when they sang another song for him he would take it down off the stick again and fasten it on someone else who would then dance. After the dance he would walk over to someone who would unfasten it and receive a present from him.[9]

After a few minutes, the Drum owners get up and divide the pile of gifts into as many parts as there are bands of visitors. As before, the Drum owners give a blanket and tobacco to each old man representing a band to keep for himself. He is also given the rest of the pile and can distribute it to any of his people. Then they dance for awhile—just to general songs, not special ones—and the head warrior gets up and announces that they will sing four more songs (this number varies) and quit. He appoints one of the singers to take the lead when they start these songs.[10] The last two songs are special songs in which the old fellow appointed will dance around the ring four times followed by the others. Before he starts, however, he blocks the doorway with a coat set up to represent a Sioux and the bull cooks start lowering the flags. After he has danced four times around the ring, he points his stick three times at the coat blocking the entrance and symbolically "shoots" it on the fourth. Then he goes out of the ring and the others follow. This used to be done by the man with the feather belt, preferably by someone who had been wounded by a Sioux. Nowadays, there isn't anyone around who has been wounded by a Sioux, so they just appoint some old man to play the role.

Then each of the singers pulls his own stake out of the ground and hands it to the head drum heater, who takes off the feathers and puts them into a box. He puts the box and stakes into a sack, covers up the Drum (only if they are not going to use the Drum that night, however), and picks up the mats. After that he picks up the Drum[11] and leads the other drum heaters (who carry the other equipment) and the singers around the ring to the east, and they all file out.[12] Sometimes they eat right in the ring after the Drums have been taken out. Then one of the warriors announces where the Drum will be used that evening.

Additional Traditions Accompanying a Drum Dance

The Drum is never put on the stakes in the evening nor are special songs performed at an evening dance, for it is just a social occasion for the people to enjoy themselves. The drum heaters decide when to stop drumming and dancing at the evening dances. Also, during the next three days they don't sing any of the special songs—just general songs.

About five years ago at a Drum Dance on "49 Hill" a fellow lost a feather from off his hat while dancing. A person is not supposed to pick up anything he has dropped, so Joe Gares (Martin) picked up the feather and told the story of how he had been wounded in the world war and then gave the feather back to the person who lost it. Dropping something from your dance costume is considered a bad sign, and the person's life would be in danger unless someone else picks up the dropped equipment and tells a story about his bravery.

Sometimes they give away a pony on the second or third day of a Drum Dance. A special song is sung for this and anyone who wants to give a horse to someone will give that person a switch when that special song is started.[13] The person will dance with the switch and imitate the motions of a horse. If a person wants to get a pony this way he will bring some bandoleer bags, moccasins, a shirt, maybe leggings or an apron and then will lay this all in front of some person he knows has a horse. If the fellow accepts these gifts he goes out and either gets his horse and brings it right into the ring or else gets a switch and gives it to the person, which is a promise that he will give him a horse within the next few days.

The second day of a Drum Dance is also used to remove mourning and to clarify instructions for Drum recipients. A mourner's bundle can be given away and the mourning removed, usually on the second day of a four-day dance. This is called "removing the mourning" and the person is "fixed up" right in the dance ring. Sometimes when they are finished "fixing up" a mourner and giving his bundle away, some old man will get up holding an eagle feather and tell a story about an act of bravery in battle with the Sioux. When he is finished, he goes over to the mourner and says, "I am giving you this feather and this story. Wear the feather on your roach at the dances and you can tell this same story in the future because it is your story from now on."[14]

Also, during the second day, if a Drum has just been presented to a group and the new owner doesn't understand all the instructions, he will go over to the leader of the donor band, give him tobacco, and ask him to repeat those instructions that he hasn't understood.

Additional Drum Songs

There must be at least forty to fifty songs for the Drum. Some of the good singers make up new ones, and sometimes visitors from the western bands bring new songs with them.[15] There are also some old ones that were given with the first Drum. Willy Bisonette says there are at least one hundred of these and that he could sing them all day, one right after another.

There are about two dozen special songs for the members. In addition, there are the following:[16]

1) The Horse-giving Song.
2) The Drum Presentation Song, performed before leaving to

give away a Drum. When this is sung, all the people who want to go on the trip get up and dance, pointing their drumsticks toward the place where they are going to present the Drum. The song is called *babaamaadizi-nagamon*, or the Going away Song.

3) The Wounded Warrior's Song.

4) The song performed when a new Drum is made or an old one "fixed up."

5) The Mourner's Song, performed after a person is "fixed up" (i.e., restored). He is required to dance to this.[17]

6) The Old Man's Song. Several old men could get up and dance during this. It is called *akiwenzii-nagamon*.

7) The song performed if a drumhead gets slack. In that case, the head drum heater gets up and dances and then takes the Drum out of the ring to a fire and heats it up to tighten the head.

Filling Vacancies

When a Drum owner dies, another Drum owner takes charge. There always used to be two owners of each Drum, but now only one of the three Drums at Lac Court Oreilles has two owners [see pp. 269]. A Drum owner's place should be filled by his son. Pete Quagon, for example, took the place of his father, Mitchell Quagon. Only the Drum owner's place is hereditary; all other positions are simply filled by ordinary appointment.

If a Drum woman dies, her partner appoints another woman to fill the place. If the chief or a warrior dies, the members get together and appoint another. A vacated singer's place is filled through appointment by his partner. Sometime during the first day of the dance, if one of the singers needs a partner to fill such a vacancy, he will ask someone there to fill it just before his song is performed. Then sometime during the second or third day, the Drum owner will announce the new position, lead the new partner over to his place at the Drum, give him a blanket, and sit him down in his new position. Other singers can give him blankets too and then they play his special song and he gets up and dances, although he doesn't have to pay for it.

When the Drum from Pine Lake was given away here, it was presented to Mitchell Quagon. After about a year, Mitchell resigned and appointed Jim Hart to take his place, whereupon Mitchell became the second Drum owner. When Mitchell died, Jim Hart appointed his son, Pete Quagon, to take the vacated place. When Jim Hart died, the members held a special meeting and sang some songs and drummed for awhile. Then the warriors got together and decided to appoint John Martin as head

Drum owner, so they set a date for a dance a week later and sent a runner with tobacco to tell John that he was wanted at that place on that date. On the appointed day, the members gathered, put up the flag, set up the Drum, and started to dance. During the dancing one of the warriors went over and sat next to John Martin, told him why they were having the Dance and asked him if he'd accept the position. John agreed and the warriors gave him blankets. Then one of the warriors led John to his place between the second chief and the first warrior and sat him down, whereupon they performed his song, while John got up and danced. Then he made a speech saying he would try to do everything that a Drum owner should do. When he sat down, all the members circled around him and shook hands with him. Then they resumed dancing.

Repairing a Drum

Years ago they used to quit if a drumhead broke during a dance. Nowadays, however, if they break a drumhead and only one Drum is being used, they turn it over and use the other side. If there is more than one Drum present and a head breaks, they just move to another Drum.

In 1938 I helped fix up the Jim Hart Drum after we broke the head at an evening dance. They stopped the dance, and after the warriors and the Drum owner talked it over, the head warrior, John Mink, got up and told the people that they had decided to take up a collection right there. They got three or four dollars and gave it to Jim Hart for the hide. When Jim got the hide they had a meeting and decided upon a date to fix up the Drum—the few who were there sending out tobacco to invite the members. Then on that date, five of us men and four women went over, the women bringing some "grub" along. First they passed tobacco and dished out food and Jim Hart spoke, offering that and telling what it was they were here for. After eating they got the untanned hide and the men scraped off the hair while the women fixed up the beadwork on the stakes and the beaded belt around the middle of the Drum.[18] During this time, they had the tobacco box set out and anyone who wished could take tobacco from it and smoke it.

After the raw hide had been scraped, as head drum heater, I laid out a blanket on the floor and put the Drum on it, and the men took off the broken hide and put on the new wet hide, sewing it onto the bottom hide.[19] They hung up the "naked" Drum in Jim's house and let it hang there for eight days to dry.

Then the members came back again, ate, put on the decorations and trappings and set a date for the next day dance, also notifying the Pine Lake band of this event.[20] On that date, after the Drum had been set up, the flag raised, and the tobacco passed, they sang a special song that is used when a new Drum is made. They then sang the head Drum owner's song, and Jim Hart got up and danced around the ring once, whereupon he went up to the drum and faked striking it three times, then on the fourth time he struck it. Then the head singer struck the Drum, then the second, third and fourth singers and the four drum heaters in order, each hitting it only once. After this they sang Jim Hart's song—he was dancing throughout all of this—and after it was over, Jim went over to the Pine Lake group and gave the head member a gift. This fellow then thanked him for the gift and wished the new Drum luck. Then they sang the Hunter's Song and food was brought in and dedicated by the bull cook. After they ate, the special songs were begun.

The Presentation of a Drum

A Drum must not be kept too long, and although any member can suggest that they give a Drum away, it is usually the Drum owner who does so. The "path of the drum" historically is represented in the following diagram:[21]

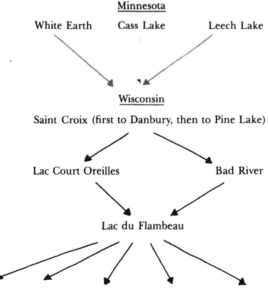

We gave one Drum to the Winnebagos some time ago, but they don't treat them the same as we do. They just use them to have fun with and the drums just go to pieces down there.[22] We took the Drum there in order to get ponies. We all took some bandoleer bags along and everyone came back riding ponies. In those days one bag equaled one pony. Winnebagos had lots of ponies that they got from Nebraska.[23] Years ago when they gave away Drums to Lac du Flambeau they would have a horse and buggy to take the Drum, but most of the people going would have to walk.[24] It took them about three or four days to get over there, and each night where they camped they would have a dance with the Drum and sing that special Drum Presentation Song and all would dance and point to the east in the direction of Flambeau with their drumsticks.

About 1934 old *mishiman* (John Apple), the owner of a Drum here, decided to give his Drum to Flambeau. The members held a meeting and agreed to do so. He picked out an old man over at Flambeau and although one usually sends a runner, he went over there himself, taking the Drum pipe along and some tobacco. He gave that fellow the pipe and tobacco and asked him if he would accept the Drum. The man agreed and smoked the pipe to seal the acceptance. John Apple returned home with a gift of tobacco that the fellow had given him and also brought that pipe back. Then he called a night dance to which all the members came. I was specially invited with tobacco because I didn't belong to that Drum. The Drum was set up and they sang some songs and then John Apple got up and announced that since old John Mike had died recently, the head drum heater's position was vacant and that he had picked out someone to fill the vacancy. Then he came over to me and led me by the hand to that vacant place at the drum, sat me down, and gave me a blanket. Nearly all the members there gave me things. Then they sang my special song and I got up and danced, but didn't have to pay anything for it. Then John Apple gave me a drumstick and I sang and drummed. (I knew most of the songs because I had belonged to a Drum at Saint Croix.)

The pipe tender filled the pipe with tobacco that had been brought back from Flambeau, turned the pipe four times above his head, passed it to the head Drum singer and then around to the other singers and the four drum heaters and then to the others in the house. The head Drum owner finished smoking the pipeful and got up to announce that this tobacco was from Flambeau and that they had accepted the Drum over there.

Then they sang a few songs followed by the special Drum Presentation Song. During that song, those members that wanted to accompany the Drum to Flambeau got up and danced, pointing their drumsticks toward Flambeau to their east, while the women who wanted to go sang through their noses (*zhaabowe*). The singers who didn't want to go dropped out of the song. Then they sang a few more songs, including the Drum Presentation Song, which we sang again and the members danced and pointed their drumsticks as before. Before these songs the Drum owner had asked the warriors when they could go and they had decided to leave in four days.

On the day of departure we drove over to Flambeau in five or six cars, and because I was head drum heater, I took the Drum in my car. Although they had made a special rule not to drink on the trip, some of them got pretty drunk. That evening we got over there and rested and all the remainder of the day and that evening we had a dance with Drum, but just for our members.

The next morning we had breakfast and waited until the Flambeau band started dancing to get into our dancing outfits and go over to the dance ring. They had just one Drum going and were dancing to it, and when we got there they stopped dancing and we marched in—the pipe tender going first and carrying the filled pipe in his two hands. Then came the Drum owner followed by me with the big Drum and then the other members in no special order. As we marched in going around clockwise we all shook hands with the people seated around the ring. When the pipe tender got to the old fellow who was to receive the Drum, he gave him the pipe to smoke and continued on around. When we got back to the entrance, the old fellow showed us where to put the Drum and I set it down on a blanket that I had brought. Then I asked the other three drum heaters to help me set up the Drum on the stakes, and we all gathered around and started a song. John Apple had already told the old fellow to watch closely to see just how the Drum would be set up.

After we had been singing for awhile, the head singer told us we could start the special songs, and we sang them; each member would dance as his song was performed and place his gift on the blanket that the head Drum owner had placed next to the Drum. The Flambeau members listened and tried to learn these songs. After the last special song—the one for the women—the four head singers pulled up their stakes and put them on that pile of gifts. Then John Apple took the bundle, went over to the old fellow, and set it in front of him. After this he went back to get the

Drum, sticks, and tobacco box, which he set on top of the bundle. The old fellow had already picked out the members for each position, so he got up and told the new head drum heater to take the Drum over to where it had been and he put in the stakes and set up the Drum. Then the new owner went over to get the new boss singer, who had the special big drumstick, and lead him by the hand to his place. Then, in order, he got the four singers, the other three drum heaters, the tobacco bag tender, the bull cook, the four warriors, the two chiefs, the sweeper, and the head speaker. When they had all been placed, he went over to the bundle of gifts and gave each member one of the gifts. Then they sang the Hunting Song and the Lac Court Oreilles bull cook brought in a pail of food to show the new members how to do it. They then performed the Bull Cook's Song and he got up, danced, and reached into the pail like he was scooping out some of the food. He offered this to the four directions and up and down and then struck his fist toward the pail of food three times. On the fourth time he went way down with his fist as though spearing the food. Then they ate. (This was around noon.)

After the feast the new members gathered around the Drum and sang the Drum owner's song, but instead of hitting the drumhead directly, they just tapped the Drum on the rim.[25] During this the Drum owner got up with a drumstick and danced around the ring and struck at the Drum without touching it. He danced around the ring again and did the same thing three times, and on the fourth time he struck the Drum once and then the boss singer hit it once, then the four head singers, and finally the others who were gathered around the Drum, and they all started drumming on the head together and finished the song.

Finally, the Drum owner said he would pay for his song and went over and gave a big beaver hide to John Apple. He spread a blanket near the Drum, whereupon they started their special songs, each one putting a gift on the blanket after his song was performed and he had danced. After all the songs were finished, the new owner got up to make a speech thanking all the members of his Drum, gathered up the bundle of gifts, and gave it to John Apple, who divided up the gifts among our members. John Apple then got up, thanked the new owner for doing this, and told him to take good care of the Drum and that he hoped they would get along well. He said that if the new owner didn't understand something he should tell him right then, whereupon the new owner asked him about the order of the special songs.

They sang a few songs and the head warrior announced how many more songs were to be sung. After these were performed, they quit. (The head warrior determines how many songs before they will quit during the daytime dance, while the head drum heater makes the announcement at night.)

That evening all the new and old members gathered at one of the homes at Flambeau and the old members went all through the special songs to teach them to the new members. They didn't use the Drum but instead just tapped on the table with a stick. They had had Drums at Flambeau before, so most of them had once known these songs, but still the old members made them practice singing them nearly all night to be sure that the Flambeau members knew them correctly.

The next day they had a general dance. No special songs were sung, and the old members joined right in with the new. We danced that night too and left the next day for home. We all had a lot of fun at the event, and I came home with two blankets.

Addressing the Drum and Its Care in the Home

They address the Drum in various ways: *manidoo omiigiwewinan* (God's gift), or *menidoowendaagozid* (someone like a spirit), or *manidoo odewe'iganan* (God's drum). I have heard John Stone say that frequently in the evening he would take tobacco and put it in the fire and talk to the Drum, which was left covered, asking for help keeping sickness away from his family, also so that he could provide for them properly.

I had the Drum here last spring for awhile. I laid out a blanket and mat and put the Drum on it. You should never lay the Drum on the bare floor or bare ground nor should any cats, dogs, or kids, or anyone be allowed to bother the Drum while you're taking care of it. The tobacco box is set next to it and must always have tobacco in it. Fresh tobacco should be put in it at least once a month and evening dances should be held about once a week for the Drum and some food and tobacco offered on such occasions. I only did this once during the month I had the Drum here. I uncovered it twice during the month and left it uncovered during the day for about an hour each time. Old John Mink told me that the Drum was like a person and wanted to be unbundled every once in awhile.

Drum Society Structures

Ritzenthaler's fieldnotes include a listing of the membership of three Drum societies—presumably the most active or prominent ones at Lac Court Oreilles circa 1940. Members are listed with the positions each held.(The equivalent positions in the Hidatsa Grass Dance society appear in the left column.) Names of members occupying more than one position are underscored; those with positions on all three drums have asterisks after their names.

Figure 106. *John Martin and his wife at Lac Court Oreilles, circa 1941. At the time, Martin was co-owner of a Drum with Pete Quagon, and his wife served on the Drum as one of the twelve ogichidaakwewag.* (Photo by Robert Ritzenthaler, courtesy Milwaukee Public Museum, neg. no. 5737.)

| Position | | Drum Societies | | |
Hidatsa	Ojibwa			
Owner	Owner	John Martin/ Pete Quagon	John Pete Cloud	John Stone
Chief	Chief	Pete Cloud	John Frog Jim Hart	Jim Billy Boy Tom Butler
Messenger	Speaker	Willie Webster*	Willie Webster	John Mustache, Jr.
	Sweeper	Louis Barber	—	—
	Warriors	John Mink Jim Bennett Joe Martin Mitchell Mustache	John Mustache, Sr. John Stone John Crow Pete Cloud	Willie Webster John Mustache, Sr. John Jack Jim Bennett
	Boss	John Dandy	—	—
(Drum heaters provide this function)	Head singer	John Jack*	Louis Coon	Henry Coon
	West stake (singer)	? John Kekik (deceased, no one now)	John Jack John Mustache, Jr.	Louis Coon John Mike
	North stake	John Barber* John Crow	Willy Billy Boy	Willy Billy Boy Charley Taylor
	East stake	Bob Jack Paul White	Willy Bisonette .	Joe Mike James Mustache
	South stake	Willy Bisonette Jim Billy Boy	John Mike Pete Quagon	John Dandy George Coon
pe tender	Pipe tender	Joe Benton*	Charlie Kaigebe	Max Grover
pe tender	Tobacco pouch tender	Joe Mike	—	—
um heater	Head drum heater	John Bisonette	John Barber	John Barber
"	Second drum heater	John Coon	George Sky	John Coon
"	Third drum heater	Frank James	—	—
"	Fourth drum heater	John Mike*	—	—
Bull cook	Bull cook	John White	Joe Benton	Joe Benton
um women	Drum women	Mrs. Jim Quagon Mrs. Willy Bisonette Mrs. John Crow Annie Dandy Ida White Mrs. Willie Webster Alice White Cadotte Mrs. Joe Martin Mrs. Mitchell Mustache Mrs. Joe Mike Mrs. Pete Quagon Mrs. John Martin	Annie Stone Mrs. John Frog Mrs. Charlie Kaigebe Julia Bisoni Sarah Wade Annie Cloud	Mrs. Sam Carl Mrs. Frank Batice Annie Dandy Mrs. Max Grover Mrs. Willy Billy Boy Mrs. Bennett Mrs. Tom Butler Mrs. Louis Quarters Mrs. John Stone Mrs. Joe Martin
	Young Warriors (Note: the functions of the Hidatsa Belt man may be carried out by the Ojibwa bull cook.)	—	—	Clifford Miller Joe Martin, Sr.
Belt man				
Belt man				
Belt man				
Belt man				
Flag man				

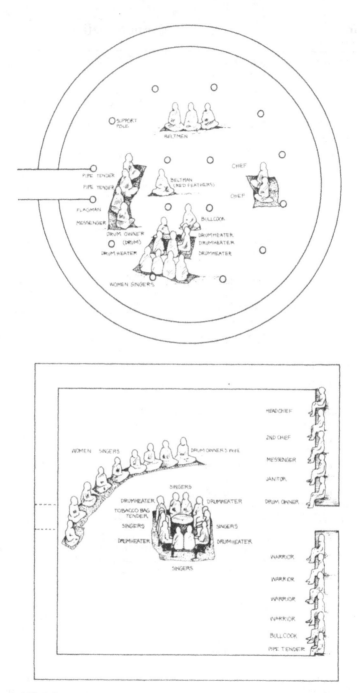

Figure 107. *Relative position of members of the Grass and Drum Dance societies during ceremonies. Big Brave's Mandan earth lodge (top), Like-a-Fishhook-Village, circa 1881, and the John Martin Drum in a Lac Court Oreilles outdoor dance enclosure (bottom), circa 1941. (Illustrations by Daphne Shuttleworth.)*

Soundtrack Transcription
of the Film *The Drummaker*

The Drummaker was filmed on the Lac Court Oreilles and Lac du Flambeau Indian reservations in northwestern Wisconsin in June and July 1974 using a Beaulieu R16 camera in combination with a spring-driven Bolex. Only available natural lighting was used for both interior and outdoor sequences. Sound was recorded with cable-sync, using a Nagra III with Sennheiser 804 (shotgun) and AKG D202 (semidirectional) microphones.

The film begins with a sequence of still photographs showing a ceremonial Dance Drum on Lac Court Oreilles Reservation, 1899; Lac du Flambeau Ojibwa drum tenders carrying a Drum, 1910; an Ojibwa Drum presentation ceremony on Menominee Reservation, 1910; a Drum presented by Lac du Flambeau Ojibwa to the Menominee, 1928; and, finally, William Bineshi Baker, Sr., Lac Court Oreilles singer/drummaker, setting up one of his drums in the Indian Bowl, a summer tourist facility on Lac du Flambeau Reservation, 1974. Except where otherwise noted, all narration is by Baker.

Baker sets up his drum.

They're losing their tradition. They don't care if they have a nice looking drum when they perform, when they have their dances. Now the people don't come down there just to see you dance, they want to see what you use, too. And that's why I don't believe in that marching-band drum for the Indian to use. I believe in our custom.

A closeup of Baker seated at his drum is shown.

There's a *shinaabe* [Indian] drum right there. If I ever take that drum out to show the public, man, I'm telling you I could make money on that fella. But I don't believe in that. I didn't make that [drum] to make money. I made it to show my people the way the drum is supposed to be used when they perform.

As other singers arrive to join Baker at his drum, they are introduced over the public address system by George Brown, Jr., who announces, finally:

And from the Lac Court Oreilles band of Chippewas [Ojibwa], Bill Baker, Bineshi [Baker's spelling of his given Indian name, Bird].

272

Preparing the Hide

Film titles are shown over animated stills of dancing at the Indian Bowl, with Baker as lead singer at the drum. The singers are performing a traditional Ojibwa Woman's Dance Song. Upon completion, the picture fades to Baker in his backyard on Lac Court Oreilles Reservation.

Baker arranges large metal washtubs in which to soak hides.

There's that board, here's that board, what did I tell you? But still that's . . . oh, no, I had it out there, that's right. I had it right here when I had it. But jeez, that trailer's supposed to . . . [a housetrailer he was having moved onto his property].

He sets up tubs on boards, pumps water into pail, and empties it into tubs.

Baker emerges from his back door with a plastic garbage can containing a fresh cowhide to be used for his drumheads.

I suppose you fellas were wondering where that hide was, eh?

He dumps hide in a cardboard box with the help of Ernie St. Germaine and drags it out onto the lawn.

That's good, there, that's good. Just follow me, follow me. . . . Drummaking is the authority that was given to each individual as a member of the Drum [religion], which was passed onto us. We're not originally the establishers of the Drum. The Drum was passed onto us in order to have peace with the other tribal people.

He stretches hide out on the ground.

No, no, you leave that, now pull that one that way. Yeh, mii'iw, mii'iw [enough].

He hands St. Germaine a tape measure.

Now, point that, point, point, no, no, over there.

The two of them measure the hide.

Now, let's see, sixty-eight inches, yeh, that's good, that's good. Now, I'm going to give you the ruler, and you hang onto that a minute. It was sixty-eight inches, now divide that in half.

St. Germaine says, "thirty-four." Baker does not hear him clearly, so he repeats it louder, "thirty-four."

Well, I want thirty-four then, from where you are.

Baker starts to cut hide in two with a penknife.

Boy, that hide dulls a knife quick. That's alright, that's alright, just half an inch.

He puts hide pieces into tubs of water, weights them down with rocks to submerge them.

But this here don't mean nothing, as long as it's the hide . . . that's good, that's it. This here one, that's only just a small piece.

He dries hands with a towel.

Every day, you know, I gotta stir them up and turn them around, you know. And then it will ferment, and then it will sour and I'll get a good scouring on that hide. Well, that's all for now.

Assembling the Drum Frame

He examines and measures metal barrel hoops hanging on a tree, takes two to a group of friends who are reassembling an old wooden washtub, using its original staves, which Baker has saved. Pat Nickens says,

This here's the bottom, up here, you know.

Baker helps to arrange staves.

Yeh, this is the bottom.

Nickens says,

You gotta raise them hoops.

Baker says,

Yeh, you gotta raise them hoops, you gotta raise them hoops up, that's what I say, and then after you get the boards in, then you'll press it down, see, and that forms the barrel, see, tight.

They have trouble holding the staves in position.

It ain't gonna work, Pat, I can see that right now. We've gotta get this [hoop] up. I'll tell you what I'm gonna do, I'm gonna put a tack in.

Baker pounds a tack into one stave to hold hoop in position.

See, we've gotta have one wide board, one at each [cardinal position] post has got to be . . . and now, this one goes in there, my boy, this one goes in there.

Baker's son, William, Jr., notes,

I've got one wide one here, Dad.

Baker arranges staves.

You've gotta have an even four all the way around, see, because that's where them straps [that suspend the drum] are going to go and . . . that's alright, Pat, leave it.

He pounds hoop down using the edge of a file and a hammer.

That's what I'm doing now, you gotta tighten that up. . . . I'm going to get that, I've got to go over there [to the other side of the tub] to get that . . . that's it, that's the way, Pat, now you got it . . . now we're going to, you . . . see, it's out [the shape of the tub], it's warped a little, see oblong this way . . . by God, I believe we got it, Pat, yeh, *mii'iw, mii'iw, mii'iw* [enough].

Further Preparation of the Drum Frame

Inside Baker's house, he rounds the upper edge of the tub with a pen knife, then sharpens knife.

When that Drum was first made, I'm going to tell you something, when that Drum was brought over, the ceremonial war powwow Drum, that was made long before I was born. And this drum I'm making is the Woman's Dance drum, same category as the ceremonial powwow Drum, same thing, and I've seen that done.

He cuts straps from an old belt.

Now it has come to the point where I see my people, they're going beyond that, the modern way of the music, but no, I don't feel that way. That's no Indian drum, that *chimookomaan* [white man's] drum. I suppose they want people to come and see the white man's drum, show the white people they're using their drum. I suppose that makes the white people happy. I'll go over there [to an Indian dance for tourists, promoted by a local white] and take a look, you know, and see. They'll have one, I'll bet there will be one or two of them marching-band drums [used by other Indians], I'll bet you, and then I'll move back home [laughs]. No, I will not participate with a drum like that, I told him [the white promoter] that. I won't sing there [laughs], no, *gaawiin* [no].

He pounds bolts through

That's the reason why, that's why this [cere-

straps to attach them to the tub.

[monial] powwow business is going to pieces, everybody's just monkeying it up. Yeh, I guess I'm too much of an Indian, I guess [laughs]. That's what I say, this [drum] is mine here. I believe in using it myself.

Further Hide Preparation

Outdoors, Baker checks condition of the soaking hides.

Goddamn it, these have been cold nights, you know, they don't . . . look at that, a whole week in there now. They don't ferment like they should, no.

He takes hide piece to hang on a pole suspended between two trees and begins to cut away fat and membrane.

You know, I want to tell you guys something, by God, you know just as well as I do, you can't rush that stuff, you know. You've got to clean the inside of that hide just as well as on the outside. It's going to take a little time, like I told you, but you can't rush that stuff. Now, look at that hide, now. Alright. Soak it. I don't know when that water is going to ferment to work into that hide to get that hair off. I have no choice. And I don't use chemicals, because if I use chemicals, might as well not even make the drum. I gotta take it up there, and I gotta hang it up there on the rack and cut all the fat off of the inside, put it back in the water again. I can't do that in one day. Takes time.

He returns hide to the tub of water and scrapes it with a knife to see if the hair will come off.

No, alright over here, some parts of it is OK, but. . . . If you're going to rush it, what the hell is the use making it, you might as well not, it's no good.

Making Decorations for the Drum

Inside his house, Baker is seated at a table working on drum decorations.

Years ago, when they first made the Drum, they didn't have material like this. They had fur, skin, and that's what they covered the Drum with. They used bear claws, teeth of animals for decoration. Now, since the white man come, well, he had different colors of all different articles. Well, then they copied that from there to decorate their Drum. . . . See, these are curtains, because, you know, the color. The color is the reason why I kept them.

He cuts cloth with scissors.

Yeh, very delicate work, I'm telling you. You don't do this in one day.

He sews seam on cloth.

See, I could use a machine, a sewing machine, but I don't want that. I want to use my own hand power, the way of doing it. And any time you want to examine my drum after it's done, being done and manufactured from machinery, *gaawiin*, no, you won't see that on my drum . . . See, there's two pieces to this [strip of cloth] . . . actually, when they make the drum, it's four pieces, there's four people work on the belt, one woman works on one piece of belt eighteen inches long. . . . And it ain't like I used to be either, you know. I can't sit there, you know, like I used to do the work. No, *gaawiin ayaabe* [no]. Yeh, my eyes get tired, you know, get watery when I look too long.

Obtaining Materials for Drum Legs

In the woods, Baker cuts sumac stems later to be carved and used for drum supports. He shows St. Germaine how he will do this.

Then I cut if off like that, and split that, and hollow that out, and whittle that this way, there, make it so long.

He hands St. Germaine a piece of sumac.

I can make a pipestem out of that, see. . . . Holy—look at the mosquitoes! *Mii'iw* [enough]. We've still got another place down here [where there is more sumac], where old Cadotte used to live, right here, you remember Frank Cadotte, eh? He lived down there, you know.

Further Hide Preparation

In the woods behind his house, Baker cuts more fat from the hides.

Pretty near done with the drum? [laughs]. Jesus Christ, pretty near done with the drum, pretty near done with the drum. . . . Boy, I'm telling you, this ain't no short time work. You know, that gets on a fella's nerves, hurry up, hurry up, hurry up [becomes angry]. You think it's easy. There's no hurry up job on this, I want you to understand that. I'll tell you when it's ready, because I've waited a long time for this stuff already in my life, and there's no sense in just going, now, tomorrow, the next day. No, *gaawiin*. It's according to that, and the way you gotta work. You can't force this thing, no you can't. Hurry up, hurry up, uh uh, I wasn't born in "hurry-up time" [laughs].

He scrapes hides in tub with knife.

Uh uh, nope, one more day, one more day and I'll take it out. One more day.

Carving Drum Leg Supports

In his front yard, Baker cuts, saws, and peels bark from sumac pieces, which will later be strapped to the drum legs from which the drum is suspended when played.

With me, I do it all alone. Years ago they used to help one another. Now it's come to the time where nobody takes interest. Not interested in this stuff.

Dehairing the Hides

Baker drags tub with hides into the woods to drape over a log he uses as a beaming post and begins to scrape hair off hide.

You say, well, we'll do it over tomorrow morning at six o'clock, no, uh uh, but you do it *then* [laughs]. Either you do it now or don't, because there ain't no rehearsal to this. When you start this stuff here, when you do this work for the Indian tradition and culture, you start and you *finish*. . . . That's why I say, you can't do this yourself, you gotta have *time* to do this stuff.

He returns scraped hide to tub, drags it through the woods back to his house. The voice of Jimmy Mustache is heard.

Here, that's something they don't do no more over here. Old Indians like Bill, he knows all about it, I know all about it, but they don't practice it. You try to tell these young kids about it and they just laugh at you, the old Indian traditional ways, you know. They more or less laugh at you now.

Making Drum Decorations

Indoors at his table, Baker jokes in Ojibwa with Pat Nickens and Jimmy Mustache,

Gee, I razz her, you know, quite a lot. You know, that woman, though, she had the right idea about her Uncle Jim, when he

while sewing ribbon onto the drum skirt.

died. And I was up there, and when they had the dinner, up there at that church, you know, at Whitefish [a community on the reservation], and she come by me, and I only spoke to her once before that, you know, when they had that funeral, and she turned around, and she says to me, she says, "Bill," she says, "there's only one thing that I regret." She says, "as much as Uncle Jim always liked Indian dance," you know, singing—he was a good singer, that Jim. He was a good singer. And she says, "Why didn't they have a dance for him with the Drum?" Well, they *could*, you know, because I seen that done at Round Lake [another community just north of the reservation], you know, they use one of them, use that Drum, you know, for a wake. That's what she was talking about. "Well," I said, "why didn't you people speak up?" I said, "You didn't have to bring him in here; he don't belong in here; he don't belong in here [in a Christian church] in the first place." And that's only one thing that I always thought, that she had the right idea for her uncle. And that's what I want them to do when *I* go, I want them to have a powwow with my Drum. Yessir, I already told the kids that. Yessir, when I go, well, that's what I want 'em, to have my wake with that Drum, 'cause I had my good time with the people, and I want them to have a good time with me when I go.

Putting Heads on the Drum Frame

Behind his house, Baker puts hides on washtub for drumheads, cuts them to size, after sharpening his knife.

He cuts slits along edges of the drumheads for the lacing and begins to lace the two heads together.

Boy, these knives you get are pretty sharp, but, by God, when you come right down to cutting these, boy, I'll tell you, it really gets dull. A hide can make a dull knife.

That's what I said before, this here film, that you're showing pictures to the people, that doesn't give them the [spiritual] authority to go ahead and make that Drum. They ain't supposed to make this Drum. They ain't got no authority to make this Drum. I wouldn't even make it if I didn't have the authority. Because it's got to come back from years, like it has been with me. Now, I had the [vision-given] authority to make this Drum a long time ago, back in the thirties. I can make four [sacred] Drums in my life, and I've already made one, and I owned one, and they stole it from me, just like they stole it from here. . . . And forty years from now, after *I'm* gone, what they do, I don't give a damn, but as far as that goes, they ain't got no right to make it.

He finishes lacing and examines it for even tautness.

That's OK, that's OK, because that's gotta be tight, you know. Yeh, that's good, that's alright, that's good. Yeh, that's the way.

Hanging the Drum for Drying

Inside his house, Baker ties drum straps to strings hanging from the ceiling.

All this weather like this, it won't take much to dry [the skin heads]. You can't dry it too fast either. Well, it should hang there at least, well, it will dry in four or five days, but you can't use it right away. You gotta wait a long time before that hide sets.

Finishing Decorations and Attaching Them to the Drum

At his table, he sews ribbon and beads on the tabs, which will hang from the belt at the four cardinal points of the drum.

Look at this, now. You ain't gonna do this all in three weeks. People done this, it took them a year at a time to do this stuff. This is not that hurry up, uh uh. . . . Look what I gotta do yet. I gotta make all them flaps [tabs], just like I got that one . . . Now, as I say, I can take, maybe it'll take me two days to make just two of them flaps, them ear-flaps there. Time, boy, oh, I'll have it done, but that [laughs], that's all hand work, I don't use no machine, all hand work. That's why I want these guys who think they're so goddamned smart, they wouldn't even start to begin to make one of them things. They don't even take time. They'd rather go and buy a drum for a hundred dollars instead of making one for the people. And they don't even dress it up [decorate it]. They ain't anywheres *near* Indian, they don't dress it. . . . See, I gotta nail that dress and then that belt on there, and the flaps, you know.

A view of the belt with the four tabs lying on it ready to be attached is shown.

Our belief is in the four corners of the earth. Everything, everything is four corners, even a song. The Indian song itself is supposed to be sung four times over.

Baker nails decorations to the drum.

And then the moccasin game, they use the same [hand] drum, but it's not painted, it's not the sacred form of the drum. They just make them [secular drums] for the purpose to use. But you take a sacred Chief Dance drum, that's decorated; it's painted with the idea of nature up above—Thunderbird and eagle—great power, spiritual power, the eagle. . . . You know, I want to tell you, I don't know, I've been thinking, like, here, they got some people in Oklahoma that's going to trial there for selling eagle feathers and decorations on their crafts, and I bet you if the Indian goes to trial to fight that case, I bet he'd win, because that honor of the eagle *was* the American eagle, not white man. The white man came over here and took the emblem of the honor of the Indian. That's *his*; that ain't *chimookomaan's* [white man's]. That's just the emblem they use. Took it from the Indian. *Chimookomaan* can't use it. All he does is use it on coins. He says, "In God we trust," and then they don't trust in God, the way they're going now [laughs].

Setting up Completed Drum for Performance

Baker carries drum in sack over his shoulder, enters the Indian Bowl, and sets up his drum in the dance circle.

And I've been denied a lot of things over such things that I've done in this world. And I've tried to help people. And I've been denied. And nothing has ever been offered to me, no. In my custom there, in my tradition of life, nothing ever come forward to me. And I ask my people, I ask people, "Do this for me," "Oh, jeez, no, I can't. Buy gas, you gotta buy gas, or do this." Nobody ever say, "here, here, here," no, *gaawiin*. And everything I get, at the end I have to pay. Always, it always has been that way with me. And then another thing, I'm going to say it right straight out, I don't give a damn if I get anything out of this [film] or not. I don't care, but I want my people to see this, and I want that film here, and I'm going to show it to my people, and after I show it to them, I'll throw the damned thing away, that's the way I feel. But you got it forever [on film], and I haven't. Because I've always got it up here [in my memory].

Glossary of Ojibwa Terms

The spelling of Ojibwa words conforms to the system used in *Ojibwewi-Ikidowinan: An Ojibwe Word Resource Book*, ed. John Nichols and Earl Nyholm, Occasional Publications in Minnesota Anthropology no. 7, Minnesota Archaeological Society, Saint Paul, Minnesota (1979). I am indebted to Earl Nyholm for spellings of words not included in the *Resource Book*.

aabikiizigewinini (-wag)	drum heater
agoogwaajigan (-an)	skirt around the drum
agwaa'isekwewinini (-wag)	bull cook (lit., someone who takes from the fire what he has cooked)
akiwenzii-nagamon (-an)	Old Man's Song
anishinaabe (-g)	Indian (lit., first man, some times shortened in speech to *shinaabe*)
asemaa-onaagan (-an)	tobacco box
baaga'akokwaan (-an)	drumstick
baagak (-og)	small doll representing a skeletal being (a Canadian term)
babaamaadizi-nagamon (-an)	Going away Song
bibigwan (-an)	end-blown duct flute used principally in courtship
bineshii̲ (-yag)	generic term for small bird
bwaan (-ag)	roasters, term applied by the Ojibwa to the Sioux, by inference dog eaters
bwaanidewe'igan (-ag)	Sioux drum, term used to describe the Drum given to Tailfeather Woman in her vision
bwaaniniimi'idiwin (-an)	Sioux dance, term used for the Drum Dance
chimookomaan (-ag)	"long knife" or white man
desaakwa'igan (-an)	frame for resting drum on

dewe'igan (-ag)	generic term for drum
dewe'iganan debenimaad (-jig)	Drum owner
dewe'iganan omiigiwen	a drum is given away, term used to describe a Drum presentation
dewe'igan-okaad (-an) .	drum leg
dewe'inaatig (-oon)	drumstick
gaagiigidoowinini (-wag)	head speaker
gaawe-nagamon (-an)	lit., he is jealous song, known at Lac Court Oreilles as the Jealous Song
gaawiin	no
gashkibidaagan (-ag)	buckskin pouch used to keep tobacco and hung from the west drum support stake
gichi-gami	"The Big Sea" or Lake Superior (cf. Longfellow's "Song of Hiawatha")
gichi-manidoo	Great Spirit
giiwedinong	in, at, or from the north
giizis (-oog)	sun spirit
gikiwe'on (-an)	flag or banner
gimishoomisinaan (-ig)	"our grandfather," name used in referring to the Drum
giniginige.	Indian tobacco made from the inner bark of the red willow and mixed with regular tobacco (lit., he mixes, sometimes spelled *kinnickinick*); more commonly used term is *apaakozigan*)
ikwe-niimi'idiwin (-an)	Woman's Dance; a circle dance accompanied by gift giving
jaasakiid (-jig)	juggler or diviner who uses the shaking tent
jiisakaan (-an)	shaking tent used for divining and prophesying

madwewechigan	musical instrument
makak (-oon)	birchbark vessel or pail used for storing food, boiling water, etc.
manidoo (-g)	spirit
manidoo odewe'iganan	God's drum
manidoo omiigiwewin (-an)	God's gift
mazinibii'igan (-an)	tabs (lit., something with drawings on it)
mazinigwaajigan (-an)	tabs or pouches sewn to the drum skirt as part of the decoration (lit., embroidered with flowers or pictures)
menidoowendaagozid (-jig)	someone like a spirit
midewigaan (-an)	lodge for *midewiwin* ceremonies
midewiwin	religious fraternity of the Ojibwa and other tribes, otherwise known as the Grand Medicine Society
miigis (-ag)	sacred cowrie shell used in *mide* initiations
miigwanigijipizoowinini (-wag)	feather belt man
miigwech	thank you (lit., it is so much)
miiyiw (var. mii'iw)	enough, term used at end of speeches, correspondence, etc.
mitigoons (-an)	little sticks beaten together to attract deer
mitigwakik (-oog)	medicine drum (lit., wooden vessel)
naagaaniinagamod (-jig)	lead singer
naanzhii'iganaatig (-oon)	scraper used for dehairing hides
nandawaabanjige-nagamon (-an)	Bull Cook's Song (lit., looking around song)
netaa-giigidod (jig)	speaker at Drum Dance
niigaanabiigizigewinini (-wag)	head drum heater

niigaaniiniimi'iwewinini (-wag)	boss or head singer
niimi'idiiwigamig	dance hall
niimi'idiiwigamig genawendang (-ig)	sweeper or janitor
ningaabi'anong	in, at, or from the west
ogichidaa (-g)	warriors (possibly a Siouan word borrowed by the Ojibwa)
ogichidaakwe (-wag)	woman warrior, one who belongs to a Drum society
ogimaa (-g)	chief
opwaaganan genawenimaad (-jig)	pipe tender
oshkaabewis (-ag)	aide or messenger, a military function as well as a position within the *midewiwin* and Drum societies
oshkinawe-ogichidaa (-g)	young warriors
waabanong	in, at, or from the east
waabanowiwin	a religious fraternity possibly older than the *midewiwin*
waaganaakobijigan (-an)	archaic term for drum legs (scalp sticks)
zhaabowe	to pierce or flow through something, term used to describe the singing of the women of the Drum meaning that the tone flows through the pinched nose
zhaabowewikwe (-wag)	female singer at the Drum Dance
zhaawanong	in, at, or from the south
zhiishiigwan (-an)	generic term for rattle (cf. *zhiishiigwe*, rattlesnake)
zhizhaakwa'igan (-an)	beaming post or log used for dehairing hides
zhooniyaa (-g)	silver, money
ziibaaska'igan (-an)	jingle, such as on a woman's dance dress

Key to Abbreviated Sources

APNH   *Anthropological Papers of the American Museum of Natural History* 11 (1916).

BI   William Bineshi Baker, Sr., tape-recorded interviews. Transcripts, Archives of the Office of Folklife Programs, Smithsonian Institution.

CC   Frances Densmore, *Chippewa Customs*. Smithsonian Institution, Bureau of American Ethnology Bulletin no. 86 (Washington, D.C., 1929).

CM   Frances Densmore, *Chippewa Music*. Smithsonian Institution, Bureau of American Ethnology Bulletin no. 45 (Washington, D.C., 1910).

CM-II   Frances Densmore, *Chippewa Music-II*. Smithsonian Institution, Bureau of American Ethnology Bulletin no. 53 (Washington, D.C., 1913).

MM   Frances Densmore, *Menominee Music*. Smithsonian Institution, Bureau of American Ethnology Bulletin no. 102 (Washington, D.C., 1932).

RF   Robert E. Ritzenthaler fieldnotes, 1940-41; expense-account books, spiralbound notebooks, photographs, etc. Archives of the Anthropology Department, Milwaukee Public Museum.

SDOH   University of South Dakota American Indian Oral History Project, Part 2. *New York Times* Oral History Program; microfiches of typed transcripts (Sanford, N.C.: Microfilming Corporation of America, 1979).

SOM   Thomas Vennum, Jr., "Southwestern Ojibwa Music" (Ph.D. diss., Harvard University, 1975).

WP   Reports, Hidatsa-Mandan 1914. Gilbert L. Wilson Papers, vol. 16. Division of Archives and Manuscripts, Minnesota Historical Society.

Notes

Editor's Preface

1. Robert H. Byington, ed., *Working Americans: Contemporary Approaches to Occupational Folklife.* Smithsonian Folklife Studies no. 3 (1978; reprint ed., Los Angeles: California Folklore Society, 1978).

2. Ralph Rinzler and Robert Sayers, *The Meaders Family: North Georgia Potters.* Smithsonian Folklife Studies no. 1 (Washington, D.C.: Smithsonian Institution Press, 1980).

3. Robert S. McCarl, "Occupational Folklife: A Theoretical Hypothesis," in Byington, pp. 3-18.

4. Ibid., p. 6.

5. Catherine Fowler, *Tule Technology: Northern Paiute Uses of Marsh Resources in Western Nevada.* Smithsonian Folklife Studies no. 4 (Washington D.C.: Smithsonian Institution Press, forthcoming).

6. Archie Green, "Industrial Lore: A Bibliographic-Semantic Query," in Byington, p. 91.

7. Margaret Mead, introduction to "Visual Anthropology in a Discipline of Words," in *Principles of Visual Anthropology,* ed. Paul Hockings (The Hague and Paris: Mouton Publishers, 1975), pp. 4-5.

History

The Ojibwa and Their Music

1. This is a fairly universal process among most tribes in preparing hides for tanning. Not all of them, however, follow the Ojibwa practice. The Northern Paiute, for example, draw the scraper toward themselves.

2. See Jaime de Angulo and M. Beclard d'Harcourt, "La musique des indiens de la Californie du nord," *Journal de la Société des Americanistes,* n.s. 23 (1931): 196; Alan P. Merriam, *Ethnomusicology of the Flathead Indians* (Chicago, 1967), pl. VI.

3. For a more complete historical coverage, see William W. Warren, "History of the Ojibway Nation," *Collections of the Minnesota Historical Society* 5 (1885): 21-394; Harold Hickerson, *The Southwestern Chippewa: An Ethnohistorical Study,* American Anthropological Association Memoir 92 (Menasha, 1962); idem, *The Chippewa and Their Neighbors: A Study in Ethnohistory* (New York, 1970); Robert Ritzenthaler, "Southwestern Chippewa," *Handbook of North American Indians,* gen. ed., William C. Sturtevant; vol. 15, *Northeast,* ed. Bruce G. Trigger (Washington, D.C.: Smithsonian Institution Press, 1978), pp. 743-59; E. S. Rogers, "Southeastern Ojibwa," *Handbook,* 15: 760-71. For an annotated bibliography, see Helen H. Tanner, *The Ojibwas: A Critical Bibliography* (Bloomington and London: Indiana University Press, 1976).

4. The Ojibwa speak an Algonquian language related to, among others, Potawatomi and Cree. Because they are so widely scattered, the Ojibwa have been referred to according to geographic subdivisions: the northern Ojibwa or Saulteaux in Canada or the central Ojibwa in Michigan. For the most part, the present monograph deals almost exclusively with the southwestern bands living in Minnesota and Wisconsin. For a complete discus-

sion of the tribe's name see Ives Goddard and E. S. Rogers, "Synonymy," in *Handbook*, 15: 768-70. Throughout this study all Ojibwa words are spelled according to the Nichols-Nyholm system currently in use by educators in Minnesota. The only exception to this is my consistent use of "Ojibwa," a widely accepted English spelling of the name for the tribe and its language. (In the Nichols-Nyholm system it would be "Ojibwe.") I am indebted to Earl Nyholm for his assistance in converting text spellings to this system. Diacritics have been omitted from all proper names and words in languages other than Ojibwa. The reader should consult the sources for their original spellings.

5. For standard sources on the *midewiwin*, see Walter J. Hoffman, "The Midewiwin; or 'Grand Medicine Society' of the Ojibwa," in *Bureau of American Ethnology, Seventh Annual Report, 1885-86* (Washington, D.C., 1891), pp. 143-300; Ruth Landes, *Ojibwa Religion and the Midewiwin* (Madison: University of Wisconsin Press, 1968).

6. See Thomas Vennum, Jr., "Ojibwa Origin-Migration Songs of the *mitewiwin*," *Journal of American Folklore* 91 (1978): 753-91. The origins of the *midewiwin* are obscure. Hickerson's conclusion, that "The Midewiwin was in fact a nativistic movement, a reaction to contact with Europeans, and not aboriginal [and] the ceremonial represented and reflected new modes of organization, not ancient ones" (Hickerson, *Chippewa*, p. 63), is by no means universally accepted, and certainly not by the Ojibwa people.

7. For a more detailed history of Lac Court Oreilles up to the 1960s, see Edmund J. Danziger, *The Chippewas of Lake Superior* (Norman: University of Oklahoma Press, 1978), p. 160.

8. George I. Quimby, *Indian Life in the Upper Great Lakes* (London and Chicago: University of Chicago Press, 1960), p. 147.

9. Catlin visited Fort Snelling during Fourth of July celebrations (see George Catlin, *Letters and Notes on the Manners, Customs, and Condition of the North American Indian* [1841; reprint ed., Minneapolis: Ross and Haines, 1965], 2: 135). The ecological factors in the Ojibwa-Sioux conflict over hunting grounds are discussed in Hickerson, *Southwestern Chippewa*, pp. 12-29.

10. Actually, the cessions of land by the Ojibwa came in stages, as did the creation of the various reservations. In Minnesota it began in 1837; by 1867 the Ojibwa had given lands in that territory to the federal government in nine treaties and would continue to relinquish even more.

11. Alexander Henry, *Travels and Adventures to Canada and the Indian Territories* (New York, 1809), pp.125-26.

12. Landes, pp. 6-7. By "storytelling" Landes must mean general gossip, for winter rather than summer was usually the season for recounting traditional stories, because then the dreaded snakes and toads were dormant.

13. SDOH, tape 341, pp. 42-43.

14. John Gillin, "Acquired Drives in Culture Contact," *American Anthropologist* 44 (1942): 549.

15. For a detailed review of the Ojibwa's early economic problems, see Danziger, particularly chap. 6, "Life on the New Reservations, 1854-1900," pp. 91-109.

16. Danziger, p. 103.

17. Red Lake, Minnesota, is one of the few Ojibwa reservations to have escaped this fate; since they never signed a treaty, the Red Lake Ojibwa have managed to retain their lands in communal ownership.

18. Danziger, p. 150.

19. Ibid., p. 94.

288

20. Gillin, p. 551.

21. Danziger, p. 149.

22. Ibid., p. 107.

23. Henry R. Schoolcraft, *Narrative Journal of Travels from Detroit Northwest through the Great Chain of American Lakes to the Sources of the Mississippi River in the Year 1820* (Albany, 1821), p. 186.

24. Johann G. Kohl, *Kitchi-Gami: Wanderings round Lake Superior* (London: Chapman and Hall, 1860), pp. 105-7.

25. *CC*, 51.

26. Ibid., p. 66.

27. BI, p. 14. Children also used discarded pans or pails for their drums (see M. Inez Hilger, *Chippewa Child Life and Its Cultural Background*, Smithsonian Institution, Bureau of American Ethnology Bulletin no. 146 [Washington, D.C., 1951], pl. 10).

28. Joseph A. Gilfillan, "The Ojibways in Minnesota," *Collections of the Minnesota Historical Society* 9 (1901): 114.

29. *CC*, p. 74. During a shaking-tent seance, the spirit of a dead girl tried to reassure her mother that everything was going well for her in the land of the dead: "I am happy. It is always bright like day where I live. . . . There are pretty flowers where I live, it's like a great garden. . . . There are great singers there, too" (cited in A. Irving Hallowell, *The Role of Conjuring in Saulteaux Society*, Publications of the Philadelphia Anthropological Society [1942], 2: 58).

30. SOM, p.104.

31. Frederick R. Burton, *American Primitive Music* (New York: Moffat, Yard and Co., 1909), pp. 126-27.

32. Henry R. Schoolcraft, *Expedition to Lake Itasca: The Discovery of the Source of the Mississippi*, ed. Philip P. Mason (1834; reprint ed., East Lansing, 1958), p. 327.

33. Kohl, p. 19.

34. Herman J. Viola, *Diplomats in Buckskin* (Washington, D.C.: Smithsonian Institution Press, 1981), pp. 145-46. For descriptions of Indian dancing in the nation's capital, see pp. 142, 147.

35. See J. Richard Haefer, "North American Indian Musical Instruments: Some Organological Distribution Problems," *Journal of the American Musical Instrument Society* 1 (1975): 60-64.

36. For more complete descriptions of Ojibwa flutes, see SOM, pp. 79-83; *CC*, pp. 167-69. For a photograph showing the various parts disassembled, such as the bridge, sounding tube, block, and birchbark "lip," see *CC*, pl. 76.

37. Paul Parthun, "Ojibwe Music in Minnesota" (Ph.D. diss., University of Minnesota, 1976), p. 51.

38. *People of the First Man: Life among the Plains Indians in Their Final Days of Glory* [Prince Maximilian of Neuwied's Expedition, 1833-34], ed. Davis Thomas and Karin Ronnefeldt (New York: E. P. Dutton and Co., 1976), p. 56; Catlin, 2: pl. 101 1/2, opposite p. 242.

39. See *CM-II*, p. 34, fig. 1. The otter-skull rattle collected by Hoffman at Luck Lake, Minnesota, circa 1891, has a wooden handle. The bone skull vessel is colored red to indicate the rattle's sacred association (National Museum of Natural History, Smithsonian Institution, cat. no. 154.318).

40. See "Stones, Bones, and Skin: Ritual and Shamanistic Art," *Artscanada* 184-87 (1974): 81; also Charles Brill, *Indian and Free: A Contemporary Portrait of Life on a Chippewa Reservation* (Minneapolis: University of Minnesota Press, 1974), p.116, for a photograph of Dan Raincloud, Ponemah medicine man, singing over a coffin in a pickup truck enroute to the cemetery; he is using a can rattle to accompany his funeral songs.

41. *MM*, p. 10.

42. *CC*, p. 166.

43. *RF*, 6: 27.

44. *CM-II*, p. 94. John M. Cooper, *Notes on the Ethnology of the Otchipwe of Lake of the Woods and Rainy Lake*, Catholic University of America Anthropological Series no. 3 (Washington, D.C., 1936), p. 9.

45. Henry R. Schoolcraft, *The Literary Voyager or Muzzeniegan*, ed. Philip P. Mason, (1826-27; reprint ed., East Lansing, 1962), p. 21.

46. Karl G. Izikowitz, *Musical and Other Sound Instruments of the South American Indians* (Göteborg, 1935), p. 178.

47. *CM*, pl. 2. Rattle drums are used by some tribes as drumsticks.

48. Fred K. Blessing, "Field Notes for 1959," *Minnesota Archaeologist* 22 (1958): 3, 5.

49. The photograph of Keeper and his Drum is published in Selwyn H. Dewdney, *The Sacred Scrolls of the Southern Ojibway* (Toronto: University of Toronto Press, 1975), p. 85.

50. *CC*, p. 169.

51. *RF*, 12: 35-36.

52. *CM*, p. 11.

53. Edward S. Curtis, *The North American Indian* (1909), 5: 75. The film *Circle of the Sun* (1961) shows Blood Indians beating on hard rawhide with rattles.

54. Fred K. Blessing, "Notes from the Field: Summer 1958," *Minnesota Archaeologist* 22 (1958): 77. Leech Lake must have had more than one peyote group. Blessing's "Twin Village" (pseudonym) appears to have been in an isolated area near Squaw Lake, but Paul Buffalo mentioned one in Bena on the same reservation (SDOH, tape 257, p. 36). Buffalo may have had in mind the "Rice Village" (pseudonym) described by Barbara D. Jackson in *Anishinabe: Six Studies of Modern Chippewa*, ed. J. Anthony Paredes (Tallahassee: University of Florida Press, 1980), chap. 4.

55. *RF*, Flambeau book, p. 7.

56. *SOM*, "Ojibwa Uses of Music," pp. 34-64.

The Origin and Early History of the Dance Drum

1. This account was written in a letter to me in 1970. I have edited it for clarity.

2. Baker's account of the origin of the Drum may be compared with that given in Samuel A. Barrett, *The Dream Dance of the Chippewa and Menominee Indians of Northern Wisconsin*, Bulletins of the Public Museum of the City of Milwaukee 1 (Milwaukee, 1911): pp. 256-57; *CM-II*, p. 144; James S. Slotkin, *The Menomini Powwow: A Study in Cultural Decay*, Milwaukee Public Museum Publications in Anthropology (Milwaukee, 1957), pp. 17-25. Many Ojibwa have their own versions of the story with varying degrees of detail. A typically sketchy account was collected from John Clark (born 1880) of Mille Lacs, as follows: "It started while they were having a war. This one women was almost starving, and it seemed like she heard someone from above speak to her [and tell her] to go to this camp where the white people were, and she got a design from there how to draw picture

on a drum, and this person spoke to her and told her that they [had] four days to live, that they were going to get all shot down or something like that, and told her to take this design [and] make a drum and have a dance. And they did this for four days, and the four days started in the morning and when the four days were over the soldiers came . . . and saw these Indians having a dance and they were going to come and wipe them out. . . . Because the Indians were not afraid, they were celebrating and dancing . . . the soldiers didn't bother them at all" (SDOH, tape 141, pp. 3-4).

3. Clay MacCauley, "The Dreamers among the North American Indians, as illustrative of the Origin of Forms of Religion," *Japan Weekly Mail* (March 18, 1893): 338-40; also Walter J. Hoffman, "The Menomini Indians," in *Bureau of American Ethnology, Fourteenth Annual Report, 1892-93* (Washington, D.C., 1896), pp. 157-61.

4. *MM*, p. 161.

5. Parthun, p. 48, n. 2.

6. Slotkin, pp. 17-25.

7. See Vennum, "Origin-Migration Songs," p. 754.

8. See here the discussion of cultism, "The Decline of the Drum Dance."

9. Truman Michelson, "On the Origin of the So-Called Dream Dance of the Central Algonkians," *American Anthropologist*, n.s. 25 (1923); idem, "Further Remarks . . . ," *American Anthropologist*, n.s. 26 (1924); idem, "Final Notes on the Central Algonkian Dream Dance," *American Anthropologist*, n.s. 28 (1926); Alanson Skinner, "A Further Note on the Origin of the Dream Dance of the Central Algonkian and Southern Siouan Indians," *American Anthropologist*, n.s. 25 (1923); idem, "Final Observations . . . ," *American Anthropologist*, n.s. 27 (1925).

10. Benjamin G. Armstrong, *Early Life among the Indians* (Ashland, Wis.: Press of A. W. Bowron, 1892), pp. 156-60. Ritzenthaler dates the spread of the Drum Dance to the Wisconsin Ojibwa somewhat earlier, circa 1876 (see Robert E. Ritzenthaler, *Potawatomi Indians of Wisconsin*, Bulletins of the Public Museum of the City of Milwaukee 19, no. 3 [Milwaukee, 1953]: p. 159).

11. This early date is challenged by James Clifton's research ("Sociocultural Dynamics of the Prairie Potawatomi Drum Cult," *Plains Anthropologist* 14 [1969]: 85-93). According to him, the Kansas Potawatomi received their first Drum between 1880 and 1885 (p. 85).

12. MacCauley, p. 338.

13. The notion that the Drum Dance is related to the Ghost Dance still persists (see George Spindler and Louise S. Spindler, *Dreamers without Power* [New York: Holt, Rinehart and Winston, Inc., 1971], p. 62).

14. Gilfillan, p. 117.

15. James Mooney, *The Ghost Dance Religion and the Sioux Outbreak of 1890*, ed. Anthony F. C. Wallace (Chicago: University of Chicago Press, 1965), originally published as *Bureau of American Ethnology, Fourteenth Annual Report, 1892–93* (Washington, D.C., 1896), 2: 60.

16. See Barrett, p. 301.

17. Mooney, p. 60. Also see p. 187 and pl. lxxxv, delimiting the area to which the Ghost Dance spread.

18. Barrett, pp. 298–99.

19. Cited in Mooney, p. 42.

20. Ibid., pp. 307-8.

21. Ibid., pp. 115-18.

22. Cited in Vivian J. L. Rohrl, "The People of Mille Lacs: A Study of Social Organization and Value Orientations" (Ph.D. diss., University of Minnesota, 1967), p. 111.

23. Warren, pp. 323-22.

24. Cited in Edwin James, *A Narrative of the Captivity and Adventures of John Tanner* (1830; reprint ed., Minneapolis: Ross and Haines, 1956), pp. 168-69.

25. Of the Woodlands contributions to the Grass Dance, some would include their elaborate pipe rituals. Clark Wissler, "General Discussion of Shamanistic and Dancing Societies," *APNH*, p. 867, sees the drum and its pipe as equally important, noting that the "highly developed" procedure of tobacco offerings among central Algonquians was incorporated by them in the Drum Dance.

26. See especially Wissler et al., *APNH*.

27. The term is geographically relevant to Wissler's argument. By "southeast" he refers to the area inhabited at the time by such tribes as the Pawnee and Iowa. The area is actually in the central part of the United States.

28. Wissler, p. 865; see also his schema of the "Diffusion of the Iruska Trait-complex" on a foldout opposite p. 868.

29. Ibid., p. 870.

30. Alice C. Fletcher and Francis La Flesche, *The Omaha Tribe* (Lincoln: University of Nebraska Press, 1972), originally published as *Bureau of American Ethnology, Twenty-Seventh Annual Report, 1905-06* (Washington, D.C., 1911), 2: 461.

31. Ibid., p. 441.

32. Wissler, p. 862.

33. Cited in WP, pp. 37-38.

34. Slotkin (citing Wissler), p. 16.

35. Regina Flannery, "The Changing Form and Function of the Gros Ventre Grass Dance," *Primitive Man* 20 (1947): 42.

36. Wissler, p. 868.

37. WP, p. 88.

38. Flannery, pp. 41-43.

39. Ibid., p. 42.

40. I do not wish to imply that group performances around a single drum were unknown before the Grass Dance, for there is ample evidence that this practice was also followed. The Woodlands medicine drum, for example, would occasionally be beaten upon by four singers using the protruding edges of the drumhead to suspend the instrument. Group performance on one drum is occasionally depicted in paintings (see for example, the lithograph *War Dance of the Sauks and Foxes* published by McKenney and Hall in the various editions of *The Indian Tribes of North America*; the lithograph was made after a painting by Peter Rindisbacher, circa 1825-35). Most of the literature, however, describes the hand-drum as the customary accompaniment to Indian song (see figs. 15, 19). Iconographic evidence prior to photography supports this as well.

41. Robert H. Lowie, "Societies of the Arikara Indians," *APNH*, p. 657; WP, p. 39; Clark Wissler, "Societies and Dance Associations of the Blackfoot Indians," *APNH*, p. 454.

42. Robert H. Lowie, "The Assiniboine," *Anthropological Papers of the American Museum of Natural History* 4 (1909): 27.

43. Alanson Skinner, "Ponca Societies and Dances," *APNH*, p. 787.

44. WP, p. 39.

45. Skinner, "Ponca," p. 787; Wissler, "Blackfoot," p. 454; Lowie, "Arikara," p. 657.

46. Flannery, p. 61.

47. WP, p. 49.

48. Pliny Earle Goddard, "Dancing Societies of the Sarsi Indians," *APNH*, p. 471.

49. Lowie, "Arikara," p. 657.

50. The one exception to this is the Chief Dance, a curing ceremony.

51. Cited in Slotkin, p. 38.

52. Wissler, "General Discussion," p. 863.

53. Cf. Densmore's experience with Bijikens (*CM-II*, p. 145).

54. Slotkin, p. 61.

55. Ibid., p. 55.

56. See Vennum, "Origin-Migration Songs," p. 767, item no. 7. The Menominee as well as the Wisconsin and Kansas Potawatomi use the same term (see Ritzenthaler, *Potawatomi*, p. 160; Clifton, p. 69).

57. Slotkin, pp. 36-37.

58. *MM*, p. 151.

59. Cited in Slotkin, p. 70.

60. Ibid., p. 124.

61. Ibid., p. 36.

62. Ibid., pp. 73-74.

63. *MM*, p. 154.

64. Cited in Slotkin, p. 119.

65. Ibid., pp. 95, 108.

66. Barrett, p. 333. The commotion caused by the partial nudity of the young man may reflect the influence of white modes of dress at the time. The young dancer may in fact have wished to express his Indian character by appearing at a dance in the manner of his ancestors.

67. Ibid., p. 279.

68. *CM-II*, p. 143.

69. Clifton, p. 89.

70. Barrett, p. 276.

71. *CM-II*, p. 169.

72. RF, 2: 67.

73. James Clifton, who has researched the Drum Dance extensively, dates it as beginning in 1872 and identifies Tailfeather Woman as a Santee, p. 85.

74. Slotkin, p. 18, n. 2.

75. Ruth Landes, *The Mystic Lake Sioux* (Madison: University of Wisconsin Press, 1968), pp. 9-10.

76. Ibid., p. 214.

77. Cited in Slotkin, p. 20.

78. Cited in ibid., p. 21. Hearing drumming and singing without visually perceiving a source is a motif that appears in the story of the origin of the Drum Dance collected from The Boy, a Gros Ventre. Cooper cautions that he obtained only fragmentary information from The Boy, who said the dance died out around 1824. From the description of the drum and its support stakes, a Grass Dance drum seems intended (see "Drum Legs," pp. 211–28; J. M. Cooper, *The Gros Ventre of Montana: Part II, Religion and Ritual*, Catholic University of America Anthropological Series 16 [Washington, D.C. 1956], pp. 221-22).

79. Landes, *Sioux*, p. 4, n. 2.

80. Ibid., p. 78.

81. WP, pp. 37–110. The Hidatsa shared Like-a-Fishhook-Village with the Mandan, and members of both tribes belonged to the Grass Dance societies there. Because the two Wilson accounts are from Hidatsa, I have used that tribal name alone. Hereinafter the reader can assume "Hidatsa" to mean "Hidatsa/Mandan."

82. Cited in WP, p. 50. It is customary for a tribe borrowing songs from another to retain the foreign texts, even though their meaning may be obscure.

83. The date is formulated from Wolf Chief's account; Wilson notes that Goodbird admitted recollecting only fragments since he was only fourteen when admitted to the dance and his village broke up soon thereafter. From Wolf Chief's account, apparently some Standing Rock Sioux around 1875 had performed an abbreviated version of the Grass Dance one evening in a Hidatsa lodge. They used only one hand-drum on the occasion and wore none of the ceremonial garb.

84. Cited in WP, p. 38.

85. Cited in ibid., pp. 60-61.

86. Cited in ibid., p. 80. The Crow were more exuberant about the gift of a horse during a Hot Dance (Grass Dance) and would ride them directly into the dance lodge to present them to elders. Lowie was very impressed with the extraordinary amount of wealth given away in these ceremonies, not only among the Crow but to visitors from other tribes as well: "In 1910 I saw one man take off all his clothes but the gee-string and give them away in the presence of a large crowd" (Robert H. Lowie, "Military Societies of the Crow Indians," *APNH*, p. 205).

87. Cited in WP, p. 83.

88. Cited in ibid., pp. 107-8.

89. Cited in Slotkin, p. 52.

90. James H. Howard, "The Henry Davis Drum Rite: An Unusual Drum Religion Variant of the Minnesota Ojibwa," *Plains Anthropologist* 11 (1966): 118.

91. *MM*, p. 152.

92. Cf. Johnny Matchokamow's remarks above; also, Clifton, p. 90.

93. Slotkin, p. 76.

94. See A. Irving Hallowell on directional orientation in ceremonialism, *Culture and Experience* (1955; reprint ed., New York: Schoken Books, 1967), pp. 200-201.

95. Ritzenthaler's dates for the Drum's arrival at Lac Court Oreilles were estimated for him by Ojibwa old enough to have been alive at the time. They range from Wase, who dated it circa 1873-78, a Louis (?), who claimed to have remembered the Drum's arrival when he was four, which would place it around 1874-75, and Prosper Guibord, who dated it circa 1882 (RF, 4: 44). Of these Ritzenthaler leaned toward accepting the earlier dates; see his "Health," p. 186. They are generally consistent with Clifton's 1872 date for Tailfeather Woman's vision and Slotkin's 1879 date for the Menominee receiving the

Drum from the Ojibwa (Slotkin, p. 17). Whether the Drum continued eastward through Ojibwa communities in Michigan is unknown to me.

96. Truman Michelson, *Contributions to Fox Ethnology—II*, Smithsonian Institution, Bureau of American Ethnology Bulletin no. 95 (Washington, D.C., 1930), p. 5.

97. RF, 3: 7.

98. Ibid.

99. *CM-II*, p. 146.

100. RF, 2: 2.

101. Ibid., 3: 12.

102. *CM*, p. 25, n. a.

103. Vennum, "Origin-Migration Songs," pp. 756-58.

104. Gilfillan, "Ojibways in Minnesota," p. 60.

105. RF, 3: 7.

106. Ibid., 3: 6, 80.

107. Clifton, p. 89.

108. To his written statement on the origin of the Drum, Baker added the following: "That [Tailfeather Woman's] drum was the last of the spiritual powwow drums of the Sioux; I have been out to see if they still have the kind of drum they passed onto the Ojibwa Indians. No, I didn't see it [even though] they [still] do the duties of what they passed on. But they still powwow the Indian way; [but] they use *chimookomaan* [the white man's] drum, bass drum, band drum."

109. Barrett, pp. 286-87.

110. Ibid., pp. 107-8.

The Drum Dance and Its Functions

1. WP, pp. 76-81.

2. Slotkin, p. 53.

3. Skinner, "Ponca," p. 786; idem, "Societies of the Iowa," *APNH*, 694.

4. Goddard, p. 470.

5. Clifton, p. 91.

6. *MM*, p. 168.

7. WP, p. 108.

8. Ibid., p. 45.

9. William Strachey, *The Historie of Travell to Virginia Britania* (1612), as cited in Robert Stevenson, "English Sources for Indian Music until 1882,"*Ethnomusicology* 17 (1973): 401. Charlotte Heth informs me that in the Southeast such people were called "dog whippers." They kept dogs out of dance enclosures and stragglers in line.

10. See Clifton, p. 90.

11. WP, p. 108.

12. See appendix "The Lac Court Oreilles Drum Dance, circa 1940."

13. M. I. Hilger, "Naming a Chippewa Indian Child," *Wisconsin Archeologist*, n.s. 39 (1958): 121. Reserve is the only real town of the five, the others are simply populated areas. Barbertown is so named because many members of the Barber family live there.

14. *MM*, pp. 150-84.

15. Occasionally there is a co-owner of a Drum. Slotkin, who knew of only one instance—the Pete Sam/Jim Beaver Drum at Zoar—considered the co-owner position more a regent than owner, since Beaver took no part in the Drum presentation. In the case of the Zoar Drum, because Pete Sam was the dominant personality, the Drum was known only as the Pete Sam Drum (see Slotkin, p. 53, n. 1).

16. Clifton, p. 90; Rohrl's names for the Mille Lacs "War Drum," "Ladies Drum," and "Thunderbird Drum" (p. 96) are generic terms without reference to ownership.

17. Densmore (*CM-II*, p. 147) numbers twenty-nine members as formerly comprising a "drum party" but says there are now (circa 1910) less. Rohrl (p. 97) counts twenty-four to thirty members.

18. Rohrl, p. 92, notes that Ojibwa kinship may once have been based on patrilineal inheritance of one's totem, but that a bilineal system is now operative in most matters—inheritance, hunting, ricing, etc.—and is reflected in Drum society membership. In the Arikara Young Dogs Society the five female singers who sat behind the men at the drum were the wives of the "drum-keeper, the conductor of the orchestra, the two leaders, and another official whose business it was to look after what had to be bought for the society" (Lowie, "Arikara," p. 659).

19. In the Grass Dance, offices could be sold, usually to a band son (WP, p. 43).

20. At Mille Lacs if an owner dies and there is no co-owner, the Drum goes to his son; if he has none, it is usually given to a brother or parallel nephew. If no adequate relative is found, the head drum heater or head singer may be chosen as the new owner (Rohrl, pp. 98, 148).

21. Slotkin, p. 53.

22. Clifton, p. 86.

23. *MM*, p. 152.

24. Cited in Slotkin, p. 66. See also Barrett, p. 279.

25. Barrett, pp. 311-12.

26. Cited in Spindler and Spindler, p. 65.

27. Cited in Slotkin, p. 64.

28. Ibid., pp. 38, 83, 101-2, 117-18; RF, 12: 7; during the Menominee food consecration, the belt man is supposed to represent the Great Spirit (Barrett, p. 287); see Clifton, p. 91, for the Potawatomi equivalents of the supernaturals, e.g., the belt man is considered standing in for the "Angel of the Lord."

29. The Potawatomi belt woman position, which exists on only one of their Drums, is exceptional (see Clifton, p. 90).

30. Cited in Slotkin, p. 66. If Rynkiewich's data are correct, at some time apparently at "Broken Reed Reservation" (Leech Lake) women began to dance as well. He describes eight female dancers (sic) entering the ring one at a time, "continuing to dance in the circle until all the women's songs had been sung" (p. 38, no source is given).

31. Ibid., p. 108.

32. Ibid., p. 117. This is at least the Menominee practice.

33. Cited in ibid., p. 88.

34. *CM-II*, p. 147.

35. Densmore, *CM-II*, says the four assistant women sit behind their partners, whereas all photographs I know picturing women and Ritzenthaler's schema for their position show them in a row shoulder to shoulder. Rohrl's "Schematic Diagram of Drum Dance" in the square dance hall at Mille Lacs has the women of the Drum along the south wall, continuing along the east wall to the door (p. 118, fig. 1).

36. Cf. in particular the Iowa Helocka arrangement (Skinner, "Iowa," p. 695). The four male singers at their drum, who were chosen by the women, occupy the same positions taken by the drum heaters in the Ojibwa Drum Dance; the four head singers at the cardinal points are in the same places as on Ojibwa Drums. See also the description of the Wahpeton matano dance (Robert H. Lowie, "Dance Associations of the Eastern Dakota," *APNH*, p. 112).

37. Lowie, "Crow," pp. 202-3.

38. Cited in WP, p. 77.

39. Kohl, p. 19.

40. MacCauley, p. 339.

41. It is difficult to describe this nasal sound. I once played a recording of it during a lecture and one person in the audience would not be dissuaded from his impression that a reed instrument was entering the song from time to time.

42. Cf. SOM, pp. 68-72.

43. Cf. Michelson, *Fox*, p. 5.

44. BI, p. 24.

45. RF, 3: 80.

46. BI, p. 24.

47. The term "squaw," an anglicized form of an Algonquian word for woman, is considered derogatory unless used by Indians themselves. For a description of the Woman's Dance in Minnesota, see Rynkiewich, p. 36.

48. Cf. SOM, pp. 106-15.

49. Barrett, p. 350. At Ball Club on Leech Lake Reservation two separate dance halls were used, one each for the Woman's Dance and the War Dance (Drum Dance); see Rynkiewich, p. 41.

50. RF, 3: 18.

51. Rohrl, p. 100.

52. BI, p. 9.

53. RF, 3: 8. Ritzenthaler's fieldnotes contain conflicting data on this. In notebook 2: 71-72, Johnny Green who was eighty years old at the time said that Mary Barber got her drum from White Earth Reservation from a Sioux (sic) around 1900. Green claimed that Barber gave the drum to him to be its "keeper" even before he was made a member of it. He added that he did not really believe in the religion but joined simply to accommodate them.

54. Cited in RF, 3: 65. Alanson Skinner claims that the Winnebago introduced the Woman's Dance to the Menominee sometime after 1911 (see his "Menomini Associations and Ceremonies," *Anthropological Papers of the American Museum of Natural History* 13 [1915]: 213). It seems unlikely, however, that the Menominee would not have known the dance from the Ojibwa before this date.

55. Barrett, pp. 341-42.

56. Rohrl, p. 97. Rohrl seems to imply that the recipients are the ones to build a Drum from a piece of the original (Sioux?) Drum. Since this is not the normal custom, she may have misunderstood the procedure, which is for the donors to retain a piece of the giveaway Drum.

57. *CM-II*, p. 146.

58. BI, p. 21. Ritzenthaler notes only that a (chief?) drumstick is "sent" when a Drum is given away so that a new Drum can be made (9: 12). I assume he means it is returned by the recipients of the Drum to the donors sometime after the transfer.

59. RF, 3: 3.

60. Alanson Skinner, "Kansa Organizations," *APNH*, p. 756.

61. *MM*, p. 155; *CM-II*, p. 148; Barrett, p. 267.

62. MacCauley, p. 338.

63. *CM-II*, p. 148.

64. Slotkin, p. 147.

65. RF, 3: 77.

66. *CM-II*, p. 165.

67. Slotkin, pp. 98-99.

68. Cited in ibid., p. 28.

69. Slotkin, p. 98, published a letter he was asked to send to the Ojibwa John M(ink?) in 1950, inviting him to a Zoar summertime Dance and asking him in turn to invite John S(tone?). Mink and Stone (both now deceased) were well-known medicine men as well as Drum members at Lac Court Oreilles.

70. Rohrl, p. 97.

71. Cited in Slotkin, p. 142.

72. Cited in ibid., p. 43.

73. Cited in ibid., p. 95.

74. Ibid., pp. 31, 111. The appearance of Ojibwa song texts in Menominee medicine songs is further indication that the Menominee accepted the Ojibwa as authorities in sacred matters.

75. Cited in WP, p. 64.

76. BI, p. 10. Baker frequently sings in his sleep. Once, he was evicted from a bus by the driver who thought he had been drinking.

77. Barrett, pp. 280-81.

78. See *MM*, p. 158. Densmore claims to have recognized only four songs in the 1928 Drum presentation as being ones she heard in the 1910 event—the songs of the Drum, pipe, painting of faces, and restoring of the mourners. We cannot infer from this, however, that the other songs were different or had changed over the years. What she probably recalled were the contexts of particular songs.

79. Cf. SOM, "The Influence of Sioux Music," p. 301.

80. Red Lake Reservation in northern Minnesota has always been particularly receptive to Siouan music.

81. *CM, CM-II.*

82. Wissler, "General Discussion," p. 870.

83. Ibid., n. 1

84. *CM-II*, p. 173.

85. *MM*, p. 155.

86. BI, pp. 2, 24.

87. Slotkin, p. 146.

88. Ibid., p. 86. Slotkin notes that as many as fifteen singers may be performing on one drum.

89. E.g., such as for striking a drum out of rhythm.

90. Slotkin, p. 87.

91. Ibid.; *MM*, p. 155.

92. BI, p. 21.

93. Slotkin, p. 96; see also Barrett, pp. 311-12.

94. Slotkin, pp. 14-15.

95. See Clark Wissler, "Societies and Ceremonial Associations in the Oglala Division of the Teton-Dakota," *APNH*, p. 52.

96. The Ojibwa have several songs to accompany the presentation of horses—one each for giving, receiving, and thanking the donor (see *CM*, pp. 164-65; *CM-II*, pp. 237-39). The Menominee evidently used only one such song at a Drum Dance (*MM*, p. 183).

97. Slotkin, p. 116.

98. RF, 3: 78.

99. Ritzenthaler was given the estimate of fifty to sixty special songs, compared to about two hundred general songs (3: 78); Slotkin was told there were "hundreds" of what the Menominee call "ordinary prayer songs" (p. 68). See also Barrett, p. 280. Bill Leaf, a Fox, recorded 123 Drum Dance songs for Truman Michelson around 1916.

100. Cf. Thomas Vennum, Jr., "A History of Ojibwa Song Form," in *Selected Reports in Ethnomusicology* 3, ed. Charlotte Heth (Los Angeles: University of California, 1980), pp. 12–75.

101. Cited in WP, p. 106.

102. Ibid., p. 86.

103. *CM-II*, p. 144.

104. Slotkin, p. 114.

105. *MM*, pp. 77, 183.

106. Densmore contrasts her impression of the Medicine Dance, which she found to be generally more loosely structured in regard to ritual exactness, with her feeling that, in the Drum Dance, "certain songs and no others must be sung, and dancing once begun must be continued the prescribed length of time regardless of conditions" (*CM-II*, p. 142).

107. Lowie, "Crow," p. 202.

108. Slotkin, p. 100.

109. Ibid., p. 106.

110. BI, p. 20.

111. Notes found inserted in the cavities of Michelson's cylinders numbers 260 and 261. The original recordings are in the Archive of Folk Culture at the Library of Congress.

112. Slotkin, p. 113.

113. Many Drum Dance songs have only the word *wananikwe, obwaanikwe*, or *pananikwe*, etc., all Algonquian variants of the name for Tailfeather Woman. The meaningful word is mixed in with their vocables (cf. SOM, "Vocables," p. 279).

114. Cited in Slotkin, p. 89.

115. Howard, p. 119.

116. Slotkin, p. 108. There are medicine songs to bring fair weather for a *midewiwin* ceremony as well. It is generally considered an ill omen if a ceremony is planned and it rains.

117. RF, 4: 15.

118. In 1954 the Menominee were terminated as a reservation and converted to county status within the state of Wisconsin. Having lost their position as federal wards, they realized quickly the economic pinch. They have since reverted to reservation status.

119. Cited in Slotkin, pp. 150-51. The "straight road" west has its parallel in the design painted on the drumhead (see "Drumhead Decorations," pp. 201–8).

120. Slotkin, pp. 20-21. Cf. Landes (*Sioux*, pp. 85-86) for a description of Shakopee meeting with the Ojibwa.

121. Evidently, by 1950 the Menominee did not perform these songs at regular song services but reserved them for special occasions, such as birthdays or doctoring sessions (Slotkin, p. 89).

122. WP, p. 83.

123. *CM-II*, p. 166.

124. Howard, p. 122.

125. Cited in Slotkin, pp. 106-7.

126. Cited in WP, pp. 93–94.

127. Slotkin, p. 129.

128. The four feather belts Densmore saw at Leech Lake in 1910 were said to have been given to them by the Sioux circa 1860 (*CM-II*, p. 173). If this date is accurate, the introduction of this military badge would predate the beginning of the Drum Dance.

129. Cited in WP, p. 55.

130. See Fletcher, pl. 55, opposite p. 441, for two examples of the Omaha Crow.

131. WP, pp. 42-43.

132. There appears to be a sacred/secular distinction made between eagle and crow feathers. The belt of the Henry Davis (Mille Lacs) Drum is of crow feathers; consequently, its owner was free to wear it at secular powwows in Saint Paul (Howard, p. 121).

133. Dancing with the belt by members in rotation was also a Grass Dance practice (see Wissler, "General Discussion," pp. 862-63).

134. Barrett, p. 287.

135. WP, p. 85.

136. Slotkin, p. 132.

137. Fletcher, p. 441. For a full discussion of the Omaha Crow belt, see pp. 441-46.

138. Cited in Slotkin, p. 62; also p. 128 (I have combined the two citations).

139. Ibid., pp. 130-33.

140. Ibid., p. 128.

141. WP, p. 77.

142. Ibid., p. 43.

143. Slotkin, p. 127; Barrett, p. 287.

144. Wissler, "General Discussion," p. 863.

145. Fletcher, p. 466.

146. WP, p. 99.

147. Wissler, "General Discussion," p. 864. He adds gathering the bones and secreting them in a safe place as a final phase.

148. Slotkin, p. 110.

149. See WP, p. 53.

150. Skinner, "Iowa," p. 723.

151. WP, p. 37ff.

152. Fletcher, p. 467; CM-II, p. 177.

153. Slotkin, p. 132.

154. CM-II, p. 150.

155. Truman Michelson, Observations on the Thunder Dance of the Bear Gens of the Fox Indians, Smithsonian Institution, Bureau of American Ethnology Bulletin no. 89 (Washington, D.C., 1929), p. 9, n. 9, notes that there are "some sins of omission and commission in Wissler's [p. 864] tables, but they are unimportant." Dogs were cooked, first their hair singed off (hence "roasting"), then the carcasses were gutted and cut into pieces for boiling. Usually the heads were discarded with the rest of the offal. The retention of a dog's head for the ceremony was totally for symbolic purposes.

156. Slotkin, p. 129; Skinner, "Menomini Associations," p. 181.

157. Slotkin, p. 135.

158. Rynkiewich, p. 73.

159. MM, p. 67. The very elaborateness of the Belt Dance among the Ojibwa and Menominee makes me question Rynkiewich's assertion that "the syncretic forms of the [Ojibwa] War dance that developed were much less distinct and less formally structured than the antecedent Plains War Dance forms" (p. 35).

160. Evon Z. Vogt, Tortillas for the Gods: A Symbolic Analysis of Zinacanteco Rituals (Cambridge, Mass., and London: Harvard University Press, 1976), p. 187.

161. Rohrl, p. 42.

162. For a photograph of a medicine lodge showing the uncovered top, see CM, pl. V. By contrast, many Menominee and Winnebago lodges were fully covered.

163. Cf. Vennum, "Origin-Migration Songs," pp. 776-77; see also Dewdney, pp. 57-80.

164. Cited in MacCauley, p. 339.

165. Barrett, p. 260.

166. Ibid.

167. Two exceptions that I know of are the southeast entrance of the dance arbor used for the 1928 Drum presentation and the southwest door to the octagonal dance hall at Lac Vieux Desert.

168. MacCauley, p. 339; Hoffman, "Menomini," pp. 158-59.

169. *CM-II*, p. 164; Barrett, p. 260.

170. Skinner, "Iowa," p. 722, fig. 2; Clifton, p. 88, fig. 1.

171. Barrett, p. 260.

172. Ibid. p. 348. Hoffman, "Menomini," p. 158, describing the Menominee practice around 1890 has the chief of the braves at the west entrance and "an appointed old man" at the east.

173. See also Slotkin, p. 102.

174. Johnny Matchokamow gave credence to this belief by stating that an invisible person stands in the doorway of the hall and one should not linger there but enter without hesitation. His mention of two bad spirits that stand there may derive from the medicine belief depicted on scrolls as two serpents (Slotkin, p. 83). For much the same reason, dead bodies are removed through the western door or window so that the spirit of the deceased cannot take the spirits of the living with him. For a recent photo of this practice, see Brill, p. 115.

175. Lowie, "Arikara," p. 658.

176. WP, p. 59.

177. Skinner, "Kansa." p. 756.

178. See James R. Murie, "Pawnee Indian Societies," *APNH*, p. 626, fig. 18.

179. Wissler, "General Discussion," p. 862.

180. Wissler, "Blackfoot," p. 454.

181. Goddard, pp. 470-71.

182. Lowie, "Crow," pp. 200-201, figs. 4-5.

183. Rohrl, p. 42.

184. I am indebted to Ernie St. Germaine for this information and his sketch of the dance grounds.

185. See Slotkin, p. 67.

186. See Vernon Kinietz, *Chippewa Village: The Story of Katikitegon*, Cranbrook Institute of Science Bulletin 25 (1947), p. 100. It was common to have more than one dance hall on a reservation. Around 1920 there were at least five on Leech Lake Reservation (Rynkiewich, p. 41). The one two miles north of Ball Club, Minnesota, was one hundred feet in diameter and had log floors. Another was so large that it required five stoves to heat it.

187. Slotkin, p. 100.

188. Rohrl, pp. 152-53.

189. Ibid., p. 118; RF, expense book, p. 34.

190. Slotkin, p. 76; Clifton, p. 88, fig. 1.

191. Cited in WP, p. 64.

192. Slotkin, p. 101, was told that the flag should be raised before dawn by a warrior. At the end of the day the west warrior requests that the man who put it up take it down while singers perform four common songs (p. 116).

193. Howard, p. 118.

194. Slotkin, pp. 79, 101; *MM*, p. 158.

195. Cited in Slotkin, p. 79.

196. Clifton, p. 87.

197. Carrie A. Lyford, *Ojibwa Crafts*, ed. Williard W. Beatty (Lawrence, Kans.: Haskell Junior College Publications, 1943), pp. 19-20.

198. RF, expense book, p. 41. The visiting spirit in this case was the South Thunderbird.

199. *MM*, p. 43, n. 45.

200. Clifton, p. 87.

201. Albert B. Reagan, "Some Notes on the Grand Medicine Society of the Bois Fort Ojibwa," *Americana* 27 (1933): 509.

202. Landes, *Sioux*, pp. 81-82.

203. Skinner, "Iowa," p. 700.

204. Rohrl, p. 99.

205. Slotkin, p. 39.

206. Ibid.

207. *MM*, p. 152.

208. See Barrett, pp. 334-35. This was during the sixth day of the Whitefish Dance described by Barrett. The young man in question had in fact been singing at the wrong Drum for some time. Instances have been reported, however, of open friction between members, particularly over the proper way of conducting a ceremony. In the course of the same dance, someone arose to criticize the omission of certain songs and the incorrect order of events. This prompted another to rebut the criticism, all of which created considerable tension at the time (see Barrett, pp. 323-25).

209. Wissler, "General Discussion," p. 862.

210. WP, pp. 80-81.

211. For the Mandan-Hidatsa practice of incorporating bits of dog and buffalo bone see WP, pp. 46-47.

212. Baker asserts that in former times an entire deer's tail was simply fastened over the head for a roach.

213. MacCauley, p. 339.

214. Barrett, p. 333. In another Frank Churchill photograph at White Earth in 1906 from the same series as figure 22 an Ojibwa is shown being introduced by one white man to another. The only basic difference in the dress of the three is that the Indian has two bandoleer bags over his suit coat and beadwork down the seams of his pants.

215. Slotkin, p. 95. Rohrl, p. 58, implies a distinct difference between the costumes worn by Ojibwa at Fort Mille Lacs during the summer tourist shows and those reserved for the Drum Dance meetings:

> The tourist season was over, and the brightly colored feathers, long and dyed, were stored away. The porcupine quills and fluff for the [roach] headdresses . . . and the elaborately beaded costumes for the autumn and winter dances were being put in order.

This seems to be a somewhat exaggerated comparison; furthermore, her illustrated (p. 250) Drum Dance costumes at Mille Lacs, which include roaches and beaded aprons, fit those worn at any secular powwow, even at Mille Lacs.

216. Slotkin, pp. 119-20. Whether or not Indian items are added to white attire, one is still expected to be in one's best dress. When Baker gave a feast for his drum in the summer of 1973, in spite of having stayed up all night preparing the food, at the last minute before his guests arrived, he carefully ironed a clean shirt and trousers to wear to the event.

The Decline of the Drum Dance

1. Cited in Slotkin, pp. 15-16.

2. BI, p. 24.

3. Slotkin, p. 54.

4. RF, Flambeau book, p. 24.

5. Slotkin, p. 52.

6. Ibid., p. 84, n. 1.

7. Cited in ibid., p. 98.

8. Cited in ibid. Although there were five Wisconsin Potawatomi Drums in 1951, meetings were infrequent. Scattered membership and lack of transportation were blamed, and Drum owners were accused of failing to hold enough meetings for members to rehearse and thereby remember the songs (see Ritzenthaler, *Potawatomi*, p. 161).

9. *CM-II*, p. 147; also Slotkin's table 1, pp. 157-58. Clifton insists that multiple membership for the Kansas Potawatomi in no way reflects a loss in viability of the societies. Rather he sees it more as "an adaptation to changed demographic circumstances and an increase in the prestige associated with active participation in ritual affairs" (p. 91). Rynkiewich, p. 41, notes the practice of multiple membership at Leech Lake in the 1930s and sees it as a sign of the dissolution of the Drum Dance.

10. Barrett, p. 311.

11. RF, 2: 63 and 3: 5.

12. The same was the case with the Menominee positions for "apprentices."

13. Slotkin, pp. 157-58.

14. Cited in ibid., pp. 50-51.

15. BI, p. 13. John Mink registered much the same complaint about the Chief Dance. John Bisonette recalls that Mink was upset by the presence of children at such a serious affair: "I also heard him tell the people right out here at a Chief Dance that they weren't doing it right and it didn't amount to anything the way they did it" (RF, 9: 5).

16. See Slotkin's description of the summmer rite which took place in 1951, pp. 119-21.

17. Ibid., p. 135.

18. Ibid., p. 99.

304

19. RF, 3: 7.

20. Slotkin, p. 82. During Densmore's, Barrett's, and Skinner's fieldwork, circa 1910-13, Drums were still kept in their owners' houses.

21. RF, Flambeau book, p. 34.

22. RF, expense book, p. 34.

23. RF, 2: 74; cf. Vennum, "Origin-Migration Songs," p. 760.

24. Norman Feder, *American Indian Art* (New York: Harry N. Abrams, Inc., 1965), p. 45. No source is given for his information.

25. Similarly, Grass Dance drums were sold or given away secretly. When the Skidi (Pawnee) drum owner Knife-Chief died, his widow kept the drum until her son was old enough to be its keeper. Once, when the members wanted the drum for a New Year's dance, the son refused to let them have the drum, to cover the fact that he had secretly given it away (Murie, p. 625).

26. Slotkin, p. 50.

27. *Saint Paul Pioneer Press*, September 7, 1969.

28. My efforts to obtain further information from the Iron River family concerning the Drum's whereabouts have been futile.

29. Robert Ritzenthaler, "The Chippewa Indian Method of Securing and Tanning Deerskin," *Wisconsin Archeologist* 27 (1947): 8. On Vermilion Lake Reservation in 1979, for example, May Pehlke was the only one keeping this tradition alive. To encourage her people to learn it, she began to teach classes in tanning, but her only students were whites from nearby Ely, Minnesota.

30. Bernard M. Coleman, *Decorative Designs of the Ojibwa of Northern Minnesota*, Catholic University of America Anthropological Series no. 12 (Washington, D.C., 1947), p. 116.

31. Clifton, p. 90.

32. Flannery, pp. 39–70.

33. Ibid., p. 59.

34. See Slotkin, p. 55; Clifton, p. 90, mentions that the expense involved made Oklahoma Indians generally unreceptive to Potawatomi drum transfers.

35. Slotkin, pp. 99-100.

36. Ibid., pp. 99, 102.

37. Cited in ibid., p. 102.

38. Cited in Slotkin, p. 151.

39. Rohrl, p. 63, n. 12 and pp. 152-53.

40. Gillin, p. 552.

41. SDOH, tape 341, p. 8.

42. Cited in Rohrl, p. 57.

43. Cited in Slotkin, p. 154.

44. Ibid., p. 135, n. 1.

45. Ibid., p. 13, n. 1. What had once been lengthy ceremonials at Lac Court Oreilles by 1941 had been reduced to a single Sunday event in July (RF, notebook ID, no. 2, p. 38).

While more than a quarter of the adults at Mille Lacs belonged at least nominally to the medicine lodge, between 1961 and 1963 only one ceremony was held because their leader was confined to a sanitorium (Rohrl, p. 90).

46. Danziger, p. 149.

47. BI, p. 22.

48. Skinner, "Kansa," p. 755.

49. Wissler, "Oglala," p. 51.

50. Murie, p. 625.

51. Lowie, "Arikara," pp. 659-60.

52. BI, film transcripts.

53. Vogt, p. 191.

54. Wissler, "General Discussion," p. 869.

55. Landes, *Ojibwa Religion*, p. 38.

56. Wissler ("General Discussion," p. 867) was one of the first to point out that central Algonquians accorded the pipe and drum attributes of medicine bundles.

57. For a more complete version, see Barrett, p. 327.

58. Cf. the biblical passage "In my Father's house are many mansions" (John 14: 2).

59. Barrett, p. 350.

60. Slotkin, p. 22.

61. Barrett, pp. 286-87.

62. For a more complete version, see "A Woman's War Vision," by Landes in *Ojibwa Religion*, pp. 207-17.

63. For a more complete account, see Howard, pp. 117-26.

64. Wissler, p. 867.

65. Published data concerning the ritual details and offices of the Maggie Wilson Dance are lacking.

66. Cited in Landes, *Ojibwa Religion*, p. 212.

67. RF, 3: 3. John Mink was also critical of Grover (see Joseph. B. Casagrande, "John Mink, Ojibwa Informant," *Wisconsin Archeologist*, n.s. 36 (1955): 116.

68. Cf. the discussion of Blessing's orthodox triangle, Vennum, "Origin-Migration Songs," p. 756.

69. Parthun, pp. 47-48.

70. Cited in Howard, p. 119.

71. Rohrl, p. 47 and p. 113, n. 11.

72. Ibid., p. 97. This is not unlike the Santee waiting for the "propitious moment" to sell the Grass Dance to the Hidatsa; they took the killing of Black Hills Dakota the previous winter as a favorable sign.

73. Some reports have the candidate at the east end of the lodge.

74. See Peter Nabokov, *Indian Running* (Santa Barbara, Calif.: Capra Press, 1981).

75. RF, 3: 72-73.

76. RF, 3: 75.

77. Clifton, pp. 92-93.

78. James A. Clifton, "Potawatomi," *Handbook*, 15: 740.

79. See Clifton, "Prairie Potawatomi," p. 87.

Construction

The Drum Proper

1. Barrett, pp. 266-67.

2. An abbreviated version by this author describing such technology, "Constructing the Ojibwa Dance Drum," appeared in *Wisconsin Archeologist*, n.s. 54 (1973): 162-74.

3. Usually a circular section is cut out. In one instance, however, the Friendship drum in the Heye Foundation collection, the builder (?) has superimposed on the circle a five-pointed star. Since there was once, but no longer, a bottom head on the Drum, the star may have been added for decorative or symbolic purposes (cf. painting on the bottom head, fig. 55).

4. Names assigned to drums throughout the text are by builder, if known; if not, then by owner or collector. The Drum collected by Albert B. Reagan is in the collections of the National Museum of Man, Ottawa, Ontario, Canada, cat. no. III-G-167.

5. According to Densmore, the distinction in sizes has social implications: the Chief Drum is presented by chiefs or leaders, the smaller Warrior Drum is given by tribal members of lesser status (*CM-II*, p. 145):

6. *CM-II*, p. 145; also *MM*, p. 154.

7. Through the gap in the skirt of the Walter Drift Drum, a small wooden peg protrudes with a leather strap attached. Possibly the drum at one time had four supporting pegs.

8. The original illustration is published in Hoffman, "The Midewiwin," p. 190, fig. 12b.

9. In 1910 some Drum members at Lac Court Oreilles claimed to be the only ones to put bells inside their Drums (Barrett, p. 261). The practice is, in fact, widespread. Menominee Drum members consider the sound of the bell to represent the voice of "the old man in the drum"; when the Drum is struck, his voice "is sent out all over, in all four directions, to all those spirits. [The Great Spirit] hears that and gives us what we ask for. That old man in the drum gets those messages out" (Spindler and Spindler, p. 66).

10. Slotkin, p. 22. The association of bells with hearts is apparent elsewhere among North American tribes. In 1868 General George Custer obtained a Cheyenne shield with four Thunderbirds painted on it. Brass bells are attached to the ends of rawhide thongs that depend from the heart area of each Thunderbird (*American Indian Art* [Summer 1979]: 57).

11. Conceivably a fall or winter hide from a buck could be used as the skin is thicker at that time of year.

12. See Lyford, p. 98, pl. 55. In the Ayer collection at Mille Lacs is a scraper with a halfted stone.

13. See D. I. Bushnell, *Villages of the Algonquian, Siouan, and Caddoan Tribes*, Bureau of American Ethnology Bulletin no. 77 (Washington, D.C., 1922), pl. 12a, showing two bone fleshers that Bushnell says were "made within a generation" of his visits, around 1900.

14. Ritzenthaler, "Tanning," p. 9.

15. Ibid., p. 13.

16. A Wisconsin drum (Milwaukee Public Museum, cat. no. 5363/2207), purchased from S. A. Barrett in 1910, has lacing but also tacks to secure both heads.

17. Ritzenthaler, "Tanning," p. 8.

18. The removal of excess flesh and membrane from deerhides is often accomplished on the beaming post by scraping the skin side after the hair has been removed.

19. Using a continuous piece of lacing is the most common method, the lacing going from one head to the other and back again. See, however, fig. 82 which shows lacing from each head joining in V shapes partway between them. As noted, however, this illustration may be fanciful.

Decorations

1. A circa 1885 velvet skirt with floral beadwork, thought to be Santee Sioux, has a scalloped fringed bottom. A photograph of it is published in the exhibition catalog *Sacred Circles: Two Thousand Years of American Indian Art* (Kansas City, Mo.: Nelson Gallery of Art, 1977), p. 177, no. 448. Ojibwa skirt bottoms, by contrast, are left straight and unadorned.

2. The Wildschut Drum skirt (Heye Foundation, cat. no.11/5864) is of four equal flannel sections sewn together, two each of blue and red on the north and south sides of the Drum respectively. Another drum in the Heye Foundation collection, the Friendship drum, has a black cotton skirt nailed around it at the top and bottom of the frame.

3. Howard, p. 22.

4. *MM*, p. 153. Slotkin, p. 72, describes such a skirt with the north half blue, the south half red. See also Milwaukee Public Museum, cat. no. 13103a/3592, said to be a Winnebago drum from Black River Falls, Wisconsin, purchased in 1913.

5. *CM-II*, p. 145.

6. Heye Foundation, cat. no. 9/1868.

7. *CC*, p. 187.

8. See Coleman, p. 59, pl. 13, identified as Cut Foot Sioux. Also Parthun, p. 49, for the description of a dance drum in the collection of Bemidji State University, said to be more than one hundred years old, and p. 306 for his photograph of a contemporary drum. The Walter Drift Drum (fig. 68) is so old that much of the beadwork of the floral stems has fallen off.

9. Cf. SOM for a discussion of the dissolution of song texts in their musical setting (pp. 257-58).

10. Rohrl, p. 98.

11. Barrett, p. 263, states that the belt is usually of beadwork but sometimes of fur. In the latter case he must be referring to the fur strip, which is a separate item and not a belt.

12. *MM*, p. 153.

13. Heye Foundation, cat.no.9/1868. The style of this beaded band suggests it might be Osage. Slotkin, p. 72, noted no consistent width for belts on Menominee drums.

14. *MM*, p. 153.

15. Coleman, p. 3. The otter-tail pattern can be represented in double and even triple bands of color. The zigzag is also used to symbolize lightning.

308

16. Slotkin, p. 72. One should be careful in interpreting the cross symbol as Christian, for it was also used in the *midewiwin* to represent one of the degrees of advancement within the medicine lodge. Furthermore, the "four steps to heaven" strongly suggest *midewiwin* tenets, as candidates strove to achieve the fourth (in some places the eighth) or highest degree.

17. Slotkin, p. 60.

18. Coleman, p. 34.

19. Lyford, p. 152; see also the beaded velvet bag with four tabs and yarn tassles, p. 126, pl. 73.

20. Canadian National Museum of Man, cat. no. III-H-408.

21. See Clark Wissler, "Decorative Art of the Sioux," *Bulletins of the American Museum of Natural History* 18 (1904): 253, pl. xl, no. 5.

22. Lyford, pp. 102-3, pl. 57.

23. McCord Museum, Montreal, cat. no. M5893, publ. *Sacred Circles*, no. 470.

24. Burton W. Thayer, "The Algonquian Trait of Asymmetry," *Minnesota Archaeologist* 8 (1942): 57.

25. For ceremonial Drums with tabs that do not have symbolic forms, see here fig. 55 and the first drum in fig. 77.

26. Howard, p. 122.

27. John M. Vlach, *The Afro-American Tradition in Decorative Arts* (Cleveland: Cleveland Museum of Art, 1978), figs. 43-44.

28. Feder, fig. 61, colorpl. 19.

29. Ibid., fig. 81, Brooklyn Museum, cat. no. 04.187.

30. Wissler, "Sioux," p. 266, pl. lv, no. 1.

31. Chandler-Pohrt collection, cat. no. 2694, published in the exhibition catalog *The Art of the Great Lakes Indians* (Flint: Flint Institute of the Arts, 1973), p. 79, no. 363 (hereinafter AGLI).

32. Coleman, p. 13.

33. Ibid.

34. See Vennum, "Origin-Migration Songs," p. 755.

35. See Fred K. Blessing, *The Ojibway Indians Observed*, Occasional Publications in Minnesota Anthropology no. 1 (1977), pp. 80-83.

36. See Barrett, pp. 263-64; Slotkin, pp. 38, 72. This interpretation was given for the two heads on tabs of a Menominee Drum, the northwest tab was said to be the Great Spirit, the southeast, the Sioux woman.

37. *MM*, p. 153.

38. RF, 5: 56.

39. Cited in Slotkin, p. 90.

40. Ibid., p. 107.

41. Cf. the Canadian Ojibwa four-to-five-foot armless *manidookanaash* put in the forest for protection (*Artscanada*, p. 69).

42. Albert B. Reagan, "Some Games of the Bois Fort Ojibwa," *American Anthropologist*, n.s. 21 (1919): 267.

43. RF, 10: 3.

44. Slotkin, p. 79. The figure with the frock is on a set of beaded decorations detached from a Drum. These were recently acquired by the Milwaukee Public Museum and may be Ojibwa, although possibly Menominee or Potawatomi. Nancy Lurie has suggested that the hat and frock might have been used to represent a white man. If so, perhaps the unusual clothing was added to signify that the flag was American or that the message of brotherhood extended to include non-Indians as well.

45. James, p. 180.

46. See the circa 1800 Minnesotan (or Canadian) Ojibwa badger bag, *Sacred Circles*, p. 99, no. 163. The Santee Sioux medicine lodge "Tree Dweller" gods were represented by wooden dolls with horns (see Feder, fig. 55).

47. Dewdney, see figs. 77-82.

48. *CM*, pl. 2b.

49. Barrett, pp. 263-64; Slotkin, p. 72.

50. Coleman, pp. 12-13. See the Mille Lacs Drum, ibid., p. 56, pl. 12a.

51. For a Red Lake Ojibwa drum of the *waabanowiwin*, see Hoffman, "The Midewiwin," p. 223, fig. 22.

52. Mooney, p. 68.

53. See *CC*, pl. 33.

54. Blessing, p. 169.

55. RF, 11: 21; for "medicine poles," see *CM-II*, pls. 40-41.

56. Blessing, *The Ojibway*, p. 165; *CC*, p. 82.

57. Paul Radin, "Ojibwa Ethnological Chit Chat," *American Anthropologist*, n.s. 26 (1924): 508.

58. *MM*, p. 183.

59. *CC*, pls. 31-32.

60. *MM*, p. 27.

61. See *CC*, p. 55, fig. 8, for such a dream token.

62. Reagan, "Some Notes," p. 508.

63. See *Artscanada*, pp. 66-67. Some smaller wooden spirit figures had movable arms. See also the circa 1875 Cree beaded bag with two dark *manidoog* against a light background (p. 68).

64. The size of Baker's tabs is about average for Ojibwa drums. By constrast, the enormous tabs of one Potawatomi Drum reach almost to the bottom of its skirt (publ. Feder, fig. 220, Wisconsin State Historical Society, cat. no. 1954.1359-c).

65. Since most Menominee Drums came from the Ojibwa, the fur strip is an integral part of their decor. Slotkin describes a 1 1/2 inch otter-fur band around "the top rim of each Drum" (p. 72). Unusually wide is the five-inch fur strip on a drum purchased in 1911 by the Milwaukee Public Museum (cat. no. 6951/2589) said to be Winnebago, but probably not. Barrett, pp. 262-63, implies that formerly the skirt was entirely of fur but that later it was replaced by velvet. I have seen no evidence to support this.

310

66. *CC*, p. 37.

67. See *CM*, pl. 9; *CM-II*, pls. 1, 9.

68. Burton, p. 254.

69. James, p. 180.

70. SDOH, tape 343.

71. Barrett, p. 263.

72. The application of cone pendants to children's furniture seems to have been widespread. See, for instance, the Blood-Blackfoot (?) willow backrest, Glenbow-Alberta Institute, cat. no. AF 3757, publ. in *American Indian Art* (Summer 1979): 66. Also, the circa 1800 Eastern Sioux (?) cradle decoration from the Lessard collection, *AGLI*, p. 4.

73. The war club is in a private collection in Spooner, Wisconsin. The author bases his date and provenance on the style of beadwork and proximity of Spooner to the reservation. The practice of attaching cone pendants to artifacts predates European contact. In the Blue Island site near present-day Chicago was found a small perched bird effigy carved of antler with copper tinkling cones beneath it, which were at one time attached to the tail of the bird through perforations in it (George I. Quimby, *Indian Culture and European Trade Goods* [Madison, Milwaukee, and London: University of Wisconsin Press, 1966], p. 39).

74. The Museum of the American Indian, Heye Foundation, cat. no. 1/6944, publ. *AGLI*, p. 1.

75. The Chandler-Pohrt collection, cat. no. 3022, publ. Feder, colorpl. 54.

76. Quimby, *Indian Culture*, p. 29. See p. 26, fig. 4, and p. 31, fig. 6.

77. Ibid., p. 127.

78. For a photograph of a Canadian Ojibwa jingle dress, see Landes, *Ojibwa Religion*, pl. 4, opposite p. 37.

79. See School of American Research, Santa Fe, cat. no. M. 478, which dates from the 1940s, publ. *American Indian Art* (Winter 1978): 36.

80. Cited in *People of the First Man*, p. 30. For Bodmer's painting, see p. 47.

81. An Iowa ceremonial Drum on exhibit in the Milwaukee Public Museum has a metal band etched with designs surrounding its skirt (cat. no. 30661/7322 a and b). Dewclaws and cones hang from the band.

82. *CC*, p. 36.

83. Quimby, *Indian Culture*, pp. 122, 154.

84. See Hoffman, "Menomini," p. 155, fig. 22.

85. *CM-II*, p. 145. See also the circa 1890 Ojibwa shoulder bag in the Lanford collection, publ. *AGLI*, p. 59, no. 228.

86. Milwaukee Public Museum cat. no. 13103a/3592, purchased at Black River Falls, Wisconsin.

87. Howard, p. 122.

88. Vogt, p. 128. See also a Sioux pouch from the early 1890s that has both bells and pennies as pendant ornaments (*Sacred Circles*, no. 506).

89. Landes, *Ojibwa Religion*, p. 209, cites Maggie Wilson who in her vision was brought "the bells to be attached to the drum and staffs [legs?]" by the Thunderbirds.

90. Cited in Barrett, p. 344.

91. See the Ojibwa knife sheaths from the Lessard collection and National Museum of Natural History (cat. no. 130.788), the latter dated circa 1835, publ. *AGLI*, pp. 90-91, nos. 411, 414.

92. Cat. no. 66.14.70, publ. *AGLI*, p. 55, no. 207.

93. Logan Museum of Anthropology, cat. no. 31309, publ. *AGLI*, p. 29, no. 107.

94. Lyford, p. 126, pl. 73.

95. See *CC*, pl. 90.

96. Moccasin game drums with symbolic designs on them were dream inspired and used when the game was considered sacred (see Densmore, "Game Songs," *CM-II*, p. 206. Also, note the hand symbol mentioned in connection with tabs).

97. See Howard, p. 122.

98. Slotkin, p. 68. The Drift Drum (fig. 68) has both heads painted; the top head has become very faded through age and use. Half of the Winnebago Friendship drum in the Museum of the American Indian, Heye Foundation, appears to have been red at one time; if the other two colors were ever present, they have now faded beyond recognition.

99. Howard, p. 121.

100. RF, expense book, p. 34.

101. Slotkin, p. 34.

102. Rohrl, p. 120.

103. Barrett, p. 264. See also p. 262, fig. 3; also, Slotkin, p. 69, for the design on the three Ojibwa/Menominee Drums studied.

104. See RF, 1: 19; also Slotkin, p. 68.

105. Rohrl (p. 118, fig. 1) gives a diagram of participants and ritual objects in the Mille Lacs Drum Dance of 1963. The Drum in the middle of the square dance hall has its yellow band oriented north and south, its red half facing west. This peculiarity and the fact that the only entrance to the hall is represented as on the south side suggest that the directional arrow indicating "north" in the diagram is incorrect and actually points west. The error is confirmed by other researchers (cf. Howard).

106. Ibid., p. 128.

107. Cf. Dewdney, figs. 78-79.

108. Slotkin, p. 70; see also Howard, p. 122.

109. Howard, p. 122.

110. Coleman, p. 60.

111. Barrett, p. 264. ·

112. RF, 12: 7.

113. Hoffman, "The Midewiwin," p. 256, describing the lower half of the westernmost of the four posts in the lodge. These associations were confirmed by Coleman's informant, Charlie Fox, some years later, except for his substitution of orange or yellow for white (Coleman, pp. 75-76). Blue was even considered a sign of evil in Grand Medicine beliefs. If someone died of "bad medicine" inflicted through witchcraft by a fourth-degree *mide*, his face, feet, and lower half of his hands would turn blue (Reagan, "Some Notes," p. 506). These color associations are so consistent that I question the Spindlers' Menominee data

showing red to indicate dangerous spirits and blue to indicate good spirits (Spindler and Spindler, p. 64)

114. Rohrl, p. 129.

115. Wissler, "Sioux," p. 270.

116. Slotkin, p. 71. It was claimed at Lac Court Oreilles that the John Stone Drum was the only one to have this design element.

117. Wissler, "Sioux," p. 270; Slotkin, p. 71.

118. Coleman, p. 98.

119. Lyford, "Use of Colors," p. 151.

120. Cited in James, p. 369.

121. *People of the First Man*, p. 120.

122. Gilfillan, p. 62.

123. McKenney, p. 284.

124. Kohl, p. 416.

125. Ibid., p. 15

126. Hoffman, "The Midewiwin," pp. 182-83, pl. vii.

127. Fletcher, *Omaha*, p. 397.

128. Barrett, pp. 335-36, 339.

129. RF, 4: 28. For some reason, John Bisonette insisted that they would never rub red paint on the red part of the drum in the removal of mourning. See also *CM-II*, p. 155, about the painting of faces at this ceremony, also *MM*, p. 163, for the Menominee practice.

Accessories

1. In 1911 Densmore (*CM-II*, p. 169) found that the pipe ritual took place "at intervals as nearly equal as possible"; thirty years later, Ritzenthaler noted that the four performances can occur anytime during the day.

2. Slotkin, p. 109.

3. See Barrett, pp. 268-76, 353. Much of Barrett's account was included verbatim in George A. West, "Uses of Tobacco and the Calumet by Wisconsin Indians," *Wisconsin Archaeologist* 10 (1911): 5-64, together with additional historical information, especially about Wisconsin practices. The Menominee use of the pipe for song services is described by Slotkin, pp. 93-94.

4. Ritzenthaler, *"Southwestern Chippewa,"* p. 754.

5. Slotkin, p. 71.

6. Ibid., p. 38. Additionally, a small purse is kept for money offerings used to purchase tobacco when the need arises (p. 71).

7. Barrett, p. 367.

8. Ibid., p. 268. When the pipe tender dances with the stem, according to Barrett, it is used "by proxy" to represent the membership of his Drum. For a photograph showing the great variety of stems in the collections of the Milwaukee Public Museum, see West, pl. 3, opposite p. 56. Also Slotkin, p. 78, fig. 9, and p. 80, fig. 10, for distinctions between

Matchokamow's short and long stems. Slotkin also mentions a special "great warrior pipe" consisting of black catlinite with lead inlay, which is kept by the Menominee west warrior as a symbol of his office (p. 79). Densmore's data on Menominee pipe stem distinctions seem at odds with the general practice: a short square stem is smoked only by the Drum owner, aide, and four singers; the longer round one, which she calls the "ordinary" pipe, is used when messages are sent concerning Drum matters (*MM*, p. 154).

9. See Howard, p. 122.

10. Publ. Hoffman, "The Midewiwin," p. 190, fig. 12b.

11. RF, 3: 3.

12. *CM-II*, p. 147.

13. *MM*, p. 175; Hoffman, p. 159.

14. Cited in Wissler, "Oglala," pp. 48-49.

15. Landes mentions bells attached to a Canadian Ojibwa Drum as well as to its legs (*Ojibwa Religion*, p. 209).

16. *CM-II*, p. 170.

17. *MM*, pp. 158-59.

18. Ibid.

19. *People of the First Man*, p. 186.

20. Skinner, "Ponca," p. 786.

21. Frances Densmore, *Mandan and Hidatsa Music*. Smithsonian Institution, Bureau of American Ethnology Bulletin no. 80. (Washington, D.C., 1923), p. 109.

22. Murie, p. 568, fig. 6; see also fig. 7 for "The Red Lance." For an Omaha example, see Fletcher, p. 155, fig. 27. Edward Curtis once posed an "Apsaroke [Crow] War Group" on horseback for a gravure. One of the three is carrying a fur-wrapped coup stick.

23. Cooper, pp. 222-23.

24. RF, expense book, pp. 46-47.

25. Howard, p. 120.

26. *MM*, p. 176.

27. The Milwaukee Public Museum has a set of legs (cat. no. 55150/16740) with aluminum hooks screwed into them that appear to have been part of nautical tackle.

28. Barrett, pp. 264-65. A set of Oto (Grass Dance?) drum legs in the Field Museum of Natural History (cat. no. 71706) is carved to resemble horses heads facing outward. The hook on each leg is effected directly behind the horse's curved neck (publ., Feder, fig. 47).

29. Barrett, p. 265.

30. The legs shown in the illustration are as follows: (left to right) Baker's in the author's collection, Lac Court Oreilles Drum leg in 1899 photograph by Jenks (builder and present location unknown), David Goss Drum leg in the collection of Museum of the American Indian, Heye Foundation, cat. no. 11/5864.

31. *MM*, p. 102.

32. *CM-II*, p. 145. See *CM*, pl. 9.

33. WP, pp. 46-47.

34. *MM*, pp. 153-54.

35. SDOH, tape 341, pp. 37-38.

36. Cited in RF, 12: 8.

37. Barrett, p. 264.

38. RF, expense book, p. 34.

39. Howard, p. 121.

40. Rohrl, p. 122.

41. For the X arrangement, see Slotkin, p. 103, fig. 15. A photograph of a Menominee Drum over a square leg stand is given in Spindler and Spindler, p. 64; the stand rests on top of a folded blanket. Ritzenthaler, *Potawatomi*, p. 160, fig. 15, published a photo of a Potawatomi Drum set up out of doors; the drum legs are simply inserted into the ground.

42. Baker sent me these directions together with a handdrawn sketch for the legs that were to go with his 1970 drum.

43. Blessing, *The Ojibway*, p. 167. See here also the 1899 Jenks photograph (fig. 34).

44. Peyotists are an exception, as they sometimes use the hand to beat the water drum; the spread of this religion, however, has been relatively recent.

45. RF, 8: 36.

46. See *CM*, pl. 2b.

47. Cf. Vennum, "Ojibwa-Migration Songs," p. 781

48. Dewdney, pp. 82-83, fig. 62.

49. Such a stick is in the Ayer collection at Mille Lacs.

50. *CC*, pl. 5b.

51. Ibid., pl. 36b.

52. Kohl, pp. 422-23.

53. Cited in RF, 8: 36.

54. Reproduced in Rogers, "Southeastern Ojibwa," p. 768, fig. 10.

55. *CC*, p. 166; *CM-II*, p. 146.

56. *CM-II*, p. 171. See also *MM*, pp. 159-60.

57. Densmore, *CC*, p. 166, describes a hand-drum stick of this type completely wrapped with cloth.

58. *People of the First Man*, pp. 207, 215. See also Densmore, *Mandan and Hidatsa Music*, pl. 9a.

59. *MM*, p. 35.

60. Ibid., p. 38.

61. Catlin, 2: pl. 224.

62. Slotkin, p. 18, n. 5.

63. *CM-II*, p. 144.

64. *CC*, p. 166; Densmore gives the hand-drum stick's length as eighteen inches.

65. Slotkin, p. 76.

66. *CC*, p. 166.

67. RF, 12: 8.

68. Slotkin, p. 76.

69. Barrett, p. 303; elsewhere, however (p. 342), he gives somewhat conflicting information about the *baaga'akokwaan*, stating that it was conferred on a younger man who was told to honor it and dance with it but never to beat the drum with it.

70. Slotkin, pp. 58, 62; see also p. 63, fig. 4.

71. Lowie, "Crow," p. 202.

72. WP, pp. 41-42, 85.

73. This is not the first instance of fishing poles converted by Woodlands Indians to musical purposes. Menominee war bundles used to contain reed whistles. Because the Menominee had to travel some distance to obtain the reed, they began to make the whistles of sections of bamboo fishing rods (*MM*, p. 69).

74. See, e.g., *CM-II*, p. 146.

75. Near the end of the final service of the seasonal rites, the Drum is heated and returned to its legs for the closing songs. All drums are then "closed" and must not be opened for four days. They are to be reopened at sunrise and left uncovered for a full day, during which there is a special song sevice, ceremonial meal, and evening song service (see Slotkin, pp. 119, 148).

76. *CM-II*, p. 145.

77. Densmore, *MM*, p. 162, described the end of one Menominee Drum Dance, during which the Drum was picked up in a clean white cloth by the owner (?), who led a procession out of the dance ring; the lead singer followed him, the other singers in a single file behind the lead.

78. Hoffman, "Menomini," p. 160, fig. 25.

79. Bushnell, pp. 11-12. Cf. suspended drums in the "heathen [non-Christian] houses" at Leech Lake described by Gilfillan, p. 79.

80. Rohrl, p. 58.

81. Conceivably it was an earlier cover for this drum that was converted into a covering for Johnny Matchokamow's tobacco box; it too had applique designs (see Slotkin, p. 77).

82. See Slotkin, p. 75, fig. 8. Rohrl, p. 98, mentions a velvet covering for drums at Mille Lacs Lake. Coleman, p. 10, speaks of *mide* drum covers with six- or eight-point stars in beadwork embroidered on them.

83. At Mille Lacs, the custom is to keep the drum near the eastern wall (Rohrl, p. 98); Baker usually keeps his drums in the southeast corner of his house.

84. Slotkin, p. 74, n. 1 and p. 76. When the Henry Davis Drum was used at Mille Lacs a large crocheted rug was placed under the instrument, with the Drum's cover on top of the rug (Howard, p. 121). In the Menominee dance hall at Zoar, two rush mats were first laid on the floor, the square frame for holding the legs placed on top of them, then a rag rug over the frame—all before the Drum was suspended (Slotkin, p. 102).

Variants

1. Samuel Bayard, "A Prolegomena to a Study of the Principal Melodic Families of British-American Folksong," *Journal of American Folklore* 63 (1950): 1-44. Bayard's original wording is as follows:

A tune family is a group of melodies showing basic interrelation by means of constant melodic correspondence, and presumably owing their mutual likeness to descent from a single air that has assumed multiple forms through processes of variation, imitation, and assimilation.

2. Rohrl, p. 129.

3. See Vogt's interpretation for the path of the sun among Mexican Indians (p. 123).

4. Rohrl, p. 129.

5. See Howard, p. 127.

6. Landes, *Ojibwa Religion*, p. 38.

7. Coleman, pp. 7, 69.

8. Cat. no. PS-3, publ. Feder, no. 26. See also the circa 1920 Cheyenne shield painted on a flour sack (ibid., no. 27). See also a Blackfoot single-headed pre-1929 medicine pipe drum, National Museums of Canada, cat. no. V-B-185, collected in Gleichen, Alberta. The head is divided by a double transverse line in black and green, separating black and red fields with dots and stylized lightning.

9. Field Museum of Natural History, cat. no. 71856, collected by George Dorsey.

10. Heye Foundation, cat. no. 11/5864. Indian people were not the only ones in America to sign percussion instruments. A tambourine found in Tuskegee, Alabama, has fifty-three signatures on its head, apparently all members of the Macon County, Alabama, singing school, and the date, December 25, 1891 (publ. *In Celebration of a Legacy: The Traditional Arts of the Lower Chattahoochee Valley* [Columbus, Ga.: Columbus Museum of Arts and Sciences, 1981]).

11. Purchased by Shirley W. Peterson, La Pointe, Wisconsin, circa 1970.

12. Purchased by William Miller, circa 1970.

13. See Vennum, "Origin-Migration Songs."

The Lac Court Oreilles Drum Dance, circa 1940

1. As described earlier in Baker's practice, attached first is the skirt around the top rim of the Drum, then the belt over this, the pads over the belt, and finally the strip of fur. Once these have been attached, pendants, ribbons, and the like are affixed to them.

2. Bisonette may be describing the John Martin Drum. (Elsewhere, however, Ritzenthaler notes that the John Martin Drum had a man holding a drum, not a flag, on one tab.) Having four different designs, one for each pad, is most unusual.

3. This is not always the practice at Lac Court Oreilles. Baker has decorated eagle feathers for drum stakes, wrapping the ends of two of them with red yarn and the other two with blue yarn to correspond with the colors on the particular stakes.

4. The clockwise movements around the dance ring conform to the general pattern of clockwise dancing around a centrally located drum, even at secular powwows. This direction has been explained as representing the legendary order of birth of the Four Winds, beginning with the East Wind, then the South Wind, the West Wind, and finally the North Wind.

5. The *oshkaabewis* traditionally held the position of messenger or runner in warfare as well as in the Grand Medicine Society. In both instances his first assignment was to make the rounds with tobacco, inviting participants to join a war party or attend a *midewiwin* ceremony. (Special invitation sticks were sometimes used for the latter event.) Baraga translates "Oshkabewiss" as "Waiter or attendant of an Indian Chief."

6. Food and tobacco are traditionally offered to six cardinal directions: the Great Spirit

above, the Good Spirit below, and to each of the Four Winds. Bisonette mentioned that at Lac Court Oreilles they began with the North Wind but noted that formerly at Saint Croix they began with the East Wind. Ritzenthaler's fieldnotes on the matter must be incorrect, for he has the bull cook making two offerings to the west, while omitting the east.

7. See appendix "Drum Society Structures."

8. Among the Menominee, the bull cook (also called waiter) holds a special baton of office while dancing to his song (Slotkin, p. 113). The same song, apparently, could be used for the belt man (Slotkin, p. 161).

9. Photographs taken at Lac Court Oreilles as early as 1899 show the feather belt being worn (see here fig. 46). Bisonette said that he had last seen the belt ritual performed sometime between 1911 and 1914. Barrett (pp. 287-88) mentions observing it in the Menominee Drum Dance but omits reference to its use among the Whitefish community at Lac Court Oreilles.

10. Typically, in Ojibwa group singing, the beginning of each song and each repetition of the melody during the course of a song is performed by one singer or lead before the rest of the group joins him in unison (see Vennum, "Song Form," SOM, pp. 47-49). The Ojibwa share this practice with most Plains tribes.

11. The Drum is usually carried by its cover, a bag deep enough to permit gathering it at its top and slinging it over one shoulder (see here figs. 98-99). When the covered Drum is kept in the home, this gathering can be tied to something to suspend the Drum in air (see Hoffman, p. 160, fig. 25, for a Menominee Drum so hung).

12. Although Ritzenthaler's fieldnotes indicate east as the exit direction, west would be more likely and in keeping with the older medicine lodge practice.

13. Densmore's study *Chippewa Music* included several songs used when ponies were given away, one of which she collected from two different singers (*CM*, pp. 202, 209; *CM-II*, pp. 238-39).

14. Formerly the Ojibwa simply used an entire deer tail for the roach.

15. Almost all new songs in the Ojibwa repertoire continue to arrive "from the west" and are probably Siouan in origin.

16. Ritzenthaler's previous list ended with number 18 and he began numbering here with number 25, probably in accordance with the informant's noting that there were "two dozen" special songs.

17. See Densmore's "Ceremony of Restoring the Mourners," (*CM-II*, pp. 153-57).

18. The belt is not, technically speaking, on the "middle" of the Drum but rather around the top edge. The informant here may have used "middle" to locate the belt somewhere between the two drumheads.

19. Sewing the heads together would be unlikely. Probably they were replaced using rope or rawhide.

20. It is not clear what "the next day dance" means here since the implication is that the dance was to be held at a future date.

21. The reader is referred to the map (fig. 21) showing the location of these communities.

22. By "down there" the informant probably means the Black River Falls, Wisconsin, area.

23. The Winnebago were removed by the United States Government from their traditional homeland in present-day Wisconsin and ultimately settled on their reservation in northeastern Nebraska. Many, however, moved back to Wisconsin, and there is continual visiting between the two groups.

318

24. To present two Drums to the Menominee in October 1910, seventy Flambeau Ojibwa traveled most of the way by train but disembarked about twenty miles from their destination in order to allow two days to walk the remainder of the distance. Presumably they danced each evening at their encampment (see *CM-II*, p. 163).

25. Singers sometimes also tap softly on the rim of a drum when they are quietly rehearsing or learning a song. In this instance, clearly the intent was to permit the ritual single strokes to stand out from the rest of the accompaniment before all the singers began to beat on the head of the Drum.

Bibliography: Sources on the Ojibwa and Their Music

Armstrong, Benjamin G. *Early Life among the Indians.* Ashland, Wis.: Press of A. W. Bowron, 1892.

Baraga, Friedrich. *A Dictionary of the Otchipwe Language, Explained in English,* 1878 and 1880. Revised ed. Edited by Albert Lacombe. Minneapolis: Ross and Haines, 1966.

Barnouw, Victor. "Reminiscences of a Chippewa Mide Priest." *Wisconsin Archeologist,* n.s. 35 (1954): 83-112.

————. "A Chippewa Mide Priest's Description of the Medicine Dance." *Wisconsin Archeologist,* n.s. 41 (1960): 77-97.

Barrett, Samuel A. *The Dream Dance of the Chippewa and Menominee Indians of Northern Wisconsin.* Bulletins of the Public Museum of the City of Milwaukee. Milwaukee, 1911, pp. 251-406.

Blessing, Fred K. *The Ojibway Indians Observed.* Occasional Publications in Minnesota Anthropology no. 1 (1977).

Bloomfield, Leonard. *Eastern Ojibwa: Grammatical Sketch, Texts, and Word List.* Ann Arbor: University of Michigan Press, 1957.

Brill, Charles. *Indian and Free: A Contemporary Portrait of Life on a Chippewa Reservation.* Minneapolis: University of Minnesota Press, 1974.

Burton, Frederick R. *American Primitive Music, with Especial Attention to the Songs of the Ojibways.* New York: Moffat, Yard, and Co., 1909.

Bushnell, David Ives, Jr. "An Ojibway Ceremony." *American Anthropologist* 7 (1905): 69-73.

Casagrande, Joseph B. "John Mink, Ojibwa Informant." *Wisconsin Archeologist,* n.s. 36 (1955): 106-28.

Coleman, Bernard. "The Religion of the Ojibwa of Northern Minnesota." *Primitive Man* 10 (1937): 33-57.

————, et al. *Ojibwa Myths and Legends.* Minneapolis: Ross and Haines, 1962.

Cooper, John M. *Notes on the Ethnology of the Otchipwe of Lake of the Woods and Rainy Lake.* Catholic University of America Anthropological Series 3. Washington, D.C., 1936, pp. 1-29.

Densmore, Frances. *Chippewa Music.* Smithsonian Institution, Bureau of American Ethnology Bulletin no. 45. Washington, D.C., 1910.

————. *Chippewa Music-II.* Smithsonian Institution, Bureau of American Ethnology Bulletin no. 53. Washington D.C., 1913.

————. *Chippewa Customs.* Smithsonian Institution, Bureau of American Ethnology Bulletin no. 86. Washington, D.C., 1929.

Dewdney, Selwyn H. *The Sacred Scrolls of the Southern Ojibway.* Toronto: University of Toronto Press, 1975.

Hallowell, Alfred Irving. *Culture and Experience.* 1955; New York: Schocken Books, 1967.

Hickerson, Harold. *The Southwestern Chippewa: An Ethnohistorical Study.* American Anthropological Association Memoir 92. Menasha, Wis., 1962.

_____. *The Chippewas and Their Neighbors: A Study in Ethnohistory.* New York: Holt, Rinehart and Winston, 1970.

Hoffman, Walter J. "The Midewiwin, or 'Grand Medicine Society' of the Ojibwa." In *Bureau of American Ethnology, Seventh Annual Report, 1885-86,* pp. 143-300. Washington D.C., 1891.

Jones, William. "Ojibwa Tales from North Shore of Lake Superior." *Journal of American Folklore* 29 (1916): 368-91.

Kinietz, William V. *Chippewa Village: The Story of Katikitegon.* Cranbrook Institute of Science Bulletin 25. Bloomfield Hills, Mich., 1947.

Kohl, Johann G. *Kitchi-Gami: Wanderings round Lake Superior.* London: Chapman and Hall, 1860.

Kuhm, Jordyce A. "Wisconsin Indian Drums and Their Uses." *Wisconsin Archeologist,* n.s. 27 (1946): 81-88.

Kurath, Gertrude P. "Chippewa Sacred Songs in Religious Metamorphosis." *Scientific American* 79 (1954): 311-17.

_____. *Michigan Indian Festivals.* Ann Arbor, Mich.: Ann Arbor Pub., 1966.

Landes, Ruth. *Ojibwa Sociology.* Columbia University Contributions to Anthropology 29. New York: Columbia University Press, 1937.

_____. *Ojibwa Religion and the Midewiwin.* Madison: University of Wisconsin Press, 1968.

Parthun, Paul. "Ojibwe Music in Minnesota." Ph.D. dissertation, Univerity of Minnesota, 1976.

Reagan, Albert B. "The Bois Fort Chippewa." *Wisconsin Archeologist,* n.s. 3 (1924): 101-32.

Ritzenthaler, Robert E. Fieldnotes, 1940-44. Archives of the Anthropology Department, Milwaukee Public Museum.

_____, and Ritzenthaler, Pat. *The Woodland Indians of the Western Great Lakes.* American Museum Science Book B 21. Garden City, N.Y.: Natural History Press, 1970.

Rohrl, Vivian J. L. "The People of Mille Lacs: A Study of Social Organization and Value Orientations." Ph.D. dissertation, University of Minnesota, 1967.

Tanner, Helen H. *The Ojibwas: A Critical Bibliography.* Bloomington and London: Indian University Press, 1976.

Vennum, Thomas, Jr. "Constructing the Ojibwa Dance Drum." *Wisconsin Archeologist,* n.s. 54 (1973): 162-74.

_____. "Southwestern Ojibwa Music." Ph.D. dissertation, Harvard University, 1975.

_____. "Ojibwa Origin-Migration Songs of the *mitewiwin.*" *Journal of American Folklore* 91 (1978): 753-91.

_____. "A History of Ojibwa Song Form." In *Selected Reports in Ethnomusicology* 3. Edited by Charlotte Heth. Los Angeles: University of California Press, 1980.

Warren, William W. "History of the Ojibways Based upon Traditions and Oral Statements." *Collections of the Minnesota Historical Society* 5 (1885): 21-394.

Winchell, Newton H. *The Aborigines of Minnesota.* Saint Paul: Minnesota Historical Society, 1911.

Afterword

Initially published in 1982 as volume two of the Smithsonian's Folklife Studies series, Thomas Vennum's *Ojibwa Dance Drum* is widely recognized as a significant ethnography of woodland Indians. His refreshing undertaking combined aging anthropological field studies with new ethnographic fieldwork and led him deep into the study of the Ojibwa[1] dance drum.

Vennum's interest in Ojibwa music grew from a childhood interest in piano and keyboard music and from summer trips to Madeline Island where his family owned a home.[2] While on Madeline Island, he would visit nearby powwows at Red Cliff and Bad River Indian reservations, and the local folklore fascinated him. As an ethnomusicologist, he began connecting his understanding of modern American music to the drum sounds and chants produced by the Indians of Lake Superior. His interest in Ojibwa music eventually led him to the Lac Courte Oreilles Reservation in 1969 where he first introduced himself to Ojibwa drummaker William Bineshi Baker Sr.

Early tempered with caution, their relationship grew into an active partnership as the two traveled, lectured, and researched together throughout the seventies. Whenever I visited Baker during this period, the first bit of news he shared was about "Tommie," and Baker always kept track of Vennum's travels, research fieldwork, and university studies. The two regularly corresponded through letters, mostly in English, though Baker sometimes interspersed Ojibwa throughout descriptions of custom craftworks from the early twentieth century.

In 1974 the two worked on *The Drummaker* for the Smithsonian, a film that documented Baker's work as a maker of custom dance drums (the completion of which, considering camera and crew costs, was a minor miracle). Despite the filming schedule, Baker, as usual, meticulously multitasked his various craft projects, carefully harvesting forest products when the seasons dictated, and Vennum's nervous coaxing to hurry Baker often incited a fervent lecture or quick rebuke from the old tribesman.

Whenever Vennum and I occasionally met to share news about our graduate studies, Baker stories were the centerpiece of our visits. Our delight in chuckling about Baker's personality antics was infused with deep and abiding respect for his knowledge of historic customs and ceremonial culture and his skill in fashioning the utilitarian objects that were once essential for survival in Ojibwa woodland settlements.

The inevitable changes that accompanied the arrival of electricity, television, and automobiles to deeply rural regions of North America took their toll on Baker's patience. He was a complex bundle of rigid beliefs, values, and mores. At times he seemed angry at the world for too quickly dissolving his notion of the good life, taking away the old people, feeding the loss of the Ojibwa who conversed with him in his tribal language, and hastening the departure of relatives and close friends who accompanied him into deep expeditions within the Anishinaabe[3] spirit realm.

Around the reservation Baker bemoaned the erosion of the old customs and was a public and harsh critic of young powwow Indians, whom he saw as the instruments of change.[4] Unfortunately, he targeted the young Ojibwa males who, in the late sixties, were working hard to learn the pan-Indian powwow music that was fast dominating popular American Indian culture while saying nothing about the Americanized Ojibwa youth who, unlike their peers, appeared completely indifferent to the evaporating Indian culture.

Baker saw in Vennum the means of preserving this vanishing heritage—or at least important elements of it—and became a willing, eager informant.[5] For his part, Baker piqued Vennum's interest and drove his research beyond his original objective. He was to Vennum what Bisonette was to Ritzenthaler and Matchokamow was to Slotkin,[6] an invaluable living resource. With the revelations that Baker provided, Vennum's research into Ojibwa music stretched outward to additional streams of subject matter. Not only was Baker the living link with the nineteenth-century Drum Dance that Vennum studied and pored over, but he added new dimensions to the story.

Vennum began this project interested in writing a historical essay about Ojibwa music, but discoveries of additional source material and descriptions of first-person involvement by Baker, whose turn-of-the-century birth placed him at the heart of the subject, added volumes of data to his research. Vennum explored "the branches that led out to exciting new parts"[7] of the Drum Dance and found clarification to questions and validation of issues that he believed were not settled by the seventy-year-old fieldwork of anthropologists at Lac Courte Oreilles, White Earth, Lac du Flambeau, and Menominee.

In 1975, six years after beginning his work with Baker, Vennum became senior ethnomusicologist with the Center for Folklife Programs and Cultural Studies at the Smithsonian Institution in Washington, DC, which afforded him the opportunity to further investigate the connection between the Northern Plains drum and the

Ojibwa dance drum. Additionally, he examined the wax cylinder collection of Ojibwa *mide* and Drum songs produced by Frances Densmore in the first decade of the twentieth century, housed in the Federal Cylinder Collection in the Library of Congress. As director of the project, Vennum oversaw the conversion of the musical recordings from fragile seventy-year-old wax to reel tape, creating a medium for returning the music to Drum Dance members in Wisconsin.

His study of Densmore's recordings uncovered big gaps and weaknesses in the collection.[8] Vennum described the limitations of her recording instruments, limitations that led to serious shortcuts in the recording of song series, abbreviating repertoires to single songs and thus violating Ojibwa adherence to spirit petitions, the practice of negotiating with spirits for good health and good will. And given Densmore's hearing impairment, Vennum questioned the accuracy and, therefore, the historical value of her musical transcriptions.[9]

Vennum's research was extraordinarily exhaustive, cross-referencing information from different regions and different eras in order to track variations in the Drum Dance. Along with Densmore's early-century fieldwork, which covered a broad swath of territory from western Minnesota to eastern Wisconsin, he studied the works of other anthropologists who focused on smaller areas within this region. From 1909 to 1911, Samuel Barrett concentrated on several Wisconsin tribes. Much later, from the late 1930s through 1944, Robert Ritzenthaler produced a rich and complex set of information from extensive interviews and observations of Lac Courte Oreilles Ojibwa ceremonial practices. In 1951, James Slotkin, whose work greatly influenced Vennum's, depicted the elaborate Drum rituals of a small Menominee village in all of its complexity.

Ritzenthaler's work was particularly fruitful for Vennum. He dug through dozens of the anthropologist's handwritten notebooks, stored in several boxes at the Milwaukee Public Museum, trying to make sense of his disjointed field notes. The notes were an information gold mine, describing the ebb and flow of a community caught in the web of a dangerous intrusion by the outside world. This little community on the Lac Courte Oreilles reservation was losing its children to boarding schools and their young men to both military service in World War II and urban relocation. Aging patriarchs told Ritzenthaler of the younger generation's growing disrespect for a way of life that, for centuries, was attuned to mores that were dictated by hundreds of spirits. The Ojibwa practice of petitioning spirits occupied dozens of Ritzenthaler's interviews with

Lac Courte Oreilles informants. Vennum tirelessly examined these erratic field notes, shaping Ritzenthaler's topic threads into a logical stream—a true feat of investigation and research.

Variously described by Ojibwa practitioners as Chideweigan, Mishomisinon, Big Drum, Dream Drum, or Ceremonial Drum,[10] the Drum movement today is widely embraced throughout Minnesota, Wisconsin, Iowa, and Kansas by thousands of Anishinaabe adherents. Few practitioners today admit to having read Vennum's treatise on the Ojibwa dance drum, but the truth is, it has been read and continues to be invaluable to the twenty-first-century generation of Drum members as they have struggled to translate their grandparents' Drum teachings and sustain an active relationship with the *manidog*[11] that aid the Anishinaabe people.

Close to thirty years have passed since Vennum's initial publication, and Ojibwa seasonal worship practices have changed drastically. On most Southwest Ojibwa[12] reservations, the *midewiwin* ceremonies are absent, but they are making a significant comeback in Minnesota and near the south shore of Lake Superior. Acculturation of Southwest Ojibwa settlements has had a deep impact on the Drum Dance culture.

The most significant development is the loss of conversational Ojibwa among the Drum membership. The Ojibwa, like most other North American tribes, believe that the use of their native language is vital to communicating with the spirit world. The Ojibwa Drum service is a seasonal, comprehensive ceremony with multiple functions that are sequentially performed over the span of several days. Song, prayer, and preaching are key features of the service. To many members today, however, much of the service is conducted in a foreign language.

The loss of the Ojibwa language by those under fifty-five years old has muted the tribal archive and deafened the younger audience. Some Drum societies have completely lost their native speakers, and with that, they have lost their means of communicating in sincerity with the manidog. Tribal elders estimate that fewer than two dozen conversant speakers remain at Lac Courte Oreilles, Bill Bineshi Baker's tribe, and that they are all over sixty-five. A recent survey conducted by tribal officials on the Mille Lacs Ojibwa reservation, long considered the most culturally prosperous of the U.S. Ojibwa tribes, revealed that there were 139 speakers remaining.[13] Nearly all of the Mille Lacs speakers are over fifty-five.

Today, when spiritual instruction is in great need, most senior Drum leaders conduct their ceremonies in the Ojibwa language but stop short of translating their messages into English, thereby depriving younger members of the history and meaning of their words. Language loss has taken its toll on the Drum Dance, though a small number of young Ojibwa are learning the language. Some are even concentrating on prayer speech so that someone will be able to perform this function in future Drum services. This recent cultural renewal still pales, however, in comparison to what has been lost, and the hope of Drum leaders is that the younger generation will create an even greater renewal.

The advent of high-stakes gaming, with casinos on all Ojibwa reservations, has changed the tribal landscape, as well. With increased wealth has come increased stakes in powwow participation. There are now numerous $100,000 powwows, both traditional and contest,[14] and as prize money has grown to phenomenal levels, the spirit of challenge has grown, resulting in a drive to gain an edge on the competition. This push for competitive advantage has led to a gross exaggeration of dance moves, regalia, and even songs. Old-time dancers now shake their heads and wonder out loud, What have we have done to ourselves?

Young powwow groups aspire to greatness, and powwow performance prowess improves their cultural prestige. Powwows are emerging everywhere across America—in Phoenix, on the Navajo reservation, California, Virginia, and Massachusetts—as demonstrations of cultural authenticity and tribal survival. In the Midwest nearly every tribe and many universities have an annual powwow.

In the past twenty years, young powwow singers have drawn the attention of Drum Keepers and have been invited to membership as singers, drum heaters, and sweepers because of their obvious interest in drums and singing. Membership in the Drum validates their cultural identity in the tribe above and beyond simple association with the secular powwow drum. The younger powwow singers are not Ojibwa-language speakers, however, and many know little about the extraordinarily complex Drum Dance history and its purpose and power.

These new, younger members have introduced new and sometimes unwelcome elements into the Drum. Though most new members have a family connection to the Drum and some understanding of Drum culture, a few younger followers also bring with them a media-inspired infatuation with inner city street culture, including hip-hop music, fashion, and slang. Elder reactions to these youthful leanings are similar to those of elders in the 1950s during the advent of rock and roll. This embrace of hip-hop represents one more step in the steady Americanization of young Ojibwa.

Amid the Drum service, singers, on short breaks and between

songs, often joke, tease one another, and laugh among themselves. The teasing is often a carryover from powwow exploits, drinking escapades, and hunting trips. Joking, teasing, and light insults have always served to build camaraderie and bind families together, but in recent years the lightheartedness has increased to the point where it would be considered, by 1950s standards, irreverent and shocking behavior. A main difference between a Drum ceremony in 1953 and one in 2008 is an often missing lack of solemnity.

Some aspects of the Drum still resemble those of the 1950s, however. When the head of a drum breaks, usually with a small tear where repeated drumstick strikes have weakened the taut hide head, the Drum chiefs meet to smoke and discuss plans for a new head. Generally, they make arrangements for the purchase of a beef hide, preferably from a young animal, and then discuss who will process the hide and replace the two heads, top and bottom. Tanning a hide and installing new heads usually require about two months. The *ogitchidakweg*[15] spend this time repairing the drum's dressing, like beadwork, ornaments, and side dressings. When the drum repairs are made, the members usually hold a service to restore the special songs into the drum. Much speaking and petitioning of the manidog accompanies the restoration project.

As generations course their way through tribal communities, Drum members regularly pass on to the spirit world. Though the Drum is not used for funerary purposes, when a Drum Keeper passes, following the funeral and mourning period, there is a time of instability for the membership. (Most Drums have a single keeper, and a few have two. The Mille Lacs Drums have two keepers, and the Wisconsin Drums once had two.) The membership holds meetings of their men and then their women to discuss replacing the Drum Keeper. They seek in the next keeper integrity, honesty, reverence, humility, sobriety, respect, and a knowledge of cultural history, with special consideration given to the sons of the departed keeper. Once a new keeper is selected from a field of finalists, the veteran chiefs visit with the nominee to give *assema*[16] and offer him the new position, as well as discuss expectations and a pledge of assistance from the veteran chiefs to the keeper. A special Drum service is then held, or if the Drum season date is close, a regular service is used to install the new Drum Keeper. The Drum Keeper is a fatherly figure on the reservation who is respected and shown great deference for his gentleness and conservative views on the political issues that today sometimes divide friends and families.

There are about twenty-seven active Drums in Anishinaabe communities across Minnesota and Wisconsin and over a dozen more in

Iowa and Kansas. Each of the active Drums follows a fairly dependable seasonal schedule of services. Some conduct their regular sessions four times a year, and others meet twice a year. For example, Mille Lacs holds eleven drum ceremonies, each on a Friday to Saturday, over eleven successive weekends. These eleven Drums often coordinate their schedules with one another and with the two White Earth Drums to avoid ceremonies being held at the same time. Several Red Lake and Leech Lake Drums hold their services on a schedule that conflicts with the Mille Lacs Drums' dates, however.

Across the St. Croix River in Wisconsin, four St. Croix Drums schedule four sessions per year, generally avoiding conflicts with the two Lac Courte Oreilles Drums. The two tribes share a historic relationship and once attended each other's Drum meetings, but in recent years the relationship has nearly dissolved. Yet they continue to hold their services on alternating weekends in April through May, June through July, October, and December.

The Mille Lacs Drums conduct their services on Friday and Saturday; the Lac Courte Oreilles Drums include Sunday as well; and the longer St. Croix services usually begin on Thursday evening and go into Sunday. Occasionally, in Wisconsin, some Drum Keepers hold a special session to harness healing power in order to aid an ailing or injured member. It is clear that today's Anishinaabe Drum ceremonies are scheduled at times of convenience for tribal communities preoccupied with midweek employment duties.

A common annoyance of Drum leaders is the chronic absence of members at regularly scheduled Drum Dance services. Larry Smallwood, a Drum Keeper at Azhoomog,[17] noted, "Our spiritual leaders and elders are becoming fewer and fewer, but yet nobody wants to put any effort into pursuing that part of life which is important to us as Anishinaabe people. It seems everyone cares more about what's happening everyday with contemporary issues [than] the way of life. 'I can't make it to the Big Drum ceremony, I have a pool tournament.'"[18]

Among other changes, the passing of drums from one community to another has nearly stopped, once an essential part of the Drum. Mille Lacs has seldom passed on a drum to an eastern Ojibwa community since the 1930s.

The practice of gift exchange or giveaway during the Drum Dance services has experienced some change, as well. On the final day of the ceremony, sometimes before the start of the special songs and sometimes at the end, the Drum Keeper or a veteran chief lays a large hand-sewn quilt on the floor and an *assema makakossag*.[19] The Keeper then puts down an assortment of hand-sewn patch quilts and tobacco and prays for acceptance of his offerings. Then the members likewise offer their assema, quilts, and money to the growing heap—at Mille Lacs the heap can number fifty blankets and $250. Following prayer to the manidog, the veteran chiefs then divide the offerings into separate piles, sometimes numbering twelve or more. Each of these bundles (or *budjidigunin*) is then distributed to the keepers or the chiefs of visiting Drum groups as signs of connection between one another and as messages of brotherhood and sisterhood, an affirmation that the Drums are all related and have a common beginning and a common purpose. Some describe the bundles as blessings from one Drum group to another.

Each of the recipients then stands and speaks in the Ojibwa language, accepting the budjidigunin, acknowledging the bonds between the members and guests, and complimenting the Drum service. Recipients finish by saying that they will distribute the blankets and goods among their own members in order to continue the tradition of gift exchange. In recent years, however, more recipients have been summoning an elder Ojibwa speaker for assistance with their acceptance speeches.

The Mille Lacs ogitchidakweg view the responsibility of blanket making as a sacred one, and hundreds and even thousands of woman hours are invested in this duty for each weekly service. Recent sparse budjidigunin offerings at Ojibwa sites in Wisconsin signal, however, an erosion of this tradition, despite repeated "preachings of generosity" offered at Drum services during the past thirty years. And today, fewer Wisconsin Ojibwa make quilts, another indication that social acculturation has changed the tribal terrain on the eastern side of the St. Croix River.

In the face of twenty-first-century encroachment, Mille Lacs Drum Keepers meet periodically to discuss issues around variations in Drum protocol, prayer, song, and history. Recently, most of their meetings have been conducted in Ojibwemowiin, with some in English in order to help younger members follow the dialogue. Their discussions include strategies for keeping the Drum Dance healthy and relevant to the tribe. Mille Lacs Drum leaders feel a strong sense of history and a duty to strengthen the ceremonial Drum practice among their own villages. These elders have claimed, with the accompanying special songs, the meeting site where Tail Feather Woman's band of Santee Indians first offered the Drum as an instrument of peace. And one tribal elder, Melvin Eagle,[20] recently publicly named the Mille Lacs Ojibwa leaders who were present at the first meeting in circa 1876.

The Drum Dance faced near dissolution during the 1950s and 1960s. Some drums fell silent, and others were lost. Numbers of drums have shown up in museums and in private collections across the Midwest, most likely having been given away in the early twentieth century. World War II and the relocation of American Indian families by the Bureau of Indian Affairs drained Ojibwa reservations of Drum members. Interest waned; absenteeism grew; and disconsolate Drum Keepers began skipping services. Early Drum Dance leaders predicted, however, that the chain of Drum groups scattered across Minnesota, Wisconsin, Iowa, and Kansas—each connected by a common ancestry—would never be broken and that continued expansion would one day reconnect these groups at the site of the Drum's origin.

During the early twentieth century, Lac du Flambeau served as a site where Drums and ritual were given to other Anishinaabe tribes, such as the Lac Vieux Desert Band, the Forest County Potowatomi, and the Menominee, but then fell silent sometime in the 1950s. Eventually, a Lac du Flambeau Drum Keeper summoned help from Lac Courte Oreilles. In response, James Pipe Mustache from Lac Courte Oreilles occasionally "feasted a silenced Drum"[21] at Lac du Flambeau, and in 1991, a small group of Lac Courte Oreilles singers met with Ojibwa singers at Lac du Flambeau to restore the special songs back into the latter's Drum.[22] The Lac du Flambeau keeper inducted new members and reinstated the Drum back into service. The broken link was repaired, and the chain of Anishinaabe Drums was renewed.

In Wisconsin, the St. Croix, Lac Courte Oreilles, Lac du Flambeau, Forest County Potowatomi, Menominee, and Wisconsin Rapids Drums have recently increased their memberships, despite the continued loss of first-language speakers. And as mentioned, younger Drum members continue to study Ojibwemowiin to improve prayers and Drum service duties. Much more needs to be done to preserve the traditional culture of the Ojibwa, however. In particular, the Ojibwa language must be learned not just by those who will perform service prayers at Drum ceremonies but by all Ojibwa youth, who have the ultimate responsibility of communicating with the spirit world.

Rick St. Germaine
University of Wisconsin–Eau Claire

Notes to the Afterword

1. In 1982, Vennum used the spelling "Ojibwa," as preferred in Wisconsin. Today, a more popular long or double-vowel system spells it "Ojibwe."

2. Madeline Island was the historic homeland of the Southwestern Ojibwa people. Current Lake Superior tourist attractions include an Indian-colonial museum, an Ojibwa cemetery, and historic lore that reaches back into the seventeenth century.

3. The Anishinaabe include the western Great Lakes Ojibwa and the Potowatomi, Menominee, Odawa, Kickapoo, and Mesquaki peoples.

4. Powwows are secular drum and dance festivals lacking spiritual function, whereas Drum Dance ceremonies have complex spiritual rituals and healing purposes.

5. In 1928, an old Navajo headman named Hasteen Tlo'tsi hee told Aileen O'Bryan: "I see my people and your people living together. In time to come my people will have forgotten their early way of life unless they learn it from white men's books. So you must write down what I tell you and you must have it made into a book that coming generations may know this truth" (Aileen O'Bryan, *The Dine: Origin Myths of the Navaho Indians*, Bureau of American Ethnology Bulletin 163 [Washington, DC: U.S. Government Printing Office, 1956], 2).

6. John Bisonette was a key informant to Robert Ritzenthaler during his five-year ethnographic research on the Lac Courte Oreilles Indian Reservation, which led to several publications about Ojibwa culture and religion. Johnny Matcholamow was the major informant to James S. Slotkin, who authored *The Menomini Pow Wow: A Study in Cultural Decay* (Milkwaukee, WI: Milwaukee Museum Publications in Anthropology, 1957).

7. Interview with Thomas Vennum on August 19, 2008.

8. Ibid.

9. Ibid.

10. The Drum is known by other names as well, many of which are cited in the Ojibwa language during prayer. They take different forms according to the context in which they are spoken.

11. Plural of *manidoo* (spirit).

12. Ojibwa ethnohistorians like Hickerson, Ritzenthaler, and Hornbeck-Tanner have mapped the Southwest Ojibwa as living in Minnesota, Wisconsin, and the Upper Peninsula of Michigan. The Southeast Ojibwa live from the Lower Peninsula of Michigan to Toronto, Ontario, including Lake Huron and Georgian Bay.

13. Interview with Joe Nayquonabe Sr., Drum Keeper, on June 19, 2008.

14. Traditional and contest powwows differ in how the $100,000 is paid out by the local powwow committee. At traditional powwows modest payments are distributed to dancers and drum groups, usually at a rate of $20 to $25 per adult dancer and $500 per drum group. At contest powwows, however, the best one hundred dancers each takes home hundreds or thousands of dollars, prestige, and much recognition, while the remaining one to two hundred dancers leave empty-handed. Contest drum groups are limited to ten or so invited groups and may be paid $1,000 or more and may also compete in a contest of their own.

15. Ogitchidakweg are the female members of the Drum and have very gender-prescribed roles and responsibilities of leadership, decision making, and support. Though there are several active women's Drums in existence, with female Drum Keepers, generally women Drum members have limited visible functions in comparison with the men's duties as drummers and singers, prayers, dancers, preachers, veteran chiefs, pipe smokers, and table setters. Behind the scenes, however, women have mother-like roles that are difficult to describe in the English language.

16. Assema is tobacco used spiritually in most Anishinaabe ceremonies.

17. Azhoomog is a Mille Lacs Band community in Minnesota that has historic ties to the St. Croix Band community in Danbury, Wisconsin.

18. The Mille Lacs Band has issued a series of articles about living Ojibwa culture on their tribal website (www.millelacsojibwe.org). Larry Smallwood is one of a dozen elders who writes about the heritage of the Ojibwa people.

19. An assema makakossag is a ceremonial wooden box used to collect members' tobacco offerings.

20. Melvin Eagle is the grandson of Migizi, the early twentieth-century hereditary chief of the Mille Lacs Ojibwa, a noted historian and respected Drum Keeper.

21. The Drum is an immensely important spirit or grandfather being. Feasting a Drum is a small ritual performed by a few members between quarterly services done to assure the grandfather (*mishomisinaan*) that his people have not forgotten him and will soon bring him back out in a service.

22. Interview with Paul DeMain on August 2, 2008.

Index

antlers, 181, 246, *246,* 248, 317n14; hair, 53, *194,* 223; hides, 17, 163–64, 166–67, 192, 215; hooves, 180. *See also* dewclaws
Delaware fire bag, 180
Densmore, Frances: on costumes, 190–91, 196, 299n128; on dance enclosures, 113, 116; on decline of Drum Dance, 133; on Dog Feast, 95, 111–13, 250, 251–53; on dream symbols, 186; on Drum decoration, 39, 173, 176, 182, 215–16; on drumsticks, 229–30, 232; on healing ceremonies, 126; informants of, 73, 128, 306n5; on Medicine Dance, 298n106; on Menominee Drum Dance, 315n77; *mide* drum collected by, 183; origin story published by, 46; on pipe rituals, 312n1, n8; on presentation ceremonies, 63, 70, 72, 79, 89–90, 99, 133, 216–17, 297n78; songs recorded by, 34, *36,* 93, 317n13, 323; on storage of Drum, 237; on women's dances, 83, 296n35
dewclaws, *15,* 37, 60, 129, 196, 310n81
Dewdney, Selwyn, 38–39, *39,* 229
Dodd, Frank, 136
Dog Feast, 69, 103–4, *109,* 149, 300n155; Densmore's observations, 95, 111–13, 250, 251–53; as part of Grass Dance, 54–55, 74, 108–9, 142
Dream Dance, 52, 154
Dream Drum, 45, 184
Dreamer's Society, 45
dreams: dances revealed in, 86, 216; Drums appearing in, 42, 85, 148, 180, 201, 202, 311n96; face painting designs in, 207; flags in, 126; influencing conversion, 143; Ojibwa belief in, 147–48; regarding drum transfers, 88, 152; songs revealed in, 31, 100–2, 147, 202; symbols appearing in, 184–87, 243
Dream Songs, 99
Drift Drum. *See* Walter Drift Drum
Drifter (Siyabas), 150, 152
Drum: accessories for, 209–40, 253–55;

anthropomorphic qualities, 61, 63, 178, 239, 267, 306n9; ceremonial, 32, 45–46, 56, 202–8, 237, 242, 244, 308n25, 325–26; children learning, 8, 32, 96; closing of, 78–79, 237, 315n75, 315n77; congregational aspects, 80–81, 88, 89, 128, 212, 241; construction of, 136–37, 151, 156–70; decoration of, 58, 137–38, *160,* 170–208, 254, 309n44; dedications of, 234; directional orientation of, *205,* 205–6; as embodiment of Indian identity, 12–13, 33; expenses related to, 136–37, 142; feasting, 331n21; first, 46, 146, 152, 172, 173, 202, 205–6, 260, 328; future of, 153–55; heart of, 161, 197, 306n10; history of, 44–75; locations of, 124, 203, 311n105; making a replacement, 70, 72, 76, 88–89, 135, 212, *213,* 254, 297n56, n58; names of, 13, 61–62, 306n4, 330n10, 331n21; origin stories, 44–52, 64, 104, 115–16, 182, 216, 232, 289n2, 294n108; path of, 71–72, *72,* 74, 95, 139, 263, 324; peace through, 45, 49, 64–65, 70, 102, 154, 161, 205–6; petitioning, 209; pipe belonging to, 209–10; power of Great Spirit in, 49, 81, 148; presentation of, 88–92, 95, 263–67, 297n78, 301n167; repair of, 262–63; rituals of, 45, 78–79, 207, 237, 324; as sacred object, 61–64, 324; sale of, 136, *137;* songs for, 260–61, 297n78, 323, 326, 328, 329; storage of, 62, 118, 119, 135–36, 237, 239, 267, 304n20, 317n11; transfer of, 70–75, 90, 128, 129, 142, 327; transporting, 160, 237–40; variants of, 241–49. *See also* drums; *and individual Drum components and personal and tribal Drums*
Drum Dance: ceremonies, 42, 113, 298n106, 330n4; clockwise motion of, 71, 86, 256, 265, 316n4; costumes, 107, 303n215; decline of, 50, 78, 100, 124, 128, 131, 132–55,